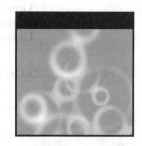

Visual Basic .NET and XML:
Harness the Power of XML in VB.NET Applications

Rod Stephens
Brian Hochgurtel

Wiley Computer Publishing

John Wiley & Sons, Inc.

Publisher: Robert Ipsen
Editor: Theresa Hudson
Developmental Editor: Kathryn A. Malm
Managing Editor: Angela Smith
New Media Editor: Brian Snapp
Text Design & Composition: John Wiley Composition Services

Designations used by companies to distinguish their products are often claimed as trade-marks. In all instances where John Wiley & Sons, Inc., is aware of a claim, the product names appear in initial capital or ALL CAPITAL LETTERS. Readers, however, should contact the appropriate companies for more complete information regarding trademarks and registration.

This book is printed on acid-free paper. ⊗

Published by John Wiley & Sons, Inc., New York

Published simultaneously in Canada.

This publication is designed to provide accurate and authoritative information in regard to the subject matter covered. It is sold with the understanding that the pub-lisher is not engaged in professional services. If professional advice or other expert assistance is required, the services of a competent professional person should be sought.

Library of Congress Cataloging-in-Publication Data:

ISBN: 0-471-12060-X

Printed in the United States of America.

10 9 8 7 6 5 4 3 2 1

For the hundreds of our colleagues and all of the others
who lost their lives on September 11, 2001.

Contents

About the Authors

Rod Stephens has been an application developer for more than 17 years. During that time he has designed and implemented more than half a dozen large commercial applications, several of which have won corporate awards. He has worked on applications in such diverse fields as repair dispatch, telephone switch maintenance, tax software for the State of Minnesota, and training for professional football players and the New York Stock Exchange. Currently a consultant and author, Rod has written 11 books and more than 160 magazine articles.

Brian Hochgurtel has been a Web application developer for six years. He has used a variety of languages including PERL, SAS, Java, C++, Cold Fusion, ASP, and Visual Basic for a diverse group of Web-based projects that included cancer research studies, environmental education, software documentation, and Web interfaces for large enterprise databases. Currently he is a Software Development Engineer on the Bobcat development team at Rogue Wave Software.

Other Books by Rod Stephens

Advanced Visual Basic Techniques   ISBN: 0-471-18881-6

Visual Basic Graphics Programming, Second Edition   ISBN: 0-471-35599-2

Bug Proofing Visual Basic   ISBN: 0-471-32351-9

Custom Controls Library   ISBN: 0-471-24267-5

Ready-to-Run Visual Basic Algorithms, Second Edition   ISBN: 0-471-24268-3

Ready-to-Run Visual Basic Code Library   ISBN: 0-471-33345-X

Ready-To-Run Delphi Algorithms   ISBN: 0-471-25400-2

Introduction

Moving data from one application to another is an extremely common programming task. Users doing their jobs with a variety of applications generate a huge amount of data. Another application extracts that data and produces reports. The reports are pulled into yet another system to create summaries, executive briefings, and so forth. All too often this exercise means wading through a labyrinth of different file formats, database interfaces, remote procedure calls, and intermediary data formats.

The extensible markup language (XML) is changing all that. XML is a simple but powerful language that lets you store data in XML files effortlessly. By standardizing data storage, XML lets any number of applications share data with little effort on the programmer's part. Data gathered by one application can be shared with other applications running anywhere on the Internet or on a private network.

Tools for working with XML files have been around for a while now, but the new release of Visual Basic .NET raises this support to a new level. Previously tools were tacked on to Visual Basic. In Visual Basic .NET, XML support is tightly integrated into the language and provides many new methods for manipulating XML data. This tight integration means Visual Basic programmers can load, manipulate, and save XML data faster and more easily than ever before.

Microsoft envisions a future Internet hosting millions of distributed applications communicating via XML. Data packaged in XML will flow to and from databases, between applications, and directly to the browser.

This book explains how you can take advantage of XML in your Visual Basic applications. It shows how you can use this new data language to position your applications at the center of a new universe of effortless data exchange.

Who Should Read This Book

This book does not assume you have previous experience with XML and its related technologies. It does assume you know at least the fundamentals of Visual Basic .NET programming so it is not for complete beginners.

This book is aimed primarily at Visual Basic database, Web, and enterprise-level programmers. XML allows database programmers to import and export data in a standard format. The XML tools provided by Visual Basic .NET make loading, manipulating, and storing data almost trivial with any database that supports XML. Developers using SQL server, Oracle, or other databases are no longer confined to compatible databases and applications. By using XML, every application is compatible with every kind of database.

XML allows Web programmers to display data easily and quickly. As the World Wide Web continues to grow, quickly displaying company data on intranets and the Internet is becoming a very important part of doing business. As more and more hand-held devices such as cell phones and personal digital assistants (PDAs) access the Internet, the importance of displaying timely corporate data in different ways increases. XML gives developers the power they need to build these flexible applications.

Enterprise-level programmers can use XML to combine data stored in different formats in different parts of the company. This kind of company-wide scope is difficult to achieve without some unifying tool like XML. Networked applications performing enterprise-level services are also a major focus in Microsoft's future programming strategy. They expect complex corporate applications to be built using a collection of small Web Services running scattered across the network communicating through XML.

Using the tools provided by Visual Basic .NET, XML programming is relatively easy. It would be far easier for a programmer to learn Visual Basic and use it to produce XML than it would be to learn another language. In some cases, it might be more cost-effective to learn Visual Basic than to continue programming with an existing language.

What Is XML?

The extensible markup language (XML) is a data storage language. It is a particularly simple data storage language often used to temporarily store data while it is transferred from one application to another. It stores data in a format defined by a series of straightforward tags created by the programmer.

By itself XML is pretty feeble because it is designed only to store data and provides no features for manipulating it. In contrast, Access, Oracle, Informix, SQL Server, and a host of other database systems provide powerful data manipulation features such as indexing, sorting, and searching. XML has only two advantages over these powerful database systems: It is simple, and it is portable. These may seem like minor benefits, but together they allow XML to add a powerful new tool to data handling enterprises.

XML syntax is easy to learn and use. It allows a programmer to quickly define complex hierarchical data structures that may contain other hierarchical data structures. Even though it is possible to build this kind of data structure using other database products, their rigid table structures force the programmer to use complicated techniques to model these data relationships. Because XML stores data definitions and values in ordinary text files, a programmer can create and modify them quickly and easily.

Less glamorous but probably more important is XML's portability. XML is easy to use in any environment that includes an XML parser. Visual Basic .NET includes extensive tools for manipulating XML files so this book focuses on them. These tools allow Visual Basic .NET programs to read XML files created by programs using another parser. Conversely, these tools allow a Visual Basic .NET program to create XML files for use by other programs that will use another parser to read them.

By running on a variety of different platforms, XML positions itself to become the lingua franca of data. Most large companies have distinct organizations that hold different key pieces of business data. Separate parts of a telephone company, for example, hold information about customers, billing, central office hardware, switch software, telephone numbers, outside plant (cables, poles, repeaters), and so forth. The data is typically stored on an assortment of hardware and software platforms scattered around the country. Trying to gather data from these diverse sources for reporting and analysis is a monumental task.

XML changes that. Each part of the business can build tools to save data in XML format. Once all of the data has been saved in the common format, reporting and analysis become trivial. Furthermore, a programmer who has a platform with an XML parser can easily read and manipulate the XML data saved by other parts of the company. Programs can reach across company networks or even the Internet to gather this information from wherever it is stored and produce a unified report.

Even this idea, that every part of the company can use a common dialect to exchange information, is nothing new. Programmers have used text files for this purpose for decades. What is new is the simplicity XML allows. It provides a solid framework that lets programmers store data in a format that any other application can understand.

The World Wide Web also provides a new opportunity for sending data from many data sources to a variety of applications and output devices. Because so many companies want the ability to display data on the Web, tools have been developed to display XML. Using a simple transformation file in XSLT and the XSLTransform class, a Visual Basic .NET application can transform data into HTML for display on the Internet or an intranet, VoiceXML for use in speech applications, or any other text-based format.

Where Visual Basic Fits In

The majority of Visual Basic's several million programmers work extensively with databases. Many work for large companies that typically have data stored in a variety of database systems. Integrating this data for reporting and analysis is one of the more common tasks these programmers face, and XML can make that task easier.

This book shows how a Visual Basic .NET program can load XML data from local files or remotely across the Internet. The program can then display and manipulate the data in a variety of ways, combining data from different sources to provide integrated reports and centralized tools for data analysis.

ASP.NET, the successor to ASP, adds dynamic content to Web pages. ASP.NET can display WebForms that a programmer builds using Visual Basic .NET. These forms can do everything other Visual Basic .NET applications can do. For example, they can load, display, and modify XML data. This lets a Visual Basic .NET programmer build dynamic Web applications that analyze and manipulate data.

Other Technologies

Microsoft's .NET initiative includes a variety of technologies including programming languages such as Visual Basic .NET, C# (pronounced "see sharp"), and Visual C++. This initiative also includes back-end solutions for such products as SQL Server 2000, Office 2000, and Internet Explorer.

This book shows how XML works with these products. It shows how you can use SQL Server 2000 and Microsoft's Internet Information Server (IIS) to display data directly on the Web with XML. Other chapters show how to use Visual Basic for Applications (VBA) to save and load XML documents in Microsoft Office 2000 applications. Using both the built-in functionality in Internet Explorer and some Microsoft plug-ins, the book shows how you can use Internet Explorer as a useful tool during XML development. All of this information will help give you a broader overview of .NET and help you design Visual Basic .NET applications as well.

Overview

This book is divided into three parts. Each part covers a major topic in using XML with Visual Basic.

Part One: XML in Visual Basic .NET

Part One explains how to use XML in Visual Basic .NET programs. It covers fundamental topics such as reading and writing XML files using Visual Basic code. These techniques are used throughout the rest of the book.

Chapter 1, "XML Overview," provides a fast introduction to XML and some of the related technologies such as DTD and XSD schemas. It gives a broad overview to help you understand where XML fits into the Visual Basic programming world.

Chapter 2, "DOM," describes the Document Object Model. The DOM forms a hierarchical data structure that lets you load, manipulate, and save XML documents, taking full advantage of their internal structure.

Chapter 3, "Forward-Only XML," explains other common models for working with XML files. Visual Basic's XmlTextReader and XmlTextWriter classes provide fast forward-only access to XML data. The Simple API for XML (SAX) provides a different, event-oriented approach to reading XML data quickly.

Chapter 4, "Serialization," tells how Visual Basic can save and restore data in simple text-based format using XML. This process, called serialization, allows a program to save extremely complex data structures almost effortlessly.

Chapter 5, "Schemas," explains different technologies for validating XML data. DTD, XDR, and XSD schemas allow an application to easily verify that XML data is correct and complete so it doesn't need to spend a lot of effort validating the data itself using Visual Basic code. Visual Basic provides the most tools for working with XSD schemas so this chapter focuses on those.

Part Two: XML on the Web

Part Two examines methods for displaying XML data on the Web using Visual Basic. Recent versions of Visual Basic have provided an increasingly sophisticated set of tools for working with the Web. These chapters show how you can take advantage of these tools to display XML data.

Chapter 6, "XSL," explains how you can use XSL (eXtensible Stylesheet Language) to automatically reformat XML data for display on the Web. It shows how a Visual Basic program can use XSL to convert XML data into a different format such as HTML, VoiceXML, or plain text.

Chapter 7, "ASP.NET," shows how you can use Visual Basic .NET code in an ASP.NET Web page to display XML data. It tells how to use client- and server-side controls to display the data automatically and how to manipulate XML data within ASP.NET code for the greatest flexibility.

Chapter 8, "Web Services," covers one of Microsoft's latest Web technologies. Using Visual Basic, you can build Web Services that a remote application can invoke to perform useful tasks.

Part Three: XML in Other Applications

Part Three describes methods for using XML to interact with some specific applications other than Visual Basic. One of XML's key benefits is its ability to facilitate data transfer from one application to another. These chapters give specific examples showing how you can move data to and from other applications.

Chapter 9, "Microsoft Office 2000," explains how you can use Visual Basic .NET to move XML data in and out of Microsoft Office 2000 applications such as Word, Excel, Access, and Outlook. These techniques are extremely useful for combining Visual Basic and Office applications to provide integrated data processing, reports, and summaries.

Chapter 10, "Internet Explorer," discusses the XML support provided by the most recent versions of Internet Explorer. Internet Explorer itself provides extensive support for XML data, and if you point an Internet Explorer browser at an XML file, it will display the data in an interactive hierarchical way.

Chapter 11, "SQL Server 2000," explains the features the database SQL Server 2000 provides for working with XML files. It tells how to integrate SQL Server with Internet Information Services (IIS) to dynamically display data on the Web.

How to Use This Book

Unless you are already familiar with XML, you should begin with Chapter 1, "XML Overview." It will give you the background you need to get started using XML in your Visual Basic applications. If you already understand XML and schemas, you can safely skip that chapter.

Chapters 2 through 5 explain the basic tools you will need to read, manipulate, and save XML data in Visual Basic. For the greatest flexibility, use the DOM methods described in Chapter 2. This chapter provides a lot of basic information on XML so it is a good chapter to study next.

If you want fast but more restricted processing of really huge XML files, use the XmlTextReader, XmlTextWriter, and SAX methods explained in Chapter 3. These techniques don't give you all the flexibility of the DOM, but for really large XML files they save a lot of memory and processing power.

If you need to save complex data structures using XML and restore them later, read about the serialization techniques described in Chapter 4. Using these techniques, you can save almost any kind of data in text files or text fields in a database.

Schemas let a program verify that data is correct and complete before trying to process it. If your application must ensure its input data is correct, read about schemas in Chapter 5.

The rest of the book is more specialized than the first five chapters. Chapters 6 through 8 deal with Web topics. Read them if you want to display XML data on the Web.

Chapters 9 through 11 explain ways to move XML data in and out of other applications including Microsoft Office 2000 applications and SQL Server 2000. Read these chapters if you need to move XML data from one program to another.

Necessary Equipment

To read this book and understand the examples, you will need no special equipment. To use XML in Visual Basic .NET or to run the examples found on the book's Web page, you need any computer that can reasonably run Visual Basic .NET. That means a reasonably modern, fast computer with a lot of memory. See the Visual Basic .NET documentation for Microsoft's exact requirements and recommendations.

To build Visual Basic .NET programs, you will also need a copy of Visual Basic .NET or the .NET SDK. Don't even bother trying to run the examples shown here if you have an earlier version of Visual Basic such as Visual Basic 6. The changes between Visual Basic 6 and Visual Basic .NET are huge. With some experience, you can translate Visual Basic 6 programs into Visual Basic .NET. It would be very difficult to translate a Visual Basic .NET XML program back into Visual Basic 6. Visual Basic .NET is tightly integrated with XML, and it provides a lot of XML tools that are missing from Visual Basic 6. You can probably use an XML library to read and write XML files using Visual Basic 6, but it will be a lot of work. If you are planning to move to Visual Basic .NET anyway, you may as well do it before you read this book.

Lots of Material

XML sits at the heart of a huge number of relatively new technologies. To really learn every nook and cranny of these new technologies, you would need to learn a host of new technologies and languages including XML itself, HTML, XSL, XPath, and XSD. To use XML to transfer data between applications, you would need to learn the quirks and expectations of those applications. Figure I.1 shows some of the relationships among the different technologies described in this book.

While this book touches on many of these technologies, it cannot cover all of them in their entirety. For instance, Chapter 5, "Schemas," describes methods you can use to validate XML data using schemas. It briefly explains how to validate data using DTD and XDR schemas, and it spends a considerable amount of time explaining how to create and use XSD schemas. This book, however, doesn't have room to cover any of these schema standards completely.

In a way, that's probably for the best. All of the technologies related to XML are evolving rapidly so any information you read in any source could quickly become obsolete.

To get more in-depth information about one of these topics, look for a book about the particular topic. For the very latest on a topic, search the World Wide Web Consortium's Web site, www.w3c.org.

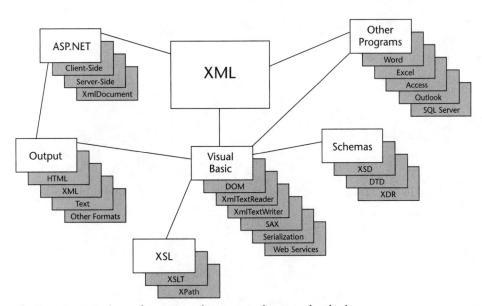

Figure I.1 XML sits at the center of a swarm of new technologies.

Samples, Updates, and Changes

At this time, writing a book about XML and Visual Basic .NET is both exciting and challenging. XML and Visual Basic .NET let Visual Basic developers build data applications faster and more easily than ever before. Unfortunately, both XML and Visual Basic .NET are currently changing on an almost daily basis. That makes it hard to pin down exactly what these technologies will do when you read this book.

This book was written using beta versions of Visual Basic .NET. Microsoft changed a lot of features between the first and second beta release and will undoubtedly make more changes before the final release. The code was checked with late release candidate versions of Visual Basic, so hopefully the examples will work in the final release with few or no changes.

At the same time, the World Wide Web Consortium (W3C) continues to develop XML, schemas, and related standards. It is likely that there will be some differences between the versions of XML and Visual Basic .NET used in this book and the version you use when you read this.

For updates, corrections, and comments, visit the book's Web page, www.vb-helper.com/xml.htm. This Web page also contains the source code for the examples in this book. If you have corrections or comments of your own, please send them to RodStephens@vb-helper.com. We will do our best to keep the Web site as up-to-date as possible.

PART One

XML in Visual Basic .NET

XML is a connecting technology. It allows diverse applications to share data with relative ease. It lets one application save data that is later read by another application, possibly running on a different computer using a different operating system and written in another programming language.

While XML can tie many different types of applications together, from a Visual Basic programmer's point of view the story begins with Visual Basic. The chapters in Part One focus on Visual Basic .NET applications that use XML. They explain how to read, write, modify, and manipulate XML data. They show how to write and process XML data quickly and efficiently and how to validate it to ensure the data is correct and complete. These techniques form the fundamental tools used by any Visual Basic .NET application that uses XML, and they are used throughout the rest of the book.

XML Overview

This chapter provides a quick overview of XML, DTD files, and schemas. It explains how these topics relate to each other and to programs that use XML data.

The sections in this chapter build and rebuild a simple example XML file that demonstrates many important XML concepts. It shows how to use elements, attributes, and comments to build a well-formed XML document. Later sections explain how to use DTD files and schemas to validate an XML file. Once you understand the basics, you will be ready to move on to later chapters that show how you can take advantage of XML in your Visual Basic applications.

Almost as long as there have been computer programs, people have been trying to move data from one program to another. The easiest way to do that is to export data from the first program into a text file and then import the text file into the second program. Unfortunately, different programs save text data in different ways. For example, Microsoft Excel can save data into a comma-separated value (CSV) file. That's great for other programs that understand CSV files, but it does little good if the program you want to load the data understands only fixed-length records. One program writes this:

```
First Name,Last Name,Street,City,State,Zip,Home Phone
Brian,Hochgurtel,123 Gold Hill Dr,Boulder,CO,80504,3035551212
Rod,Stephens,323 Nederland Pl,Boulder,CO,80013,3035551133
```

The second program expects this:

```
First Name Last Name  Street          City    State Zip   Home Phone
Brian      Hochgurtel 123 Gold Hill Dr Boulder CO    80504 3035551212
Rod        Stephens   323 Nederland Pl Boulder CO    80013 3035551133
```

Other files may separate fields with semi-colons, tabs, vertical bars, or other special characters. Each of these data representations is relatively simple, but handling every one of them can be a big chore. If you wanted to load one of these text-based data files into a program that does not understand the format, you would need to write some sort of translator program. If you wanted to transfer data between a dozen different programs, each using a different data format, you might need to write more than a hundred translators.

XML standardizes data representation to help programs move text-based data across heterogeneous systems. It defines a simple set of rules that let you represent almost any kind of data in a uniform way. Most importantly, XML is extensible so you can define your own set of tags to represent your data.

Converting data from a comma-delimited file into an XML file is a good way to gain an understanding of how powerful XML is. Consider the following author contact information CSV file written by Excel:

```
First Name,Last Name,Street,City,State,Zip,Home Phone
Brian,Hochgurtel,123 Gold Hill Dr,Boulder,CO,80504,3035551212
Rod,Stephens,323 Nederland Pl,Boulder,CO,80013,3035551133
```

Programs that understand CSV files, such as Microsoft Access, can easily read this file. Other programs, like those you write in Visual Basic, do not automatically understand the information this file contains. If you want to load this data into a Visual Basic program, you need to write code to open the file, read the lines of text it contains, break the lines into fields, and store the field values in variables.

If you convert this CSV file into XML, any program that understands XML can easily load the data. It's no coincidence that Visual Basic .NET includes many tools for reading, manipulating, and writing XML files. As you'll see in later chapters, using Visual Basic you can load, modify, and save XML documents (Chapter 2, "DOM"); process XML data more efficiently when you don't need to have the entire document loaded at once (Chapter 3, "Forward-Only XML"); serialize and deserialize program information (Chapter 4, "Serialization"); build schemas to validate XML data (Chapter 5, "Schemas"); and transform documents using XSL (Chapter 6, "XSL").

Once you translate data into XML, a Visual Basic program can load and display the data almost effortlessly. It can modify the data and save it as a new XML file, ready for any other program that understands XML to load it.

Before you build an XML file, you should understand that XML does nothing on its own except store data. To use an XML file, a program needs to use a parser to read the file and turn the file's text and tags into usable values. You could write a parser yourself, but Visual Basic provides all the tools you need to read and parse XML so you needn't bother. Visual Basic gives you a couple of parsing options that you can use to manipulate the data in different ways. Chapters 3 and 4 discuss parser types in detail and give you some guidelines for selecting the parsing method that is best for a particular project.

For now, keep in mind that some parser will read the XML file and try to make sense of it. To help the parser understand what kind of document it is reading, an XML file begins with a version tag like this:

```
<?xml version="1.0"?>
```

XML tags that begin with a question mark contain processing instructions (PI). This is an instruction to the parser itself and is not part of the data you are storing in the file. This statement tells the parser that the XML document follows version 1.0 of the W3C XML standard.

This introductory tag can also tell the parser whether the XML document stands alone or has a related DTD (Document Type Definition) or XSD (XML Schema Definition) schema file. Both DTD and XSD files help a parser verify that the data in the XML document fits some desired format. For example, an XSD schema file might tell the parser to require a properly formatted telephone number in each record. If the XML data does not include the right phone numbers, the parser rejects the file.

After the initial version tag, it's easy to translate the previous CSV file into an XML file. Each data field begins with a tag named after the field and ends with a corresponding tag with the same name but starting with a slash (/).

```
<?xml version="1.0"?>
<Contacts>
<Author>
<FirstName>Brian</FirstName>
<LastName>Hochgurtel</LastName>
<Street>123 Gold Hill Drive</Street>
<City>Boulder</City>
<State>CO</State>
<Zip>80504</Zip>
<HomePhone>3035551212</HomePhone>
<WorkPhone>3035551213</WorkPhone>
<FaxPhone>3035551214</FaxPhone>
</Author>
<Author>
<FirstName>Rod</FirstName>
<LastName>Stephens</LastName>
<Street>323 Nederland Place</Street>
<City>Boulder</City>
<State>CO</State>
<Zip>80013</Zip>
<HomePhone>3035551133</HomePhone>
<WorkPhone>3035551144</WorkPhone>
<FaxPhone>3035551155</FaxPhone>
</Author>
</Contacts>
```

An XML file must have a single root element that contains all of the other data elements. In this example, the root element Contacts contains two Author elements. Each Author element represents one data record and contains several other elements holding the real text data.

Notice that this file does not contain separate entries to define column headings the way the CSV file does. The XML file knows what each field represents by the tag that surrounds it. For example, it knows the value "Brian" has the type "FirstName" because it is surrounded by a <FirstName> tag. The only indication that "Brian" is a first name in the CSV file was the fact that it is the first field in a line and the value "First Name" is the first field in the file's first line.

This XML file isn't very pretty. In fact, it is downright hard to read. That's because XML is really designed for the convenience of parsers, not human beings. If you wade through this file, you'll see that every piece of data makes sense, but the formatting is downright unpleasant. Once your Visual Basic program loads an XML document, you can manipulate it using normal program objects so this ungainly format no longer matters.

You can improve the readability by adding some white space outside of the data tags. The extra spaces are not inside the data tags so they are not considered part of those elements. On the other hand, white space that appears within tags and attributes is considered part of the data. For example, the spaces between words and numbers in an address are actually part of the data.

The following code shows the same XML file with white space added to make the file easier to read.

```xml
<?xml version="1.0"?>
<Contacts>
  <Author>
    <FirstName>Brian</FirstName>
    <LastName>Hochgurtel</LastName>
    <Street>123 Gold Hill Drive</Street>
    <City>Boulder</City>
    <State>CO</State>
    <Zip>80504</Zip>
    <HomePhone>3035551212</HomePhone>
    <WorkPhone>3035551213</WorkPhone>
    <FaxPhone>3035551214</FaxPhone>
  </Author>
  <Author>
    <FirstName>Rod</FirstName>
    <LastName>Stephens</LastName>
    <Street>323 Nederland Place</Street>
    <City>Boulder</City>
    <State>CO</State>
    <Zip>80013</Zip>
    <HomePhone>3035551133</HomePhone>
    <WorkPhone>3035551144</WorkPhone>
    <FaxPhone>3035551155</FaxPhone>
  </Author>
</Contacts>
```

When a program builds an XML file, however, this kind of extra formatting tends to disappear. For example, if a program loads an XML file, makes some changes, and then saves the changes back into the file, the tools that write the new version of the file usually strip out all the white space.

Elements and Attributes

Elements are the basic building blocks of any XML document. The following sections describe elements, empty elements, element nesting, and attributes.

Elements

Each of the tags in the example XML file contains elements. An element is the chunk of data between the start and end tags. The name that appears within the start and end tags defines the element's type.

In many ways, an element in an XML document is similar to the markup codes found in an HTML document. The difference is that HTML tells a browser how to format data while an XML element tells a browser or a parser what the data is. To see the difference, consider this snippet of HTML:

```
<B>Boulder</B>
```

Here the browser receives an instruction to make the text Boulder bold. The browser doesn't really know what lies between the <B> and </B> tags. The browser doesn't know whether Boulder is the name of a city, a description of a large rock, or just a random string of characters.

In XML this example might read:

```
<City>Boulder</City>
```

Now the browser knows that the value "Boulder" is a City. The browser still doesn't really know what a City is, but given some extra programming, it can learn how to display a city properly. For example, a stylesheet might tell the browser to display all City objects in bold type. Chapter 6 has more to say about using XSL stylesheets to display XML documents in a browser.

Notice that a person reading the XML file can easily understand that Boulder is a city, not a big rock or a random series of characters. The <City> tag invented just for this XML document gives useful information to both the browser and to someone reading the file.

Empty Elements

Sometimes an XML document uses a tag that holds all of its information inside the tag itself. These tags specify such things as database connections, remote procedure calls (RPC), image file locations, processing instructions, and more. For example, the following statement specifies the URL of an image file.

```
<IMG SRC="http://www.vb-helper.com/images/brian.gif"></IMG>
```

Even though this is an HTML tag, it can still be part of an XML file. Although the image tag's path data is specified in the tag itself and there is no data between the starting and closing tags, this statement still needs a closing tag </IMG>.

This statement is perfectly valid in XML, but there's a shortcut. If a tag contains no data outside of the tag itself, you can end the field by simply adding a slash (/) right before the closing bracket. The previous statement becomes:

```
<IMG SRC="http://www.vb-helper.com/images/brian.gif"/>
```

Any HTML tag you include in an XML document must end with a slash (/). For example, to use a simple <BR> break tag within an XML document, you need to use <BR/> or
</BR> to make a well-formed document. You cannot simply say <BR> as you can in HTML.

Element Nesting

In addition to having elements that contain nothing, an XML element can contain other elements. For example, the Author tag in the previous XML file contains FirstName, LastName, and other subelements.

Each Author element in the file includes a series of related address elements: Street, City, State, and Zip. These go together so you could give the document a little more structure by grouping these elements into their own nested Address element like this.

```
<Address>
  <Street>323 Nederland Place</Street>
  <City>Boulder</City>
  <State>CO</State>
  <Zip>80013</Zip>
</Address>
```

Using nested elements does not make a huge difference in this example. If each Author element contained more than one address, however, it could be very helpful. In that case, you could use separate Address elements to represent the home address, work address, and any other addresses you needed.

Attributes

The previous example contains three kinds of phone numbers: HomePhone, WorkPhone, and FaxPhone. Instead of giving each of these fields a separate tag with a different name, the XML standard lets you use the same tag with different *attributes*. Instead of making separate <HomePhone>, <WorkPhone>, and <FaxPhone> tags, the XML file can use the single tag type <Phone>. Each <Phone> entry uses an attribute that defines the kind of phone number contained in the tag. For example:

```
<Phone type="home">3035551133</Phone>
<Phone type="work">3035551144</Phone>
<Phone type="fax">3035551155</Phone>
```

Similarly, if you modified the Author element to contain separate home and work addresses, you could assign them all to Address tags and give them different type attributes.

With these improvements, the contact information file becomes this:

```
<?xml version="1.0"?>
<Contacts>
  <Author>
    <IMG SRC="http://www.vb-helper.com/images/brian.gif"/>
    <FirstName>Brian</FirstName>
    <LastName>Hochgurtel</LastName>
    <Address type="home">
      <Street>123 Gold Hill Drive</Street>
      <City>Boulder</City>
      <State>CO</State>
      <Zip>80504</Zip>
    </Address>
    <Phone type="home">3035551212</Phone>
    <Phone type="work">3035551213</Phone>
    <Phone type="fax">3035551214</Phone>
  </Author>
  <Author>
    <IMG SRC="http://www.vb-helper.com/images/rod.gif"/>
    <FirstName>Rod</FirstName>
    <LastName>Stephens</LastName>
    <Address type="home">
      <Street>323 Nederland Place</Street>
      <City>Boulder</City>
      <State>CO</State>
      <Zip>80013</Zip>
    </Address>
    <Address type="work">
      <Street>869 Bug Blvd</Street>
      <City>Programmersville</City>
      <State>CO</State>
      <Zip>80808</Zip>
    </Address>
    <Phone type="home">3035551133</Phone>
    <Phone type="work">3035551144</Phone>
    <Phone type="fax">3035551155</Phone>
  </Author>
</Contacts>
```

Whether you should give two data items different tags or make them share a single tag with different attributes is largely a matter of style. If two items are different kinds of the same thing, like work and home phone numbers, use one tag with different attributes. If two items are different kinds of things, like Street and City, give them their own tags.

When you read an XML file, you will probably be able to figure out what the different pieces of data represent whichever way you do things. Using a system of tags that makes sense can be a big help when you load the data into a Visual Basic program. Programs often need to group values that are different kinds of the same thing, like different kinds of phone numbers. If you give these items the same name and different attributes, processing the items as a group is a little easier.

Comments

You should comment your code in any programming language. While XML is a data description language, not a programming language, you should still use comments to make it easier to understand. Comments are an important part of the documentation process. Without comments, you may have trouble understanding what your code was supposed to do when you look at it later. Other people who read your code will certainly understand it more easily if you include comments.

XML comments are identical to those found in HTML. A one-line comment in XML looks like this:

```
<?xml version="1.0">
<!-- This Is a comment -->
<Database>Oracle</Database>
```

Comments can also span multiple lines, as in this code.

```
<?xml version="1.0">
<!-- This is a comment
     spanning multiple lines
     in this simple XML document. -->
<Database>Oracle</Database>
```

XML is not a procedural language. That means it doesn't do anything; it just sits there holding data. In that case, you may need to use a different commenting style than the one you use when you write Visual Basic code. Instead of explaining what the code does, you need to explain what the data represents. For example, you might break the XML file into sections and use comments to describe the data in each section, as in this example:

```
<?xml version="1.0">
<!-- Program Parameters -->
 . . .
<!-- Customer Data -->
 . . .
<!-- Inventory Data -->
 . . .
<!-- Pricing Data -->
 . . .
```

Using Namespaces

Namespaces give you a method of guaranteeing that the elements in an XML document are unique. If two XML documents use the same element name to describe two different types of data, a program using the data may become confused. Consider the following snippet of XML:

```
<State>Frozen</State>
```

This would cause a conflict with the earlier example that used the State element to hold the value Colorado. A namespace prevents this kind of name collision by adding a unique identifier to the elements.

To add a namespace to a document, add the following code to the root element:

```
<Contacts xmlns:vbhelper="www.vb-helper.com/XML">
```

This code assigns the namespace name vbhelper to the URL www.vb-helper.com/ XML. Namespaces use URLs to guarantee uniqueness. As long as different developers use URLs that they own and control, no two developers will use the same URLs.

The namespace could just as easily use an invalid URL, also called a pseudo-url, as in this example:

```
<Contacts xmlns:vbhelper="www-vb-helper-com/XML">
```

Here the URL is invalid, but it still gives a unique identifier for the namespace. Note that the URL doesn't need to contain any information relevant to the namespace, though there has been some discussion about creating some sort of standard on what kinds of URLs to use.

Once the namespace is declared, the XML file can use it to prefix tag names like this:

```
<?xml version="1.0"?>
<Contacts xmlns:vbhelper="www.vb-helper.com/XML">
  <vbhelper:Author>
    <vbhelper:IMG SRC="http://www.vb-helper.com/images/brian.gif"/>
    <vbhelper:FirstName>Brian</vbhelper:FirstName>
    <vbhelper:LastName>Hochgurtel</vbhelper:LastName>
    <vbhelper:Address type="home">
      <vbhelper:Street>123 Gold Hill Drive</vbhelper:Street>
      <vbhelper:City>Boulder</vbhelper:City>
      <vbhelper:State>CO</vbhelper:State>
      <vbhelper:Zip>80504</vbhelper:Zip>
    </vbhelper:Address>
    <vbhelper:Phone type="home">3035551212</vbhelper:Phone>
    <vbhelper:Phone type="work">3035551213</vbhelper:Phone>
    <vbhelper:Phone type="fax">3035551214</vbhelper:Phone>
  </vbhelper:Author>
</Contacts>
```

This adds complexity to the document but guarantees the document's element names will not conflict with any other element names the application comes across. To simplify this code, the document can use a default namespace. The root element declares its namespace like this:

```
<Contacts xmlns="www.vb-helper.com/XML">
```

Notice that no colon follows the keyword xmlns in this declaration. That means this namespace applies to all of the elements inside the Contacts element.

When an element uses a default namespace, the items it contains don't need to give their namespace explicitly. The parser is smart enough to give all the tags the default namespace.

Unfortunately, XML development isn't always this straightforward. A single document often requires more than one namespace. A document can declare multiple namespaces, as in the following example. This code declares the vbhelper and advocate namespaces, and it sets the Contact element's default namespace to www.wiley.com.

```
<Contact
  xmlns:vbhelper = "www.vb-helper.com"
  xmlns:advocate  = "www.advocatemedia.com"
  xmlns = "www.wiley.com">
</Contact>
```

The following example is also valid. It declares the same namespaces and also indicates that the Contact element itself is part of the vbhelper namespace.

```
<vbhelper:Contact
  xmlns:vbhelper = "www.vb-helper.com"
  xmlns:advocate  = "www.advocatemedia.com"
  xmlns = "www.wiley.com">
</vb-helper:Contact>
```

A parser reading this file can keep track of all of the namespaces in use at any given moment. Consider the following XML document with several namespaces:

```
<Contacts
  xmlns:Authors = "www.vb-helper.com/XML"
  xmlns:Microsoft = "www.microsoft.com/NET"
  xmlns = "www.wiley.com">
    <Authors:City>Boulder</Authors:City>
    <Authors:State>Colorado</Authors:State>
    <Authors:Zip>80015</Authors:Zip>
    <Microsoft:Product>VB.Net</Microsoft:Product>
</Contacts>
```

A parsing program could read this file and list the elements with their namespaces like this:

```
Begin Parsing Document
----------------------------------------------------------------
Start Element:Contacts          Namespace: www.wiley.com
Start Element:City              Namespace: www.vb-helper.com/XML
        Value:Boulder
  End Element:City              Namespace: www.vb-helper.com/XML
Start Element:State             Namespace: www.vb-helper.com/XML
        Value:Colorado
```

```
      End Element:State              Namespace: www.vb-helper.com/XML
   Start Element:Zip                 Namespace: www.vb-helper.com/XML
            Value:80015
      End Element:Zip                Namespace: www.vb-helper.com/XML
   Start Element:Product             Namespace: www.microsoft.com/NET
            Value:80015
      End Element:Product            Namespace: www.microsoft.com/NET
      End Element:Contact            Namespace: www.wiley.com
   ------------------------------------------------------------
End Parsing Document
```

Notice that the parser knows that the Contacts element is part of the default namespace of www.wiley.com because it does not have a namespace prefix. If the XML data did not declare a default namespace, the Contacts element and any other elements with a namespace prefix would be considered part of the *global default namespace*.

Because namespaces add complexity to XML documents, you should use them only when necessary. If you might need to merge one XML file with another, you may want to give the two documents namespaces so their element names do not collide. An XML file also needs to use namespaces to refer to special processing elements. For example, schemas and stylesheets use special prefixes to indicate processing elements.

Using the XML Editor in Visual Studio .NET

Although creating an XML document is a relatively simple task, creating a document within a text editor such as notepad can be tedious. Notepad also provides no hints or validation so you can easily add mistakes to the file. Two common mistakes are not spelling an element's start and end tags the same way (<Authors>...</authors>) and omitting the / in the closing tag (<Authors>...<Authors>).

Fortunately, the Visual Basic .NET development environment includes an XML editor to make editing XML files easier. This editor includes several nice features including text and data views, automatic indentation, and automatic generation of correctly spelled closing tags.

To use the XML editor, create a new Visual Basic Windows application project within Visual Studio .NET and select the project menu's Add New Item command. This displays the dialog shown in Figure 1.1. On the left side of the dialog, click on Local Project Items. On the right side of the dialog, select XML File from the list of file types and click Open. This brings up a blank XML editor window for the new XML document you added to the project.

Type an opening tag in the XML editor. Notice how the editor automatically creates the closing tag for you. Figure 1.2 shows the XML editor displaying the file Author-Contacts.xml.

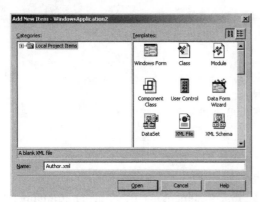

Figure 1.1 Use the Project menu's Add New Item command to add an XML file to a project.

The XML editor's data view lets you work with the data without worrying about the XML file's tags and processing instructions. To use the data view, click the Data button in the XML editor's lower left corner. Figure 1.3 shows the XML editor's data view. Click on a cell to change the cell's value. Click on any field in the bottom row marked with an asterisk to add a new data record. Click on the leftmost column in a row to select it and then press the Delete key to remove that record.

When you finish editing the data, click the XML button in the editor's lower left corner to view the XML file's text. You should see any changes you made using the data view.

Figure 1.2 You can use Visual Basic's XML editor to enter XML data.

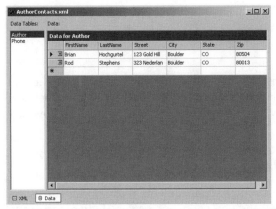

Figure 1.3   The XML editor's data view lets you edit XML data as records.

Validation

When a program *validates* an XML document, it verifies that the document contains the correct data and is in the correct format. The following sections discuss valid XML documents. They explain how a document might be well-formed but not valid. They also tell how you can use DTD and XSD schema files to validate an XML document.

Well-Formed Documents

A *well-formed* XML document follows the rules of the W3C standard for XML. All that really means is an XML parser should be able to read the file without getting confused.

To be well-formed, every tag must have a corresponding closing tag. For example, if a data element begins with the tag <HomePhone>, it must end with the closing tag </HomePhone>. The exception is the shortcut tag for an empty element where the closing slash (/) is inside the tag itself.

Attributes in a tag must be surrounded by quotes, as in this example.

```
<Address type="work"></Address>
```

Tags can strictly contain each other, but they cannot overlap. In the contact file, the Author tag contains the FirstName, LastName, Address, and other tags. It could not contain only part of a tag like this:

```
<Author>
    <Address type="work">
        <Street>869 Bug Blvd</Street>
        <City>Programmersville</City>
```

```
</Author>
        <State>CO</State>
        <Zip>80808</Zip>
    </Address>
```

Here the Author tag contains some but not all of the Address tag. One tag can contain all or none of another tag, but it cannot contain just part of the other tag. Consistent indentation, as shown in this example, makes this kind of partial overlap easy to see.

Validating and Non-Validating Parsers

Before you get into a deep discussion of valid XML documents, it's important to understand the difference between validating and non-validating parsers. Both report errors in the document's well-formedness. Only a validating parser will check the correctness of the document against a DTD (Document Type Definition) or XSD (XML Schema Definition) schema file. The schema contains the rules the parser uses to validate the XML file.

A non-validating parser checks an XML document for well-formedness, but it will not report any errors that occur if values in the XML document violate the rules set in the associated schema. It ignores the rules in the schema file.

Although Visual Basic .NET does not provide tools for building DTD files, it can validate an XML file against a DTD schema. The Web is full of XML documents that use DTD files so it's important for you to understand what's happening within the DTD.

The following section briefly describes DTD files. There are several other kinds of schema files including XDR and XSD schemas. Chapter 5, "Schemas," briefly discusses DTD and XDR schemas and describes XSD schemas in detail.

Valid Documents and DTD

A *valid* XML document's contents conform to the rules found in the associated DTD or XSD schema file. Before a document can be considered valid, it must pass all the well-formedness rules explained earlier in this chapter. This section focuses on how a DTD works and its syntax.

The DTD file uses *element type declarations* that describe the allowed elements in the XML document. For example, you might want to require the first name, last name, and work address fields. The IMG, home, and fax phone numbers fields might be optional.

The DTD file's first element type declaration is for Contacts, the XML file's outermost tag.

```
<!ELEMENT Contacts (Author+)>
```

This statement means the XML document has a Contacts tag that contains at least one Author element. The parentheses indicate that the list of Authors must occur inside the Contacts element. The plus sign indicates the file must contain one or more Authors.

The following statement says the Author tag includes zero or more IMG elements and one or more FirstName, LastName, Address, and Phone elements. A comma between the child elements indicates that the order of the children is required. If the DTD file used a vertical bar (|) instead of a comma, the order would be unimportant.

A plus sign (+) after the name of a child element means one or more of that element will be present in the document. An asterisk (*) means zero or more of that element appears. A question mark (?) means the element is optional.

```
<!ELEMENT Author (IMG*, FirstName+, LastName+, Address+, Phone+)>
```

The following statements define rules for each of the Author's simple child elements. Each of these elements contains parsed character data (PCDATA) so these fields contain text. The ATTLIST statement forces the Phone tag to have an attribute named "type." This attribute is required and is character data (CDATA).

```
<!ELEMENT FirstName (#PCDATA)>
<!ELEMENT LastName  (#PCDATA)>
<!ELEMENT Phone     (#PCDATA)>
<!ATTLIST Phone type CDATA #REQUIRED>
```

Unfortunately, DTDs have a number of shortcomings that make them an incomplete solution for validating data. For example, they do not allow you to verify that a field contains a value that looks like a phone number. If the DTD cannot validate the data completely, your program must still perform its own data validation. In that case, you might wonder why you should bother with a DTD.

While some validation is generally better than none, XSD (XML Schema Definition) provides a more comprehensive solution. An XSD schema has much more power and flexibility than a DTD file. Microsoft has chosen XSD as its validation method of choice so Visual Basic provides more tools to work with XSD than with other kinds of schemas. Because Visual Basic focuses on XSD, this book doesn't cover DTD in great detail. For more information on DTD, look at the W3C specification at www.w3c.org. For more information on XSD and schemas in general, see Chapter 5, "Schemas."

Using DTD Files

Once you have created a DTD file, you can attach it to an XML file. One way to do that is to add a DOCTYPE statement to the beginning of the XML file. The following statement tells the parser to look for the DTD file named ContactInfo.dtd in the same directory as the XML file.

```
<!DOCTYPE Contacts SYSTEM "ContactInfo.dtd">
```

If the DTD file is not in the same directory as the XML file, this statement can give the DTD file's complete location.

```
<!DOCTYPE Contacts SYSTEM "http://www.vb-
helper.com/XML/ContactInfo.dtd">
```

You can also include the DTD file text directly inside the XML file.

```
<?xml version="1.0"?>
<!--The DTD along with the PI Is called the prolog -->
<!--of the XML document -->
```

```
<!DOCTYPE Contacts [
<!ELEMENT Contacts (Author+ )>
<!ELEMENT Author (IMG?,FirstName+, LastName+, Address+, Phone+)>
<!ELEMENT FirstName (#PCDATA )>
<!ELEMENT LastName (#PCDATA )>
<!ELEMENT Address (Street+,City+, State+, Zip+ )>
<!ATTLIST Address type CDATA #REQUIRED>
<!ELEMENT City   (#PCDATA)>
<!ELEMENT Street (#PCDATA)>
<!ELEMENT State  (#PCDATA)>
<!ELEMENT Zip    (#PCDATA)>
<!ELEMENT Phone  (#PCDATA)>
<!ATTLIST Phone type CDATA #REQUIRED>
<!ELEMENT IMG EMPTY>
<!ATTLIST IMG SRC CDATA #REQUIRED>
]>
<Contacts>
  <Author>
    <IMG SRC="http://www.vb-helper.com/images/brian.gif"/>
    <FirstName>Brian</FirstName>
    <LastName>Hochgurtel</LastName>
    <Address type="home">
      <Street>123 Gold Hill Drive</Street>
      <City>Boulder</City>
      <State>CO</State>
      <Zip>80504</Zip>
    </Address>
    <Phone type="home">3035551212</Phone>
    <Phone type="work">3035551213</Phone>
    <Phone type="fax">3035551214</Phone>
  </Author>
  <Author>
    <IMG SRC="http://www.vb-helper.com/images/rod.gif"/>
    <FirstName>Rod</FirstName>
    <LastName>Stephens</LastName>
    <Address type="home">
      <Street>323 Nederland Place</Street>
      <City>Boulder</City>
      <State>CO</State>
      <Zip>80013</Zip>
    </Address>
    <Address type="work">
      <Street>869 Bug Blvd</Street>
      <City>Programmersville</City>
      <State>CO</State>
      <Zip>80808</Zip>
    </Address>
    <Phone type="home">3035551133</Phone>
    <Phone type="work">3035551144</Phone>
    <Phone type="fax">3035551155</Phone>
  </Author>
</Contacts>
```

When a parser reads this XML file, it either loads the DTD file from the specified location or gets it directly from the XML file. As it loads the XML data, the parser can verify that it follows the rules specified in the DTD file. If the XML data doesn't follow the rules, the parser rejects it.

For instance, if you have Internet Explorer's XML Utility Plug-In installed, Internet Explorer automatically validates the XML files it reads if it can find the DTD data. For more information on obtaining and installing this plug-in, see Chapter 10, "Internet Explorer."

Entity Definitions

An entity is an abbreviation for data within an XML document. After an entity is defined, the XML data can refer to its value easily. Consider the following example:

```
<!DOCTYPE Contacts SYSTEM
  "http://www.vb-helper.com/examples/rolodex.dtd" [
  <!ENTITY ROD "<Author>Rod Stephens</Author>">
  <!ENTITY BRIAN "Brian Hochgurtel">
]>
```

In this example, the DTD is external and is located at the specified URL. After specifying the DTD file's location, the file defines two entities: ROD and BRIAN. ROD contains an Author element holding the text Rod Stephens. Note an entity that contains an opening element must also contain the corresponding closing element. The file cannot open an element in one entity and close it in another.

The BRIAN entity contains the text Brian Hochgurtel.

An XML file uses an entity by including an ampersand, the entity's name, and a semi-colon. For example, the XML data might contain the text &ROD;. When it reads the data, a parser expands the entity to <Author>Rod Stephens</Author>.

The following XML document uses several entities.

```
<!DOCTYPE Contacts SYSTEM
  "http://www.vb-helper.com/examples/rolodex.dtd" [
  <!ENTITY HOME "http://www.vb-helper.com">
  <!ENTITY BRIAN "Brian">
  <!ENTITY ROD "<FirstName>Rod</FirstName>">
  <!ENTITY STEPHENS "<LastName>Stephens</LastName>">
  <!ENTITY CITY "<City>BOULDER</City>">
  <!ENTITY STATE "<State>CO</State>">
]>
<Contacts>
  <Author>
    <IMG SRC="&HOME;/images/brian.gif"/>
    <FirstName>&BRIAN;</FirstName>
    <LastName>Hochgurtel</LastName>
    <Address type="home">
      <Street>123 Gold Hill Drive</Street>
      &CITY;
      &STATE;
```

```
        <Zip>80504</Zip>
      </Address>
      <Phone type="home">3035551212</Phone>
      <Phone type="work">3035551213</Phone>
      <Phone type="fax">3035551214</Phone>
    </Author>
    <Author>
      <IMG SRC="&HOME;/images/rod.gif"/>
      &ROD;
      &STEPHENS;
      <Address type="home">
        <Street>323 Nederland Place</Street>
        &CITY;
        &STATE;
        <Zip>80013</Zip>
      </Address>
      <Address type="work">
        <Street>869 Bug Blvd</Street>
        <City>Programmersville</City>
        &STATE;
        <Zip>80808</Zip>
      </Address>
      <Phone type="home">3035551133</Phone>
      <Phone type="work">3035551144</Phone>
      <Phone type="fax">3035551155</Phone>
    </Author>
  </Contacts>
```

XSD Schemas

You may have noticed that the syntax for DTD files is even less friendly than the syntax of XML files. One of the biggest problems with DTD files is that they are not based on XML. They originate from the Standard Generalized Markup Language (SGML) that was created for the publishing industry. DTDs don't always fit the needs of an XML developer perfectly because they were originally designed for one specific industry rather than for broad use. To use DTD files, you need to learn to speak both XML and DTD.

XSD schemas offer an alternative to DTD files. An XSD schema uses XML itself to verify the contents and order of fields in an XML document. It accomplishes roughly the same thing as a DTD file but uses a syntax that is similar to that of an XML document.

Of the schema languages available, Microsoft has chosen XSD schemas to use in validating XML documents. While Visual Basic provides some tools for validating XML documents using DTD and XDR schemas, it provides the most support for XSD schemas. Because XSD is the schema language of choice for Visual Basic, the term schema usually means XSD schema unless specified otherwise.

The first step in building an XSD schema is to define the xsd namespace, as in this example.

```
<xsd:schema xmlns:xsd="http://www.w3.org/2000/08/XMLSchema">
    <!-- Rules will appear within the schema root element -->
</xsd:schema>
```

This namespace identifies the name xsd with the URL http://www.w3.org/2000/08/XMLSchema. The URL is just an address that should be unique within the document. In other words, no other namespace should use the same URL.

By convention, you should use the name "xsd" for the schema's namespace. You could use some other name, but "xsd" is standard. The W3C has reserved this particular URL for schemas. If you use it to define your namespace, you should not have a problem with other namespaces using it for different purposes. Using the standard URL also helps other developers understand your code.

After you have defined the schema namespace, schema tags should begin with its name. For example, the following statement defines a tag named complexType. The xsd prefix tells the parser that this is the complexType tag in the xsd namespace. If the XML document has some other tag named complexType, the parser will be able to tell them apart as long as they are in different namespaces.

```
<xsd:complexType></xsd:complexType>
```

You can also define additional namespaces inside the schema. To do that, you would add more xmlns arguments. In the following code, the default namespace is set by defining xmlns ="http://www.vb-helper.com/XMLFile1.xsd". Any tag that appears in the schema without a prefix is considered part of the default namespace.

This code also defines the namespace vbhelper. Any tags that you want to be part of the vbhelper namespace should begin with the vbhelper prefix.

```
<xsd:schema
    xmlns ="http://www.vb-helper.com/XMLFile1.xsd"
    xmlns:vbhelper = "http://www.vb-helper.com/XMLFile1.xsd"
    xmlns:xsd="http://www.w3.org/2001/XMLSchema">
</xsd:schema>
```

Note that a namespace URL does not need to have any content. It just acts as a placeholder that other XML files and schemas are unlikely to use. Some developers place a file that says "XML Schema namespace" at the namespace's URL.

Building Schemas

The following code shows a schema that validates the file AuthorContacts.xml. All schemas begin with a schema tag. This tag uses xmlns attributes to declare its default namespace and the standard xsd namespace.

The XML file's data root node is named Contacts so the schema element contains an element named Contacts. Because this element contains other elements, it is a complex type so the Contacts element contains a complexType element.

The complexType element contains a choice element. A choice element allows the XML file to contain one of the items inside the choice element. In this case, the choice element contains only an element named Author. Allowing the XML file to contain any

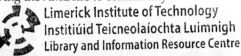

item selected from a list containing the single item Author doesn't seem like much help. This statement is needed to satisfy the rules of XSD. The choice element also includes the attribute maxOccurs="unbounded" to indicate that the Contacts element can contain any number of Author elements.

Author also contains other elements so it is also a complex type. The corresponding element contains a complexType element.

This complexType element contains a sequence element. A sequence requires the XML document to contain the items inside the sequence in order.

The sequence element contains elements representing FirstName, LastName, Street, City, State, Zip, and Phone. By default, each of these elements must appear exactly once. The Phone element overrides this default, using the minOccurs and maxOccurs attributes to indicate it can occur any number of times (including zero).

Unlike the other elements inside the sequence, the Phone element is not simple. If you look at the AuthorContacts.xml code shown earlier in this chapter, you will see that the Phone element has a type attribute. To build that into the schema, the Phone element contains a complexType element.

This complexType element contains a simpleContent element. A simpleContent element can contain only a simple element, not another complexType. In this case, the simpleContent element uses an extension based on the string data type. The extension contains an attribute element named type. This combination of elements (complexType, simpleContent, extension, attribute) adds the type attribute to the Phone element.

```
<xsd:schema
xmlns="http://www.vb-helper.com/AuthorContacts.xsd"
xmlns:xsd="http://www.w3.org/2001/XMLSchema">
  <xsd:element name="Contacts">
    <xsd:complexType>
      <xsd:choice maxOccurs="unbounded">
        <xsd:element name="Author">
          <xsd:complexType>
            <xsd:sequence>
              <xsd:element name="FirstName" type="xsd:string" />
              <xsd:element name="LastName" type="xsd:string" />
              <xsd:element name="Street" type="xsd:string" />
              <xsd:element name="City" type="xsd:string" />
              <xsd:element name="State" type="xsd:string" />
              <xsd:element name="Zip" type="xsd:string" />
              <xsd:element name="Phone" minOccurs="0"
                                       maxOccurs="unbounded">
                <xsd:complexType>
                  <xsd:simpleContent>
                    <xsd:extension base="xsd:string">
                      <xsd:attribute name="type" type="xsd:string" />
                    </xsd:extension>
                  </xsd:simpleContent>
                </xsd:complexType>
              </xsd:element>
            </xsd:sequence>
```

```
            </xsd:complexType>
          </xsd:element>
        </xsd:choice>
      </xsd:complexType>
    </xsd:element>
  </xsd:schema>
```

Schemas are difficult to program by hand in a text editor such as Notepad. Fortunately, tools in Visual Basic .NET and third-party tools such as XML Spy can generate schemas for a given XML document. After you generate the schema, you can change the result by hand to provide a better representation of the data.

Unlike DTD files, schemas cannot be contained within an XML document. That would require two root elements: Contacts and xsd:schema. Having the two root elements would cause an error when parsing the document because the XML standard allows only one root element.

There are several ways you can validate an XML document with a schema. First, you can validate the document at design time using the XML editing tools in the development environment. Second, you can call Visual Basic routines to validate the file at run time. Chapter 5, "Schemas," explains how to use these two methods.

You can also refer to a schema file in the XML document's root element. That makes the parser automatically validate the document when it reads the data. The following code shows how an XML file's Contacts element can refer to the document's schema.

```
<Contacts
  xmlns:xsi="http://www.w3c.org/2000/10/XMLSchema-instance"
  xsi:schemaLocation="http://www.vb-helper.com/XML/Schemas
    file:contacts.xsd">
```

The xmlns:xsi statement defines the xsi schema instance namespace. By convention, you should call the schema namespace xsi inside the XML document. Like the namespace URL in the schema itself, this URL is just a placeholder that makes the namespace unique.

The xsi:schemaLocation contains two values. While they don't fit on one line here, the URL and the string file:contacts.xsd are contained in the same set of quotation marks. The first value is a URL that acts as a unique placeholder for the schema. The second value tells validating parsers where to find the document's schema. In this case, file:contacts.xsd means that the schema is in the same directory as the XML document. This value could have included a complete URL to indicate the schema's location on the Web.

Creating Schemas in Visual Studio .NET

If it looks difficult to create a good schema, don't worry because the XML editor discussed earlier has a built-in tool to create schemas quickly. Open the project you created earlier in this chapter and open the XML document.

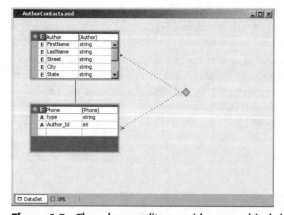

```
AuthorContacts.xsd
    <xsd:schema id="Contacts" targetNamespace="http://www.vb-helper.c
      <xsd:element name="Contacts" msdata:IsDataSet="true" msdata:Enf
        <xsd:complexType>
          <xsd:choice maxOccurs="unbounded">
            <xsd:element name="Author">
              <xsd:complexType>
                <xsd:sequence>
                  <xsd:element name="FirstName" type="xsd:string" min
                  <xsd:element name="LastName" type="xsd:string" minO
                  <xsd:element name="Street" type="xsd:string" minOcc
                  <xsd:element name="City" type="xsd:string" minOccur
                  <xsd:element name="State" type="xsd:string" minOccu
                  <xsd:element name="Zip" type="xsd:string" minOccurs
                  <xsd:element name="Phone" minOccurs="0" maxOccurs="
                    <xsd:complexType>
                      <xsd:simpleContent msdata:ColumnName="Phone_Tex
                        <xsd:extension base="xsd:string">
                          <xsd:attribute name="type" form="unqualifie
                          <xsd:attribute name="Author_Id" type="xsd:i
                        </xsd:extension>
                      </xsd:simpleContent>
  Schema    XML
```

Figure 1.4   Visual Basic can automatically create a schema for an XML file.

While viewing your XML file, note that an XML menu appears on the menu bar. Open this menu and select Create Schema. This automatically builds a schema for the XML document. Double-click on the .xsd file in the Solution Explorer to open the file in the schema editor shown in Figure 1.4.

Just as you can view text and data versions of an XML document, you can see text and graphical views of a schema. Click the Schema button on the editor's lower left corner to see a graphical representation of the schema. Figure 1.5 shows the editor's graphical view.

Unfortunately, the schema editor's graphical view does not give you access to every feature provided by a schema. For example, it will not let you set an item's minOccurs and maxOccurs values. To modify these items, you need to display the schema's text and make the changes manually.

```
AuthorContacts.xsd
  E Author      (Author)
  E FirstName   string
  E LastName    string
  E Street      string
  E City        string
  E State       string

  E Phone       (Phone)
  A type        string
  A Author_Id   int

  DataSet    XML
```

Figure 1.5   The schema editor provides a graphical view where you can modify the schema.

Conclusion

XML doesn't do anything by itself—it simply allows you to define data in a standard way. That lets different programs load and understand the data relatively easily.

While XML does nothing more than define data, it does that with remarkable flexibility. It lets you define tags that describe your data in your own terms. By using meaningful tag names and comments, you can make an XML file self-documenting and easy to understand.

DTD and XSD schema files let you further determine how data must be stored in an XML file. You can require that values appear in a certain order, specify their data types, and give them minimum and maximum allowed values. All these features give the data extra structure that a program can use to manipulate the data more effectively.

This chapter is not intended to tell you everything there is to know about XML, DTD files, or XSD schemas. These are each large topics, and their standards are continuously evolving. For more information, see the W3C and Microsoft Web sites. Other chapters later in this book also provide more detailed information on topics such as XSL and schemas.

This chapter gives a fast overview so you know how these topics fit together. It should be enough to let you follow the examples later in this book that show how you can take advantage of XML in your Visual Basic applications.

The Document Object Model (DOM) is a representation of the data in an XML document held in memory. It represents the document's tree-like hierarchy explicitly.

In contrast, the XmlTextReader and XmlTextWriter classes discussed in Chapter 3, "Forward-Only XML," store only local information about an XML document. They process the document's nodes one at a time without storing information about the document's structure as a whole.

From a Visual Basic program's point of view, the DOM includes a collection of object classes that represent various pieces of an XML document. For example, the XmlDocument class represents the XML document itself, and the XmlComment class represents a comment inside the document.

This chapter explores the DOM classes provided by Visual Basic. Using these classes your programs can build, load, modify, and save complicated XML documents quickly and easily.

The following sections describe the DOM classes. The sections after that show how you can wrap DOM object creation functions in separate routines to make building documents easier. The final sections in this chapter present several examples that use the DOM to perform useful programming tasks.

DOM Objects

Before you can use the DOM objects to manipulate XML files, you need to know what those objects are. The following sections describe the DOM classes roughly in their order of importance.

XmlNode

The XmlNode class is an abstract class. That means you cannot directly create an instance of this class. Instead you can create instances of classes derived from the XmlNode class.

That may make the XmlNode class seem to be of secondary importance. Actually XmlNode is very useful for two reasons. First, you can use an XmlNode object to "walk" over an XML document's representation. The XmlNode object you declare can represent the objects contained in the document without knowing what kind of objects it represents. It can "walk" over XmlElements, XmlComment, or XmlWhitespace objects. The following code shows how a program might list the values of the nodes contained within a document's root node.

```
Dim root As XmlNode
Dim xml_node As XmlNode

' Get the document's root node.
root = xml_doc.FirstChild

' Walk over the root's children.
For Each xml_node In root.ChildNodes
    Debug.WriteLine(xml_node.InnerText)
Next xml_node
```

The second reason the XmlNode class is useful is that it defines a lot of functionality that is common to all of the objects that make up a document's representation. For example, the XmlNode class defines the ChildNodes collection used in the previous code. All of the classes that represent parts of the document provide similar ChildNodes collections so you can navigate through the document uniformly. You don't need to worry about what kind of object you are visiting because they all provide this collection.

For example, the DisplayNodeInformation function shown in the following code returns a string showing the structure of a node and its child nodes. The routine begins by adding the node's name and value to a result string. Then, if the node has a ChildNodes collection, the routine calls the DisplayNodeInformation function for each child node and adds the results to its result string. The routine adds four to the indent parameter in the calls to DisplayNodeInformation so the child information is indented farther than this node's information.

```
' Return indented information about this node and its descendants.
Private Function DisplayNodeInformation(ByVal xml_node As XmlNode, _
    Optional ByVal indent As Integer = 0) As String
    Dim results As String
    Dim child_node As XmlNode

    ' Add this node to the results
    results = Space(indent) & xml_node.Name & " [" & _
        xml_node.Value & "]" & vbCrLf

    ' Add the child nodes to the results.
```

```
    ' Make sure we have a ChildNodes collection.
    If Not (xml_node.ChildNodes Is Nothing) Then
        ' Display each child node.
        For Each child_node In xml_node.ChildNodes
            results = results & _
                DisplayNodeInformation(child_node, indent + 4)
        Next child_node
    End If


    Return results
End Function
```

The WalkDom example program described a little later uses this code to display an XML file's structure.

Subclass Differences

While this apparent uniformity is very helpful, it can be a little misleading, particularly for the Attributes method. An object's Attributes method returns a collection of XmlAttribute objects that apply to the object. Although all of the objects derived from XmlNode provide an Attributes method, only the XmlElement class actually has attributes because only an XML element can have attributes. The Attributes method provided by all of the other DOM classes returns Nothing.

If an XmlElement object has no attributes, its Attributes method still returns a collection, but the collection is empty. On the other hand, an XmlAttribute object's Attributes method returns Nothing. That means you cannot use the same code to decide whether a DOM object has attributes in both cases.

The XmlElement class provides a HasAttributes property that returns True if the element has any attributes. Unfortunately, that method doesn't exist for the other DOM classes so you cannot use HasAttributes to look for attributes uniformly. You must first see if the Attributes method returns Nothing or verify that the object is an XmlElement before you can use its HasAttributes method.

Different kinds of DOM objects also handle child nodes slightly differently. In particular, some classes cannot have children belonging to certain classes. For example, an XmlAttribute object cannot have an XmlElement object as a child; however, an XmlAttribute object can have any number of XmlText objects as children. These children are essentially concatenated into a single value.

Identifying Nodes

An XML document has a basically tree-like structure. The document may begin with an XML declaration, preprocessing instructions, and a DOCTYPE section, but once the actual data starts the document seems more or less tree-shaped.

While the idea is straightforward, an XML document as read into DOM objects may contain a lot of objects that you would not normally think of as nodes in the tree. For example, consider the following simple XML document.

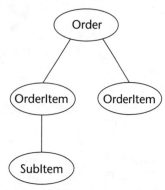

Figure 2.1   An XML file's logical structure can seem deceptively simple.

```
<Order>
    <OrderItem>Item 1
        <SubItem />
    </OrderItem>
    <OrderItem>Item 2</OrderItem>
</Order>
```

You might diagram the logical structure of this document as shown in Figure 2.1. Actually, this document's DOM structure is a little more complex. First, the text values inside the OrderItem nodes are actually contained in child nodes. XML also preserves whitespace so there are hidden whitespace nodes between each node's closing bracket and the following node's starting bracket. Figure 2.2 shows this document's DOM structure.

Even if you ignore the whitespace, you probably think of the text inside a node as being the node's value, not a separate XmlText child node.

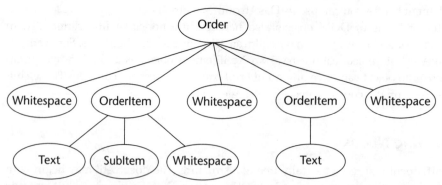

Figure 2.2   An XML file's DOM structure can contain hidden whitespace.

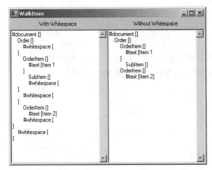

Figure 2.3 Program WalkDom displays an XML document's structure.

The XmlDocument class described in the following section represents an XML document as a whole. If you set the XmlDocument object's PreserveWhitespace property to False, the object strips whitespace out of any XML file it loads. If you set Preserve-Whitespace to True, the XmlDocument puts any whitespace in separate nodes.

The WalkDom example program shown in Figure 2.3 uses the PreserveWhitespace property to display an XML file's DOM structure. The output on the left shows the file's DOM structure when PreserveWhitespace is True. The output on the right shows the document's structure when PreserveWhitespace is False.

Notice that even when PreserveWhitespace is False, the structure contains some space that you might normally consider whitespace. On the right side in Figure 2.3, the first OrderItem's text value contains the text "Item 1" followed by a carriage return, linefeed, and eight spaces.

If you look closely at the document's XML code shown earlier, you will see that those characters appear between the text "Item 1" and the following SubItem node's opening bracket. If there had been no text in this position, the XmlDocument object would have considered these characters whitespace and removed them. As the file is, those characters are added to the "Item 1" text value.

Example program ReadPIs traverses an XML file much as program WalkDom does, but it displays information only about processing instructions. When it finds any other type of node, it recursively traverses that node's subtree looking for other processing instructions.

XmlDocument

The XmlDocument class is the root of the DOM. This class represents an in-memory copy of an XML document and all of the other objects that define the document's data. XmlDocument provides methods for creating, loading, saving, and manipulating an XML document in memory. It also provides methods to create the other objects that represent the document's data.

Load

The XmlDocument object's Load method loads an XML file into the object, creating any other objects that it needs to represent the document. For example, the following code declares an XmlDocument and makes it load the XML file Order.xml.

```
' Declare and allocate a new XmlDocument.
Dim xml_doc As New XmlDocument()

' Load an XML file into the XmlDocument.
xml_doc.Load("Order.xml")
```

Example program Load uses the Load method to initialize an XmlDocument object. Use the File menu's Open command to load an XML file. The program displays the file's contents, the document's InnerXml and OuterXml values, and its InnerText value.

Save

The XmlDocument object's Save method is just as easy to use as Load. This method takes as its only parameter the name of the file in which it should save the XML document.

```
' Create the XmlDocument.
...

' Save the XmlDocument into an XML file.
xml_doc.Save("Order.xml")
```

LoadXml

The XmlDocument object's LoadXml method creates a new XML document model using text passed into the routine. For example, the following code creates a new order document.

```
' Compose the XML text.
xml_text = _
    "<?xml version=""1.0""?>" & vbCrLf & _
    "<AllItems Customer=""Rod"" OrderDate=""4/1/3000"">" & vbCrLf & _
    "  <OrderedItem>" & vbCrLf & _
    "    <Item>Brownies</Item>" & vbCrLf & _
    "    <Price>1.25</Price>" & vbCrLf & _
    "    <Quantity>3</Quantity>" & vbCrLf & _
    "  </OrderedItem>" & vbCrLf & _
    "  <OrderedItem>" & vbCrLf & _
    "    <Item>Cookies</Item>" & vbCrLf & _
    "    <Price>0.25</Price>" & vbCrLf & _
    "    <Quantity>12</Quantity>" & vbCrLf & _
```

```
"     </OrderedItem>" & vbCrLf & _
"     <OrderedItem>" & vbCrLf & _
"         <Item>Cupcakes</Item>" & vbCrLf & _
"         <Price>0.5</Price>" & vbCrLf & _
"         <Quantity>6</Quantity>" & vbCrLf & _
"     </OrderedItem>" & vbCrLf & _
"</AllItems>"

' Declare and allocate a new XmlDocument.
Dim xml_doc As New XmlDocument()

' Load the document.
xml_doc.LoadXml(xml_text)
```

The LoadXml method allows you to create some or all of a document quickly and intuitively. It is common for programs to use LoadXml to initialize a document before using DOM objects to build the main body of the document. The following code uses LoadXml to define a document's XML declaration without using an XmlDeclaration object.

```
' Start the document.
xml_doc.LoadXml("<?xml version=""1.0""?><AllItems/>")

' Add orders to the document using DOM objects.
...
```

Note that the text you pass to the LoadXml method must represent a complete, valid XML document. For instance, you could not pass the method the string "<?xml version=""1.0""?>" because that doesn't define the document's root node.

Example program LoadXml uses similar code to build an XML file at run time.

InnerXml

The XmlDocument object's InnerXml property contains the XML markup that represents the document's children. Because the entire XML document is contained in children of the XmlDocument object, setting InnerXml does the same thing as using LoadXml. The following code has the same result as the previous version that uses LoadXml.

```
' Start the document.
xml_doc.InnerXml = "<?xml version=""1.0""?><AllItems/>"

' Add orders to the document using DOM objects.
...
```

For clarity, it is probably better to use LoadXml to initialize an XmlDocument; however, you can use InnerXml in a similar way to initialize other DOM objects quickly and easily. While an XmlElement object doesn't have a LoadXml method, it does have an InnerXml property.

Suppose a program creates a new XmlElement named new_order. It could then use the following code to give the new element two OrderItems.

```
new_order.InnerXml = _
    "<OrderItem>Cookie</OrderItem>" & _
    "<OrderItem>Milk</OrderItem>"
```

Creating the OrderItems using InnerXml would be slightly easier than using new XmlElement objects.

Creating Nodes

Before a program can add a new item to an XML document, it must create that item. The XmlDocument object provides methods for creating new document nodes. Table 2.1 lists the most useful node creation functions provided by the XmlDocument class.

All of the DOM objects provide a CloneNode method that creates a copy of the object. CloneNode's parameter, *deep*, is a Boolean indicating whether the copy should include the object's child nodes. If *deep* is False, CloneNode makes a copy of the object only. If *deep* is True, CloneNode makes a copy of the object and all of its descendants.

Table 2.1   Node Creation Functions

FUNCTION	OBJECT CREATED	XML EQUIVALENT
CreateAttribute	XmlAttribute	<Item *Attr="AttrValue"*>
CreateCDataSection	XmlCDataSection	<![CDATA[X > Y]]>
CreateComment	XmlComment	<!-- Comment text -->
CreateDocumentType	XmlDocumentType	<!DOCTYPE Root[<!ENTITY us "United States">]>
CreateElement	XmlElement	<Item>...</Item>
CreateEntityReference	XmlEntityReference	&us;
CreateProcessingInstruction	XmlProcessingInstruction	<?xml-stylesheet type="text/xsl" href="Test.xsl"?>
CreateTextNode	XmlText	<Item>*Item text*</Item>
CreateWhitespace	XmlWhitespace	This adds blank spaces, carriage returns, and so forth
CreateSignificantWhitespace	XmlSignificantWhitespace	This adds blank spaces, carriage returns, and so forth
CreateXmlDeclaration	XmlDeclaration	<?xml version="1.0"?>

All DOM objects also provide a Clone method that is equivalent to CloneNode(True).

The XmlDocument class also provides a method for copying nodes. The ImportNode method makes a copy of a node contained in another XmlDocument object. Like CloneNode, ImportNode takes a parameter that determines whether it creates a deep or a shallow copy. Use Clone or CloneNode when you want to make a copy of a node within the same XmlDocument object. Use ImportNode when you want to copy a node from one XmlDocument to another.

Attaching Nodes

After the program creates a new DOM object, it must attach the object to the document. Because of the document's tree-like structure, the new object must be added as a child of another object. The parent object can be another object in the document hierarchy, or it can be the XmlDocument itself. The XmlDocument can have only one XmlElement child, however. All of the XmlDocument's other children must be XML declarations, comments, processing instructions, and other non-XmlElements.

The XmlDocument class and the other DOM classes that can contain child nodes provide several methods for adding a node as a child. The AppendChild method adds the new child at the end of the child list. When you build an XML document from scratch, you usually start at the beginning and add items on one at a time. In that case, AppendChild is the only method you will need.

The PrependChild method inserts the child at the beginning of the parent node's child list. InsertBefore and InsertAfter add the new child before or after an existing child node, respectively.

The following code shows how a program might build a simple XmlDocument.

```
Dim xml_document As XmlDocument
Dim root As XmlElement
Dim child As XmlElement
Dim grandchild As XmlElement

' Make the document itself.
xml_document = New XmlDocument()

' Make a root node.
root = xml_document.CreateElement("AllItems")

' Add the root node to the document.
xml_document.AppendChild(root)

' Create a child element.
child = xml_document.CreateElement("Child")

' Add the child node to the root node.
root.AppendChild(child)

' Create a child element.
grandchild = xml_document.CreateElement("Grandchild")

' Add the child node to the root node.
```

```
child.AppendChild(grandchild)

' Save the XML document.
xml_document.Save("Test.xml")
```

This code produces the following XML document.

```
<AllItems>
  <Child>
    <Grandchild />
  </Child>
</AllItems>
```

Notice that the Grandchild node uses a single empty token rather than separate starting and ending tokens. As far as the DOM objects are concerned, there is no difference between these two possible representations. The object representing the Grandchild's ChildNodes collection is empty. When you save the document into an XML file or examine its InnerXml or OuterXml properties, the document represents nodes with no children using an empty token as in this example.

XmlElement

An XmlElement object represents a node defined by a normal XML token in the document. The following XML code corresponds to three XmlElement objects that represent the AllItems, Child, and Grandchild nodes.

```
<AllItems>
  <Child>
    <Grandchild />
  </Child>
</AllItems>
```

XmlElements define an XML document's tree-like hierarchy. Unlike many other DOM objects, they can include child objects and have attributes. The following code shows how a program might create a new XmlElement object and assign it an attribute.

```
' Create an XmlDocument and its root node.
...

' Create an OrderItem element.
order_item = xml_document.CreateElement("OrderItem")
root.AppendChild(order_item)

' Give the OrderItem a Quantity attribute.
order_attribute = xml_document.CreateAttribute("Quantity")
order_item.Attributes.Append(order_attribute)
order_attribute.Value = "50"

' Give the OrderItem some text.
order_text = xml_document.CreateTextNode("CD-R disc")
order_item.AppendChild(order_text)
```

Figure 2.4 Visual Basic displays this error message when a program tries to add a second root node to a document.

This code produces the following XML text.

```
<OrderItem Quantity="50">CD-R disc</OrderItem>
```

Usually it is easiest to create an element and immediately add it to the document before you work with the element. The previous example appends the new order_item element to the root node before it gives the new element a text value or attribute. Similarly, this example adds the new order_attribute to the order_item's Attributes collection before it assigns the order_attribute a value. Adding these objects to the document right away helps ensure that you don't forget to add them later.

One of the more common mistakes when adding elements to a document is giving the new element the wrong parent. The syntax for creating a new element is complicated enough that cut and paste can make programming easier. If you forget to change the parent node, you will add the new element to the wrong part of the document hierarchy.

A common variation on this error is adding the new element to the document itself rather than to another element in the tree, as shown in this code.

```
order_item = xml_document.CreateElement("OrderItem")
xml_document.AppendChild(order_item)
```

You should only make the document's root node a child of the document itself. Because XML documents can have only one root node, trying to add another element to the document raises an error at run time. In Visual Basic .NET Beta 2, the program displays the error message shown in Figure 2.4. The XmlDocument's DocumentElement property is a reference to the document's root element so this message is saying the program tried to add a new root node to the document. This error is easy to make but at least the error message makes it easy to find.

XmlAttribute

This object represents an XmlElement object's attribute. The XmlElement object's Attributes collection contains all of the XmlAttribute objects that apply to the XmlElement. The following code shows how a program can add an attribute to the element named xml_element in the document xml_document.

```
Dim xml_attribute As XmlAttribute

xml_attribute = xml_document.CreateAttribute("Quantity")
xml_attribute.Value = "12"
xml_element.Attributes.Append(xml_attribute)
```

If the element's name is OrderItem, this code produces the following XML.

```
<OrderItem Quantity="12">
```

XmlAttribute objects cannot have their own attributes, although you may be surprised to learn they can have children. In the previous example, the xml_attribute object's ChildNodes collection contains one XmlText object. That object's name is #text, and its value is 12.

You can use the XmlAttribute object's AppendChild method to add other XmlText objects to the attribute's ChildNodes collection. The XmlText objects are stored separately in the collection, but their values are concatenated when you invoke the attribute's Value method.

If you give an XmlAttribute object more than one XmlText child, you can combine them by invoking the XmlAttribute object's Normalize method. Normalize concatenates the XmlText objects into a single XmlText object.

XmlText

An XmlText object represents text within an element or attribute. For a simple token such as the one in the following code, the text is what you might think of as the token's value. In this example, the text is Pizza.

```
<Item>Pizza</Item>
```

Text can span multiple lines, and if it does it includes the carriage returns and linefeeds between the lines. The text also includes any whitespace between the text value's opening and closing tokens. For example, in the following code, the text includes a carriage return, linefeed, and two spaces before the string Pizza, and it contains a carriage return and linefeed after Pizza.

```
<Item>
  Pizza
</Item>
```

An element can contain more than one XmlText object separated by other elements. In the following code, the strings Pizza and Deep Dish are represented by two XmlText objects separated by an XmlElement.

```
<Item>
  Pizza
  <Topping>Peperoni</Topping>
  Deep Dish
</Item>
```

XmlText objects cannot have children or attributes.

XmlComment

The XmlComment class represents an XML comment.

Comments can include almost any text but they cannot contain two dashes in a row (--) and they cannot end in a single dash (-). To make a comment span multiple lines, include carriage returns and linefeeds as shown in this code.

```
xml_comment = xml_document.CreateComment( _
    vbCrLf & " *** The data starts here *** " & vbCrLf)
root.AppendChild(xml_comment)
```

This code produces the following XML output.

```
<!--
 *** The data starts here ***
-->
```

To prevent the comment from starting on the same line as the previous token, you may want to insert a whitespace element before the comment.

XmlDeclaration

The XmlDeclaration class represents an XML declaration statement. The following code shows how a program might create the document's declaration.

```
xml_declaration = xml_document.CreateXmlDeclaration( _
    "1.0", "UTF-16", "yes")
xml_document.AppendChild(xml_declaration)
```

This code produces the following XML.

```
<?xml version="1.0" encoding="UTF-16" standalone="yes"?>
```

If the program sets the encoding or standalone values to Nothing, they are also omitted from the XML declaration. For example, setting both values to Nothing produces the following XML code.

```
<?xml version="1.0"?>
```

The encoding parameter tells a program reading the XML file what kinds of characters are contained in the XML file. If this parameter is missing, the program assumes the document uses the UTF-8 encoding.

The standalone parameter tells a program whether the document contains all of the entity declarations it needs. Set this value to no if the document uses an external DTD file.

XmlDeclaration is the strictest of the DOM objects. An XML document can have only one declaration. That declaration must come at the very beginning of the document.

That doesn't mean you need to create it first, however. The following code shows one way a program might add the XML declaration at the beginning of the document after it has created other nodes.

```
xml_declaration = xml_document.CreateXmlDeclaration( _
    "1.0", Nothing, Nothing)
xml_document.PrependChild(xml_declaration)
```

The last XmlDeclaration requirement is that the XML version must be 1.0. If you set the version to any other value, the program raises an error.

While the XmlDeclaration object is quite finicky about its placement in the document and its parameter values, it is also optional. If you don't want to worry about the details, just leave it out.

XmlProcessingInstruction

An XmlProcessing instruction object represents an XML processing instruction (PI). A processing instruction gives information that is not part of the document's actual data. Some of this information is used only by specific programs that might read the XML file. Other processing instructions are relatively standardized. The following code shows how a program might create a processing instruction that tells where to find the XSL file related to this document.

```
xml_processing_instruction = _
    xml_document.CreateProcessingInstruction( _
        "xml-stylesheet", _
        "type=""text/xsl"" href=""test.xsl""")
xml_document.AppendChild(xml_processing_instruction)
```

This code produces the following XML statement.

```
<?xml-stylesheet type="text/xsl" href="test.xsl"?>
```

If you look again at the XML declarations in the previous section, you will see that they are actually a special kind of processing instruction.

The formats of some processing instructions, such as XML declarations and stylesheet definitions, are predefined. Others are defined by particular applications that read XML files. In fact, you can even create your own processing instructions to attach data to the file as a whole without putting it in the data area. For example, the following XML file uses a processing instruction to tell the My Order Processor application where to look to resolve abbreviations. This instruction is meaningless to other programs, such as browsers, that read the file

```
<?xml version="1.0" encoding="UTF-8" standalone="yes"?>
<?mop-abbreviations href="abbrevs.txt"?>
<AllItems>
  <OrderedItem>
    <Item>Brownies</Item>
    <Price>1.25</Price>
```

```
    <Quantity>3</Quantity>
  </OrderedItem>
</AllItems>
```

Processing instructions are intended to modify the state of a program reading the XML file rather than to add more information to the data. An XML declaration tells the reader what kind of text it will find in the file. A stylesheet statement tells a browser where to find the stylesheet it should use to display the file's data. The mop-abbreviations statement shown in the previous example tells the My Order Processor program where to locate abbreviations used in the file so it can process the file's data correctly.

Contrast these examples with an order date for a file full of order data. The order date applies to the entire file rather than a single element so it may be tempting to put it in a processing instruction. The date really adds more information to the data, however. It does not tell a data reading program how to read the data. Instead, it gives the date when the order was placed. Because this information is really data, it should be placed inside the data elements. Because the information applies to the document as a whole instead of to just a node within the document, it makes sense to add the information as an attribute of the document's root node as shown in the following code.

```
<?xml version="1.0" encoding="UTF-8" standalone="yes"?>
<?mop-abbreviations href="abbrevs.txt"?>
<AllItems OrderDate="4/1/2010">
  <OrderedItem>
    <Item>Brownies</Item>
    <Price>1.25</Price>
    <Quantity>3</Quantity>
  </OrderedItem>
</AllItems>
```

When you think you need to make a new processing instruction, think carefully about whether the information tells some sort of file reading program what to do or whether the information really modifies the data itself. If the information modifies the data, put it in the data area instead of creating a processing instruction. This keeps more structure in the data where it belongs.

Processing instructions can appear anywhere within an XML file, not just at the beginning. For example, some of the values in a file used by the My Order Processor application might use one set of abbreviations while other parts of the file use different abbreviations. In that case, you could use different mop-abbreviations statements to tell the program when to load different abbreviation files.

XmlCDataSection

The XmlCDataSection object represents CDATA. An XML CDATA section contains text that should not be processed as XML markup code. That allows the text to contain brackets (< and >) and other characters that would otherwise confuse programs that read the XML file. This makes it much easier to include XML examples within an XML file.

The following XML code shows how a document might include code that creates an OrderedItem object.

```
<CodeExample>
<![CDATA[
<OrderedItem>
  <Item>Brownies</Item>
  <Price>1.25</Price>
  <Quantity>3</Quantity>
</OrderedItem>
]]>
</CodeExample>
```

You can put most strings in a CDATA section although a CDATA section cannot contain the string]]> that normally ends a CDATA section. Oddly, a CDATA section can contain the string <![CDATA[that normally begins a CDATA section. That could be extremely confusing, however, so you should avoid this rather odd situation if possible.

XmlEntity and XmlEntityReference

An XML file can include a DOCTYPE section that, among other things, defines entities. When the program later refers to the entity, the browser replaces the reference with the entity's value. For example, the following XML code defines the entity co to be an abbreviation for the value Colorado. The State token refers to the entity with the &co; statement. When a browser reads this reference, it will replace the reference to produce <State>Colorado<State>.

```
<?xml version="1.0"?>
<!DOCTYPE Address[<!ENTITY co "Colorado">]>

<Address>
  <Street>1234 Programmer Way</Street>
  <City>Bugville</City>
  <State>&co;</State>
  <ZipCode>81587</ZipCode>
</Address>
```

While Visual Basic has an XmlEntity class that a program can use to examine the entities defined in a document, the XmlDocument class does not have a CreateEntity method so you cannot create an entity. Once a document contains an entity, however, the XmlDocument's CreateEntityReference method will let you use it.

To create the entity itself, the program can use the XmlDocument's CreateDocumentType method to create the DOCTYPE section. The following example shows how a program can create the &co; entity reference inside the state_node element.

```
entity_reference = xml_document.CreateEntityReference("co")
state_node.AppendChild(entity_reference)
```

Example program Entity uses similar code to create the previous XML document.

You can simplify an XML file that contains a long list of abbreviations by moving the abbreviations into a separate file. For example, the following code shows how an XML file can load and process a file containing a list of state abbreviations.

```
<?xml version="1.0"?>
<!DOCTYPE Address[
  <!-- Load the file -->
  <!ENTITY % states SYSTEM "states.ent">

  <!-- Process the file so the entities are defined -->
  %states;
]>

<Address>
  <Street>1234 Programmer Way</Street>
  <City>Bugville</City>
  <State>&co;</State>
  <ZipCode>81587</ZipCode>
</Address>
```

The file states.ent looks like this.

```
<!ENTITY ak "Alaska">
<!ENTITY al "Alabama">
<!ENTITY ar "Arkansas">
...
<!ENTITY wy "Wyoming">
```

Putting abbreviations in a separate file like this makes the main XML file easier to read and allows more than one XML file to share the abbreviations.

XmlWhitespace and XmlSignificantWhitespace

Whitespace is text that is not normally visible. In XML, whitespace can include only these characters:

- Space
- Carriage return
- Linefeed
- Tab

Significant whitespace is whitespace that should be preserved by the XML document. Other whitespace sometimes called insignificant whitespace, may be discarded. Whitespace inside an element's text is considered significant while whitespace between elements is not. For example, consider the following XML code.

```
<Root>
  <Child>
    This child element
```

```
    contains four lines of text!
  </Child>
</Root>
```

The carriage return, linefeed, and two spaces between the <Root> tag and the <Child> tag are insignificant. Similarly the carriage return and linefeed between the </Child> and </Root> tags is also insignificant.

If a program loads this file into an XmlDocument object with the PreserveWhitespace property set to False (the default), the document discards these pieces of insignificant whitespace. If the document's PreserveWhitespace property is set to True, the document creates XmlWhitespace objects to represent these pieces of whitespace.

On the other hand, the carriage return, linefeed, and four spaces between the words "element" and "contains" inside the Child element are significant whitespace. This whitespace is part of the element's text value so it cannot be discarded whether the document's PreserveWhitespace property is True or False.

In fact, the carriage return, linefeed, and four spaces after the <Child> tag and the carriage return, linefeed, and two spaces before the </Child> tag are also significant whitespace so the document will not discard them either. These nonprinting characters are included in the Child element's text. To prevent the Child's text from beginning and ending with whitespace, you would need to remove the whitespace from the XML file as in this example.

```
<Root>
  <Child>This child element
    contains two lines of text!</Child>
</Root>
```

Setting an XmlDocument's PreserveWhitespace property to True or False makes a big difference in the structure of the document. When an XmlDocument object with PreserveWhitespace set to True loads the previous XML examples, it converts the whitespace it finds into XmlWhitespace objects. It pulls any whitespace inside an element's text into the text. For the previous example, the XmlDocument would create these objects:

- XmlElement to represent the <Root> node
- XmlWhitespace to represent the insignificant whitespace between <Root> and <Child>
- XmlElement to represent the <Child> node
- XmlText to hold the Child element's text including the embedded carriage return and spaces
- XmlWhitespace to represent the insignificant whitespace between </Child> and </Root>

Figure 2.5 shows the document's hierarchical structure graphically.

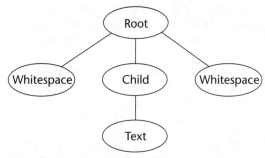

Figure 2.5 The XmlDocument object preserves whitespace between elements when its PreserveWhitespace property is True.

Notice that this document structure doesn't include any XmlSignificantWhitespace objects. At first this doesn't seem to make much sense because the document clearly includes both significant and insignificant whitespace. The Child element's text contains significant whitespace between the words "element" and "contains." Just looking at the XML code, however, the XmlDocument object cannot tell if this whitespace should be part of the text itself or if it should be placed in a separate XmlSignificant-Whitespace object so it takes the first approach. All whitespace that could be included in an XmlText object is. All other whitespace is placed in XmlWhitespace objects.

Note that the XmlDocument would have created no XmlWhitespace objects if its PreserveWhitespace property were set to False. In that case, the document would contain only the following three objects:

- XmlElement to represent the <Root> node
- XmlElement to represent the <Child> node
- XmlText to hold the Child element's text including the embedded whitespace

Figure 2.6 shows the document's new structure graphically.

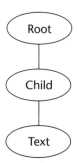

Figure 2.6 The XmlDocument object discards whitespace between elements when its PreserveWhitespace property is False.

When a program builds an XML document using the DOM, it doesn't matter too much whether it adds whitespace using XmlWhitespace or XmlSignificantWhitespace objects. When the XmlDocument writes the document into an XML file, both appear as nonprintable characters.

When a program loads the document, whitespace within a text element is included in the text. Whitespace between elements is stored in XmlWhitespace objects if PreserveWhitespace is True, and it is discarded if PreserveWhitespace is False. Even if the program originally wrote nonprinting characters using an XmlSignificantWhitespace object, it is reloaded in an XmlWhitespace object.

The one time when an XmlDocument will load space into an XmlSignificantWhitespace object is if the XML code itself marks nonprinting characters as significant. Consider the following XML code.

```
<Root>
    <Child xml:space="preserve">
        <GrandChild>Grandchild text</GrandChild>
    </Child>
    <Child>
        <GrandChild>Grandchild text</GrandChild>
    </Child>
</Root>
```

In this document, the first Child tag sets the predefined xml:space entity to preserve. That means the whitespace inside this Child element should be considered significant. When an XmlDocument object loads this file, it creates XmlSignificantWhitespace objects to represent the whitespace within this Child element. When it reads the second Child element, the XmlDocument discards whitespace if its PreserveWhitespace property is False, or it stores the whitespace in XmlWhitespace objects if PreserveWhitespace is True.

Figure 2.7 shows this document's structure if PreserveWhitespace is False.

If the XmlDocument's PreserveWhitespace property is true, the second Child element's subtree is very similar to the first Child element's subtree. The difference is that the second child's whitespace is stored in XmlWhitespace objects instead of XmlSignificantWhitespace objects. The document's Root element also contains XmlWhitespace objects between its Child elements, as shown in Figure 2.8.

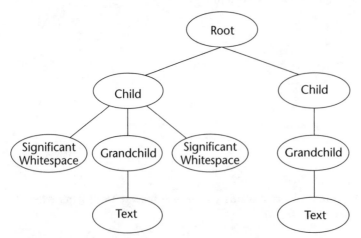

Figure 2.7 The xml:space="preserve" attribute makes the XmlDocument create XmlSignificantWhitespace objects.

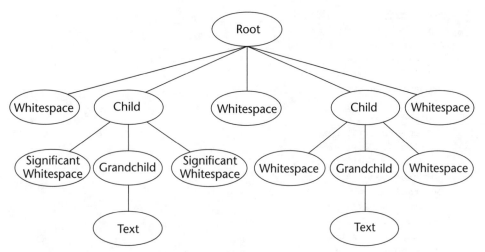

Figure 2.8 When PreserveWhitespace is True, nonprinting characters might be included in XmlSignificantWhitespace or XmlWhitespace objects.

When you build a document using DOM objects, it usually doesn't matter whether you use XmlWhitespace or XmlSignificantWhitespace objects because they are both converted into nonprinting characters when the XmlDocument object writes the XML code into a file.

When you read an XML document, you should be aware of the difference between significant and insignificant whitespace. If you just need to display the document, you can probably treat the two in the same way. You just need to be aware that the document may include XmlSignificantWhitespace objects if an element has an xml:space="preserve" attribute.

XmlNodeList

An XmlNodeList is an ordered collection of references to XmlNode objects. Your program will usually obtain an XmlNodeList by calling a function that selects some of the nodes in an XML document. For example, the XmlDocument object's GetElementsBy-TagName method returns an XmlNodeList containing references to nodes in the document with a certain tag name. For example, look at the following XML code.

```
<?xml version="1.0"?>
<AllItems Customer="Rod" OrderDate="4/1/3000">
  <OrderedItem>
    <Item>Brownies</Item>
    <Price>1.25</Price>
    <Quantity>3</Quantity>
  </OrderedItem>
  <OrderedItem>
    <Item>Cookies</Item>
    <Price>0.25</Price>
```

```
        <Quantity>12</Quantity>
    </OrderedItem>
    <OrderedItem>
      <Item>Cupcakes</Item>
      <Price>0.5</Price>
      <Quantity>6</Quantity>
    </OrderedItem>
    <OrderedItem>
      <Item>Bread</Item>
      <Price>3.40</Price>
      <Quantity>1</Quantity>
    </OrderedItem>
    <OrderedItem>
      <Item>Donuts</Item>
      <Price>0.25</Price>
      <Quantity>13</Quantity>
    </OrderedItem>
  </AllItems>
```

A call to xml_document.GetElementsByTagName("Item") would return an Xml-NodeList containing the five Item nodes. Similarly a call to xml_document. GetElementsByTagName("OrderedItem") would return an XmlNodeList containing the five OrderedItem nodes.

The following code shows how a program might iterate through the returned XmlNodeList and display the nodes' InnerText values in a message box.

```
Dim xml_node As XmlNode
Dim results As String

For Each xml_node In xml_document.GetElementsByTagName("Item")
    results = results & xml_node.InnerText & vbCrLf
Next xml_node

MsgBox(results)
```

Note that the items in the XmlNodeList are references to the document nodes, not copies of those nodes. That means if you change the properties of the items in the list, the document is immediately changed as well.

The section *Finding Nodes* later in this chapter says more about functions that return XmlNodeLists.

Wrapping Object Creation

You probably noticed in earlier examples that creating a new node for a document requires three steps. First, the program uses one of the XmlDocument object's Create methods to create the new node object. Second, it appends the new object to its parent node in the document tree. Third, the program assigns properties to the new object.

Adding an attribute to an element requires similar steps. First, the program uses the XmlDocument object's CreateAttribute method to create the new attribute object.

Second, it appends the attribute to the parent element's Attributes collection. Third, the program sets the new attribute's value.

The following code shows how a program might add a new XmlElement node as a child of the existing node named root and give the new element an attribute.

```
Dim child As XmlElement
Dim xml_attribute As XmlAttribute

' Create a child element.
child = xml_document.CreateElement("Child")

' Add the child node to the root node.
root.AppendChild(child)

' Make a new attribute.
xml_attribute = xml_document.CreateAttribute("attribute-name")

' Add the attribute to the child.
child.Attributes.Append(xml_attribute)

' Set the attribute's value.
xml_attribute.Value = "Attribute Value"
```

All that code adds this single line to the XML file:

```
<Child attribute-name="Attribute Value" />
```

It is not too difficult to write routines to wrap the DOM node creation functions into simpler packages. For example, the AddXmlElement function shown in the following code creates a new XmlElement object and adds it as a child of a specified parent node. Similarly, the AddXmlAttribute function creates a new XmlAttribute object, sets the attribute's value, and adds it to an element's Attribute's collection.

```
' Add a new XmlElement to the node.
Public Function AddXmlElement(ByVal xml_document As XmlDocument, _
  ByVal parent_node As XmlNode, ByVal element_name As String) _
  As XmlElement

    Dim xml_element As XmlElement

    xml_element = xml_document.CreateElement(element_name)
    parent_node.AppendChild(xml_element)
    Return xml_element
End Function

' Add an XmlAttribute to the node.
Public Function AddXmlAttribute(ByVal xml_document As XmlDocument, _
  ByVal xml_node As XmlNode, ByVal attribute_name As String, _
  ByVal attribute_value As String) As XmlAttribute

    Dim xml_attribute As XmlAttribute

    xml_attribute = xml_document.CreateAttribute(attribute_name)
```

```
      xml_attribute.Value = attribute_value
      xml_node.Attributes.Append(xml_attribute)
      Return xml_attribute
End Function
```

Using these functions, a program can create a new node and give it an attribute with the following simplified code.

```
Dim child As XmlElement

' Create the child node.
child = AddXmlElement(xml_document, root, "Child")

' Give the child an attribute.
AddXmlAttribute(xml_document, child, "attribute-name", "Attribute
Value")
```

The module XmlStuff.vb shown in the following code defines 12 functions that make it easier for a program to build XML files. The functions are listed in Table 2.2. All of the functions return the newly created DOM object so the program can set its properties, add child nodes and attributes to it, and otherwise modify it.

Table 2.2 Functions Defined in Module XmlStuff.vb

FUNCTION	PURPOSE
AddXmlDeclaration	Adds an XML declaration statement as in <?xml version="1.0"?>.
AddXmlXSLFile	Adds a processing instruction that associates the XML file with an XSL file.
AddXmlDocumentType	Adds a DOCTYPE section.
AddXmlElement	Adds a new element.
AddXmlAttribute	Adds a new attribute to an element.
AddXmlNewLine	Adds an XmlWhitespace object representing a carriage return, linefeed, and a specified number of spaces. A program can use this to indent the document.
AddXmlComment	Adds a comment as in <!-- This is the comment text -->.
AddXmlCdataSection	Adds a CDATA section.
AddXmlText	Adds an XmlText object.
AddXmlEntityReference	Adds a reference to an entity defined in the DOCTYPE section as in &us;.
AddXmlWhitespace	Adds an XmlWhitespace object.
AddXmlSignificantWhitespace	Adds an XmlSignificantWhitespace object.

```vb
Imports System.Xml

Module XmlStuff

    ' Add an XML declaration to the document.
    Public Function AddXmlDeclaration( _
      ByVal xml_document As XmlDocument, _
      Optional ByVal version As String = "1.0", _
      Optional ByVal encoding As String = Nothing, _
      Optional ByVal standalone As String = Nothing) _
      As XmlDeclaration

        ' Make the declaration.
        Dim xml_declaration As XmlDeclaration
        xml_declaration = xml_document.CreateXmlDeclaration( _
            version, encoding, standalone)

        ' Prepend the child so we know it's in the right place.
        xml_document.PrependChild(xml_declaration)
        Return xml_declaration
    End Function

    ' Create an XmlProcessingInstruction.
    Public Function AddXmlProcessingInstruction( _
      ByVal xml_document As XmlDocument, _
      ByVal parent_node As XmlNode, _
      ByVal target As String, _
      ByVal data As String) _
      As XmlProcessingInstruction

        ' Make the processing instruction.
        Dim xml_processing_instruction As XmlProcessingInstruction
        xml_processing_instruction = _
            xml_document.CreateProcessingInstruction(target, data)
        parent_node.AppendChild(xml_processing_instruction)
        Return xml_processing_instruction
    End Function

    ' Associate the XML file with an XSL file.
    Public Function AddXmlXSLFile( _
      ByVal xml_document As XmlDocument, _
      ByVal xsl_file As String) _
      As XmlProcessingInstruction

        Return AddXmlProcessingInstruction( _
            xml_document, xml_document, _
            "xml-stylesheet", _
            "type=""text/xsl"" href=""" & xsl_file & """")
    End Function

    ' Create a DOCTYPE section.
    Public Function AddXmlDocumentType( _
```

```vb
  ByVal xml_document As XmlDocument, _
  ByVal document_name As String, _
  ByVal internal_subset As String, _
  Optional ByVal public_id As String = Nothing, _
  Optional ByVal system_id As String = Nothing) _
  As XmlDocumentType

      ' Make the DOCTYPE section.
      Dim xml_document_type As XmlDocumentType
      xml_document_type = xml_document.CreateDocumentType( _
          document_name, public_id, system_id, _
          internal_subset)
      xml_document.AppendChild(xml_document_type)
      Return xml_document_type
End Function


' Add a new XmlElement to the node.
Public Function AddXmlElement( _
  ByVal xml_document As XmlDocument, _
  ByVal parent_node As XmlNode, _
  ByVal element_name As String) _
  As XmlElement

      ' Make the new element.
      Dim xml_element As XmlElement
      xml_element = xml_document.CreateElement(element_name)
      parent_node.AppendChild(xml_element)
      Return xml_element
End Function


' Add an XmlAttribute to the node.
Public Function AddXmlAttribute( _
  ByVal xml_document As XmlDocument, _
  ByVal xml_node As XmlNode, _
  ByVal attribute_name As String, _
  ByVal attribute_value As String) _
  As XmlAttribute

      ' Make the new attribute.
      Dim xml_attribute As XmlAttribute
      xml_attribute = xml_document.CreateAttribute(attribute_name)
      xml_attribute.Value = attribute_value
      xml_node.Attributes.Append(xml_attribute)
      Return xml_attribute
End Function


' Add an XmlWhitespace object containing a vbCrLf and the
' indicated number of spaces to the parent node.
Public Function AddXmlNewLine( _
  ByVal xml_document As XmlDocument, _
  ByVal parent_node As XmlNode, _
  ByVal num_spaces As Integer) _
```

```
    As XmlWhitespace

        ' Make the XmlWhitespace object.
        Dim xml_whitespace As XmlWhitespace
        xml_whitespace = xml_document.CreateWhitespace( _
            vbCrLf & Space(num_spaces))

        ' Add it to the parent node.
        parent_node.AppendChild(xml_whitespace)
        Return xml_whitespace
End Function

' Add a comment to the node.
Public Function AddXmlComment( _
  ByVal xml_document As XmlDocument, _
  ByVal parent_node As XmlNode, _
  ByVal comment_value As String) _
  As XmlComment

        ' Make the new comment.
        Dim xml_comment As XmlComment
        xml_comment = xml_document.CreateComment( _
            " " & comment_value & " ")
        parent_node.AppendChild(xml_comment)
        Return xml_comment
End Function

' Add some CDATA to the node.
Public Function AddXmlCdataSection( _
  ByVal xml_document As XmlDocument, _
  ByVal parent_node As XmlNode, _
  ByVal cdata_text As String) _
  As XmlCDataSection

        ' Make the new CDATA section.
        Dim xml_cdata_section As XmlCDataSection
        xml_cdata_section = xml_document.CreateCDataSection(cdata_text)
        parent_node.AppendChild(xml_cdata_section)
        Return xml_cdata_section
End Function

' Add a new XmlText node to the node.
Public Function AddXmlText( _
  ByVal xml_document As XmlDocument, _
  ByVal parent_node As XmlNode, _
  ByVal element_text As String) _
  As XmlText

        ' Make the new XmlText object.
        Dim xml_text As XmlText
        xml_text = xml_document.CreateTextNode(element_text)
        parent_node.AppendChild(xml_text)
```

```
      Return xml_text
   End Function


   ' Add an entity reference to the node.
   Public Function AddXmlEntityReference( _
      ByVal xml_document As XmlDocument, _
      ByVal parent_node As XmlNode, _
      ByVal entity_name As String) _
      As XmlEntityReference

         ' Make the new entity reference.
         Dim xml_entity_reference As XmlEntityReference
         xml_entity_reference = _
             xml_document.CreateEntityReference(entity_name)
         parent_node.AppendChild(xml_entity_reference)
         Return xml_entity_reference
   End Function


   ' Add an XmlWhitespace object.
   Public Function AddXmlWhitespace( _
      ByVal xml_document As XmlDocument, _
      ByVal parent_node As XmlNode, _
      ByVal whitespace As String) _
      As XmlWhitespace

         ' Make the XmlWhitespace object.
         Dim xml_whitespace As XmlWhitespace
         xml_whitespace = xml_document.CreateWhitespace(whitespace)

         ' Add it to the parent node.
         parent_node.AppendChild(xml_whitespace)
         Return xml_whitespace
   End Function

   ' Add an XmlSignificantWhitespace object.
   Public Function AddXmlSignificantWhitespace( _
      ByVal xml_document As XmlDocument, _
      ByVal parent_node As XmlNode, _
      ByVal whitespace As String) _
      As XmlSignificantWhitespace

         ' Make the XmlSignificantWhitespace object.
         Dim xml_whitespace As XmlSignificantWhitespace
         xml_whitespace = _
             xml_document.CreateSignificantWhitespace(whitespace)

         ' Add it to the parent node.
         parent_node.AppendChild(xml_whitespace)
         Return xml_whitespace
   End Function
End Module
```

Example program BuildDocument uses the following code to build an XML document. The functions provided by XmlStuff.vb make the code easy to follow.

```
' Make the XML document.
Private Function CreateXmlFile() As XmlDocument
    Const INDENT As Integer = 4

    Dim xml_document As XmlDocument
    Dim root As XmlElement
    Dim child As XmlElement
    Dim grandchild As XmlElement

    ' Create a new XmlDocument object.
    xml_document = New XmlDocument()
    xml_document.PreserveWhitespace = True

    ' Define the file's version information.
    AddXmlDeclaration(xml_document)
    AddXmlNewLine(xml_document, xml_document, 0)

    ' Associate the XML file with an XSL file.
    AddXmlXSLFile(xml_document, "Test.xsl")

    ' Make the DOCTYPE section.
    AddXmlDocumentType(xml_document, "Root", _
        "<!ENTITY us ""United States of America"">")

    ' Add a blank line before the real data.
    AddXmlNewLine(xml_document, xml_document, 0)

    ' Add a comment.
    AddXmlComment(xml_document, xml_document, _
        "*** The data starts here ***")

    ' Create the root element.
    AddXmlNewLine(xml_document, xml_document, 0)
    root = AddXmlElement(xml_document, xml_document, "Root")

    ' Give the root element some attributes.
    AddXmlAttribute(xml_document, root, "Attr-1", "Value 1")
    AddXmlAttribute(xml_document, root, "Attr-2", "Value 2")

    ' Give the root element some text.
    AddXmlText(xml_document, root, "Root inner text")

    ' Create a child element.
    AddXmlNewLine(xml_document, root, INDENT)
    child = AddXmlElement(xml_document, root, "Child-1")
    AddXmlText(xml_document, child, "Child inner text")
    AddXmlAttribute(xml_document, child, "Child-Attr-1", "Child Value
```

```
1")

        ' Create another child element.
        AddXmlNewLine(xml_document, root, INDENT)
        child = AddXmlElement(xml_document, root, "Child-2")

        ' Add some CDATA inside Child 2.
        AddXmlNewLine(xml_document, child, 2 * INDENT)
        AddXmlCdataSection(xml_document, child, vbCrLf & _
            "<Example>" & vbCrLf & _
            "    CDATA text can contain whitespace" & vbCrLf & _
            "    & characters that look like markup!" & vbCrLf & _
            "</Example>")
        AddXmlNewLine(xml_document, child, INDENT)

        ' Create a comment inside the root.
        AddXmlNewLine(xml_document, root, INDENT)
        AddXmlComment(xml_document, root, _
            "The following text and entity reference are in the Root node")

        ' Create a text node inside the root.
        AddXmlNewLine(xml_document, root, INDENT)
        AddXmlText(xml_document, root, "Country = ")

        ' Create an entity reference.
        AddXmlEntityReference(xml_document, root, "us")

        ' Create another child node.
        AddXmlNewLine(xml_document, root, INDENT)
        child = AddXmlElement(xml_document, root, "Child-3")

        ' Create a grandchild.
        AddXmlNewLine(xml_document, child, 2 * INDENT)
        grandchild = AddXmlElement(xml_document, child, "Grandchild-1")

        ' Create a comment inside the grandchild.
        AddXmlNewLine(xml_document, grandchild, 3 * INDENT)
        AddXmlComment(xml_document, grandchild, _
            "This comment is inside Grandchild-1")
        AddXmlNewLine(xml_document, grandchild, 2 * INDENT)
        AddXmlNewLine(xml_document, child, INDENT)

        ' Create a final root-level comment.
        AddXmlNewLine(xml_document, root, 0)
        AddXmlNewLine(xml_document, xml_document, 0)
        AddXmlComment(xml_document, xml_document, "That's all folks!")

        ' Return the document.
        Return xml_document
    End Function
```

This code produces the following XML document.

```
<?xml version="1.0"?>
<?xml-stylesheet type="text/xsl" href="Test.xsl"?>
<!DOCTYPE Root[<!ENTITY us "United States of America">]>
<!-- *** The data starts here *** -->
<Root Attr-1="Value 1" Attr-2="Value 2">Root inner text
    <Child-1 Child-Attr-1="Child Value 1">Child inner text</Child-1>
    <Child-2>
        <![CDATA[
<Example>
    CDATA text can contain whitespace
    & characters that look like markup!
</Example>]]>
    </Child-2>
    <!-- The following text and entity reference are in the Root node --
>
    Country = &us;
    <Child-3>
        <Grandchild-1>
            <!-- This comment is inside Grandchild-1 -->
        </Grandchild-1>
    </Child-3>
</Root>
<!-- That's all folks! -->
```

Admittedly this isn't a very pretty document, but it does show how to use most of the functions provided in the module XmlStuff.vb.

Example program BuildDocument2 uses the following code to create a much more realistic XML document. If you remove the calls to AddXmlNewLine from this code, the program is even simpler. The resulting XML code is harder to read, however.

Notice how this program's MakeOrderItem function wraps up the code that creates an OrderItem. You can usually simplify the code that builds a complex XML document by wrapping pieces of the document hierarchy in subroutines.

Also notice that the MakeOrderItem function returns the object that forms the root of the subtree that this function creates. This gives the routine calling the function the ability to easily modify the subtree if necessary. The returned value isn't used in this program, but this technique may make the function a little easier to use under different circumstances.

```
' Make the XML document.
Private Function CreateXmlFile() As XmlDocument
    Dim xml_document As XmlDocument
    Dim root As XmlElement

    ' Create a new XmlDocument object.
    xml_document = New XmlDocument()
    xml_document.PreserveWhitespace = True

    ' Define the file's version information.
```

```
        AddXmlDeclaration(xml_document)
        AddXmlNewLine(xml_document, 0)

        ' Associate the XML file with an XSL file.
        AddXmlXSLFile(xml_document, "Order.xsl")

        ' Add a blank line before the real data.
        AddXmlNewLine(xml_document, 0)

        ' Create the root element.
        AddXmlNewLine(xml_document, 0)
        root = AddXmlElement(xml_document, "AllItems")

        ' Save the order date as a root attribute.
        AddXmlAttribute(root, "OrderDate", "4/1/2009")

        ' Add order items.
        MakeOrderItem(root, "Brownies", "1.25", "3")
        MakeOrderItem(root, "Cookies", "0.25", "12")
        MakeOrderItem(root, "Cupcakes", "0.50", "6")

        ' Add a final new line.
        AddXmlNewLine(root, 0)

        ' Return the document.
        Return xml_document
End Function

' Make a new OrderItem.
Private Function MakeOrderItem( _
  ByVal parent_node As XmlNode, _
  ByVal item_name As String, _
  ByVal price As String, _
  ByVal quantity As Integer) _
  As XmlElement

    Dim order_item As XmlElement
    Dim subitem As XmlElement

    ' Make the OrderItem node.
    AddXmlNewLine(parent_node, 4)
    order_item = AddXmlElement(parent_node, "OrderedItem")

    ' Make the Item subitem.
    AddXmlNewLine(order_item, 8)
    subitem = AddXmlElement(order_item, "Item")
    subitem.InnerText = item_name

    ' Make the Price subitem.
    AddXmlNewLine(order_item, 8)
    subitem = AddXmlElement(order_item, "Price")
```

```
        subitem.InnerText = price

        ' Make the Quantity subitem.
        AddXmlNewLine(order_item, 8)
        subitem = AddXmlElement(order_item, "Quantity")
        subitem.InnerText = quantity

        ' Add a new line.
        AddXmlNewLine(order_item, 4)

        ' Return the Order object.
        Return order_item
End Function
```

Program BuildDocument2 generates the following XML file.

```
<?xml version="1.0"?>
<?xml-stylesheet type="text/xsl" href="Order.xsl"?>

<AllItems OrderDate="4/1/2009">
    <OrderedItem>
        <Item>Brownies</Item>
        <Price>1.25</Price>
        <Quantity>3</Quantity>
    </OrderedItem>
    <OrderedItem>
        <Item>Cookies</Item>
        <Price>0.25</Price>
        <Quantity>12</Quantity>
    </OrderedItem>
    <OrderedItem>
        <Item>Cupcakes</Item>
        <Price>0.50</Price>
        <Quantity>6</Quantity>
    </OrderedItem>
</AllItems>
```

This is a much more sensible document. You can imagine using something similar in a real application.

Navigating the DOM

The DOM objects provide several methods for moving through an XML document hierarchy. The ChildNodes method, which returns a list of a node's children, makes it easy to traverse the entire document tree or a subtree. Other properties including NextSibling, PreviousSibling, and ParentNode let a program navigate through the document at a more local scale.

The following sections explain how to use the DOM objects' properties and methods to move through an XML document's structure.

Using ChildNodes

The XmlNode class and the classes derived from it provide a ChildNodes method that returns an XmlNodeList containing references to a node's children. Using this list of children, you can easily traverse the document's nodes. The following code fragment shows how a program can use the ChildNodes list to do something with each of a node's children.

```
Dim child_node As XmlNode

    ' Add the child nodes to the results.
    For Each child_node In xml_node.ChildNodes
    ' Do something with child_node ...
    Next child_node
```

Example program WalkDom uses the following code to traverse an entire XML document. When the main form loads, the Form1_Load event handler loads the document Test.xml preserving whitespace. It then calls the DisplayNodeInformation function, passing it the xml_document object as a parameter. That object is of type XmlDocument. The XmlDocument class inherits from XmlNode so xml_document provides a ChildNodes method just as other XmlNode objects do.

The DisplayNodeInformation function adds the name and type of the object it was passed to a result string. It then recursively calls itself to process each of the object's child nodes. It adds the results of those calls to its output string.

When the initial call to DisplayNodeInformation finishes, Form1_Load displays the results and repeats the process, this time loading the XML document without preserving spaces.

```
' Read the nodes in Test.xml and list them.
Private Sub Form1_Load(ByVal sender As System.Object, _
    ByVal e As System.EventArgs) Handles MyBase.Load

    Dim xml_document As New XmlDocument()
    Dim new_item As ListViewItem

    ' Load the XML document with whitespace.
    xml_document.PreserveWhitespace = True
    xml_document.Load(DataSubdirectory() & "\Test.xml")
    txtWithWhitespace.Text = DisplayNodeInformation(xml_document)
    txtWithWhitespace.Select(0, 0)

    ' Load the XML document without whitespace.
    xml_document.PreserveWhitespace = False
    xml_document.Load(DataSubdirectory() & "\Test.xml")
    txtWithoutWhitespace.Text = DisplayNodeInformation(xml_document)
    txtWithoutWhitespace.Select(0, 0)
End Sub

' Return indented information about this node and its descendants.
```

```
Private Function DisplayNodeInformation(ByVal xml_node As XmlNode, _
    Optional ByVal indent As Integer = 0) As String

    Dim results As String
    Dim child_node As XmlNode

    ' Add this node to the results
    results = Space(indent) & xml_node.Name & " (" & _
        xml_node.NodeType.GetName( _
            xml_node.NodeType.GetType, xml_node.NodeType) & _
        ")" & vbCrLf

    ' Add the child nodes to the results.
    For Each child_node In xml_node.ChildNodes
        results = results & DisplayNodeInformation( _
            child_node, indent + 4)
    Next child_node

    Return results
End Function
```

Figure 2.9 shows program WalkDom displaying information about the following XML document. If you look closely, you can identify the document element, declaration, document type, elements, text, and entity reference objects. You can also see the significant and insignificant whitespace objects in the two versions of the loaded file.

```
<?xml version="1.0"?>
<!DOCTYPE Root[<!ENTITY us "United States of America">]>
<Root>
    <Child xml:space="preserve">
        <GrandChild>Grandchild text in &us;</GrandChild>
    </Child>
    <Child>
        <GrandChild>Grandchild text</GrandChild>
    </Child>
</Root>
```

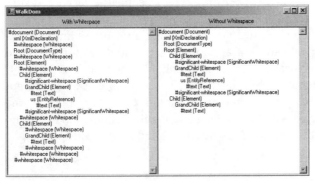

Figure 2.9   Program WalkDom uses the ChildNodes method to traverse an XML document.

The HasChildNodes method returns True if a node has children. You can use this method to decide whether you need to examine the node's children, but in practice you often don't need to. The code used by program WalkDom simply tries to process the node's children using the code:

```
For Each child_node In xml_node.ChildNodes
    results = results & DisplayNodeInformation( _
        child_node, indent + 4)
Next child_node
```

If a node has no children, the ChildNodes method returns an empty XmlNodeList and the For Each loop does nothing. This is similar to the way the loop For i = 1 To -1 executes the code it contains zero times.

Local Navigation

Using the ChildNodes method, a program can traverse an XML document hierarchy or one of its subtrees. For more localized movement, the DOM classes provide FirstChild, LastChild, NextSibling, PreviousSibling, ParentNode, and OwnerDocument methods.

FirstChild and LastChild are references to a node's first and last children. If a node has no children, FirstChild and LastChild are both Nothing.

NextSibling and PreviousSibling are references to a node's nearest sibling (brother or sister) nodes. If a node is its parent's first child, PreviousSibling is Nothing. Similarly if a node is its parent's last child, NextSibling is Nothing.

A program could use a node's FirstChild property to move to its first child node and then use the child nodes' NextSibling methods to move from one child node to the next. If you need to visit all of the child nodes, however, it is easier to use the ChildNodes method.

A node's ParentNode method returns a reference to the node's parent in the document hierarchy. If necessary, you can use the parent node's ParentNode method to move even higher up the hierarchy. You can continue using the nodes' ParentNode methods to climb to the top of the document hierarchy.

Each node's OwnerDocument method also returns a reference to that topmost node. If you need to find the top of the hierarchy, using OwnerDocument is faster and simpler than climbing to the top using ParentNode.

Figure 2.10 shows the FirstChild, LastChild, NextSibling, PreviousSibling, ParentNode, and OwnerDocument references graphically. Parent-child relationships are shown in dashed lines. This picture focuses on the highlighted node and its parent. It does not show all of the links between the other nodes. For example, every node except the document's root node also has an OwnerDocument link pointing to the root; the root's two children are connected with NextSibling and PreviousSibling links; and the picture doesn't show the NextSibling and PreviousSibling links with value Nothing.

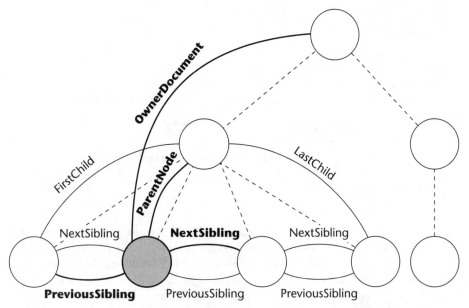

Figure 2.10 The FirstChild, LastChild, NextSibling, PreviousSibling, ParentNode, and OwnerDocument methods provide local navigation through a document hierarchy.

The one node that behaves differently from the others is the topmost node itself. That node is the XmlDocument representing the entire document, and its OwnerDocument method returns Nothing. If the program doesn't know whether a node is the XmlDocument node, it can find this node using the following code.

```
xml_document = xml_node.OwnerDocument
If xml_document Is Nothing Then xml_document = xml_node
```

To be well-formed, an XML document must have a single root data element; however, that node is not the root of the DOM object hierarchy. That node may have siblings containing such things as an XML declaration, a DOCTYPE section, and whitespace. Above all of these objects is an XmlDocument object representing the entire document. This is the same document returned by a node's OwnerDocument method. It's also the same XmlDocument object the program must use to create new document nodes with functions such as CreateElement and CreateAttribute.

You can use this fact to add a new node to a document hierarchy completely locally. For example, the following code adds a new XmlElement to a node without needing the XmlDocument passed in as a parameter.

```
' Add a new XmlElement to the node.
Public Function AddXmlElement( _
  ByVal parent_node As XmlNode, _
```

```
      ByVal element_name As String) _
    As XmlElement

        ' Find the XmlDocument.
        Dim xml_document As XmlDocument
        xml_document = parent_node.OwnerDocument
        If xml_document Is Nothing Then xml_document = parent_node

        ' Create the new element.
        Dim xml_element As XmlElement
        xml_element = xml_document.CreateElement(element_name)
        parent_node.AppendChild(xml_element)
        Return xml_element
    End Function
```

Example programs BuildDocumentLocally and BuildDocumentLocally2 use code similar to the code used by programs BuildDocument and BuildDocument2 to create XML documents. They use the element creation wrapper functions shown in the following code and contained in the module XmlStuffLocal.vb. These routines are similar to those described earlier in module XmlStuff.vb except most of them do not need to receive an XmlDocument object as a parameter.

```
Imports System.Xml

Module XmlStuff

    ' Return this node's document root object.
    Private Function FindXmlDocument( _
      ByVal xml_node As XmlNode) _
      As XmlDocument

        Dim xml_document As XmlDocument

        xml_document = xml_node.OwnerDocument
        If xml_document Is Nothing Then xml_document = xml_node
        Return xml_document
    End Function

    ' Add an XML declaration to the document.
    Public Function AddXmlDeclaration( _
      ByVal xml_node As XmlNode, _
      Optional ByVal version As String = "1.0", _
      Optional ByVal encoding As String = Nothing, _
      Optional ByVal standalone As String = Nothing) _
      As XmlDeclaration

        ' Create the new XmlDeclaration.
        Dim xml_declaration As XmlDeclaration
        xml_declaration = _
            FindXmlDocument(xml_node).CreateXmlDeclaration( _
```

```
                    version, encoding, standalone)

            ' Prepend the child so we know it's in the right place.
            FindXmlDocument(xml_node).PrependChild(xml_declaration)
            Return xml_declaration
End Function


' Create an XmlProcessingInstruction.
Public Function AddXmlProcessingInstruction( _
  ByVal xml_node As XmlNode, _
  ByVal target As String, _
  ByVal data As String) _
  As XmlProcessingInstruction

        ' Create the new processing instruction.
        Dim xml_processing_instruction As XmlProcessingInstruction
        xml_processing_instruction = _
            FindXmlDocument(xml_node).CreateProcessingInstruction( _
                target, data)
        xml_node.AppendChild(xml_processing_instruction)
        Return xml_processing_instruction
End Function


' Associate the XML file with an XSL file.
Public Function AddXmlXSLFile( _
  ByVal xml_node As XmlNode, _
  ByVal xsl_file As String) _
  As XmlProcessingInstruction

        ' Add the appropriate processing instruction to
        ' the document.
        Return AddXmlProcessingInstruction( _
            FindXmlDocument(xml_node), "xml-stylesheet", _
            "type=""text/xsl"" href=""" & xsl_file & """")
End Function


' Create a DOCTYPE section.
Public Function AddXmlDocumentType( _
  ByVal xml_node As XmlNode, _
  ByVal document_name As String, _
  ByVal internal_subset As String, _
  Optional ByVal public_id As String = Nothing, _
  Optional ByVal system_id As String = Nothing) _
  As XmlDocumentType

        ' Create the new DOCTYPE section.
        Dim xml_document_type As XmlDocumentType
        xml_document_type = _
            FindXmlDocument(xml_node).CreateDocumentType( _
                document_name, public_id, system_id, _
```

```
                        internal_subset)
          FindXmlDocument(xml_node).AppendChild(xml_document_type)
          Return xml_document_type
End Function

' Add a new XmlElement to the node.
Public Function AddXmlElement( _
  ByVal parent_node As XmlNode, _
  ByVal element_name As String) _
  As XmlElement

     ' Create the new element.
     Dim xml_element As XmlElement
     xml_element = _
         FindXmlDocument(parent_node).CreateElement(element_name)
     parent_node.AppendChild(xml_element)
     Return xml_element
End Function

' Add an XmlAttribute to the node.
Public Function AddXmlAttribute( _
  ByVal xml_node As XmlNode, _
  ByVal attribute_name As String, _
  ByVal attribute_value As String) _
  As XmlAttribute

     ' Create the new attribute.
     Dim xml_attribute As XmlAttribute
     xml_attribute = _
         FindXmlDocument(xml_node).CreateAttribute(attribute_name)
     xml_attribute.Value = attribute_value
     xml_node.Attributes.Append(xml_attribute)
     Return xml_attribute
End Function

' Add an XmlWhitespace object containing a vbCrLf and the
' indicated number of spaces to the parent node.
Public Function AddXmlNewLine( _
  ByVal parent_node As XmlNode, _
  ByVal num_spaces As Integer) _
  As XmlWhitespace

     ' Make the XmlWhitespace object.
     Dim xml_whitespace As XmlWhitespace
     xml_whitespace = FindXmlDocument(parent_node).CreateWhitespace( _
         vbCrLf & Space(num_spaces))
     parent_node.AppendChild(xml_whitespace)
     Return xml_whitespace
End Function

' Add a comment to the node.
```

```
Public Function AddXmlComment( _
  ByVal parent_node As XmlNode, _
  ByVal comment_value As String) _
  As XmlComment

    ' Make the comment.
    Dim xml_comment As XmlComment
    xml_comment = FindXmlDocument(parent_node).CreateComment( _
        " " & comment_value & " ")
    parent_node.AppendChild(xml_comment)
    Return xml_comment
End Function

' Add some CDATA to the node.
Public Function AddXmlCdataSection( _
  ByVal parent_node As XmlNode, _
  ByVal cdata_text As String) _
  As XmlCDataSection

    ' Make the CDATA section.
    Dim xml_cdata_section As XmlCDataSection
    xml_cdata_section = _
        FindXmlDocument(parent_node).CreateCDataSection(cdata_text)
    parent_node.AppendChild(xml_cdata_section)
    Return xml_cdata_section
End Function

' Add a new XmlText node to the node.
Public Function AddXmlText( _
  ByVal parent_node As XmlNode, _
  ByVal element_text As String) _
  As XmlText

    ' Make the XmlText node.
    Dim xml_text As XmlText
    xml_text = _
        FindXmlDocument(parent_node).CreateTextNode(element_text)
    parent_node.AppendChild(xml_text)
    Return xml_text
End Function

' Add an entity reference to the node.
Public Function AddXmlEntityReference( _
  ByVal parent_node As XmlNode, _
  ByVal entity_name As String) _
  As XmlEntityReference

    ' Make the entity reference.
    Dim xml_entity_reference As XmlEntityReference
    xml_entity_reference = _
        FindXmlDocument(parent_node).CreateEntityReference( _
            entity_name)
```

```
        parent_node.AppendChild(xml_entity_reference)
        Return xml_entity_reference
End Function


' Add an XmlWhitespace object.
Public Function AddXmlWhitespace( _
  ByVal parent_node As XmlNode, _
  ByVal whitespace As String) _
  As XmlWhitespace

     ' Make the XmlWhitespace object.
     Dim xml_whitespace As XmlWhitespace
     xml_whitespace = _
         FindXmlDocument(parent_node).CreateWhitespace(whitespace)
     parent_node.AppendChild(xml_whitespace)
     Return xml_whitespace
End Function


' Add an XmlSignificantWhitespace object.
Public Function AddXmlSignificantWhitespace( _
  ByVal parent_node As XmlNode, _
  ByVal whitespace As String) _
  As XmlSignificantWhitespace

     ' Make the XmlSignificantWhitespace object.
     Dim xml_whitespace As XmlSignificantWhitespace
     xml_whitespace = _
         FindXmlDocument(parent_node).CreateSignificantWhitespace( _
             whitespace)
     parent_node.AppendChild(xml_whitespace)
     Return xml_whitespace
End Function


End Module
```

Finding Nodes

Using the ChildNodes, FirstChild, LastChild, NextSibling, PreviousSibling, ParentNode, and OwnerDocument methods a program can navigate through a document hierarchy. You could use these methods to build a function that searches the hierarchy for specific nodes. Happily, the DOM objects save you the trouble of writing your own routines by providing several functions that search for nodes within an XML document.

The DOM objects provide GetElementsByTagName, SelectNodes, SelectSingleNode, and GetElementById methods for finding specific nodes. The following sections describe these methods in detail.

GetElementsByTagName

The GetElementsByTagName method returns an XmlNodeList containing references to nodes that have a given name. Both the XmlDocument and XmlElement classes provide a GetElementsByTagName method. The XmlDocument version searches the entire document for nodes with the given name. The XmlElement version of GetElementsBy-TagName searches the document subtree rooted at the element.

Note that GetElementsByTagName may return nodes at different levels of the subtree, and some nodes may be descendants of others. For example, the following XML code defines a Part node that contains two child nodes that are also named Part. If a program searched this document for nodes named Part, GetElementsByTagName would return all three nodes. Depending on what you want to do with the nodes, you may need to be careful not to process a node more than once. For example, if you list the nodes' InnerText values, the subitems' values will appear separately and within the parent node's InnerText.

```xml
<?xml version="1.0"?>
<AllParts>
  <Part>
    <Item>Speaker Assembly</Item>
    <InventoryNumber>K-6437</InventoryNumber>
    <Quantity>1</Quantity>
    <Part>
      <Item>Left Speaker</Item>
      <InventoryNumber>K-6437-L</InventoryNumber>
      <Quantity>1</Quantity>
    </Part>
    <Part>
      <Item>Right Speaker</Item>
      <InventoryNumber>K-6437-R</InventoryNumber>
      <Quantity>1</Quantity>
    </Part>
  </Part>
</AllParts>
```

The following code displays a list of the InnerText values for all of the document's nodes named Item.

```vb
Dim xml_node_list As XmlNodeList
Dim xml_node As XmlNode
Dim results As String

' Get a list of the matching nodes.
xml_node_list = xml_document.GetElementsByTagName("Item")

' Display the nodes' InnerText values.
For Each xml_node In xml_node_list
    results = results & xml_node.InnerText & vbCrLf
```

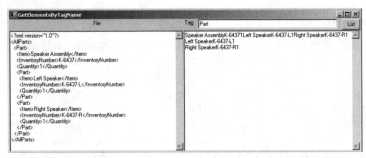

Figure 2.11   Program GetElementsByTagName demonstrates one method for locating nodes in a document.

```
Next xml_node

MsgBox(results)
```

Example program GetElementsByTagName, shown in Figure 2.11, demonstrates this function. When you enter a tag name and click the List button, the program searches the document for nodes with that tag name. It then lists the InnerText value for each of the nodes it finds. If you look closely at Figure 2.11, you will see that the subitems Left Speaker and Right Speaker appear separately and in their parent node's InnerText value.

SelectNodes

The SelectNodes method returns an XmlNodeList containing references to nodes that match a specified XML Path Language (XPath) expression. An XPath expression gives a node's location within an XML document much as a file path describes a file's location on a disk. While file paths are relatively simple, XPath allows you to specify a very complex set of nodes. See Chapter 6, "XSL," for more information on XPath.

Example program SelectNodes, shown in Figure 2.12, uses the following code to select nodes. Enter an XPath expression for the loaded XML document and click the List button. The program uses the XmlDocument object's SelectNodes method to find the nodes you selected. It then displays the nodes' names and InnerText values.

```
' Display the values of the matching elements.
Private Sub btnList_Click( _
  ByVal sender As System.Object, _
  ByVal e As System.EventArgs) _
  Handles btnList.Click

    Dim xml_node_list As XmlNodeList
    Dim xml_node As XmlNode
```

```
    Dim results As String

    ' Get a list of the matching nodes.
    Try
        xml_node_list = xml_document.SelectNodes(txtTagName.Text)

        ' Display the elements.
        For Each xml_node In xml_node_list
            results = results & xml_node.Name & _
                " (" & xml_node.InnerText & ")" & vbCrLf
        Next xml_node

    Catch exc As Exception
        MsgBox(exc.Message, _
            MsgBoxStyle.Exclamation Or MsgBoxStyle.OKOnly, _
            "SelectNodes Error")
    End Try

    txtResults.Text = results
End Sub
```

XPath is a remarkably flexible language that lets a program select an incredible number of different combinations of document nodes. For more details, see Chapter 6, "XSL," and the W3C XML Path Language Recommendation at .

SelectSingleNode

The SelectSingleNode method is very similar to SelectNodes except it returns only the first node that matches an XPath expression instead of all of the nodes that match. After a program has located the matching node, it can use other document navigation methods such as NextSibling, PreviousSibling, and ParentNode to move through the document. In some cases this can be more efficient than using SelectNodes.

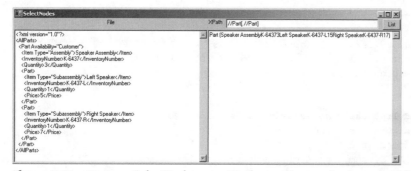

Figure 2.12   Program SelectNodes uses XPaths to select nodes from an XML document.

For example, suppose an XML document has the structure shown in Figure 2.13 and a program must process the nodes at level B. The simple XPath expression //B would select those nodes. To find those nodes, however, SelectNodes would have to traverse every node in the document hierarchy. On the other hand, SelectSingleNode would stop after it had found the first matching node. While SelectNodes might need to search thousands of nodes, SelectSingleNode would search only two before it found a match and stopped. The program could then use the B-level nodes' NextSibling properties to find the other nodes at level B.

Example program SelectSingleNode uses the following code to search the document shown in Figure 2.13 for B-level nodes using SelectNodes and SelectSingleNode.

```
' Find and list the B nodes using SelectNodes.
Private Sub btnSelectNodes_Click( _
  ByVal sender As System.Object, _
  ByVal e As System.EventArgs) Handles btnSelectNodes.Click

    Dim xml_node_list As XmlNodeList
    Dim xml_node As XmlNode
    Dim results As String
    Dim start_time As Single
    Dim stop_time As Single

    ' Get a list of the matching nodes.
    start_time = Timer
    Try
        xml_node_list = xml_document.SelectNodes("//B")

        ' Display the elements.
        For Each xml_node In xml_node_list
            results = results & xml_node.Name & " (" & _
                xml_node.Attributes(0).Value & ")" & vbCrLf
        Next xml_node

    Catch exc As Exception
        MsgBox(exc.Message, _
            MsgBoxStyle.Exclamation Or MsgBoxStyle.OKOnly, _
            "SelectNodes Error")
    End Try
    stop_time = Timer

    txtResults.Text = "Ellapsed time: " & _
        Format(stop_time - start_time, "0.00") & _
        " seconds" & vbCrLf & results
End Sub

' Find and list the B nodes using SelectSingleNode.
Private Sub btnSelectSingleNode_Click( _
  ByVal sender As System.Object, _
  ByVal e As System.EventArgs) Handles btnSelectSingleNode.Click

    Dim xml_node As XmlNode
```

```
Dim results As String
Dim start_time As Single
Dim stop_time As Single

' Get the first matching node.
start_time = Timer
Try
    xml_node = xml_document.SelectSingleNode("//B")

    ' Display the elements.
    Do Until xml_node Is Nothing
        ' Display this element.
        results = results & xml_node.Name & " (" & _
            xml_node.Attributes(0).Value & ")" & vbCrLf

        ' Move to the next element.
        xml_node = xml_node.NextSibling
    Loop

Catch exc As Exception
    MsgBox(exc.Message, _
        MsgBoxStyle.Exclamation Or MsgBoxStyle.OKOnly, _
        "SelectSingleNode Error")
End Try
stop_time = Timer

txtResults.Text = "Ellapsed time: " & _
    Format(stop_time - start_time, "0.00") & _
    " seconds" & vbCrLf & results
End Sub
```

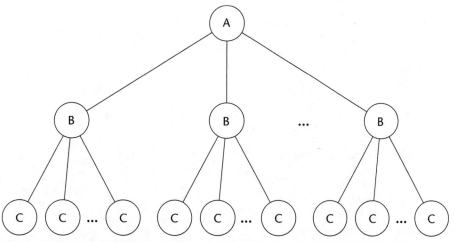

Figure 2.13 This XML document has one level A root node, dozens of nodes at level B, and hundreds or thousands at level C.

Note that SelectNodes is still very fast even for documents like the one shown in Figure 2.13. In one test on a 1GHz Pentium III where the document contained 12 level B nodes and 10,000 level C nodes for each B node, SelectNodes took only 0.11 seconds to locate the B nodes.

When SelectSingleNode searches the document hierarchy for a level B node, however, it needs to examine only two nodes. It is so fast that the time needed by SelectSingleNode is undetectable.

On a relative scale, SelectSingleNode is much faster than SelectNodes. On an absolute scale, however, the difference between 0.11 seconds and 0.00 seconds is small and was noticeable only on a huge XML file. For smaller files, the difference will be almost imperceptible so you should probably use whichever method makes your code easier to debug and maintain unless you are working with really enormous XML documents.

Example program BuildABCDocument builds large documents for program SelectSingleNode to manipulate.

GetElementById

The GetElementById method returns the first node it finds with a specified ID attribute. Like GetElementsByTagName, this method searches for nodes that have a certain property. Unlike GetElementsByTagName, however, this method only returns the first match it finds rather than an XmlNodeList containing all of the nodes that have the correct ID.

GetElementById examines each node's attributes looking for one that is marked as an ID. Simply naming the attribute ID is not enough. The XML document must identify the attribute as having type ID. For example, the following XML file identifies the OrderItem's Index property as an ID.

```
<?xml version="1.0"?>
<!DOCTYPE AllItems [
 <!ELEMENT OrderedItem ANY>
 <!ATTLIST OrderedItem Index ID #REQUIRED>]>
<AllItems Customer="Rod" OrderDate="4/1/3000">
  <OrderedItem Index="1">
    <Item sku="10">Brownies</Item>
    <Price>1.25</Price>
    <Quantity>3</Quantity>
  </OrderedItem>
  <OrderedItem Index="2">
    <Item sku="11">Cookies</Item>
    <Price>0.25</Price>
    <Quantity>12</Quantity>
  </OrderedItem>
  <OrderedItem Index="3">
    <Item sku="12">Cupcakes</Item>
    <Price>0.5</Price>
    <Quantity>6</Quantity>
  </OrderedItem>
  <OrderedItem Index="4">
    <Item sku="13">Bread</Item>
```

```
      <Price>3.40</Price>
      <Quantity>1</Quantity>
    </OrderedItem>
    <OrderedItem Index="5">
      <Item sku="14">Donuts</Item>
      <Price>0.25</Price>
      <Quantity>13</Quantity>
    </OrderedItem>
  </AllItems>
```

Example program GetElementById, shown in Figure 2.14, uses the following code
to locate a node with a given ID attribute. Enter the ID you want to select and click the
Find button. The program uses GetElementById to find first the OrderedItem element
with that ID and displays its OuterXml value.

```
' Display the first node with the given ID.
Private Sub btnFind_Click( _
  ByVal sender As System.Object, _
  ByVal e As System.EventArgs) Handles btnFind.Click

    Dim xml_node As XmlNode

    ' Find the first element with the entered ID.
    Try
        xml_node = xml_document.GetElementById(txtID.Text)
        If xml_node Is Nothing Then
            txtResults.Text = "Node not found"
        Else
            txtResults.Text = xml_node.OuterXml
        End If
    Catch exc As Exception
        MsgBox(exc.Message, _
            MsgBoxStyle.Exclamation Or MsgBoxStyle.OKOnly, _
            "SelectNodes Error")
    End Try
End Sub
```

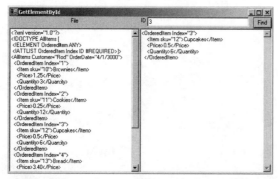

Figure 2.14 Program GetElementById locates an item with a particular Index.

Once you find a node with a matching ID, you can use local navigation methods such as NextSibling, PreviousSibling, and Parent to move to different parts of the document, as explained in the previous section.

GetElementById returns only the first element with an ID attribute that has the value you specified. If you want to examine all matching nodes, you can use SelectNodes to do something similar. For example, SelectNodes("//*[@Index='3']") returns an XmlNodeList containing all nodes that have Index attributes with value 3. Note that this statement does not verify that the attributes are marked with the ID type so it's not exactly the same as GetElementById.

Moving Nodes within Trees

Moving a node from one part of an XML document to another is relatively straightforward. A program can use the RemoveAll and RemoveChild methods to remove a child and its subtree from a document node. It can use the AppendChild, PrependChild, InsertAfter, and InsertBefore methods to add an element to the document.

Combining these routines, a program can use RemoveChild to remove an element from one position in the document and then use AppendChild, PrependChild, InsertAfter, or InsertBefore to replace it in another position.

In fact, the DOM object methods make moving a node and its subtree even easier. If a program uses AppendChild, PrependChild, InsertAfter, or InsertBefore to add a node to the document tree and that node is already part of the tree, it is automatically removed from its current location. That means the program need not explicitly use RemoveChild to remove the node from the document before repositioning it in the tree. It can just insert the node where it belongs, and the DOM objects do the rest.

If you want to make a copy of a node and leave the original node intact, use the node's Clone or CloneNode method. When you insert the new copy of the node into the document, the original node is left where it started.

Example program MoveNodes uses these facts to swap two nodes in the following XML document. When you click the program's Swap button, MoveNodes swaps the first and second OrderedItem document subtrees.

```xml
<?xml version="1.0"?>
<AllItems Customer="Rod" OrderDate="4/1/3000">
  <OrderedItem Index="1">
    <Item>Brownies</Item>
    <Price>1.25</Price>
    <Quantity>3</Quantity>
  </OrderedItem>
  <OrderedItem Index="2">
    <Item>Cookies</Item>
    <Price>0.25</Price>
    <Quantity>12</Quantity>
  </OrderedItem>
  <OrderedItem Index="3">
    <Item>Cupcakes</Item>
    <Price>0.5</Price>
```

```
        <Quantity>6</Quantity>
    </OrderedItem>
</AllItems>
```

Program MoveNodes uses the following code to swap the nodes.

```
' Swap the positions of the first and second elements.
Private Sub btnSwap_Click( _
  ByVal sender As System.Object, _
  ByVal e As System.EventArgs) Handles btnSwap.Click

    Dim root As XmlNode
    Dim child2 As XmlNode
    Dim space2 As XmlNode

    ' Get the root.
    root = m_XmlDocument.DocumentElement

    ' Get the root's second whitespace and
    ' OrderedItem children.
    space2 = root.ChildNodes(2)
    child2 = root.ChildNodes(3)

    ' Insert these before the first whitespace and
    ' OrderedItem children.
    root.PrependChild(child2)
    root.PrependChild(space2)

    ' Redisplay the document's XML.
    txtFileContents.Text = m_XmlDocument.OuterXml
    txtFileContents.Select(0, 0)
End Sub
```

The program loads its document with PreserveWhitespace set to True so the data elements in the document are separated by whitespace elements. Keeping in mind that the ChildNodes list is indexed starting with zero, the root node's children are as follows:

0. A whitespace element

1. An OrderedItem element

2. A second whitespace element

3. A second OrderedItem element

This code begins by saving references to the root node's children number 2 and 3: the second whitespace element and the second OrderedItem element. It then uses PrependChild to insert child number 3 (the second OrderedItem element) at the beginning of the list. The DOM objects automatically remove the element from its previous position in the document to give this arrangement:

3. A second OrderedItem element

0. A whitespace element

1. An OrderedItem element

2. A second whitespace element

Next, the code uses PrependChild again to move child number 2 (the second white-space element) to the beginning of the list. Again, the DOM automatically removes the node from its current position in the document leaving the nodes in this arrangement:

2. A second whitespace element

3. A second OrderedItem element

0. A whitespace element

1. An OrderedItem element

If you ignore the whitespace elements, the program has swapped the positions of the first and second OrderedItem nodes.

Moving Nodes between Trees

Moving a node from one XML document structure to another is not quite as straight-forward as moving a node within a single tree. A program can insert a node in a document only if it was created in the context of that document. If you try to simply insert a node from one tree into another, the system raises an error message saying, "The node to be inserted is from a different document context."

To move a node from one XmlDocument object to another, use the ImportNode method to make a copy of the node in the new document. You can then add the node to the new document using AppendChild, PrependChild, InsertAfter, or InsertBefore.

When you insert a node in a new position within the same document tree, the DOM objects automatically remove the node from its original position. When you create a copy of the node in a different document tree, however, the original node remains. If you want to move the node into a new document and remove it from its original document, you need to perform two steps. First import the node and insert it into the new document. Then use RemoveChild to remove the original node from its document tree.

Example program CombineOrders, shown in Figure 2.15, shows how a program can combine node subtrees from different documents. It takes the OrderedItem subtrees from the two documents on the left and combines them into the single document on the right.

Program CombineOrders uses the following code to build its new document. It begins by loading the two existing XML files Order1.xml and Order2.xml. Next the program uses the first document's CloneNode method to make a copy of the XmlDocument representing that document. Using the parameter True makes CloneNode create a "deep copy" of the XmlDocument node. A deep copy includes all of the descendants of the node so the copy includes all of the nodes in the entire document.

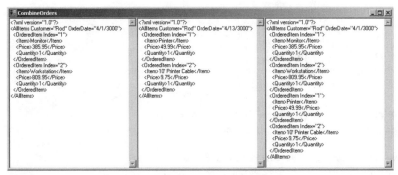

Figure 2.15 Program CombineOrders combines the nodes in two XML files to create a third.

The program then gets a reference to the new document's root AllItems node and removes that node's last child element. The two existing documents were loaded with PreserveWhitespace equal to True so the first document's data ends with a whitespace element and the second document's data begins with a whitespace element. If the program did not remove this whitespace element, the file would contain two whitespace elements in a row where the first document's data ends and the second document's data begins.

Next the program loops through the second document's OrderedItem elements. For each of those nodes, the program uses the new document's ImportNode method to make a deep copy of the node. It then adds the copied node to the new document.

Finally, the program displays the OuterXml properties of all three documents. Notice that the two original documents are unchanged.

```
' Load and combine the orders.
Private Sub Form1_Load( _
  ByVal sender As System.Object, _
  ByVal e As System.EventArgs) Handles MyBase.Load

    Dim xml_document1 As XmlDocument
    Dim xml_document2 As XmlDocument
    Dim xml_combined_document As XmlDocument
    Dim combined_root As XmlNode
    Dim old_node As XmlNode
    Dim new_node As XmlNode

    ' Load the first order.
    xml_document1 = New XmlDocument()
    xml_document1.PreserveWhitespace = True
    xml_document1.Load(DataSubdirectory() & "\Order1.xml")

    ' Load the second order.
    xml_document2 = New XmlDocument()
```

```
xml_document2.PreserveWhitespace = True
xml_document2.Load(DataSubdirectory() & "\Order2.xml")

' Clone the first order.
xml_combined_document = _
    CType(xml_document1.CloneNode(True), XmlDocument)

' Get a reference to the new document's root.
combined_root = xml_combined_document.DocumentElement

' Remove the root's last whitespace child.
combined_root.RemoveChild(combined_root.LastChild)

' Examine all the children of the second order's root.
For Each old_node In xml_document2.DocumentElement.ChildNodes
    ' Import the node into the new document.
    new_node = xml_combined_document.ImportNode(old_node, True)

    ' Add the new node to the new document's root element.
    combined_root.AppendChild(new_node)
Next old_node

' Display the documents.
txtOrder1.Text = xml_document1.OuterXml
txtOrder1.Select(0, 0)

txtOrder2.Text = xml_document2.OuterXml
txtOrder2.Select(0, 0)

txtCombinedOrder.Text = xml_combined_document.OuterXml
txtCombinedOrder.Select(0, 0)
End Sub
```

There are other approaches you could take to merging two documents. For example, instead of creating a duplicate of the first document and then adding to it, the program could load the first document and then add to it directly. Unless the program needs to use the first document directly, it doesn't need to keep a copy of it.

There are also usually other issues to address when you merge two documents like this. In this example, the documents' AllItems elements have two attributes, Customer and OrderDate, that may not be the same. In that case, what values should the new document have for these attributes?

Similarly, the OrderedItem elements have an Index attribute giving the index of those elements within their AllItems parent node. When the program combines the elements from the two original documents, it creates duplicated attributes. In the example files included with the CombineOrders program, the resulting document contains two OrderedItem nodes with Index 1 and two nodes with Index 2.

In this case, it would probably make more sense to renumber the items with Indexes 1 through 4. An even better solution might be to omit these attributes entirely because a program can deduce the element's Index values by their positions within the AllItems node.

In other applications, the solution may not be as obvious. If an inventory code or some other attribute or tag cannot duplicate a value used by another element, the program will need to do some more work to figure out what to do.

Other Examples

The examples presented in this chapter so far have manipulated XML documents that look more or less like database entries. They contain a series of records that include fields describing data used by the program. This document structure is relatively wide and flat. A root element contains many data record elements. The record elements contain several fields each. Generally, the field elements contain text values but not other child elements so the document hierarchy goes no deeper. These documents have a structure similar to a relational database or an HTML table so they are useful for programs that need to process that kind of data.

Storing Configuration Data

In addition to the table-like data, applications often need to save and restore a series of unique values. For example, a program might need to store configuration and user preferences and reload them when it starts. When it closes, example program Form-Properties saves its form's position and size into the XML file Settings.xml shown in the following code.

```
<?xml version="1.0"?>
<settings>
    <x>25</x>
    <y>18</y>
    <width>179</width>
    <height>507</height>
</settings>
```

When program FormProperties starts, it reads these values from the file and puts the form back where it was last. Using similar techniques, you could write a program that saved and restored the position and contents of every form in an application. Each time the user started the application, it would look just as it did the last time the user closed it.

A single XML file can combine both hierarchical data and this kind of setting information. To be well-formed, the document must have a single root node. That node can have two children: Settings and Data. The Settings node can contain whatever configuration information the program needs, and the Data node can hold hierarchical data.

Editing XML Documents

Example program TreeEdit, shown in Figure 2.16, lets you use a TreeView control to edit XML documents. Use the File menu's Open command to load an XML file. Use the Save As command to save any changes you make. Right-click on TreeView nodes to

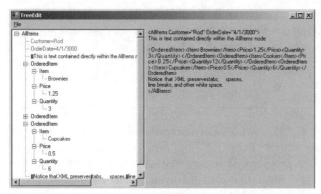

Figure 2.16   Program TreeEdit lets you use a TreeView control to edit XML documents.

add child nodes, attributes, and text elements or to delete a node. The program makes the changes in the TreeView and then generates an XML file corresponding to the nodes you have created.

Program TreeEdit is not really intended to be a great XML editor. Visual Basic's XML editor or even a text editor is usually easier to use. This program is intended to demonstrate some of the flexibility of Visual Basic's DOM objects. It's worth spending some time studying the code to see how it works. For an even greater understanding, you might try modifying the program to add processing instructions, XML declarations, and other elements to the document.

Conclusion

Editing an XML file is easier using an XML or text editor than a Visual Basic program, but the DOM objects Visual Basic provides give you the power you need to automatically modify documents without manual editing. That makes them ideal for building applications that periodically build or examine documents.

These objects let a program manipulate any part of an XML file. They let a program create XML declarations, processing instructions, elements, and attributes. They let a program add, remove, modify, and rearrange the nodes that make up an XML document's structure.

XSL, described in Chapter 6, provides a means for transforming XML documents in a wide variety of ways with remarkably little work. When XSL is insufficient, the DOM provides all the features you need to tear an XML file apart and rebuild it from the ground up.

Forward-Only XML

The XmlDocument object described in Chapter 2, "DOM," represents an XML document by implementing the XML Document Object Model (DOM). It lets a program examine and manipulate every part of an XML document's structure. Using the DOM, a program can add and delete elements, add and remove attributes for an element, move one part of an XML document to another, and even import parts of one XML document into another.

The DOM provides tremendous flexibility, but that flexibility comes at a price. To manipulate an XML document, the XmlDocument object must load the entire document into memory and keep it there. Modern desktop computers may have more than 100 MB of memory so that isn't a problem for many XML documents. For a really huge document, however, that can pose quite a problem.

For example, suppose a program wants to search an XML document containing telephone directory entries for 1 million customers to find a specific phone number. Depending on the structure of the file and the amount of information stored for each entry, this file could use a few hundred bytes per entry to store name, address, phone number, fax number, and so forth. That would make the total file occupy several hundred megabytes of space.

While some computers have enough memory to load this huge file into an XmlDocument object, using hundreds of megabytes to load this file would be a burden on the operating system. This seems particularly wasteful when you consider that the program really wants to find only a single record. It doesn't need to use the structure of the document hierarchy loaded by the DOM. It needs only local information to decide whether a specific record is the one it wants. It could examine the records one-at-a-time to see which one matches the phone number it is trying to find.

For other examples, imagine a program that needs to search an inventory database and list items with fewer than 10 units in stock. Or a program that scans an XML document containing sales information and makes summaries grouping sales by date and region. Or an application that searches an employee database looking for technicians who have a certain set of skills. While the XML documents used in some of these examples may be small enough to load into the DOM, none of these examples need to use the documents' global structure so using the DOM is overkill.

This chapter describes three approaches to reading and writing this kind of huge XML document. All three provide fast forward-only access to XML data. All three rely on the fact that the program can read or write the document locally without using the document's global structure. Because they do not store and manipulate the structure of the XML document the way the DOM does, these methods can read and write extremely large XML documents quickly using relatively small amount of memory.

The first approach is to use Visual Basic's file routines to write the XML document "by hand." This approach is simple but unstructured so it is easier to make mistakes with this method than with the others.

The second approach uses Visual Basic's XmlTextReader and XmlTextWriter classes. These two classes provide methods that let a program tell them how to move through a document. The XmlTextWriter provides more structure than writing files by hand, and it handles XML syntax more consistently.

The third approach uses SAX (Simple API for XML). SAX uses a reader object to scan an XML document. When the SAX reader encounters different kinds of nodes in the document, it raises events that let the program take action.

Writing XML Documents by Hand

Writing XML documents "by hand" is relatively simple. You can easily build an application that writes the appropriate strings into a text file. The program begins by writing an XML declaration into the file. It then writes an opening tag, any data the XML file should contain, and a closing tag.

One disadvantage to this method is that it is easy to forget to properly close a tag. If the document is long and complicated, it can be difficult to verify that every opening tag has a corresponding closing tag. If the document contains a complex hierarchy of nested elements, it can be difficult to ensure that the structure is consistent.

You can make this a little easier by using separate subroutines to write each tag. For example, the WriteOrder subroutine starts by writing an opening <Order> tag, writes the Order item's data possibly calling other subroutines to write subitems, and finishes by writing the closing </Order> tag. If every routine that writes data starts and ends with the item's start and end tag, it is easy to verify that each opening tag has a corresponding closing tag.

Example program WriteOrderByHand shown in Figure 3.1 uses this technique to create an XML file. When you click the Add button, the program displays a dialog where you can enter a new item's name and quantity. Select an item in the list and click the Delete button to remove it from the list. When you have the items you want, click the Write XML button to make the program generate the corresponding XML file.

Figure 3.1   Program WriteOrderByHand uses a FileStream and a StreamWriter to write an XML document.

Program WriteOrderByHand uses the following code to write its XML document. The program uses separate subroutines to write each tag and its contents. The program starts by creating a new text file and writing an XML declaration into it. It then calls subroutine WriteOrder to write an Order tag and its contents.

Subroutine WriteOrder adds the opening tag <Order> to the file. It then calls the WriteItem subroutine to write Item tags for each of the items in the program's ListBox. WriteOrder finishes by adding the closing tag </Order> to the file.

Subroutine WriteItem adds the Item element's opening tag to the file, adds an attribute containing the item's quantity, and finishes the opening Order tag. It then writes the Item elements text into the file and finishes with the closing tag </Item>.

```
Private Sub btnWriteXml_Click( _
  ByVal sender As System.Object, _
  ByVal e As System.EventArgs) Handles btnWriteXml.Click

    Dim file_name As String = DataSubdirectory() & "\Order.xml"
    Dim file_stream As New FileStream(file_name, FileMode.Create)
    Dim stream_writer As New StreamWriter(file_stream)

    ' Start the document.
    stream_writer.WriteLine("<?xml version=""1.0"" _
        encoding=""utf-8""?>")

    ' Write the Order element and its contents.
    WriteOrder(stream_writer)

    ' Finish the document.
    stream_writer.Flush()
    stream_writer.Close()

    ' Display the results.
    txtResults.Text = GetFileContents(file_name)
End Sub

' Write an Order element and its contents.
```

```
Private Sub WriteOrder(ByVal stream_writer As StreamWriter)
    Dim item_values() As String
    Dim i As Integer

    ' Write the Order's start tag.
    stream_writer.WriteLine("<Order>")

    ' Write the Items.
    For i = 0 To lstItems.Items.Count - 1
        ' Get the Item's text and quantity from the ListBox.
        item_values = lstItems.Items(i).Split(vbTab)

        ' Write the Item.
        WriteItem(stream_writer, item_values(0), item_values(1))
    Next i

    ' Write the Order's end tag.
    stream_writer.WriteLine("</Order>")
End Sub

' Write the Item element and its contents.
Private Sub WriteItem(ByVal stream_writer As StreamWriter, _
  ByVal item_text As String, ByVal quantity As String)

    ' Start the Item.
    stream_writer.Write("    <Item")

    ' Add the attribute.
    stream_writer.Write(" Quantity=""" & quantity & """")

    ' Close the Item starting tag.
    stream_writer.Write(">")

    ' Add the Item object's Text.
    stream_writer.Write(item_text)

    ' Add the Item closing tag.
    stream_writer.WriteLine("</Item>")
End Sub
```

This method is fast and effective, and it has low resource requirements. It is not without its dangers, however. If the program fails to close a tag, it produces an invalid XML document.

The program can easily create an invalid tag name such as <Sub Item>. This tag is invalid because its name contains a space character.

To make the resulting document readable, the program must keep track of the levels of indentation whenever it writes new tags. This isn't too hard, particularly if the document has a simple structure that you can model with subroutine calls as program WriteOrderByHand does. It's one more thing that can go wrong, however.

All of these problems are more annoyances than showstoppers, and fixing them is just a matter of debugging the code. The errors they generate, however, are in the XML file so the program itself cannot easily catch them. It is only later when another program tries to read the file that the error may become apparent. At that point, it may be hard to figure out what the problem is and where it was introduced into the file.

While all of these problems are surmountable, the XmlTextWriter make them easier to avoid. XmlTextWriter won't do all of your work for you, but it will make writing XML documents easier and less error-prone.

XmlTextWriter

Building an XML file using the DOM is relatively straightforward. A program creates an XmlDocument object and uses its methods to add new elements to the document. When the document is complete, it calls the XmlDocument object's Save method to write the document into a file.

Writing an XML document using the DOM is practically foolproof. The program cannot make simple mistakes such as forgetting to close a tag because the XmlDocument object creates the tags automatically. If the program tries to make a tag with an illegal name, such as <Root Node>, which contains a space character, the DOM raises an error so the illegal name cannot slip into the resulting XML document.

On the other hand, if a program simply needs to write an XML file, the DOM is overkill. It provides features for manipulating an XML document's structure in ways that are unnecessary in an application that simply writes an XML file. That flexibility comes at the price of increased overhead. In particular, the DOM builds the entire document in memory before it writes the XML file. If the document is large, that could require huge amounts of memory.

The XmlTextWriter class provides properties and methods a program can use to build an XML file quickly and with relative safety with much less overhead than the XmlDocument class. It provides methods to write starting tags, closing tags, attributes, text values, processing instructions, and everything else a program needs to write well-formed XML. These methods encapsulate XML syntax to make building correct XML statements easier.

The XmlTextWriter also helps ensure that the resulting file is well-formed. For example, if a program tries to add an attribute to a text string, the XmlTextWriter raises the following error.

```
Token StartAttribute in state Content would result in an invalid XML
document.
```

The program encounters the error at run time so you can debug it rather than writing incorrect statements into the XML document where they may not be found until much later.

XmlTextWriter Methods

The XmlTextWriter provides properties and methods for writing different XML elements into a file. The following sections describe some of its more useful methods.

Close

The Close method flushes the XmlTextWriter's output and closes the output stream. If any elements or attributes are still open, this automatically closes them. That can be very confusing, however, because the code doesn't explicitly close these items. It also means if you forget to close a tag, the XmlTextWriter will do it for you, probably with unexpected results.

For example, suppose a program creates an Order element that contains a series of Item elements. If it forgets to close the Item elements, the Close method closes them all at the end of the document producing the following strangely nested result.

```
<?xml version="1.0" encoding="utf-8"?>
<Order>
    <Item Quantity="6">Apple
        <Item Quantity="2">Apricot
            <Item Quantity="10">Banana
                <Item Quantity="24">Cherry
                    <Item Quantity="4">Peach
                    </Item>
                </Item>
            </Item>
        </Item>
    </Item>
</Order>
```

Because the Close method raises an error if any elements or attributes are still open, you need to be careful to close them yourself.

Flush

The Flush method writes anything in the XmlTextWriter's output buffer into its output stream and then flushes the output stream. Most programs don't need to call Flush directly because the Close method automatically flushes the output.

Calling Flush is necessary only under rather strange conditions. For example, you can use Flush if you want to write into the underlying stream using some method other than the XmlTextWriter and you need to be sure the XmlTextWriter's output has been sent to the output stream first.

The following code uses an XmlTextWriter to start a document. It then writes XXX into the file, flushes the XmlTextWriter, and writes YYY into the file.

```
Dim file_name As String = DataSubdirectory() & "\Order.xml"
Dim file_stream As New FileStream(file_name, FileMode.Create)
Dim xml_text_writer As New XmlTextWriter(file_stream, Encoding.UTF8)
Dim stream_writer As New StreamWriter(file_stream)

' Start the document.
xml_text_writer.WriteStartDocument()
```

```
' Write some unformatted text.
stream_writer.Write("XXX")
stream_writer.Flush()

' Flush the XmlTextWriter.
xml_text_writer.Flush()

' Write some more unformatted text.
stream_writer.Write("YYY")
stream_writer.Flush()
```

Because this code doesn't flush the XmlTextWriter before it writes the string XXX, that string may appear before the XML declaration, as in the following output.

```
XXX<?xml version="1.0" encoding="utf-8"?>YYY
```

If you write using only the XmlTextWriter, you can ignore this whole bizarre issue and never use Flush.

LookupPrefix

The LookupPrefix method returns the prefix for a namespace's URI. For example, the following code defines the bk namespace and then uses LookupPrefix to find the prefix from the URI to which it is assigned.

```
' Start a Book element.
xml_text_writer.WriteStartElement("Book")

' Define the bk namespace for the Book element.
xml_text_writer.WriteAttributeString("xmlns", "bk", Nothing, _
    "http://www.vb-helper.com/Book")

' Start a bk:Title element.
xml_text_writer.WriteStartElement("bk:Title")

' Write a string containing the namespace assigned to
' the URI http://www.vb-helper.com/Book. In this case, bk.
xml_text_writer.WriteString( _
    xml_text_writer.LookupPrefix("http://www.vb-helper.com/Book"))

' End the Title element.
xml_text_writer.WriteEndElement()

' End the Book element.
xml_text_writer.WriteEndElement()
```

An alternate strategy would be to define the prefix characters in a Visual Basic variable when you need the prefix.

WriteAttributeString

This method adds an attribute statement to the XML document. If the XmlTextWriter has not just opened an item that can have an attribute, this method raises an error. For example, the following code writes an element start tag, two attributes, and a text value. It then tries to write another attribute value, but it fails because the previous node, a text value, cannot have attributes.

```
' Write an IceCream start tag.
xml_text_writer.WriteStartElement("IceCream")

' Write the Size attribute.
xml_text_writer.WriteAttributeString("Size", Nothing, "Large")

' Write the ConeType attribute.
xml_text_writer.WriteAttributeString("ConeType", Nothing, "Waffle")

' Write the text string.
xml_text_writer.WriteString("Chocolate")

' Write the HasChips attribute. This fails because the
' previous node, a string, cannot have attributes.
xml_text_writer.WriteAttributeString("HasChips", Nothing, "False")

' Write the IceCream end tag.
xml_text_writer.WriteEndElement()
```

If you remove the attempt by WriteAttributeString to create a HasChips attribute, the output looks like this.

```
<IceCream Size="Large" ConeType="Waffle">Chocolate</IceCream>
```

The third call to WriteAttributeString essentially tries to place an attribute between the string Chocolate and the closing tag </IceCream>, and that is not allowed.

WriteBase64

XML files are text-based so they cannot contain binary data. The WriteBase64 method translates binary data stored in an array of bytes into text using the base64 encoding. It then writes the resulting text into the XML document.

Note that the data is not automatically marked as encoded. If you want to mark the data as encoded, you can place special flags in the element's name or attributes. For example, the following code writes a Data element with an Encoding="Base64" attribute. When you write the program that loads this data, you can check the Encoding attribute to see how the data was encoded.

```
' Start a Data element.
xml_text_writer.WriteStartElement("Data")

' Make an Encoding="Base64" attribute.
```

```
xml_text_writer.WriteAttributeString("Encoding", Nothing, "Base64")

' Write the encoded data.
xml_text_writer.WriteBase64(data_buffer, 0, buffer_length)

' Close the Data element.
xml_text_writer.WriteEndElement()
```

For more information on WriteBase64 and to see an example program, see the *Writing Binary Data* section later in this chapter.

WriteBinHex

The WriteBinHex method encodes binary data and writes it into the XML document exactly as WriteBase64 does except using a binhex encoding instead of the base64 encoding. For more information on WriteBinHex and to see an example program, see the *Writing Binary Data* section later in this chapter.

WriteCData

This method creates a CDATA section. For example, consider the following code.

```
xml_text_writer.WriteStartElement("Example")
xml_text_writer.WriteCData("An empty item looks like: <Item/>")
xml_text_writer.WriteEndElement()
```

This code generates the following XML data.

```
<Example><![CDATA[An empty item looks like: <Item/>]]></Example>
```

In Visual Basic .NET Beta 2, WriteCData confuses the XmlTextWriter's indentation in the element that contains it. For example, consider the following code.

```
' Start the Example element.
xml_text_writer.WriteStartElement("Example")

' Add an Intro child element.
xml_text_writer.WriteStartElement("Intro")
xml_text_writer.WriteString("Describe example here")
xml_text_writer.WriteEndElement()

' Add the XML example text.
xml_text_writer.WriteCData("An empty item looks like: <Item/>")

' Add a Conclusion child element.
xml_text_writer.WriteStartElement("Conclusion")
xml_text_writer.WriteString("Wrap up here")
xml_text_writer.WriteEndElement()

' Close the Example element.
xml_text_writer.WriteEndElement()
```

This code produces the following XML statements. All of the Example element's child nodes are run together on the same line, although the rest of the XML file looks correct.

```
<Example>
    <Intro>Describe example here</Intro><![CDATA[An empty item looks
like: <Item/>]]><Conclusion>Wrap up here</Conclusion></Example>
```

This will probably be fixed in a future release of Visual Basic. It may even be fixed before the final release of Visual Basic .NET.

WriteCharEntity

This method writes a hexadecimal character entity into the XML document. For example, this statement:

```
xml_text_writer.WriteCharEntity(":"c)
```

produces this output:

```
&#x3A;
```

Here 3A is the hexadecimal Unicode value of the colon character.

Note that the WriteCharEntity method takes a character as input, not a string. The value ":"c is a character containing the colon character. The value ":" would be a string containing the colon character.

The XmlTextWriter raises an error if the character entity is illegal at that point in the XML document. For example, a character entity cannot appear before the XML declaration or the root data node.

WriteChars

The WriteChars method writes an array of characters into the XML document. For example, the following code writes a group of three characters twice: first as characters and then as hexadecimal character entities using WriteCharEntity.

```
' Define an array of characters.
Dim chars() As Char = { _
    Convert.ToChar(&H1124), _
    Convert.ToChar(&H10DC), _
    Convert.ToChar(&H11BE), _
    Convert.ToChar(&H11CE), _
    Convert.ToChar(&H10EC), _
    Convert.ToChar(&H111B) _
}

' Write as characters.
xml_text_writer.WriteStartElement("Characters")
xml_text_writer.WriteChars(chars, 0, chars.Length)
```

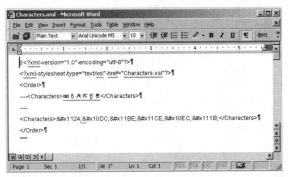

Figure 3.2 Characters written by WriteChars are included directly in the XML output while those written by WriteCharEntity are not.

```
xml_text_writer.WriteEndElement()

' Write as character entities.
xml_text_writer.WriteStartElement("Characters")
Dim c As Integer
For c = 0 To chars.Length - 1
    xml_text_writer.WriteCharEntity(chars(c))
Next c
xml_text_writer.WriteEndElement()
```

Figure 3.2 shows this code's output in Microsoft Word. Notice that the first six characters, written by WriteChars, are contained directly in the XML document. The next six characters, written by WriteCharEntity, are represented by hexadecimal character entities.

XML-enabled browsers such as Internet Explorer 6 should be able to display both character entities and characters included directly in the XML document. Figure 3.3 shows Internet Explorer 6 displaying this example's output.

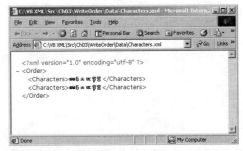

Figure 3.3 Internet Explorer 6 can display character entities and characters written directly into the XML file.

Internet Explorer can also display character entity and character data using an XSL stylesheet. Figure 3.4 shows Internet Explorer using the following XSL stylesheet to display characters in a table.

```
<?xml version="1.0"?>
<xsl:stylesheet version="1.0"
  xmlns:xsl="http://www.w3.org/1999/XSL/Transform">
    <xsl:template match="/">
        <!-- Start the HTML document. -->
        <HTML>
        <HEAD>
        <TITLE>Characters</TITLE>
        </HEAD>
        <BODY>

        <!-- Start a TABLE. -->
        <TABLE BORDER="1" CELLPADDING="5" CELLSPACING="1">
        <TR>
            <TH>String</TH>
            <TH ALIGN="Right">Length</TH>
        </TR>

        <!-- Process the subelements. -->
        <xsl:apply-templates/>

        <!-- Finish the TABLE and the document. -->
        </TABLE>
        </BODY>
        </HTML>
    </xsl:template>

    <xsl:template match="Characters">
        <TR>
            <TD><xsl:value-of select="."/></TD>
            <TD ALIGN="Right">
                <xsl:value-of select="string-length(.)"/>
            </TD>
        </TR>
    </xsl:template>
</xsl:stylesheet>
```

Figure 3.4 Internet Explorer 6 can display character entities and characters written directly into the XML file using an XSL stylesheet.

Note also that some text editors cannot save these special characters correctly in a plaintext file. If you load an XML document built by XmlTextWriter, modify the file, and save the results, the special characters may be removed or transformed by the editor. You will probably get good results editing these files with Microsoft Word treating the file as a Unicode (UTF-8) encoding. You will get the best results if you modify the program that built the file so you don't need to edit the file at all.

WriteComment

This method adds a comment to the XML document. For example, this code:

```
xml_text_writer.WriteComment("Orders for August")
```

produces this result:

```
<!--Orders for August-->
```

A program can create a multiline comment by embedding a carriage return and linefeed in the comment string. For example, this code:

```
xml_text_writer.WriteComment(vbCrLf & "  Orders for August" & vbCrLf)
```

generates this three line comment:

```
<!--
   Orders for August
-->
```

You may also want to place whitespace containing a carriage return and linefeed before and after the comment so it starts and ends on its own lines instead of being squeezed between two other document nodes.

WriteDocType

The WriteDocType method creates a DOCTYPE section. For example, this code:

```
xml_text_writer.WriteDocType("Addresses", Nothing, Nothing, _
    "<!ENTITY us ""United States of America"">")
```

generates this XML statement:

```
<!DOCTYPE Addresses[<!ENTITY us "United States of America">]>
```

This example defines an entity that the program can later use with the WriteEntityRef method.

WriteElementString

This method adds an element with a string value to the XML document. For example, this statement:

```
xml_text_writer.WriteElementString("Flavor", "Chocolate")
```

generates this XML code:

```
</Flavor>Chocolate</Flavor>
```

In this example, WriteElementString is equivalent to the following code.

```
xml_text_writer.WriteStartElement("Flavor")
xml_text_writer.WriteString("Chocolate")
xml_text_writer.WriteEndElement()
```

If the element will contain only simple text and won't have any attributes, WriteElementString is simpler and makes the code easier to understand.

WriteEndAttribute

This method closes an attribute opened using WriteStartAttribute. For example, this code:

```
xml_text_writer.WriteStartElement("Item")
xml_text_writer.WriteStartAttribute("Quantity", Nothing)
xml_text_writer.WriteString("12")
xml_text_writer.WriteEndAttribute()
xml_text_writer.WriteString("Cookie")
xml_text_writer.WriteEndElement()
```

generates this XML output:

```
<Item Quantity="12">Cookie</Item>
```

The WriteAttributeString method is a bit easier to use in many cases. The following code is equivalent to the previous longer version.

```
xml_text_writer.WriteStartElement("Item")
xml_text_writer.WriteAttributeString("Quantity", Nothing, "12")
xml_text_writer.WriteString("Cookie")
xml_text_writer.WriteEndElement()
```

The WriteEndAttribute method raises an error if it is called when no attribute is open. For example, it raises an error if it is called right after a call to WriteString or WriteStartElement.

WriteEndDocument

The WriteEndDocument method closes any open tags or attributes and ends the document. See the earlier description of the Close method for an explanation of why this can be confusing.

WriteEndElement

This method closes an element opened by WriteStartElement. For an example, this code:

```
xml_text_writer.WriteStartElement("Item")
xml_text_writer.WriteString("Cookie")
xml_text_writer.WriteEndElement()
```

produces this result:

```
<Item>Cookie</Item>
```

If the item will contain a text value and nothing else, the WriteElementString method is simpler than WriteStartElement, WriteString, and WriteEndElement.

WriteEntityRef

This method writes an entity reference. For example, this statement:

```
xml_text_writer.WriteEntityRef("cp")
```

generates this XML code:

```
&cp;
```

This method does not check whether the entity has been defined before it writes the reference.

WriteFullEndElement

The WriteFullEndElement method writes an end element into the XML document. This statement uses a separate end tag even if the element is empty. For example, the following code writes an abbreviated empty element and an empty element with a separate end tag.

```
' The following lines write:
'    <IceCream />
xml_text_writer.WriteStartElement("IceCream")
xml_text_writer.WriteEndElement()

' The following lines write:
'    <IceCream>
'    </IceCream>
xml_text_writer.WriteStartElement("IceCream")
xml_text_writer.WriteFullEndElement()
```

The first version, without a separate end tag, takes less space in the document so most developers prefer that form.

WriteName

This method checks that its argument is a valid name according to the XML specification (for example, it contains no spaces) and then adds it to the XML document. You can use this method to catch invalid names at run time so they aren't written into the XML code. Note that routines such as WriteStartElement also verify that their arguments are valid names.

WriteProcessingInstruction

The WriteProcessingInstruction method adds a processing instruction to the XML document. For example, this statement:

```
xml_text_writer.WriteProcessingInstruction( _
    "xml-stylesheet", "type='text/xsl' href='Orders.xsl'")
```

produces this XML output:

```
<?xml-stylesheet type='text/xsl' href='Orders.xsl'?>
```

While the XML declaration looks like any other processing instruction, it has a special place in the file. The WriteStartDocument method automatically creates the XML declaration so you should not try to create it using the WriteProcessingInstruction method.

WriteRaw

This method lets a program write raw, unformatted text into the XML document. You can use this to circumvent the other XmlTextWriter methods that a program normally uses to write into the XML document.

WriteRaw will write anything, however, even if it invalidates the document. For example, this code:

```
xml_text_writer.WriteStartElement("Dangerous")
xml_text_writer.WriteRaw("Raw XML can be risky & >>> dangerous <<<")
xml_text_writer.WriteEndElement()
```

produces this invalid XML output:

```
<Dangerous>Raw XML can be risky & >>> dangerous <<</Dangerous>
```

To avoid writing incorrect values like this one, you should use the other XmlTextWriter methods whenever possible.

Like the WriteCData method, WriteRaw confuses the XmlTextWriter's indentation in Visual Basic .NET Beta 2.

WriteStartAttribute

The WriteStartAttribute method starts writing an attribute. The program should then use WriteString to add the attribute's value to the output and close the attribute with WriteEndAttribute. For example, this code:

```
xml_text_writer.WriteStartElement("Item")
xml_text_writer.WriteStartAttribute("Quantity", Nothing)
xml_text_writer.WriteString("12")
xml_text_writer.WriteEndAttribute()
xml_text_writer.WriteString("Cookie")
xml_text_writer.WriteEndElement()
```

produces this result:

```
<Item Quantity="12">Cookie</Item>
```

If the program does not call WriteString, the attribute is empty as in this code:

```
<Item Quantity="">Cookie</Item>
```

If the program omits the call to WriteEndAttribute, the XmlTextWriter automatically closes the attribute when the program calls its WriteEndElement method. For example, this code:

```
xml_text_writer.WriteStartElement("Item")
xml_text_writer.WriteStartAttribute("Color", Nothing)
xml_text_writer.WriteString("Car")
xml_text_writer.WriteEndElement()
```

generates this XML code:

```
<Item Color="Car" />
```

Letting the XmlTextWriter automatically close the attribute can be very confusing, however. When you read the code in this example, it is easy to mistake the attribute value Car for the Item element's value. The code is much easier to understand if it explicitly closes the attribute.

WriteStartDocument

The WriteStartDocument method adds an XML declaration with version "1.0" to the output. If the program passes this method a Boolean argument, WriteStartDocument adds an appropriate "standalone" field to the declaration.

WriteStartElement

This method begins writing an element. After the element is open, the program can add attributes, text, and subelements.

If the element will contain only text and will not need attributes, you can use the WriteElementString method to write the element all in one statement instead of using separate calls to WriteStartElement, WriteString, and WriteEndElement.

WriteString

WriteString writes a string into the XML output. Like the WriteCData and WriteRaw methods, WriteString confuses the XmlTextWriter's indentation in Visual Basic .NET Beta 2. For example, this code:

```
xml_text_writer.WriteStartElement("Pub")
xml_text_writer.WriteElementString("Child", "Before")
xml_text_writer.WriteString("Slug & Lettuce")
xml_text_writer.WriteElementString("Child", "After")
xml_text_writer.WriteEndElement()
```

produces this result:

```
<Pub>
    <Child>Before</Child>Slug &amp; Lettuce<Child>After</Child></Pub>
```

Notice that unlike WriteRaw, WriteString replaces the ampersand (&) in the original string with the & escape sequence so the resulting XML is safe.

WriteWhitespace

The WriteWhitespace method adds whitespace to the XML document. WriteWhitespace behaves much as the WriteString method does except it verifies that its argument is a string that contains only whitespace characters.

You can use WriteWhitespace to format output in the XML file, but it is easier to set the XmlTextWriter's Formatting property to Formatting.Indented so that the object automatically indents the resulting XML code. That will also produce a more consistent result.

XmlTextWriter Properties

While most of the XmlTextWriter's methods write different kinds of elements into an XML document, many of its properties determine the appearance of those elements. The following sections describe this object's most useful properties.

Formatting

When this property is set to Formatting.Indented, the XmlTextWriter indents the XML code to show the document's structure as shown in the following code.

```
<?xml version="1.0" encoding="utf-8" standalone="yes"?>
<?xml-stylesheet type="text/xsl" href="Order.xsl"?>
<Order>
    <Item Quantity="6">Apple</Item>
    <Item Quantity="2">Apricot</Item>
    <Item Quantity="10">Banana</Item>
    <Item Quantity="24">Cherry</Item>
    <Item Quantity="4">Peach</Item>
</Order>
```

When this Formatting is set to Formatting.None, the XmlTextWriter places all of its output on one line as in the following code.

```
<?xml version="1.0" encoding="utf-8" standalone="yes"?><?xml-stylesheet
type="text/xsl" href="Order.xsl"?><Order><Item
Quantity="6">Apple</Item><Item Quantity="2">Apricot</Item><Item
Quantity="10">Banana</Item><Item Quantity="24">Cherry</Item><Item
Quantity="4">Peach</Item></Order>
```

Setting Formatting to Formatting.None can save a little space in a deeply nested document that will be read only by programs and not by people. Eliminating the formatting removes one of the major benefits of XML: It is easy to read. Unless a program is writing a file that will be immediately transformed into some other format, for example by XSL, the small saving in space is usually not worth the document's reduced readability.

Indentation

The Indentation property determines the number of characters the XML code is indented when Formatting is set to Formatting.Indented. The default value is two.

IndentChar

IndentChar is the character used by the XmlTextWriter to indent its output. This character can be any whitespace character, although some whitespace characters such as carriage return make poor choices. Normally IndentChar is the space character.

Another useful combination of properties is to set Indentation to 1 and IndentChar to vbTab. That produces readable XML code while using only one indentation character per level of indentation. As long as the document hierarchy isn't too deep, the result is easy to read and takes less disk space than a document with Indentation set to 2 or 4 and IndentChar set to the space character.

Namespaces

When Namespaces is set to True, the XmlTextWriter provides support for namespaces. When Namespaces is False, the XmlTextWriter does not support namespaces.

Setting Namespaces to False doesn't really help the program do anything new. It does make the XmlTextWriter raise an error if the program tries to declare a namespace. If you know the program will not need to use namespaces, you can set Namespaces to False to watch for possible errors.

QuoteChar

QuoteChar determines the character the XmlTextWriter uses to quote attribute values. This character must be a single or double quote.

WriteState

This property gives the XmlTextWriter's state. It can have the values listed in Table 3.1.

If a program keeps track of what it is doing, it should generally not need to use WriteState.

XmlLang

XmlLang returns the current language value set by an xml:lang statement. For example, the following XML code sets the language inside the Item tag to English in Great Britain.

```
<Item xml:lang="en-GB">Colour</Item>
```

The following Visual Basic code shows how a program might produce this XML code. The comments give the value of XmlLang after each statement.

```
' XmlLang = ""
xml_text_writer.WriteStartElement("Item")
' XmlLang = ""
xml_text_writer.WriteAttributeString("xml", "lang", Nothing, "en-GB")
' XmlLang = "en-GB"
xml_text_writer.WriteString("Colour")
' XmlLang = "en-GB"
xml_text_writer.WriteEndElement()
' XmlLang = ""
```

When no xml:lang statement is in effect, a call to XmlLang returns an empty string.

XmlSpace

XmlSpace returns the value XmlSpace.None, XmlSpace.Preserve, or XmlSpace.Default to indicate the document's current xml:space value. For example, in the following code the first item's whitespace is preserved. In the second item, the whitespace is insignificant so a program reading the XML document may remove it.

```
<Item xml:space="preserve">In this Item,
whitespace is significant</Item>
<Item xml:space="default">In this Item,
whitespace is insignificant</Item>
```

If no xml:space statement is in effect, the XmlSpace method returns XmlSpace.None.

Table 3.1   WriteState Values

VALUE	MEANING
Attribute	The XmlTextWriter is writing an attribute. The program has called WriteStartAttribute but not WriteEndAttribute.
Closed	The XmlTextWriter's Close method has been called.
Content	The XmlTextWriter is writing content. The program has finished opening an element, for example by calling WriteString or by closing a nested element.
Element	The XmlTextWriter is writing an element. The program has called WriteStartElement but not WriteEndElement and has not started writing content for the element.
Prolog	The XmlTextWriter is writing the prolog. The program has called WriteStartDocument, may have written processing instructions or a DOCTYPE section, but has not yet written the root data node.
Start	The program is not writing anything. This occurs after the XmlTextWriter has been created but before the program calls WriteStartDocument. It also occurs after the program closes the root data node.

An XmlTextWriter Example

Example program WriteOrder, shown in Figure 3.5, uses the XmlTextWriter to build an XML document. When you click the Add button, the program displays a small dialog where you can enter a name and quantity for a new item. Select an item in the list and click the Delete button to remove the item from the list. When you have finished building the list of items, click the Write XML button to generate the XML file. Use the Formatting Indented check box to tell the XmlTextWriter whether it should indent the result.

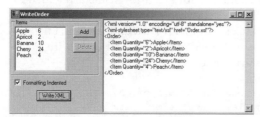

Figure 3.5   Example program WriteOrder uses the XmlTextWriter to build an XML document.

Program WriteOrder uses the following code to build XML files. The btnWriteXml_Click event handler starts the process. This routine creates the new Xml-TextWriter object, associating it with a file name and setting its encoding to Unicode (UTF-8).

It checks the chkFormattingIndented check box to see if it should set the XmlText-Writer's Formatting property to Formatting.Indented or Formatting.None. The program sets the object's Indentation and IndentChar properties to indent the XML code by four spaces for each level of nesting in the XML document's hierarchy. The XmlTextWriter ignores these properties if its Formatting property is set to Formatting.None.

Next the routine starts the XML document by calling WriteStartDocument. This statement creates the document's XML declaration statement. The XML declaration specifies the encoding UTF-8 assigned to the XmlTextWriter when it was created. Passing the WriteStartDocument method the value True makes the declaration include the standalone="yes" clause.

The program then uses the WriteProcessingInstruction method to create a stylesheet reference. The code uses multiple sets of double quotes to insert single double quotes into the result strings. For example, this Visual Basic code:

```
"type=""text/xsl"" href=""Order.xsl"""
```

represents this string:

```
type="text/xsl" href="Order.xsl"
```

Alternatively, the program could have surrounded the processing instruction's parameter values with single quotes like this:

```
"type='text/xsl' href='Order.xsl'"
```

After it has finished creating the document's prolog, the program calls subroutine WriteOrder to write the root data node and its contents. It then calls the XmlTextWriter object's WriteEndDocument and Close methods to finish the document. The program displays the resulting XML file in its txtResults text box.

Subroutine WriteOrder writes an Order element and its contents. It starts the Order element by calling WriteStartElement. For each entry in the program's list box, Write-Order calls subroutine WriteItem to write an Item element describing that entry. Write-Order finishes by calling WriteEndElement to close the Order element. Making this routine start with a call to WriteStartElement and finish with a call to WriteEndElement makes it easy to see that the Order element is started and closed properly.

Subroutine WriteItem opens an Item element with a call to WriteStartElement. It gives the element an attribute with WriteAttributeString, builds the Item's body by calling WriteString, and then closes the Item element with WriteEndElement. Like subroutine WriteOrder, this routine starts with WriteStartElement and ends with Write-EndElement so it is easy to see that it is started and closed properly.

```
Private Sub btnWriteXml_Click(ByVal sender As System.Object, _
    ByVal e As System.EventArgs) Handles btnWriteXml.Click

    Dim file_name As String = DataSubdirectory() & "\Order.xml"
```

```
Dim xml_text_writer As New XmlTextWriter(file_name, Encoding.UTF8)

    ' Tell the XmlTextWriter whether to indent.
    If chkFormattingIndented.Checked Then
        xml_text_writer.Formatting = Formatting.Indented
    Else
        xml_text_writer.Formatting = Formatting.None
    End If
    xml_text_writer.Indentation = 4
    xml_text_writer.IndentChar = " "

    ' Start the document.
    xml_text_writer.WriteStartDocument(True)

    ' Write a stylesheet reference.
    xml_text_writer.WriteProcessingInstruction( _
        "xml-stylesheet", "type=""text/xsl"" href=""Order.xsl""")

    ' Write the Order element and its contents.
    WriteOrder(xml_text_writer)

    ' Finish the document.
    xml_text_writer.WriteEndDocument()
    xml_text_writer.Close()

    ' Display the results.
    txtResults.Text = GetFileContents(file_name)
    txtResults.Select(0, 0)
End Sub

' Write an Order element and its contents.
Private Sub WriteOrder(ByVal xml_text_writer As XmlTextWriter)

    ' Start the Order element.
    xml_text_writer.WriteStartElement("Order")

    ' Write the Items.
    Dim item_values() As String
    Dim i As Integer
    For i = 0 To lstItems.Items.Count - 1
        ' Get the Item's text and quantity from the ListBox.
        item_values = lstItems.Items(i).Split(vbTab)

        ' Write the Item element and its contents.
        WriteItem(xml_text_writer, item_values(0), item_values(1))
    Next i

    ' End the Order element.
    ' Actually the XmlTextWriter will automatically add this
    ' closing element if you omit it but that could be confusing.
    xml_text_writer.WriteEndElement()
```

```
End Sub

' Write the Item element and its contents.
Private Sub WriteItem(ByVal xml_text_writer As XmlTextWriter, _
  ByVal item_text As String, ByVal quantity As String)

    ' Write the Item's start tag.
    xml_text_writer.WriteStartElement("Item")

    ' Write the Quantity attribute.
    xml_text_writer.WriteAttributeString("Quantity", quantity)

    ' Write the Item's text value.
    xml_text_writer.WriteString(item_text)

    ' Add the Item closing tag.
    xml_text_writer.WriteEndElement()
End Sub
```

The structure of the btnWriteXml_Click, WriteOrder, and WriteItem subroutines used by program WriteOrder mimics the structure of the document it is writing. Subroutine btnWriteXml_Click opens the document, writes its prolog, and closes the document when it is finished. Subroutine WriteOrder starts an Order element, calls WriteItem to build subelements, and closes the Order element. Subroutine WriteItem starts, builds, and closes an Item element.

Making these routines duplicate the XML document's structure makes them easy to debug. Each opens a document object and then later closes it. Each works at a single level in the document tree so it is relatively easy to understand. While you could write the entire document in the btnWriteXml_Click event handler, distributing the work among the subroutines makes it easier to understand and verify.

Writing Binary Data

XML is a text-based data description language. If you want to store binary data in an XML file, you need to encode the data in some sort of textual way. The XmlTextWriter's WriteBase64 and WriteBinHex methods automatically convert binary data into textual representations. As their names imply, these routines write binary data using the Base64 and binhex encodings, respectively.

Example program WriteEncodedPicture, shown in Figure 3.6, writes a picture into an XML file using either the Base64 or binhex encodings.

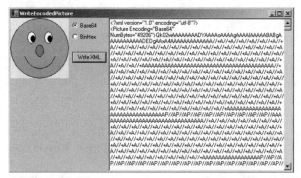

Figure 3.6 Example program WriteEncodedPicture saves an image into a file using the Base64 or binhex encoding.

When you select the Base64 option and click the WriteXML button, program WriteEncodedPicture saves the picture in the file PictureBase64.xml using a Base64 encoding. The following code shows what this file looks like. It contains a root Picture data element with attributes Encoding set to Base64 and NumBytes set to 49206. The element itself contains 65,608 characters of encoded data.

```
<?xml version="1.0" encoding="utf-8"?>
<Picture Encoding="Base64"
NumBytes="49206">Qk02wAAAAAAADYAAAAoAAAAgAAAAIAAAAABABgAAAAAAAAAAAAAADED
gAAxA4AAAAAAAAAAAAA//+A//+A//+A//+A//+A//+A//+A//+A//+A//+A//+
    ... lots of encoded data deleted here ...
+A//+A//+A//+A//+A//+A//+A//+A//+A//+A//+A//+A//+A//+A//+A//+A
//+A//+A//+A//+A//+A//+A//+A//+A//+A//+A//+A//+A//8=</Picture>
```

Because the encoding uses only text characters, it cannot represent all 256 possible byte values with a single character. That means the encoding must take up more room than the original data. In this case, 49,206 bytes of image data take up 65,608 characters when encoded.

When you Select the WriteEncodedPicture program's BinHex option and click the WriteXML button, the program saves the picture in the file PictureBinHex.xml using a binhex encoding. The following code shows what this file looks like. This file contains a root Picture data element with attributes Encoding set to BinHex and NumBytes set to 49206. The element itself contains 98,410 characters of encoded data.

```
<?xml version="1.0" encoding="utf-8"?>
<Picture Encoding="BinHex"
NumBytes="49206">424D36C0000000000000360000002800000080000000800000000
```

```
10018000000000000000000000C40E0000C40E00000000000000000000000FFFF80FFFF80FFF
    ... lots of encoded data deleted here ...
FFFF80FFFF80FFFF80FFFF80FFFF80FFFF80FFFF80FFFF80FFFF80FFFF80FFFF80FFFF80FFFF
80FFFF80FFFF80FFFF80FFFF80FFFF80FFFF80FFFF80FFFF80FFFF</Picture>
```

Like the Base64 encoding, the binhex encoding must expand the data because it cannot represent all possible byte values in a single character. In this case, the expansion is from 49,206 bytes of image data to 98,410 characters of binhex encoded data.

Program WriteEncodedPicture uses the following code to save its image into an XML file. The program initializes the file_name variable to the value PictureBase64.xml or PictureBinHex.xml, depending on which encoding is selected.

Next the program opens an XmlTextWriter attached to that filename, writes the document's XML declaration, and starts a Picture element. It gives the new element an attribute indicating the picture's encoding so an application that reads the document can tell how to decode it.

The program then creates a MemoryStream and saves the picSmiley PictureBox's Image into it. The program creates an array of bytes big enough to hold the Memory Stream data and uses the MemoryStream's ToArray method to copy the data into the array.

The program saves the array's length in the Picture element's NumBytes attribute so a program reading the file later can easily tell how much data it will need to load. That program could use the ReadBase64 and ReadBinHex methods to read the data in chunks and then combine the chunks. Saving the number of bytes lets the reading program load the data all at once and simplifies the code.

At this point, the image data is stored in an array of bytes as required by the XmlText-Writer object's WriteBase64 and WriteBinHex methods. Program WriteEncodedPicture calls WriteBase64 or WriteBinHex to encode the array and add it to the XML file.

The application finishes by closing the Picture element and the document and displaying the resulting XML file in a text box.

```vb
' Save the picture into an XML file.
Private Sub btnWriteXML_Click(ByVal sender As System.Object, _
  ByVal e As System.EventArgs) Handles btnWriteXML.Click

    Me.Cursor = Cursors.WaitCursor
    Refresh()


    ' Set the filename depending on the type of encoding.
    Dim file_name As String
    If optBase64.Checked Then
        file_name = DataSubdirectory() & "\PictureBase64.xml"
    Else
        file_name = DataSubdirectory() & "\PictureBinHex.xml"
    End If


    ' Make an XmlTextWriter attached to this file.
    Dim xml_text_writer As New XmlTextWriter(file_name, Encoding.UTF8)


    ' Start the document.
```

```
xml_text_writer.Formatting = Formatting.Indented
xml_text_writer.WriteStartDocument()

' Make a Picture element.
xml_text_writer.WriteStartElement("Picture")

' Save the encoding type in an attribute.
If optBase64.Checked Then
    xml_text_writer.WriteAttributeString( _
        "Encoding", Nothing, "Base64")
Else
    xml_text_writer.WriteAttributeString( _
        "Encoding", Nothing, "BinHex")
End If

' Copy the picture into a MemoryStream.
Dim memory_stream As New MemoryStream()
picSmiley.Image.Save(memory_stream, ImageFormat.Bmp)

' Copy the MemoryStream data into a byte array.
Dim bytes(memory_stream.Length - 1) As Byte
bytes = memory_stream.ToArray()

' Save the array's length in an attribute.
xml_text_writer.WriteAttributeString( _
    "NumBytes", Nothing, bytes.Length)

' Write the byte data into the XML document.
If optBase64.Checked Then
    xml_text_writer.WriteBase64(bytes, 0, bytes.Length)
Else
    xml_text_writer.WriteBinHex(bytes, 0, bytes.Length)
End If

' Finish the Picture element.
xml_text_writer.WriteEndElement()

' Finish the XML document.
xml_text_writer.WriteEndDocument()
xml_text_writer.Close()

' Display the results.
txtResults.Text = GetFileContents(file_name)
txtResults.Select(0, 0)

Me.Cursor = Cursors.Default
End Sub
```

The section *Reading Binary Data* later in this chapter explains how the ReadEncodedPicture program uses the XmlTextReader class to load the pictures saved by program WriteEncodedPicture.

XmlConvert

The XmlTextWriter class provides methods and properties that help a program write a well-formed XML document. Unfortunately, those methods do not guarantee the document is well-formed. While the XmlTextWriter will not let a program close an element when none is open, it will let the program create elements and attributes with invalid names. For example, consider the following Visual Basic code fragment.

```
xml_text_writer.WriteStartElement("Online Order")
xml_text_writer.WriteStartElement("1 Item")
xml_text_writer.WriteAttributeString("Inches/Feet", "Feet")
xml_text_writer.WriteAttributeString("Width+Height", "4x8")
xml_text_writer.WriteAttributeString("Thickness", "5/16""")
xml_text_writer.WriteString("Plywood")
xml_text_writer.WriteEndElement()
xml_text_writer.WriteEndElement()
```

This code produces the following result.

```
<Online Order>
    <1 Item Inches/Feet="Feet" Width+Height="4x8"
Thickness="5/16&quot;">Plywood</1 Item>
</Online Order>
```

This XML code is not well-formed for several reasons. Online Order is an invalid element name because it contains a space character, 1 Item is an invalid element name because it begins with a number and it contains a space, Inches/Feet is an invalid attribute name because it contains the / character, and Width+Height is an invalid attribute name because it contains the + character. The XmlTextWriter generously converts the double quote character in the value 5/16" into the " entity reference and ensures that all of the elements are closed, but otherwise this XML is garbage.

It would be nice if the XmlTextWriter raised errors so these problems couldn't slip into the XML document, but it doesn't. The mistakes in this XML file might remain unnoticed for quite a while until some other application tries to read the file.

It is easy to blame these invalid results on poor source code. A programmer should know better than to name an XML element Online Order. On the other hand, if the program generates these item names at run time, it may not be as obvious that it is creating invalid values. For example, the program might obtain element names from database tables or column names. A database table or column name can legally contain spaces and other characters that are prohibited in XML names.

The XmlConvert class provides methods for converting names to and from a safe XML format. When you write a program that creates XML elements or attributes and you have any doubts about whether the names are valid, you can use an XmlConvert object to ensure they are safe.

The XmlConvert object's EncodeName method converts a name into a safe XML name. When it encounters an invalid character, EncodeName replaces the character with the hexadecimal code for that character surrounded by underscores. For example, the hexadecimal code for the space character is x0020 so the name Online Order encodes to Online_x0020_Order.

If EncodeName finds a sequence that it could confuse for a character encoding, it converts the leading underscore into the string _x005F_. For example, the string A_x002F_B looks as if it contains an encoding for the space character. If the Encode-Name routine receives this string as an input, it encodes it as A_x005F_x002F_B. This is the letter A, followed by the encoding for the underscore character, followed by x002F_B. It is extremely unlikely that you will ever need to make an element or attribute name include a string such as _x002F_, but XmlConvert can handle it.

The following revised Visual Basic code fragment shows how a program can use an XmlConvert object to write element and attribute names safely. Note that attribute and string values are quoted in the resulting XML so they are allowed to contain characters that are disallowed in element and attribute names.

```
Dim xml_convert As New XmlConvert()
xml_text_writer.WriteStartElement( _
    xml_convert.EncodeName("Online Order"))
xml_text_writer.WriteStartElement( _
    xml_convert.EncodeName("1 Item"))
xml_text_writer.WriteAttributeString( _
    xml_convert.EncodeName("Inches/Feet"), "Feet")
xml_text_writer.WriteAttributeString( _
    xml_convert.EncodeName("Width+Height"), "4x8")
xml_text_writer.WriteAttributeString( _
    xml_convert.EncodeName("Thickness"), "5/16""")
xml_text_writer.WriteString("Plywood")
xml_text_writer.WriteEndElement()
xml_text_writer.WriteEndElement()
```

This Visual Basic code produces the following XML output. The result isn't pretty, but it is legal.

```
<Online_x0020_Order>
    <_x0031__x0020_Item Inches_x002F_Feet="Feet"
Width_x002B_Height="4x8"
Thickness="5/16&quot;">Plywood</_x0031__x0020_Item>
</Online_x0020_Order>
```

The XmlConvert object's EncodeName method does not assume the name you pass it is a local name. In other words, it allows the name to contain a colon character. For example, the following code starts a new element named wood:1_x0020_Item.

```
xml_text_writer.WriteStartElement( _
    xml_convert.EncodeName("wood:1 Item"))
```

The EncodeLocalName method is similar to EncodeName except it also encodes the colon character. For example, the following Visual Basic code starts an element named wood_x003A_1_x0020_Item.

```
xml_text_writer.WriteStartElement( _
    xml_convert.EncodeLocalName("wood:1 Item"))
```

Use EncodeLocalName when you want to use an element or attribute name that contains a colon other than the colon used to specify a namespace.

The XmlConvert object's DecodeName method restores an encoded name to its original value. For example, the following code recovers an encoded element name.

```
element_name = xml_convert.DecodeName("_x0031__x0020_Item")
' Now element_name is "1 Item".
```

An application can use DecodeName to recover encoded names when it reads an XML file using the XmlTextReader described later in this chapter.

The XmlConvert class also provides several methods for converting string values into other data types. For example, the following code converts the value of the Price attribute into a Double variable.

```
Dim price As Double
Dim xml_convert As XmlConvert
price = xml_convert.ToDouble(xml_text_reader.GetAttribute("Price"))
```

Other methods the XmlConvert class provides to convert strings into typed values include ToBoolean, ToByte, ToChar, ToDateTime, ToDecimal, ToDouble, ToGuid, ToInt16, ToInt32, ToInt64, ToSByte, ToSingle, ToTimeSpan, ToUInt16, ToUInt32, and ToUInt64.

XmlTextReader

The XmlTextReader class provides a fast, forward-only, read-and-forget approach to processing XML documents. While SAX, described later in this chapter, provides an event-oriented solution, the XmlTextReader uses a procedural approach. SAX reads an XML document and uses events to tell the program what it finds. The program uses the XmlTextReader's methods to see what data it is reading and to tell it what to do.

For example, a program can make the XmlTextReader ignore all insignificant white-space. It can then make the XmlTextReader skip to the beginning of the content elements. The program can examine the nodes in the document as it encounters them and decide what to do. For instance, the program can make the XmlTextReader skip all nodes except Item nodes. When it sees an Item node, the program can use the XmlText-Reader's methods to read the Item's QuantityAvailable child to see how many units of the item are in inventory. It can then display those where QuantityAvailable is less than 10.

XmlTextReader Methods

The XmlTextReader class provides several methods for moving through an XML document and examining its nodes. The following sections describe some of the more useful of these methods.

Close

The Close method closes the XmlTextReader's associated XML document.

GetAttribute

GetAttribute gets an attribute value from the current node. For example, xml_text_reader. GetAttribute("Color") returns the value of the current node's Color attribute. The statement xml_text_reader.GetAttribute(2) returns the value of the current node's third attribute. Remember that the numbering starts at zero.

IsStartElement

IsStartElement calls MoveToContent (described shortly) and then returns True if the node is either a start tag or an empty element such as <Item/>.

Note that the implicit call to MoveToContent might change the XmlTextReader's position in the file and that can be very confusing. For example, if a program calls IsStartElement while reading an attribute, the XmlTextReader's position is reset to the element that contains the attribute. If the program then examines that node's attributes, it might call IsStartElement again for the attribute. That moves the XmlTextReader back to the element again, and the program enters an infinite loop.

It's less confusing to check whether xml_text_read.NodeType = XmlNodeType. Element to see if the current node is a start element without changing the position of the XmlTextReader.

LookupNamespace

The LookupNamespace method returns the definition of a namespace in the current node's context. For example, suppose a program is processing the following XML code fragment.

```
<Item xmlns:bk="http://www.vb-helper.com/Books">
    ... Sub items, text values, and so forth ...
</Item>
```

While the XmlTextReader is inside the Item element, LookupNamespace("bk") returns the string http://www.vb-helper.com/Books.

MoveToAttribute

MoveToAttribute moves to the current node's indicated attribute. For example, xml_text_reader.MoveToAttribute("Title") moves to the current node's Title attribute. The statement xml_text_reader.MoveToAttribute(2) moves to the current node's third attribute. Remember that numbering starts at zero.

MoveToContent

If the current node is not content (Element, EndElement, non-whitespace text, CDATA, EntityReference, or EndEntity), the MoveToContents method makes the XmlText-Reader skip to the next content node. If the current node is an attribute, the XmlText-Reader moves to the element that contains the attribute. This can be very confusing so it's usually better not to use MoveToContent while the XmlTextReader is reading attributes.

MoveToContent is most commonly used when the file is first opened to skip processing instructions, a document type section, comments, and whitespace before the body of the data starts.

MoveToElement

MoveToElement moves the XmlTextReader back to the element that contains the attribute it is currently reading. If the current node is not an attribute, MoveToElement leaves the current node unchanged.

MoveToFirstAttribute

The MoveToFirstElement method moves the XmlTextReader to the current node's first attribute. This method returns True if the current node has an attribute and False otherwise. A program can use MoveToFirstAttribute with MoveToNextAttribute to loop through all of the node's attributes.

MoveToNextAttribute

MoveToNextAttribute moves the XmlTextReader to the current node's next attribute. This method returns True if it can find a next attribute and False otherwise.

If the current node is an element or an XML declaration, this method moves to the node's first attribute just as MoveToFirstAttribute does. The following code uses this fact to list all of the current node's attributes. When it is finished, the code returns the XmlTextReader's position to the element.

```
Do While xml_text_reader.MoveToNextAttribute()
    DescribeNode(xml_text_reader)
Loop
xml_text_reader.MoveToElement
```

Note that the program doesn't need to check whether the current node is an Element, XML declaration, or something else. If the node is neither an element nor an XML declaration, MoveToNextAttribute immediately returns False so the loop does nothing. If the call to MoveToNextAttribute did not move the XmlTextReader to an attribute, the MoveToElement statement leaves the position of the XmlTextReader unchanged.

Read

The Read method makes the XmlTextReader read the next node from the XML document. This method returns True if it successfully reads a node and False if there are no more nodes to read.

When the XmlTextReader first opens, it has no current node. The program should call Read to move to the first node.

If the current node is an attribute, Read makes the XmlTextReader skip any other attributes and move to the next nonattribute node.

ReadAttributeValue

If the current node is an attribute, this method converts it into a Text node or an Entity Reference node containing the attribute's value. The program can then treat the attribute as a node.

The following code shows how a program could print the values of all of a node's attributes. Note that this prints only the attribute values, not the attribute names.

```
xml_text_reader.MoveToFirstAttribute()
Do While xml_text_reader.ReadAttributeValue()
    If (xml_text_reader.NodeType = XmlNodeType.EntityReference) Then
        Debug.WriteLine("EntityReference: " & xml_text_reader.Name)
    Else
        Debug.WriteLine("Text: " & xml_text_reader.Value)
    End If
    xml_text_reader.MoveToNextAttribute()
Loop
```

The GetAttribute method and the MoveToNextAttribute method provide less confusing attribute access so you probably won't need to use ReadAttributeValue often.

ReadBase64

The ReadBase64 method reads data encoded with a Base64 encoding and returns an array of bytes containing the decoded binary data. ReadBase64 takes as parameters the byte array, the offset in the array where ReadBase64 should put the data, and the maximum number of bytes the method should copy into the array.

ReadBase64 returns the number of bytes it actually copied. This will be the maximum number of bytes specified by ReadBase64's parameter if there are that many bytes left to copy, a smaller number if there are fewer bytes left to copy, or zero if previous calls to ReadBase64 have read all of the data.

For example, the following code fragment reads the data in 1,000-byte chunks. It starts by calling ReadBase64 to get the first buffer full of data. Then it loops, processing a buffer full of data, and calling ReadBase64 to get the next buffer of data until it has read all of the data. The last time through the loop, bytes_read will be less than 1,000 unless the amount of data is an exact multiple of 1,000 bytes.

```
Const BUF_LEN = 1000
Dim buffer(BUF_LEN) As Byte
Dim bytes_read As Integer

' Get the first buffer load of data.
bytes_read = xml_text_reader.ReadBase64(buffer, 0, BUF_LEN)

' Process the buffer loads.
Do While bytes_read > 0
```

```
' Do something with the bytes in the buffer
' array's entries 0 through bytes_read.
   :

' Get the next buffer load of data.
bytes_read = xml_text_reader.ReadBase64(buffer, 0, BUF_LEN)
Loop
```

For more information on ReadBase64 and to see an example program, see the *Reading Binary Data* section later in this chapter.

ReadBinHex

The ReadBinHex method reads data encoded with a binhex encoding much as Read-Base64 reads data encoded with the Base64 encoding. The example code in the previous section will work for binhex encodings if you replace the calls to ReadBase64 with calls to ReadBinHex.

For more information on ReadBinHex and to see an example program, see the *Reading Binary Data* section later in this chapter.

ReadChars

The ReadChars method reads characters from an element node into a character array much as the ReadBase64 and ReadBinHex methods read binary data into a byte array. ReadChars parameters indicate the character array, the offset in the array where Read-Chars should put the characters, and the maximum number of characters ReadChars should read.

ReadChars returns the number of bytes it actually copied. This will be the maximum number of bytes specified by ReadChars's parameter if there are that many bytes left to copy, a smaller number if there are fewer bytes left to copy, or zero if previous calls to ReadChars have read all of the data.

Note that ReadChars works only when the XmlTextReader is positioned on an element. If it is reading some other kind of node, ReadChars returns zero and doesn't copy any characters into the array.

Normally a program can use the XmlTextReader's ReadString method to read an element's text. ReadChars can be useful when the element's text is really large and the program doesn't need to use all of it at once. For example, suppose a program needs to copy the text into a text file. It can read the text value in 1,000-byte chunks and write them into the file one at a time. The program never needs to load the entire string into memory all at once. While the text may be enormous, the program needs to have only 1,000 bytes of it loaded at any time.

This buffered processing is awkward for many string operations. It is usually much easier to read the entire string at once using the ReadString method. Remember, however, that the point of the XmlTextReader class is to let an application process an XML document locally without loading the entire document into an XmlDocument object.

The ReadChars method takes this idea one step further, letting the program process a string in localized chunks instead of all at once.

Example program ReadChars, shown in Figure 3.7, uses ReadChars to determine whether a target string is in an XML document's Section node. Enter a target string in the text box and click the Find button. The program reads the Section node's text using ReachChars and searches for the string you entered. If the program finds the target string, it displays the buffers in which it found the target, highlighting the target.

Program ReadChars searches the following XML document for target strings. The Section node's text contains 3,568 characters so it wouldn't be too hard to load all of the text into a single string. If the text were much larger, however, using ReadChars would be more important.

```
<?xml version="1.0" standalone="yes"?>
<Book>
  <Chapter Number="5" Title="Forward-Only XML">
    <Section Name="" xml:space="preserve">The XmlDocument object
described in Chapter 2 ... <lots of text deleted here> ... let the
program
take action.</Section>
  </Chapter>
</Book>
```

Program ReadChars uses the following code to search for the target string. The program begins by getting the value of the target string entered in the txtTarget TextBox. It allocates a data buffer that is 10 bytes long or the length of the target string, whichever is greater. Later it will consider two adjacent buffer's worth of data at a time looking for the target. Making the buffer at least as long as the target means the target will fit within two adjacent buffers no matter how the target is aligned within the text. For example, the target may span the boundary between two buffers, lying partly in one and partly in the next. Making each buffer at least as long as the target guarantees that the target must fit in an adjacent two-buffer pair.

The program connects the XmlTextReader to the XML document and uses the XmlTextReader's Read method to process nodes until it finds one named Section. It then enters a loop, using ReadChars to fill the buffer with data. It converts the buffer into a string, concatenates it with the previous buffer's text, and searches the result for the target string. If the program finds the target, it displays the text that contains it, highlighting the target.

Figure 3.7 Program ReadChars uses the ReadChars method to see if a target string is in an XML document.

```
Private Sub btnFind_Click( _
  ByVal sender As System.Object, _
  ByVal e As System.EventArgs) Handles btnFind.Click
    Dim target As String
    Dim buffer_length As Integer
    Dim xml_text_reader As XmlTextReader
    Dim buffer() As Char
    Dim characters_read As Integer
    Dim old_text As String
    Dim new_text As String
    Dim combined_text As String
    Dim target_found As Boolean

    ' Clear previous values.
    rchResult.Text = ""
    Me.Cursor = Cursors.WaitCursor
    Refresh()

    ' Get the target string.
    target = txtTarget.Text

    ' Allocate the buffer.
    buffer_length = target.Length
    If buffer_length < 10 Then buffer_length = 10
    ReDim buffer(buffer_length)

    ' Attach the XmlTextReader to the XML document.
    xml_text_reader = New XmlTextReader(DataSubdirectory() &
"\Book.xml")

    ' Read looking for the Section tag.
    xml_text_reader.MoveToContent()
    Do Until xml_text_reader.Name = "Section"
        ' Skip this node.
        xml_text_reader.Read()

        ' Stop if we've run out of file.
        If xml_text_reader.EOF Then Exit Do
    Loop

    ' See if we found the Section node.
    If xml_text_reader.Name = "Section" Then
        ' There is no old text yet.
        old_text = ""

        ' Process the text one buffer at a time.
        characters_read = _
            xml_text_reader.ReadChars(buffer, 0, buffer_length)
        Do Until characters_read = 0
            ' Convert the array of characters into a string.
            new_text = New String(buffer, 0, characters_read)

            ' See if the target string is here.
```

```
                  If InStr(old_text & new_text, target) > 0 Then
                      ' We found the target.
                      ' Display the text where we found it.
                      combined_text = old_text & new_text
                      rchResult.Text = combined_text
                      rchResult.Select( _
                          InStr(combined_text, target) - 1, target.Length)
                      rchResult.Focus()

                      target_found = True
                      Exit Do
                  End If

                  ' Save the latest text for next time.
                  old_text = new_text

                  ' Get the next buffer load of text.
                  characters_read = _
                      xml_text_reader.ReadChars(buffer, 0, buffer_length)
              Loop
          End If

          ' Close the XmlTextReader.
          xml_text_reader.Close()

          ' If we didn't find the text, say so.
          If Not target_found Then
              rchResult.Text = "<Not found>"
              rchResult.Select(0, 0)
          End If

          Me.Cursor = Cursors.Default
      End Sub
```

Program ReadChars reads its string using relatively small buffers. In a real application, it would make sense to use the largest buffers the program can comfortably allocate. For example, it could read the data 1,000 or even 10,000 characters at a time. That will mean fewer trips through the program's Do loop so it will make the program run faster. The additional 1K or 10K of memory used by the buffer should be no problem for most computers.

ReadElementString

The ReadElementString method reads the contents of a simple textual element and moves to the next node in the document. For instance, consider the following XML document.

```
<?xml version="1.0" encoding="ISO-8859-1"?>
<Flavors>
  <Flavor cone="No">Chocolate</Flavor>
```

```
    <Flavor>Vanilla</Flavor>
    <Flavor>Pistachio</Flavor>
  </Flavors>
```

A program could display the three flavor values Chocolate, Vanilla, and Pistachio using the following code.

```
xml_text_reader.Read()      ' Move to the XML declaration.
xml_text_reader.Read()      ' Move to Flavors.
xml_text_reader.Read()      ' Move to the first Flavor.
Debug.WriteLine(xml_text_reader.ReadElementString)
Debug.WriteLine(xml_text_reader.ReadElementString)
Debug.WriteLine(xml_text_reader.ReadElementString)
```

Actually, in some versions of Visual Basic, the program can omit the initial calls to the Read method, and ReadElementString automatically skips down to the first text element. This does not work for all XML documents, however, and does not seem to fit the intent of the ReadElementString method so you should not rely on this behavior. It would be safer to verify that the XmlTextReader is positioned on the correct text element before calling ReadElementString.

ReadEndElement

The ReadEndElement method verifies that the current node is an element's end tag and then advances the XmlTextReader to the next document node. For example, consider the following XML document.

```
<?xml version="1.0" encoding="ISO-8859-1"?>
<Computer>
  <CPU>Pentium</CPU>
</Computer>
```

The following code reads this document and displays the text inside the CPU tag.

```
xml_text_reader.Read()
xml_text_reader.ReadStartElement("Computer")
xml_text_reader.ReadStartElement("CPU")
Debug.WriteLine(xml_text_reader.ReadString())
xml_text_reader.ReadEndElement()
```

Note that a program can use ReadElementString method to read a simple text element's value more concisely than the calls to ReadStartElement, ReadString, and ReadEndElement shown here.

ReadInnerXml

The ReadInnerXml method returns the XML markup for the current node's contents.

If the current node is an attribute, ReadInnerXml returns the attribute's value and leaves the current node pointing to the attribute. If the current node is an element,

ReadInnerXml returns the markup for the element's contents and moves the XmlText-Reader to the node after the element's end tag.

It might seem that ReadInnerXml would be more useful if it left the XmlTextReader at the element's start tag when it was finished. Then the program could call the Skip method explicitly if it wanted to skip the element. Remember that the XmlTextReader is designed to provide forward-only access to the XML document. Reading an element's contents might make the XmlTextReader move a long way through the document. While XmlTextReader could probably have been designed to allow it to return to the element's start, that would certainly have violated the intent of its forward-only access.

ReadOuterXml

The ReadOuterXml method behaves exactly as the ReadInnerXml method does except it returns the node's XML markup as well as the markup of its contents. For example, suppose the XmlTextReader is reading the Equipment node in the following XML document.

```
<?xml version="1.0" encoding="ISO-8859-1"?>
<Equipment Type="individual">
  <Item>tent</Item>
  <Item>stove</Item>
  <Item>trebuchet</Item>
</Equipment>
```

At this point, the ReadInnerXml method returns the following string. Notice that this string begins and ends with a carriage return and linefeed because those characters are inside the Element tags.

```
  <Item>tent</Item>
  <Item>stove</Item>
  <Item>trebuchet</Item>
```

In contrast, the ReadOuterXml method returns the following string.

```
<Equipment Type="individual">
  <Item>tent</Item>
  <Item>stove</Item>
  <Item>trebuchet</Item>
</Equipment>
```

ReadOuterXml has the same effect on the XmlTextReader's current position as the ReadInnerXml method.

ReadStartElement

The ReadStartElement method reads an element's starting tag.

The most basic version of ReadStartElement takes no parameters. It verifies that the current node is an element's start node and then reads that node.

A second overloaded version of ReadStartElement takes a name as a parameter and verifies that the current node has that name before it reads the node. A third version of this method takes as parameters the node's name and namespace URI. This version verifies that the node has the indicated name and namespace before it reads the node.

The second and third versions of this method help the program verify that it is reading the node it thinks it is reading. That can help expose possible errors in the Visual Basic code and make debugging easier. Without this sort of verification, the program could wander off into the document structure without giving you a clue about where it actually was.

ReadString

The ReadString method concatenates the text, whitespace, and CDATA values contained by the current element or text node and returns the result.

When it finishes, ReadString leaves the XmlTextReader positioned at the element's end tag.

Skip

The Skip method makes the XmlTextReader skip the current node and any child nodes it contains. This moves the XmlTextReader to the current node's next sibling. If the current node has no sibling, calling Skip is equivalent to calling the Read method.

For example, take a look at the following XML code.

```
<?xml version="1.0" encoding="ISO-8859-1"?>
<Drinks>
  <Beverage>Water</Beverage>
  <Beverage>Milk</Beverage>
  <Beverage>Soda</Beverage>
  <Beverage>Orange Juice</Beverage>
</Drinks>
```

If the XmlTextReader is positioned on the Drinks element's opening tag, calling skip bypasses all of the Beverage elements and moves the XmlTextReader to the end of the document.

If the current node is the first Beverage element's opening tag, calling skip moves the XmlTextReader to the second Beverage element's opening tag.

If the current node is the first text node (the one with value Water), calling skip is the same as calling Read because the text node has no siblings. In this case, calling Skip moves the XmlTextReader to the first Beverage element's closing tag. Similarly that closing tag has no siblings so calling Skip again moves the XmlTextReader to the second Beverage element's opening tag.

XmlTextReader Properties

As it moves through an XML document, the XmlTextReader's properties give information about the XmlTextReader's current node. The following sections describe the XmlTextReader's most useful properties.

AttributeCount

AttributeCount gives the number of attributes the current node has. A program can use the following code to display the values of the current node's attributes.

```
For i = 0 to xml_text_reader.AttributeCount - 1
    Debug.WriteLine(xml_text_reader.GetAttribute(i))
Next i
```

Note that the program need not check whether the node could have attributes before it uses AttributeCount. If the node is a text node or some other node that cannot have attributes, AttributeCount returns zero.

See the section *MoveToNextAttribute* earlier in this chapter for another method of accessing a node's attributes.

Depth

The Depth property returns the depth of the current node in the XML document hierarchy. A program can use the Depth property together with the Skip method to move up the document hierarchy quickly. The following code shows how a program might move from a low level in the tree to the level of nodes that are children of the data root node.

```
Do While xml_text_reader.Depth > 1
    xml_text_reader.Skip
Loop
```

Because this code checks the Depth property before it skips any nodes, it does nothing if the current Depth is already 1 or less.

Encoding

The Encoding property returns the document's encoding attribute object. The Encoding object includes several methods that may be useful if you need to look carefully at the data's encoding. Its most basic method, EncodingName, returns a readable description of the encoding. For example, suppose an XML document uses the following XML declaration.

```
<?xml version="1.0" encoding="ISO-8859-1"?>
```

In this case, Encoding.EncodingName returns the string Western European (ISO).

The Encoding object also provides methods to translate strings and arrays from one encoding to another.

The XmlTextReader's Encoding property returns Nothing before the encoding is set in the document. For example, consider the following XML file. This file explicitly declares the document's encoding. The XmlTextReader's Encoding property is Nothing until the program reads the XML declaration.

```
<?xml version="1.0" encoding="ISO-8859-1"?>
<!-- This version sets the encoding to ISO-8859-1 -->
<Body/>
```

The following XML file does not explicitly declare the document's encoding so it defaults to Unicode (UTF-8). As in the previous example, the Encoding property returns Nothing until the XmlTextReader reads the XML declaration.

```
<?xml version="1.0"?>
<!-- This version does not specify the encoding -->
<Body/>
```

The following XML file doesn't have any XML declaration. In this case, the Encoding property returns Nothing until the XmlTextReader has read the document's first node, in this case a comment element. As in the previous example, the encoding defaults to Unicode (UTF-8).

```
<!-- This version doesn't even have an XML declaration -->
<Body/>
```

The Encoding property also returns Nothing after the XmlTextReader reaches the end of the file. See the following section for information on when the program reaches the end of the file.

EOF

EOF returns True if the XmlTextReader has reached the end of the XML document. This happens when the XmlTextReader reads the document's last node and then tries to read some more. Because the XmlTextReader makes a forward-only trip through the document, it does not look ahead to know if it has read the last node in the document. Usually the closing tag that matches the data root node is the last node in the file, but a document can contain other nodes after that tag. For example, the following XML code ends with a comment after the data root's closing tag.

```
<?xml version="1.0" encoding="ISO-8859-1"?>
<Sales>
  <Employee Name="Andrews">120.00</Employee>
  <Employee Name="Axle">8473.39</Employee>
  <Employee Name="Banner">3998.12</Employee>
     :
  <Employee Name="Zachary">1487.17</Employee>
</Sales>
<!-- Report finished 8/20/2010 -->
```

Because it cannot tell which node is the last one, the XmlTextReader doesn't know it has read the last node until it tries to read something and cannot find anything more to read. After that point, EOF returns True.

What this means for practical purposes is that a program should be prepared to stop processing nodes when the EOF property returns True. The XmlTextReader's Read method also returns False when it tries to read past the end of the document so the program can check its return value, if it uses Read instead of other reading methods such as ReadStartElement and ReadElementString.

HasAttributes

HasAttributes returns True if the current node has attributes. Often a program doesn't need to explicitly check HasAttributes because the other attribute properties and methods can handle nodes without attributes implicitly. For example, the following code lists a node's attributes.

```
For i = 0 to xml_text_reader.AttributeCount - 1
    Debug.WriteLine(xml_text_reader.GetAttribute(i))
Next i
```

This code doesn't need to check HasAttributes because the AttributeCount property returns zero if the node has no attributes.

HasValue

The HasValue property returns True if the current code can have a value. This does not mean the node actually has an interesting value. For example, the following XML file defines an empty comment. When the XmlTextReader is reading this node, HasValue returns True because a comment node can have a value even though this node's value is an empty string.

```
<?xml version="1.0" encoding="ISO-8859-1"?>
<!---->
<Body/>
```

Table 3.2 lists node types that can have values and for which HasValue returns True. Because HasValue doesn't really tell you whether the node has an *interesting* value, you may just want to look at the XmlTextReader's Value property.

Table 3.2 Node Types That Can Have Values

NODE TYPE	CONTENTS OF VALUE
Attribute	The attribute's value. For example, in the statement <Order Qty="12">, the value of the Qty attribute node is 12.
CDATASection	The contents of the CDATA section.
Comment	The contents of the comment.
DocumentType	The contents of the DOCTYPE. For example, in the statement <!DOCTYPE Root[<!ENTITY us "United States of America">]>, the value is <!ENTITY us "United States of America">.
ProcessingInstruction	The contents of the instruction. For example, in the statement <?xml-stylesheet type="text/xsl" href="Test5.xsl" ?>, the value is type="text/xsl" href="Test5.xsl".
SignificantWhitespace	The contents of the whitespace.
Text	The contents of the text.
Whitespace	The contents of the whitespace.
XmlDeclaration	The contents of the declaration. For example, in the statement <?xml version="1.0" encoding="UTF-8"?>, the value is version="1.0" encoding="UTF-8". Note that this may be different from the value returned by the Encoding object's EncodingName property. In this example, the EncodingName property would be Unicode (UTF-8).

IsEmptyElement

The IsEmptyElement property returns True if the current node is an empty element as in <Body/>.

Note that IsEmptyElement returns False if the node is the opening tag in an empty combination such as <Body></Body>. When the XmlTextReader reads the opening tag <Body>, it doesn't yet know whether the closing tag follows immediately so it cannot tell whether there will be any content between the two tags.

Item

The Item property returns the value of an attribute. For example, xml_text_reader. Item("Cost") returns the value of the current node's Cost attribute, and xml_text_reader. Item(2) returns the value of the current node's third attribute (numbering starts at zero).

LineNumber

The LineNumber property returns the line number of the current node in the XML document. If the node spans multiple lines, LineNumber returns the line where the node begins.

LinePosition

The LinePosition property returns the character in the XML document where the current node begins. Unlike the usual case in Visual Basic, the first character in a line is at position 1. LineNumber and LinePosition are mostly used for reporting errors.

Note also that a node starts at the first character that is actually part of the node and not the tag syntax that surrounds it. For example, consider the following XML statement.

```
<?xml version="1.0" encoding="ISO-8859-1"?>
```

Here the XML declaration node starts at position 3 because that's where the "x" is. The version attribute node starts at position 7 where the "v" is. The encoding attribute starts at position 21 where the "e" is.

LocalName

The LocalName property returns the current node's name without its namespace prefix. For example, if the current node's Name is bk:pages, then LocalName returns pages.

Name

The Name property returns the current node's name including its namespace prefix if it has one.

NamespaceURI

The NamespaceURI property returns the URI of the node's namespace. For example, suppose the bk namespace is defined in the following XML code.

```
<Book xmlns:bk="http://www.vb-helper.com/books">
  <bk:Title>Rasins of Wrath</bk:Title>
</Book>
```

Then when the XmlTextReader is reading the bk:Title node, its NamespaceURI property returns http://www.vb-helper.com/books.

The Prefix property described shortly returns the namespace name bk.

NodeType

The NodeType property returns an enumeration value giving the current node's type. For example, the following code determines whether the current node is a Text node.

```
If xml_text_reader.NodeType = XmlNodeType.Text Then ...
```

A program can use the ToString method to convert the type into a string as in Msg-Box(xml_text_reader.NodeType.ToString).

Prefix

The Prefix property returns the current node's namespace prefix. For example, the prefix of the node bk:Price is bk. The NamespaceURI property described earlier returns the namespace's defining URI.

Value

The Value property returns the current node's value. See the *HasValue* section earlier in this chapter for a list of node types that have values and what their values represent.

WhitespaceHandling

WhitespaceHandling is one of the few XmlTextReader properties that does not describe the XmlTextReader's state or its current node. This property is a Whitespace-Handling enumeration value that tells the XmlTextReader which kinds of whitespace it should visit as nodes. This property can have the values WhitespaceHandling.All, WhitespaceHandling.Significant, and WhitespaceHandling.None to indicate that the XmlTextReader should visit all of the whitespace, only the significant whitespace, or no whitespace.

If a program changes this value while the XmlTextReader is in the middle of processing a document, the new value takes effect for the nodes that the XmlTextReader has not yet processed. It is more common to set this value before starting to process the file.

XmlLang

The XmlLang property returns the current node's xml:lang value. For example, consider the following XML statement.

```
<Item xml:lang="en-GB">Colour</Item>
```

While the XmlTextReader is reading the element (Item), attribute (xml:lang), text (Colour), and end element (/Item), its XmlLang property returns en-GB indicating English as spoken in Great Britain.

XmlSpace

The XmlSpace property returns an XmlSpace enumeration value indicating whether whitespace is marked as preserved in the XML document at this node. For example, consider the following XML code.

```
<Item xml:space="preserve">...</Item>
```

While the XmlTextReader is reading the Item node and its contents, whitespace is marked as significant and the XmlSpace property returns the value XmlSpace.Preserve.

An XmlTextReader Example

Example program ReadOrder, shown in Figure 3.8, uses an XmlTextReader object to read an XML document. For each Item tag it finds in the document, the program creates an entry in its list box.

Program ReadOrder reads an order file similar to the following. This file was created by program WriteOrder. See the section *An XmlTextWriter Example* earlier in this chapter for more information on the WriteOrder program.

```
<?xml version="1.0" encoding="utf-8" standalone="yes"?>
<?xml-stylesheet type="text/xsl" href="Order.xsl"?>
<Order>
    <Item Quantity="6">Apple</Item>
    <Item Quantity="2">Apricot</Item>
    <Item Quantity="10">Banana</Item>
    <Item Quantity="24">Cherry</Item>
    <Item Quantity="4">Peach</Item>
</Order>
```

Program ReadOrder uses the following code to load order information. The program starts by connecting the XmlTextReader to the file Order.xml. It then sets the XmlTextReader's WhitespaceHandling property to WhitespaceHandling.None so it ignores all whitespace. Figuring out where whitespace lies in an XML file can be challenging so ignoring all whitespace makes the rest of the routine much simpler.

Figure 3.8 Program ReadOrder uses an XmlTextReader object to read an XML document.

Next the routine calls the XmlTextReader's MoveToContent method to find the root data node. This makes the XmlTextReader skip the XML declaration, the XSL stylesheet processing instruction, and any other comments or processing instructions at the beginning of the document. Many programs use MoveToContent to skip to the interesting part of the XML file. This not only simplifies the code, but also lets a program continue to work even if changes are made to the XML document's prolog.

Next the program uses the XmlTextReader's Read method to read the Order element's start tag. That makes the first Item element the XmlTextReader's current node.

The program then enters a Do loop that continues until it finds a node that is not named Item. For each node named Item, the program uses the GetAttribute method to get the Item's Quantity attribute value. It then calls ReadStringElement to read the Item element's string value, and it adds the value and the previously saved quantity to the program's ListBox.

The call to ReadStringElement automatically moves the XmlTextReader to the node following the current node's closing tag. In this case, that means the next Item element's start tag becomes the current node so the program is ready to read the next Item.

When it encounters a node that is not named Item, the program has finished reading all of the data it cares about so it closes the XmlTextReader.

```
Private Sub btnReadXml_Click( _
  ByVal sender As System.Object, _
  ByVal e As System.EventArgs) Handles btnReadXml.Click
    Dim file_name As String = DataSubdirectory() & "\Order.xml"
    Dim xml_text_reader As New XmlTextReader(file_name)
    Dim quantity As String

    Me.Cursor = Cursors.WaitCursor
    lstItems.Items.Clear()
    Refresh()

    ' Skip all whitespace.
    xml_text_reader.WhitespaceHandling = WhitespaceHandling.None

    ' Move to the data root node.
    xml_text_reader.MoveToContent()

    ' Read the Order start tag.
    xml_text_reader.Read()

    ' Process each Item tag.
    Do While xml_text_reader.Name = "Item"
        ' Save the quantity.
        quantity = xml_text_reader.GetAttribute("Quantity")

        ' Get the value.
        ' The call to ReadElementString moves to the next element.
        lstItems.Items.Add( _
            xml_text_reader.ReadElementString("Item") & vbTab & _
```

```
            quantity)
    Loop
    xml_text_reader.Close()

    Me.Cursor = Cursors.Default
End Sub
```

Program ReadOrder uses code that is quite closely tied to the structure of the XML document it will read. If you make nontrivial changes to Order.xml, the program will not read it correctly. For example, if you insert a comment between two of the Item elements, the program will not read any of the Items that come after it.

You can modify the code to make it a little more robust. For example, you could make the program use a Do loop to examine every node in the file and process those named Item. Still, program ReadOrder depends heavily on the structure of the file created by WriteOrder.

If you publish an XML file's structure for others to use, it is likely they will write programs that depend on its structure. If you later change the structure, you will probably break their programs. You can help protect yourself from complaints by documenting the parts of the file that are likely to change later.

Testing XmlTextReader Properties

Example program XmlTextReaderProperties, shown in Figure 3.9, shows the XmlTextReader object's properties that describe the nodes it reads. Use the combo box to tell the program whether it should display all, significant, or no whitespace. Then use the File menu's Open command to load an XML document. The program uses the XmlTextReader's Read method to move through the document. When it visits a node, the program displays the XmlTextReader's node-related properties in a ListView control.

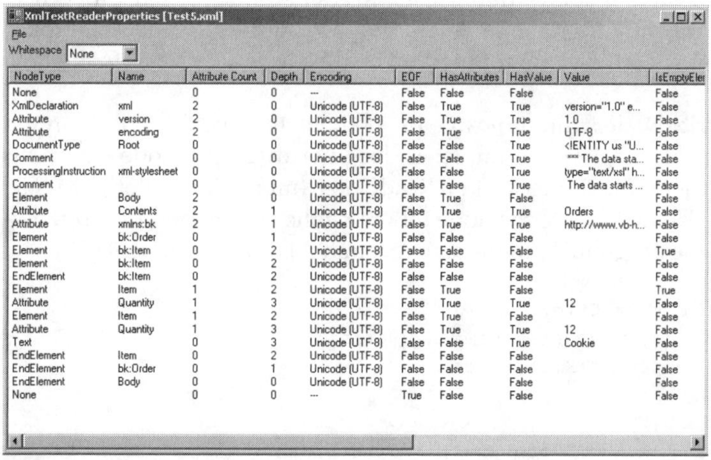

NodeType	Name	Attribute Count	Depth	Encoding	EOF	HasAttributes	HasValue	Value	IsEmptyEler
None		0	0	---	False	False	False		False
XmlDeclaration	xml	2	0	Unicode (UTF-8)	False	True	True	version="1.0" e...	False
Attribute	version	2	0	Unicode (UTF-8)	False	True	True	1.0	False
Attribute	encoding	2	0	Unicode (UTF-8)	False	True	True	UTF-8	False
DocumentType	Root	0	0	Unicode (UTF-8)	False	False	True	<!ENTITY us "U...	False
Comment		0	0	Unicode (UTF-8)	False	False	True	*** The data sta...	False
ProcessingInstruction	xml-stylesheet	0	0	Unicode (UTF-8)	False	False	True	type="text/xsl" h...	False
Comment		0	0	Unicode (UTF-8)	False	False	True	The data starts ...	False
Element	Body	2	0	Unicode (UTF-8)	False	True	False		False
Attribute	Contents	2	1	Unicode (UTF-8)	False	True	True	Orders	False
Attribute	xmlns:bk	2	1	Unicode (UTF-8)	False	True	True	http://www.vb-h...	False
Element	bk:Order	0	1	Unicode (UTF-8)	False	False	False		False
Element	bk:Item	0	2	Unicode (UTF-8)	False	False	False		True
Element	bk:Item	0	2	Unicode (UTF-8)	False	False	False		False
EndElement	bk:Item	0	2	Unicode (UTF-8)	False	False	False		False
Element	Item	1	2	Unicode (UTF-8)	False	True	False		True
Attribute	Quantity	1	3	Unicode (UTF-8)	False	True	True	12	False
Element	Item	1	2	Unicode (UTF-8)	False	True	False		False
Attribute	Quantity	1	3	Unicode (UTF-8)	False	True	True	12	False
Text		0	3	Unicode (UTF-8)	False	False	True	Cookie	False
EndElement	Item	0	2	Unicode (UTF-8)	False	False	False		False
EndElement	bk:Order	0	1	Unicode (UTF-8)	False	False	False		False
EndElement	Body	0	0	Unicode (UTF-8)	False	False	False		False
None		0	0	---	True	False	False		False

Figure 3.9 Program XmlTextReaderProperties reads XML documents and lists every node with its property values.

Program XmlTextReaderProperties uses the following code to display the XmlText-Reader's properties. Subroutine ListNodes adds column titles naming the XmlText-Reader's properties to the ListView control. It then opens the XML file and sets the XmlTextReader's WhitespaceHandling property depending on the value of the cboWhitespace ComboBox.

ListNodes then calls subroutine DescribeNode to display the XmlTextReader's node-related properties. It makes this first call to DescribeNode before the XmlText-Reader has read any of the document's nodes. If you look closely at the first line of output in Figure 3.9, you can see that the Encoding property is not yet defined at this point.

Next ListNodes enters a While loop where it calls the XmlTextReader's Read method to read the XML document's next node. The Read method returns True if it successfully read a node from the document. Read returns False when it reaches the end of the file and there are no more nodes to read.

Each time the Read method returns True, the ListNodes subroutine calls subroutine DescribeNode to display the XmlTextReader's node-related properties. It uses the XmlTextReader's MoveToNextAttribute method to loop through the node's attributes. MoveToNextAttribute returns True as long as it successfully reads one of the node's attributes. If MoveToNextAttribute does not read an attribute, either because it has already read all of the node's attributes or because the node has no attributes, Move-ToNextAttribute returns False and the loop ends.

Subroutine ListNodes exits its main Do loop when it has read every node in the file and then called the XmlTextReader's Read method again. At that point, the XmlText-Reader realizes it has run out of nodes so its Read method returns False, exiting the loop.

Subroutine ListNodes calls the DescribeNode routine one final time to display the XmlTextReader's node-related properties after XmlTextReader has read the entire document. If you look closely at the last line of output shown in Figure 3.9, you will see that at this point the Encoding property is undefined and the EOF property returns True.

Subroutine DescribeNode displays the XmlTextReader's node-related properties. It adds a new item giving the current node's name to the lvsResults ListView control. It then adds subitems showing the values of the XmlTextReader's properties to the new item.

Note that the DescribeNode subroutine avoids methods that would reposition the XmlTextReader's current node. For example, it does not display a node's markup using the XmlTextReader's ReadInnerXml or ReadOuterXml methods. Both of those methods move the XmlTextReader to the node following the current node's subtree so they would interrupt the program's progression through the XML document.

```
' List the nodes in this file.
Private Sub ListNodes(ByVal file_name As String)
    Dim xml_text_reader As XmlTextReader

    lvwResults.Clear()
    lvwResults.Columns.Add("NodeType", 100, HorizontalAlignment.Left)
    lvwResults.Columns.Add("Name", 100, HorizontalAlignment.Left)
    lvwResults.Columns.Add("Attribute Count", 100, _
        HorizontalAlignment.Left)
    lvwResults.Columns.Add("Depth", 100, HorizontalAlignment.Left)
```

```
lvwResults.Columns.Add("Encoding", 100, HorizontalAlignment.Left)
lvwResults.Columns.Add("EOF", 100, HorizontalAlignment.Left)
lvwResults.Columns.Add("HasAttributes", 100, _
    HorizontalAlignment.Left)
lvwResults.Columns.Add("HasValue", 100, HorizontalAlignment.Left)
lvwResults.Columns.Add("Value", 100, HorizontalAlignment.Left)
lvwResults.Columns.Add("IsEmptyElement", 100, _
    HorizontalAlignment.Left)
lvwResults.Columns.Add("LineNumber", 100, HorizontalAlignment.Left)
lvwResults.Columns.Add("LinePosition", 100, _
    HorizontalAlignment.Left)
lvwResults.Columns.Add("LocalName", 100, HorizontalAlignment.Left)
lvwResults.Columns.Add("NamespaceURI", 100, _
    HorizontalAlignment.Left)
lvwResults.Columns.Add("Prefix", 100, HorizontalAlignment.Left)

' Open the XmlTextReader.
Try
    ' Open the XML file.
    xml_text_reader = New XmlTextReader(file_name)

    ' Set the WhitespaceHandling property appropriately.
    Select Case cboWhitespace.Text
        Case "All"
            xml_text_reader.WhitespaceHandling = _
                WhitespaceHandling.All
        Case "Significant"
            xml_text_reader.WhitespaceHandling = _
                WhitespaceHandling.Significant
        Case "None"
            xml_text_reader.WhitespaceHandling = _
                WhitespaceHandling.None
    End Select
Catch exc As Exception
    MsgBox("Error opening file '" & file_name & "'" & _
        vbCrLf & exc.Message())
    Exit Sub
End Try
m_FileName = file_name
Text = "XmlTextReaderProperties [" & FileTitle(file_name) & "]"

' Display node information after opening the file.
DescribeNode(xml_text_reader)

' Read every node and report on it.
Try
    Do While xml_text_reader.Read()
        ' Display the node-related properties.
        DescribeNode(xml_text_reader)

        ' Display the node's attributes if it has any.
        Do While xml_text_reader.MoveToNextAttribute
            ' Display the attribute's properties.
            DescribeNode(xml_text_reader)
        Loop
```

```
        Loop

        ' Display the information after the end of the file.
        DescribeNode(xml_text_reader)
    Catch exc As Exception
        MsgBox("Error reading nodes" & vbCrLf & exc.Message, _
            MsgBoxStyle.Exclamation Or MsgBoxStyle.OKOnly, "Error")
    Finally
        ' We are done reading everything. Close the file.
        xml_text_reader.Close()
    End Try
End Sub

' Display information about this node.
Private Sub DescribeNode(ByVal xml_text_reader As XmlTextReader)
    Dim new_item As ListViewItem

    new_item = lvwResults.Items.Add(xml_text_reader.NodeType.ToString)
    new_item.SubItems.Add(xml_text_reader.Name)
    new_item.SubItems.Add(xml_text_reader.AttributeCount)
    new_item.SubItems.Add(xml_text_reader.Depth)
    If xml_text_reader.Encoding Is Nothing Then
        new_item.SubItems.Add("---")
    Else
        new_item.SubItems.Add(xml_text_reader.Encoding.EncodingName)
    End If
    new_item.SubItems.Add(xml_text_reader.EOF)
    new_item.SubItems.Add(xml_text_reader.HasAttributes)
    new_item.SubItems.Add(xml_text_reader.HasValue)
    new_item.SubItems.Add(xml_text_reader.Value)
    new_item.SubItems.Add(xml_text_reader.IsEmptyElement)
    new_item.SubItems.Add(xml_text_reader.LineNumber)
    new_item.SubItems.Add(xml_text_reader.LinePosition)
    new_item.SubItems.Add(xml_text_reader.LocalName)
    new_item.SubItems.Add(xml_text_reader.NamespaceURI)
    new_item.SubItems.Add(xml_text_reader.Prefix)
End Sub
```

The XmlTextReaderProperties example program is useful for understanding the nodes in an XML document. It can be particularly helpful when you want to build an application to read an XML document using the XmlTextReader. You can use the program's output to determine how the new application must step through the document to find the information it needs.

This example can also help you understand where whitespace appears in an XML document. Locating whitespace by hand can be tricky. This program makes it obvious where the whitespace lies.

Summarizing Data

Example program TotalOrders, shown in Figure 3.10, uses an XmlTextReader to read an XML document containing information about 100 orders. It calculates and displays the total cost of the items in each order. When it has processed every order, the program displays a grand total that includes all of the orders.

Figure 3.10 Program TotalOrders uses an XmlTextReader to display total order amounts and a grand total.

Program TotalOrders processes the following XML file. The test file contains 100 randomly generated Order elements that contain one or more Item elements. Each Item element includes attributes giving the Item's name, unit price, and quantity. The program multiplies the unit price by the quantity to get the Item's total price and then adds the prices of the Items in each Order to calculate the Order's total price.

```xml
<?xml version="1.0" standalone="yes"?>
<Orders>
  <Order>
    <Customer>
      <Name>Ulaf</Name>
      <Address>9596 Date Ave</Address>
    </Customer>
    <Item ItemName="Cake, Slice" UnitPrice="1.25" Quantity="5" />
    <Item ItemName="Cruller" UnitPrice="0.35" Quantity="1" />
    <Item ItemName="Danish" UnitPrice="0.65" Quantity="2" />
  </Order>
  <Order>
    <Customer>
      <Name>Stephens</Name>
      <Address>1467 Lake Ln</Address>
    </Customer>
    <Item ItemName="Brownie" UnitPrice="0.45" Quantity="9" />
  </Order>

  ... (98 Orders omitted) ...

</Orders>
```

Program TotalOrders uses the following Visual Basic code to compute and display its totals. The btnTotalOrders_Click event handler opens the XML document containing the order information. It sets the XmlTextReader's WhitespaceHandling property to WhitespaceHandling.None so it can safely ignore any whitespace in the file. It then calls the reader's MoveToContent method to skip the XML declaration and any comments or processing instructions that may later be added at the beginning of the file.

Next the program checks the XmlTextReader's Name property to verify that the current node is an Orders element. If this node is not an Orders element, there is something wrong with the XML file's format so there is no point in the program continuing.

After verifying that the XML file makes at least a little sense, the program uses the XmlTextReader's Read method to move to the first Order element. The program next enters a Do loop that repeats until the XmlTextReader finds the </Orders> tag that ends the data.

Within the Do loop, the program examines the current node's name. If the node's name is Order, the program calls subroutine GetOrderTotal to read the Order element and return its total cost. It adds the order's cost to the results string and to the grand total.

If the node's name is Orders, the program has reached the </Orders> tag ending the data. It exits the Do loop and stops processing the file.

If the program finds any other node name, there is an error in the XML document's structure. In that case, the program displays an error message.

When the program has finished reading the order data, it closes the XmlTextReader and displays the grand total.

Function GetOrderTotal reads an Order element. It begins by using the XmlText-Reader's Read method to get the next node. This is an Item element, the closing </Order> tag, or some other element such as <Customer> that is uninteresting to the program.

If the node is an Item element, the program uses the GetAttribute method to get the Item's unit price and quantity. It multiplies these values, adds the result to the Order's total cost, and calls the XmlTextReader's Read method to move to the next node.

If the node is the closing </Order> tag, the GetOrderTotal function calls the Xml-TextReader's Read method to move to the node following the </Order> tag. It then returns the order's total cost.

If the node is some other element such as <Customer>, the program doesn't care about that element. The GetOrderTotal function calls the XmlTextReader's Skip method to skip this element and any others it contains.

```
' Calculate the total of all orders.
Private Sub btnTotalOrders_Click( _
  ByVal sender As System.Object, _
  ByVal e As System.EventArgs) Handles btnTotalOrders.Click

    Dim xml_text_reader As XmlTextReader
    Dim results As String
    Dim order_total As Decimal
    Dim grand_total As Decimal

    ' Open the XmlTextReader.
    Dim file_name As String = DataSubdirectory() & "\Orders.xml"
    Try
        xml_text_reader = New XmlTextReader(file_name)
    Catch exc As Exception
        MsgBox("Error opening file '" & file_name & "'" & _
            vbCrLf & exc.Message())
        Exit Sub
```

```
        End Try

        ' Skip over processing instructions and other noncontent nodes.
        xml_text_reader.WhitespaceHandling = WhitespaceHandling.None
        xml_text_reader.MoveToContent()

        ' The first node should be Orders.
        If xml_text_reader.Name <> "Orders" Then
            MsgBox("Error reading file '" & DataSubdirectory() & _
                "\Orders.xml' at line number " & _
                xml_text_reader.LineNumber.ToString & "." & _
                vbCrLf & "Found '" & xml_text_reader.Name & _
                "' node when expecting an 'Orders' node.")
            Exit Sub
        End If

        ' Move to the next node (the first Order).
        xml_text_reader.Read()

        ' Read until we find the </Orders> tag.
        Do
            ' See what kind of node we are reading.
            ' This should be either an Order element or the
            ' closing </Orders> tag.

            If xml_text_reader.Name = "Order" Then
                ' This is an Order node. Process it.
                ' Note that GetOrderTotal moves xml_text_reader
                ' so it points to the node after </Order>.
                ' That will be either another Order element or the
                ' closing </Orders> tag.
                order_total = GetOrderTotal(xml_text_reader)

                ' Add the order total to the results.
                results = results & Format(order_total, "$#,##0.00") & _
                    vbCrLf
                grand_total = grand_total + order_total
            ElseIf xml_text_reader.Name = "Orders" Then
                ' This is the </Orders> closing tag for the document.
                ' Stop processing the file.
                xml_text_reader.Skip()
                Exit Do
            Else
                ' This should never happen.
                MsgBox("Error processing orders file. Found '" & _
                    xml_text_reader.Name & _
                    "' when expecting 'Order' or 'Orders'", _
                    MsgBoxStyle.Exclamation Or MsgBoxStyle.OKOnly, _
                    "Parsing Error")
            End If
        Loop

        ' We are done reading everything. Close the file.
```

```
        xml_text_reader.Close()

        ' Display the results.
        results = results & "--------------------" & vbCrLf & _
            "Grand Total: " & Format(grand_total, "$#,##0.00")
        txtOrders.Text = results
        txtOrders.Focus()
        txtOrders.Select(txtOrders.Text.Length, 0)
        txtOrders.ScrollToCaret()
End Sub


' Read this Order node and return the order total.
Private Function GetOrderTotal(ByVal xml_text_reader As XmlTextReader)
        Dim order_total As Decimal

        ' Get the next node (the first node inside the Order).
        xml_text_reader.Read()

        ' Examine nodes until we find the </Order> closing tag.
        Do
            Select Case xml_text_reader.Name
                Case "Item"
                    ' This is an order item.
                    ' Add its cost to the total.
                    order_total = order_total + _
                        xml_text_reader.GetAttribute("UnitPrice") * _
                        xml_text_reader.GetAttribute("Quantity")

                    ' Move to the next node.
                    xml_text_reader.Read()
                Case "Order"
                    ' This is the </Order> closing tag.
                    ' Move to the next node before we return.
                    xml_text_reader.Read()

                    ' Return the order total.
                    Return order_total
                Case Else
                    ' This is something like <Customer> that
                    ' we want to ignore. Skip it.
                    xml_text_reader.Skip()
            End Select
        Loop
End Function
```

At any given moment, program TotalOrders needs to have information loaded only
for the single node it is currently reading. The only nodes it really cares about are the
Item nodes. When it finds an Item node, it simply reads the node's UnitPrice and
Quantity attributes.

Contrast this with a DOM implementation of this program. That version would
need to load the entire XML document into memory before it could start processing the

data. Loading the DOM might take only a few dozen kilobytes of memory for this example, but loading larger files might be impractical.

Reading Binary Data

The section *Writing Binary Data* earlier in this chapter explains how to use the XmlText-Writer's WriteBase64 and WriteBinHex methods to save encoded binary data into an XML file. The XmlTextReader's ReadBase64 and ReadBinHex methods read data saved by those routines.

Both of these functions take as parameters an array to hold the coded data, an offset in the array where the data should be placed, and the number of bytes that should be copied into the array. ReadBase64 and ReadBinHex return the number of bytes actually read.

If a program doesn't know how many bytes of encoded data it must read, it can call these routines repeatedly until it has read all of the data. For example, the following code fragment shows how a program can read binary data in 1,000-byte chunks. Note that the last time the program passes through the loop, bytes_read will not be 1,000 unless the total number of encoded bytes happens to be an exact multiple of 1,000.

```
' Get the first buffer full of bytes.
Dim bytes(1000) As Byte
bytes_read = xml_text_reader.ReadBase64(bytes, 0, bytes.Length)

Do While bytes_read > 0
    ' Do something with the bytes_read bytes.
    ...

    ' Get the next buffer full of bytes.
    bytes_read = xml_text_reader.ReadBase64(bytes, 0, bytes.Length)
Loop
```

Example program ReadEncodedPicture, shown in Figure 3.11, loads an image stored in a Base64 or binhex encoding from an XML file into a PictureBox. Use the File menu's Open command to load one of the test XML files. Click the Clear button to clear the picture before you load a new file so you can tell the file is really loaded.

Figure 3.11 Program ReadEncodedPicture loads an image stored in an XML file into a PictureBox.

ReadEncodedPicture loads XML files written by the WriteEncodedPicture example program described in the *Writing Binary Data* section earlier in this chapter. That program writes Base64 and binhex encoded files similar to the following.

```
<?xml version="1.0" encoding="utf-8"?>
<Picture Encoding="Base64"
NumBytes="49206">Qk02wAAAAAAADYAAAAoAAAAgAAAAIAAAAABABgAAAAAAAAAADED
gAAxA4AAAAAAAAAAAA//+A//+A//+A//+A//+A//+A//+A//+A//+A//+A//+
    ... lots of encoded data deleted here ...
+A//+A//+A//+A//+A//+A//+A//+A//+A//+A//+A//+A//+A//+A//+A
//+A//+A//+A//+A//+A//+A//+A//+A//+A//+A//+A//+A//8=</Picture>
```

The file contains a Picture element that contains the encoded data. This element's Encoding attribute tells the program whether the data uses the Base64 or binhex encoding. Its NumBytes attribute gives the number of bytes stored in the encoding.

Example program ReadEncodedPicture uses the following code to read the files saved by program WriteEncodedPicture. The program uses an OpenFileDialog to let the user select the XML file to load. It creates a new XmlTextReader, associating it with the file the user selected. It then uses the XmlTextReader's Read method to read nodes from the XML file until it finds a node named Picture.

The program uses the XmlTextReader's GetAttribute method to read the Picture element's NumBytes attribute. It uses that value to allocate an array of bytes large enough to hold all of the data.

Then the program checks the Picture element's Encoding attribute to determine whether the data was saved using Base64 or binhex encoding. The program calls the XmlTextReader's ReadBase64 or ReadBinHex methods as appropriate to read the encoded data into the byte array.

Next the program creates a MemoryStream object and attaches a new BinaryWriter object to it. It uses the BinaryWriter's Write method to copy the byte array's data into the MemoryStream. It resets the MemoryStream's position to the beginning of the stream and uses the Image class's FromStream method to load an Image object from the memory stream.

Having read the encoded data, the program exits its Do loop so it stops processing the XML document. If the XML file contained more than one encoded picture, the program could continue reading nods looking for other Picture elements.

```
' Let the user select an XML file and open it.
Private Sub mnuFileOpen_Click( _
  ByVal sender As System.Object, _
  ByVal e As System.EventArgs) Handles mnuFileOpen.Click

    ' Present the dialog and let the user select a file.
    If dlgXmlFile.ShowDialog() = DialogResult.Cancel Then Exit Sub

    picSmiley.Image = Nothing
    Me.Cursor = Cursors.WaitCursor
    Refresh()

    ' Load the file's picture.
```

```
        Dim xml_text_reader As New XmlTextReader(dlgXmlFile.FileName)

        ' Skip until we find the Picture node.
        Do While xml_text_reader.Read()
            ' See if this is the Picture node.
            If xml_text_reader.Name = "Picture" Then
                ' Allocate room for the byte data.
                Dim num_bytes As Integer = _
                    xml_text_reader.GetAttribute("NumBytes")
                Dim bytes(num_bytes - 1) As Byte

                ' Translate the encoded data back into byte data.
                Select Case xml_text_reader.GetAttribute("Encoding").ToLower
                    Case "base64"
                        xml_text_reader.ReadBase64(bytes, 0, num_bytes)
                    Case "binhex"
                        xml_text_reader.ReadBinHex(bytes, 0, num_bytes)
                    Case Else
                        MsgBox("Unknown image encoding '" & _
                            xml_text_reader.GetAttribute("Encoding") & _
                            "'", MsgBoxStyle.Exclamation, _
                            "Unknown Encoding")
                        Exit Sub
                End Select

                ' Allocate a MemoryStream and
                ' a BinaryWriter attached to it.
                Dim memory_stream As New MemoryStream()
                Dim binary_writer As BinaryWriter = _
                    New BinaryWriter(memory_stream)

                ' Copy the bytes into the BinaryWriter
                ' and thus the MemoryStream.
                binary_writer.Write(bytes, 0, num_bytes)
                binary_writer.Flush()

                ' Load the picture from the memory stream.
                memory_stream.Position = 0
                picSmiley.Image = Image.FromStream(memory_stream)
                Refresh()

                binary_writer.Close()
                Exit Do
            End If
        Loop

    xml_text_reader.Close()
    Me.Cursor = Cursors.Default
End Sub
```

Program ReadEncodedPicture uses the Picture element's NumBytes attribute to determine how large to make its data array. It then reads all of the data in a single call to ReadBase64 or ReadBinHex.

Instead of reading all of the data at once, the program could use the code fragment shown earlier in this section to read the data a chunk at a time. Because program Read-EncodedPicture displays the data as an image, the image data must eventually all be loaded into memory at the same time so there would be little value in reading the data in chunks in this case.

On the other hand, if the program could examine the data locally, it might make sense to load a buffer at a time. For instance, suppose the data contains a large array of numbers and the program needs to locate a particular value. The program could read the data 100 values at a time to minimize its memory use. When it found the value it wanted, it could skip the rest of the element and make the XmlTextReader jump to the next node.

XmlNodeReader

The XmlNodeReader class provides functionality similar to the XmlTextReader class. While the XmlTextReader class provides a fast, forward-only, read-and-forget method for reading an XML document, the XmlNodeReader provides similar methods for processing a DOM subtree represented by an XmlNode object.

Using the XmlDocument object, a program can build or load an XML file. The program can then use an XmlNodeReader object to perform XmlTextReader-style operations on subtrees in the DOM document represented by the XmlDocument object's nodes.

Example program XmlNodeReader, shown in Figure 3.12, demonstrates this technique. When the program starts, it loads customer names from a large XML file containing order information. When you click on a name, the program locates the corresponding Order node in the XmlDocument, attaches an XmlNodeReader to it, and uses the XmlNodeReader to process the information contained in that node's subtree. It displays the Order's items together with their unit prices, quantities, and calculated total costs.

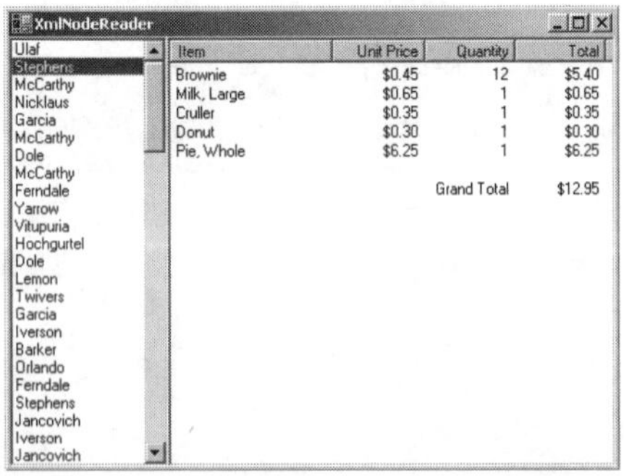

Figure 3.12 Program XmlNodeReader uses an XmlNodeReader object to process subtrees representing Orders in an XML file.

Program XmlNodeReader loads the following XML document.

```
<?xml version="1.0" standalone="yes"?>
<Orders>
  <Order>
    <Customer>
      <Name>Ulaf</Name>
      <Address>9596 Date Ave</Address>
    </Customer>
    <Item ItemName="Cake, Slice" UnitPrice="1.25" Quantity="5" />
    <Item ItemName="Cruller" UnitPrice="0.35" Quantity="1" />
    <Item ItemName="Danish" UnitPrice="0.65" Quantity="2" />
  </Order>
  <Order>
    <Customer>
      <Name>Stephens</Name>
      <Address>1467 Lake Ln</Address>
    </Customer>
    <Item ItemName="Brownie" UnitPrice="0.45" Quantity="12" />
    <Item ItemName="Milk, Large" UnitPrice="0.65" Quantity="1" />
    <Item ItemName="Cruller" UnitPrice="0.35" Quantity="1" />
    <Item ItemName="Donut" UnitPrice="0.3" Quantity="1" />
    <Item ItemName="Pie, Whole" UnitPrice="6.25" Quantity="1" />
  </Order>
  ... (Lots of orders deleted) ...
</Orders>
```

The program uses the following code to display this file. The form's Load event handler loads the XML document into the XmlDocument object named m_AllOrders. It then creates an XmlNodeReader, associating it with the XmlDocument's DocumentElement node. The routine enters a Do loop that repeats until the XmlNodeReader runs out of document to process.

Each time the loop executes, the program determines whether the XmlNodeReader is reading a node named Name. When it finds a Name node, the program uses the XmlNodeReader's ReadString method to read the node's text contents and it adds the value to the lstOrders ListBox. The ReadString method advances the XmlNodeReader to the close </Name> tag.

The code in the loop then calls the XmlNodeReader's Read method to move on to the next node. If the program just added a name to its ListBox, this moves the XmlNodeReader off of the </Name> end tag. That is important because the program would get confused if it encountered that tag at the beginning of the loop. It would see that the node </Name> is named Name and would try to add its text value to the output.

After the program finishes adding all of the XML document's Name values to its ListBox, it creates headers for the ListView control where it will display order information.

When you click a name in the program's name list, the lstOrders_IndexChanged event handler fires. This routine finds the XmlDocument Order node corresponding to the item you clicked, and it creates a new XmlNodeReader associated with that node.

The program could do this all in one step because it will not need to use the document's XmlNode, but creating the XmlNodeReader in two steps makes the code a little easier to understand.

The program clears its ListView control and enters a loop that repeats until the XmlNodeReader has finished reading the selected Order's subtree. Each time through the loop, the program examines the XmlNodeReader's name to see if it is processing an Item node. When it finds an Item node, the program uses the XmlNodeReader's GetAttribute method to get the item's ItemName, UnitPrice, and Quantity attributes and displays the attribute values in the ListView control.

After it has examined the node, adding information to the ListView if the node is an Item node, the program calls the XmlNodeReader's Read method to move to the next node. When it has read the Order node's entire subtree, the program adds a grand total to the ListView.

```
' Load the list of customer names.
Private Sub Form1_Load( _
  ByVal sender As System.Object, _
  ByVal e As System.EventArgs) Handles MyBase.Load

    Dim xml_node_reader As System.Xml.XmlNodeReader

    ' Load the document Orders.xml.
    m_AllOrders = New XmlDocument()
    m_AllOrders.Load(DataSubdirectory() & "\Orders.xml")

    ' Display the Orders' Customer names.
    lstOrders.Items.Clear()

    ' Assign an XmlNodeReader to the node.
    xml_node_reader = New System.Xml.XmlNodeReader( _
        m_AllOrders.DocumentElement)

    ' Process the nodes.
    Do Until xml_node_reader.EOF
        ' If this is an Order node, process it.
        If xml_node_reader.Name = "Name" Then
            lstOrders.Items.Add(xml_node_reader.ReadString())
        End If

        ' Get the next node.
        xml_node_reader.Read()
    Loop

    ' Create ListView headers.
    lvwOrder.Columns.Add("Item", 125, HorizontalAlignment.Left)
    lvwOrder.Columns.Add("Unit Price", 70, HorizontalAlignment.Right)
    lvwOrder.Columns.Add("Quantity", 70, HorizontalAlignment.Right)
    lvwOrder.Columns.Add("Total", 70, HorizontalAlignment.Right)
End Sub

' Display information on the selected order.
```

```
Private Sub lstOrders_SelectedIndexChanged( _
  ByVal sender As System.Object, _
  ByVal e As System.EventArgs) Handles lstOrders.SelectedIndexChanged

    Dim xml_node As XmlNode
    Dim xml_node_reader As System.Xml.XmlNodeReader
    Dim unit_price As Single
    Dim quantity As Single
    Dim grand_total As Single
    Dim lvw_item As ListViewItem

    ' Get the corresponding node.
    xml_node = _
        m_AllOrders.DocumentElement.ChildNodes(lstOrders.SelectedIndex)

    ' Attach an XmlNodeReader to the Order subtree.
    xml_node_reader = New System.Xml.XmlNodeReader(xml_node)

    ' Process the subtree looking for item information.
    lvwOrder.Items.Clear()
    Do Until xml_node_reader.EOF
        ' If this is an Item, process this node.
        If xml_node_reader.Name = "Item" Then
            ' Get the unit price and quantity.
            unit_price = CSng(xml_node_reader.GetAttribute("UnitPrice"))
            quantity = CSng(xml_node_reader.GetAttribute("Quantity"))
            grand_total = grand_total + unit_price * quantity

            ' Display the values for this Item.
            lvw_item = lvwOrder.Items.Add( _
                xml_node_reader.GetAttribute("ItemName"))
            lvw_item.SubItems.Add(Format$(unit_price, "$#,##0.00"))
            lvw_item.SubItems.Add(quantity.ToString)
            lvw_item.SubItems.Add( _
                Format(unit_price * quantity, "$#,##0.00"))
            lvw_item.EnsureVisible()
        End If

        ' Get the next node in the Order.
        xml_node_reader.Read()
    Loop

    lvw_item = lvwOrder.Items.Add("")
    lvw_item = lvwOrder.Items.Add("")
    lvw_item.SubItems.Add("")
    lvw_item.SubItems.Add("Grand Total")
    lvw_item.SubItems.Add(Format(grand_total, "$#,##0.00"))
    lvw_item.EnsureVisible()
End Sub
```

Note that the particular XML document used by this program contains only empty
Item elements so the program never encounters closing </Item> tags. If it contained

separate </Item> closing tags, the Do loop in the ListBox's SelectedIndexChanged event handler would need modification. As it is written, the routine would find the </Item> end element and think it had encountered a new Item. It would use the XmlNodeReader's GetAttribute method and add another copy of the Item element's values to the output.

If all of the XML document's Item elements had separate closing tags, the program could call the XmlNodeReader's Read or Skip method after adding the Item's information to the ListView control. That would skip the closing </Item> tag.

If the document contained a mix of Item tags both with and without separate closing tags, the program would need a more robust test in the event handler's loop. The following code would add information to the ListView control only when it found an Item node's start element.

```
If xml_node_reader.Name = "Item" And _
    xml_node_reader.NodeType = XmlNodeType.Element _
Then
    :
End If
```

Although the XmlNodeReader provides forward-only access to a document subtree, it does not modify the document hierarchy that it examines. The program can continue to use the XmlDocument object containing the data and the nodes visited by the XmlNodeReader. Program XmlNodeReader relies on this fact. If you click on a name, the program uses an XmlNodeReader to display information in the corresponding Order's subtree. If you click on the same name later, the program's XmlDocument is still correct so the program can display the information again.

There is no reason why you have to use the XmlNodeReader if you don't want to. The DOM objects XmlDocument, XmlNode, XmlElement, and so forth also provide navigation methods that let you traverse the XML document's structure. You could rewrite the XmlNodeReader example program to use only the DOM objects without much difficulty.

Use whichever method you find more comfortable. If you prefer to use only DOM methods, skip the XmlNodeReader. If you have been writing a lot of code using the XmlTextReader and you like the way it works, use XmlNodeReader.

SAX

SAX (Simple API for XML) is a library of routines that provide fast, forward-only read access to XML files. While Visual Basic itself doesn't provide an implementation of SAX, it is easy to install SAX so that it works with Visual Basic. Even if you don't want to use SAX, it is useful to know a little about it so you can understand what other developers are talking about on Internet newsgroups.

The XmlTextReader provides methods that a program uses to tell the XmlTextReader how to move through an XML file. The program essentially gives the XmlTextReader instructions such as the following:

- Read the start of an element
- Skip a node
- Read the current node's attributes
- Skip another node
- And so forth

When a SAX reader processes an XML document, it reads the document and raises events to tell the main program what it is reading. The program can then take action based on the local information the SAX routines provide. The SAX reader essentially tells the program the following:

- I am reading the start of an element
- I am reading some text
- I am reading the end of an element
- Et cetera

You can think of these two strategies as proactive or reactive. With an XmlText-Reader, the program proactively tells the XmlTextReader how to move through the XML document. With a SAX reader, the program reacts to what the SAX reader finds as it moves through the document. Both approaches work. Which one you should use is largely a matter of preference. XmlTextReader is more closely integrated into Visual Basic, however, so support for it may be slightly better.

Installing SAX

SAX was developed jointly by members of the XML-DEV mailing list and has no official relationship with the W3C. It is a popular library used by many XML developers.

There are several different versions of SAX written for different languages including Java, C++, Python, Perl, and COM. Unfortunately, there are also several different versions for the same languages. For example, there are several C++ implementations of SAX. There have been some efforts to standardize these versions, and newer implementations of SAX are extensible so developers should be able to add to the core implementation instead of building their own from scratch.

You can find more information on SAX and links to implementations for several different languages at www.megginson.com/SAX.

Microsoft's SAX Web site is msdn.microsoft.com/downloads/webtechnology/xml/msxml.asp. Go to that site, download the latest Microsoft SAX implementation, and follow the installation instructions.

To use SAX in a program, start a new project. Open the Project menu and select Add Reference. Click on the COM tab, find the component named Microsoft XML, v4.0, and double-click it. If you cannot find this component, click the Browse button and locate its DLL yourself. You will probably find it at C:\WINNT\System32\msxml4.dll. The version number 4 may vary depending on the latest release available at Microsoft's Web site.

After you have selected the component, click the OK button. At that point, the system will probably present a message similar to the following.

Could not find a primary interop assembly for the COM component 'Microsoft XML, v4.0'. A primary interop assembly is not registered for this type library. Would you like to have a wrapper generated for you?

Because this component is COM-based and not native to the .NET environment, the program needs a wrapper to use the component. Click Yes to make Visual Basic generate this wrapper for you. When you have finished adding SAX to the project, the Solution Explorer's References section should list MSXML2 (again, the version may vary).

Now the application can use SAX objects defined in the MSXML2 namespace. Two key interfaces defined in this namespace are IVBSAXContentHandler and IVBSAXErrorHandler.

The IVBSAXContentHandler interface defines the methods a class must provide to be a SAXContentHandler. An application uses a SAXContentHandler object to receive events as the SAX reader processes an XML document.

Similarly, IVBSAXErrorHandler defines the methods a SAXErrorHandler class must provide. A program uses this class to respond to errors that occur when the SAX reader processes the document.

SAX Order Processing

Example program SAXOrders, shown in Figure 3.13, uses a SAX reader to process an XML document containing Order records. For each Order, the program loops through the Order's Items, multiplying the Item's unit price and quantity. It then displays the total cost for the order. After it has processed all of the Orders, the program displays a grand total.

The main SAXOrders program shown in the following code is relatively straightforward. The program imports the MSXML2 namespace to make declarations easier. It then creates a new SAXXMLReader object. This is the object that reads through the XML document.

Figure 3.13 Program SAXOrders uses a SAX reader to display Order totals.

The SAXXMLReader class provides the most recent version of the SAX reader. The MSXML library also includes more specific versions of the SAX reader for backward compatibility. The SAXXMLReader30 class provides version 3.0 of the SAX reader, and the SAXXMLReader40 class provides version 4.0 of the SAX reader (the most recent version at the time of this writing). Generally, you should use the more general SAXXMLReader class to get the latest version of the SAX reader. You will need to use a specific version such as SAXXMLReader40 only when a newer version appears that doesn't provide the features you used when you built your application.

After creating its SAXXMLReader, the program creates new OrderErrorHandler and OrderContentHandler objects. The program declares these classes using the WithEvents keyword so that it can receive events raised by these objects. The OrderErrorHandler and OrderContentHandler classes are defined in this project and are described shortly.

When you click the Total Orders button, the program attaches its content handler and error handler objects to its SAXXMLReader. It then calls the SAXXMLReader's ParseURL method to make it load and process an XML document. When ParseURL is done, the program adds the grand total to the output. All the rest of the work is performed by the error handler and content handler classes.

If the error handler object raises its OrderError event, the program displays an error message. You can edit the program's XML file and introduce mistakes into it to see how the error handler deals with your changes.

When the SAXXMLReader processes an Order, the content handler object examines the Order data and raises an OrderTotaled event. The main program's event handler displays the Order's total and adds it to the grand total.

```
Imports MSXML2


' The SAX XML Reader.
Private m_SaxReader As New SAXXMLReader()


' The SAX reader's error handler.
Private WithEvents m_ErrorHandler As New OrderErrorHandler()


' The SAX reader's content handler.
Private WithEvents m_ContentHandler As New OrderContentHandler()


' The grand total of all orders.
Private m_GrandTotal As Double


' Process the XML file.
Private Sub btnTotalOrders_Click( _
  ByVal sender As System.Object, _
  ByVal e As System.EventArgs) Handles btnTotalOrders.Click

    ' Set the SAX XML Reader's content handler.
    m_SaxReader.contentHandler = m_ContentHandler

    ' Set the SAX XML Reader's error handler.
```

```
    m_SaxReader.errorHandler = m_ErrorHandler

    ' Clear out any previous results.
    Me.Cursor = Cursors.WaitCursor
    m_GrandTotal = 0
    txtOrders.Text = ""
    Refresh()

    ' Make the SAX reader parse the document.
    Try
        m_SaxReader.parseURL(DataSubdirectory() & "\Orders.xml")
    Catch exc As Exception
        MsgBox("Error parsing file " & _
            DataSubdirectory() & "\Orders.xml" & _
            vbCrLf & exc.Message, _
            MsgBoxStyle.Exclamation Or MsgBoxStyle.OKOnly, _
            "Parse Error")
    End Try

    ' Display the grand total.
    txtOrders.Text = txtOrders.Text & _
        "--------------------" & vbCrLf & _
        "Grand Total: " & Format(m_GrandTotal, "$#,##0.00")
    txtOrders.Focus()
    txtOrders.Select(txtOrders.Text.Length, 0)
    txtOrders.ScrollToCaret()
    Me.Cursor = Cursors.Default
End Sub

' The error handler is reporting an error.
Private Sub m_ErrorHandler_OrderError( _
  ByVal oLocator As MSXML2.IVBSAXLocator, _
  ByRef strErrorMessage As String, _
  ByVal nErrorCode As Integer) Handles m_ErrorHandler.OrderError

    MsgBox("Error parsing XML document." & _
        vbCrLf & "Line: " & oLocator.lineNumber & _
        vbCrLf & "Column: " & oLocator.columnNumber, _
        MsgBoxStyle.Information Or MsgBoxStyle.OKOnly, _
        "Parse Error")
End Sub

' Record an order total.
Private Sub m_ContentHandler_OrderTotaled( _
  ByVal order_total As Double) Handles m_ContentHandler.OrderTotaled

    ' Add the order total to the output text.
    txtOrders.Text = txtOrders.Text & _
        Format(order_total, "$#,##0.00") & vbCrLf

    ' Add the order total to the grand total.
    m_GrandTotal = m_GrandTotal + order_total
End Sub
```

The OrderContentHandler and OrderErrorHandler classes are described in the following sections.

OrderContentHandler

The OrderContentHandler class is a specialized class designed to process the content of this application's Order data. When you build your own SAX programs, you will need to create a similar content handling class.

OrderContentHandler implements the IVBSAXContentHandler interface. It must implement this interface if the main program is going to assign an instance of this class to the SAX reader's contentHandler property.

The OrderContentHandler declares its own OrderTotaled event. After it finishes totaling the Items in an Order, the class raises this event to let the main program know what's happening.

Because this class implements the IVBSAXContentHandler interface, it must implement several methods even if it doesn't really want to use them. These are the methods the SAX reader invokes as it processes different parts of the XML document. These methods tell the content handler when the SAX reader starts reading the document, starts reading an element, encounters ignorable whitespace, reads a processing instruction, and so forth.

You can read the code that follows to see all of the required methods, but the OrderContentHandler doesn't care about most of these events. This class takes action only when the SAX reader starts reading an element and when it ends reading an element.

When the SAX reader starts reading an element, it calls the OrderContentHandler's startElement method. This method examines the new element's name. If the element's name is Order, the SAX reader is starting to read a new Order element. The OrderContentHandler resets its m_OrderTotal value to 0 so it can begin totaling the Order's Item costs.

If the new element's name is Item, the SAX reader is starting to read an Item element inside an Order element. The startElement method includes a parameter oAttributes that represents the new element's attributes. The startElement method uses the oAttributes object's getValueFromName method to get the values of the Item element's UnitPrice and Quantity attributes. It multiplies those values and adds the result to the value m_OrderTotal.

When the SAX reader is reading an element's end tag, it calls the OrderContentHandler's endElement method. This method examines the element's name to see if the SAX reader is reading the end of an Order element. If the name is Order, the OrderContentHandler object raises its OrderTotaled event to tell the main program the Order's total cost.

```
Imports MSXML2

Public Class OrderContentHandler
    Implements IVBSAXContentHandler

    ' Raise this event when we finish processing an Order.
    Public Event OrderTotaled(ByVal order_total As Double)

    ' The current Order's total price so far.
```

```
Private m_OrderTotal As Double

' documentLocator is the first method called when the SAX reader
' opens the XML document. Because this is the first event, it is
' a good place to initialize the class.
'
' The parameter Value provides access to the XML document.
Overridable WriteOnly Property CatchDocumentLocator() _
  As IVBSAXLocator _
Implements IVBSAXContentHandler.documentLocator
    Set(ByVal Value As IVBSAXLocator)

    End Set
End Property

' startDocument is called when the SAX reader
' starts reading the document.
Overridable Sub CatchStartDocument() _
Implements IVBSAXContentHandler.startDocument

End Sub

' endDocument is called when the SAX reader is done reading
' the document, either because it has reached the end of the
' document or because it had a fatal error.
Overridable Sub CatchEndDocument() _
Implements IVBSAXContentHandler.endDocument

End Sub

' startElement is called when the SAX reader
' reads start of an element.
Overridable Sub CatchStartElement( _
    ByRef strNamespaceURI As String, _
    ByRef strLocalName As String, _
    ByRef strQName As String, _
    ByVal oAttributes As MSXML2.IVBSAXAttributes) _
Implements IVBSAXContentHandler.startElement
    ' See what kind of element this is.
    If strLocalName = "Order" Then
        ' Order.
        ' Start a new total.
        m_OrderTotal = 0
    ElseIf strLocalName = "Item" Then
        ' Item element.
        ' Add to the current total.
        m_OrderTotal = m_OrderTotal + _
            CDbl(oAttributes.getValueFromName("", "UnitPrice")) * _
            CDbl(oAttributes.getValueFromName("", "Quantity"))
    End If
End Sub

' endElement is called when the SAX reader
```

```
' reads an element's closing tag.
Overridable Sub CatchEndElement( _
    ByRef strNamespaceURI As String, _
    ByRef strLocalName As String, _
    ByRef strQName As String) _
Implements IVBSAXContentHandler.endElement
    ' See if this is the end of an Order element.
    If strLocalName = "Order" Then
        ' This is the end of an Order element.
        ' Send out the accumulated total for the Order.
        RaiseEvent OrderTotaled(m_OrderTotal)
    End If
End Sub


' The characters method is passed the characters that appear
' between an element's start and end tags.
Overridable Sub CatchCharacters(ByRef strChars As String) _
Implements IVBSAXContentHandler.characters

End Sub


' startPrefixMapping is called when a URI namespace prefix
' mapping starts. Occurs after the startElement call for the
' element that contains it, but the order of the startPrefixMapping
' and corresponding endPrefixMapping is not guaranteed.
Overridable Sub CatchStartPrefixMapping( _
    ByRef strPrefix As String, _
    ByRef strURI As String) _
Implements IVBSAXContentHandler.startPrefixMapping

End Sub


' endPrefixMapping is called when a URI namespace prefix
' mapping is ending. Occurs after the endElement call for the
' element that contains it, but the order of the startPrefixMapping
' and corresponding endPrefixMapping is not guaranteed.
Overridable Sub CatchEndPrefixMapping( _
    ByRef strPrefix As String) _
Implements IVBSAXContentHandler.endPrefixMapping

End Sub


' ignorableWhitespace is not called by SAX2 because SAX2 is
' nonvalidating.
Overridable Sub CatchIgnorableWhitespace( _
    ByRef strChars As String) _
Implements IVBSAXContentHandler.ignorableWhitespace

End Sub


' processingInstruction is called when the SAX reader reads
' a processing instruction.
```

```
Overridable Sub CatchProcessingInstruction( _
    ByRef strTarget As String, _
    ByRef strData As String) _
Implements IVBSAXContentHandler.processingInstruction

End Sub


' skippedEntity is called when the SAX reader skips an external
' DTD declaration and when it skips an entity. It skips an entity
' when it did not read that entity's declaration, for example
' if the entitiy was defined in an external declaration.
Overridable Sub CatchSkippedEntity( _
    ByRef strName As String) _
Implements IVBSAXContentHandler.skippedEntity

End Sub
End Class
```

Most of the code in this class contains empty methods that must be present to satisfy the IVBSAXContentHandler implementation. Building all of those methods is inconvenient so, when you build your own content handling classes, you may want to copy this class and modify it to suit your needs.

OrderErrorHandler

The OrderErrorHandler class processes errors for this application's SAX reader. This class doesn't do anything specific to this application so you can reuse it in your own applications if you like (though you may want to change its name).

OrderErrorHandler implements the IVBSAXErrorHandler interface. It must implement this interface if the main program is going to assign an instance of this class to the SAX reader's errorHandler property.

The OrderErrorHandler declares its own OrderError event. If the SAX reader encounters an error, this class raises the OrderError to tell the main program that something is wrong.

Because this class implements the IVBSAXErrorHandler interface, it must implement three methods: ignorableWarning, error, and fatalError. The MSXML2 implementation of SAX2 doesn't call the ignorableWarning or error methods so they can be empty. The fatalError method simply raises the object's OrderError event so the main program can tell the user something is wrong.

```
Imports MSXML2


Public Class OrderErrorHandler
    Implements IVBSAXErrorHandler

    ' When our error method is called, we raise this error.
    Public Event OrderError( _
        ByVal oLocator As MSXML2.IVBSAXLocator, _
        ByRef strErrorMessage As String, _
```

```
        ByVal nErrorCode As Integer)


    ' This method is called when the SAX reader encounters
    ' an igorable warning.
    '
    ' Note: SAX2 doesn't call this method.
    Overridable Sub CatchIgnorableWarning( _
        ByVal oLocator As MSXML2.IVBSAXLocator, _
        ByRef strErrorMessage As String, _
        ByVal nErrorCode As Integer) _
    Implements IVBSAXErrorHandler.ignorableWarning

    End Sub


    ' This method is called when the SAX reader encounters
    ' a nonfatal error.
    '
    ' Note: SAX2 doesn't call this method.
    Overridable Sub CatchError( _
        ByVal oLocator As MSXML2.IVBSAXLocator, _
        ByRef strErrorMessage As String, _
        ByVal nErrorCode As Integer) _
    Implements IVBSAXErrorHandler.error

    End Sub


    ' This method is called when the SAX reader encounters
    ' a fatal error.
    Overridable Sub CatchFatalError( _
        ByVal oLocator As MSXML2.IVBSAXLocator, _
        ByRef strErrorMessage As String, _
        ByVal nErrorCode As Integer) _
    Implements IVBSAXErrorHandler.fatalError
        RaiseEvent OrderError(oLocator, strErrorMessage, nErrorCode)
    End Sub
End Class
```

If you wanted, you could build a single class to play the role of both content handler and error handler. The combined class would implement both the IVBSAXContent-Handler and IVBSAXErrorHandler interfaces and provide all of the required methods for both interfaces. This would place all of the SAX information handler code in one class, but it would make the class a bit more cluttered.

Wrapping the SAX Wrapper

Building classes that implement the IVBSAXContentHandler and IVBSAXError-Handler interfaces is straightforward but messy. These classes must contain subroutines to respond to quite a few SAX events whether or not you actually care about those events. For example, the error handling class must contain subroutines that implement the IVBSAXErrorHandler.error and IVBSAXErrorHandler.ignorableWarning interface routines even though the current implementation of SAX never invokes those routines.

Filling your classes with these events that you don't really want makes your code more cluttered and harder to read. It would be nice if you could use events to process these occurrences instead of subroutines. Then if you don't care about an event, you simply don't provide an event handler for it.

SAXContentEvents

Example program SAXEvents uses two classes that follow this approach. The SAX-ContentEvents class shown in the following code implements the IVBSAXContent-Handler interface. When the SAX reader calls one of its subroutines, the subroutine raises an event. The main program can provide an event handler to process the event if it is interested.

```
Imports MSXML2

Public Class SAXContentEvents
    Implements IVBSAXContentHandler

    ' Events we reraise so the main program can handle them.
    Public Event SAXDocumentLocator(ByVal Value As IVBSAXLocator)
    Public Event SAXStartDocument()
    Public Event SAXEndDocument()
    Public Event SAXStartElement( _
        ByRef strNamespaceURI As String, _
        ByRef strLocalName As String, _
        ByRef strQName As String, _
        ByVal oAttributes As MSXML2.IVBSAXAttributes)
    Public Event SAXEndElement( _
        ByRef strNamespaceURI As String, _
        ByRef strLocalName As String, _
        ByRef strQName As String)
    Public Event SAXCharacters(ByRef strChars As String)
    Public Event SAXStartPrefixMapping( _
        ByRef strPrefix As String, _
        ByRef strURI As String)
    Public Event SAXEndPrefixMapping( _
        ByRef strPrefix As String)
    Public Event SAXIgnorableWhitespace( _
        ByRef strChars As String)
    Public Event SAXProcessingInstruction( _
        ByRef strTarget As String, _
        ByRef strData As String)
    Public Event SAXSkippedEntity( _
        ByRef strName As String)

    ' documentLocator is the first method called when the SAX reader
    ' opens the XML document. Because this is the first event, it is
```

```
' a good place to initialize the class.
'
' The parameter Value provides access to the XML document.
Overridable WriteOnly Property CatchDocumentLocator() _
  As IVBSAXLocator _
Implements IVBSAXContentHandler.documentLocator
    Set(ByVal Value As IVBSAXLocator)
        RaiseEvent SAXDocumentLocator(Value)
    End Set
End Property


' startDocument is called when the SAX reader
' starts reading the document.
Overridable Sub CatchStartDocument() _
Implements IVBSAXContentHandler.startDocument
    RaiseEvent SAXStartDocument()
End Sub


' endDocument is called when the SAX reader is done reading
' the document, either because it has reached the end of the
' document or because it had a fatal error.
Overridable Sub CatchEndDocument() _
Implements IVBSAXContentHandler.endDocument
    RaiseEvent SAXEndDocument()
End Sub


' startElement is called when the SAX reader
' reads start of an element.
Overridable Sub CatchStartElement( _
    ByRef strNamespaceURI As String, _
    ByRef strLocalName As String, _
    ByRef strQName As String, _
    ByVal oAttributes As MSXML2.IVBSAXAttributes) _
Implements IVBSAXContentHandler.startElement
    RaiseEvent SAXStartElement( _
        strNamespaceURI, _
        strLocalName, _
        strQName, _
        oAttributes)
End Sub


' endElement is called when the SAX reader
' reads an element's closing tag.
Overridable Sub CatchEndElement( _
    ByRef strNamespaceURI As String, _
    ByRef strLocalName As String, _
    ByRef strQName As String) _
Implements IVBSAXContentHandler.endElement
    RaiseEvent SAXEndElement( _
        strNamespaceURI, _
```

```
            strLocalName, _
            strQName)
End Sub


' The characters method is passed the characters that appear
' between an element's start and end tags.
Overridable Sub CatchCharacters(ByRef strChars As String) _
Implements IVBSAXContentHandler.characters
     RaiseEvent SAXCharacters(strChars)
End Sub


' startPrefixMapping is called when a URI namespace prefix
' mapping starts. Occurs after the startElement call for the
' element that contains it, but the order of the startPrefixMapping
' and corresponding endPrefixMapping is not guaranteed.
Overridable Sub CatchStartPrefixMapping( _
    ByRef strPrefix As String, _
    ByRef strURI As String) _
Implements IVBSAXContentHandler.startPrefixMapping
     RaiseEvent SAXStartPrefixMapping(strPrefix, strURI)
End Sub


' endPrefixMapping is called when a URI namespace prefix
' mapping is ending. Occurs after the endElement call for the
' element that contains it, but the order of the startPrefixMapping
' and corresponding endPrefixMapping is not guaranteed.
Overridable Sub CatchEndPrefixMapping( _
    ByRef strPrefix As String) _
Implements IVBSAXContentHandler.endPrefixMapping
     RaiseEvent SAXEndPrefixMapping(strPrefix)
End Sub


' ignorableWhitespace is not called by SAX2 because SAX2 is
' non-validating.
Overridable Sub CatchIgnorableWhitespace( _
    ByRef strChars As String) _
Implements IVBSAXContentHandler.ignorableWhitespace
     RaiseEvent SAXIgnorableWhitespace(strChars)
End Sub


' processingInstruction is called when the SAX reader reads
' a processing instruction.
Overridable Sub CatchProcessingInstruction( _
    ByRef strTarget As String, _
    ByRef strData As String) _
Implements IVBSAXContentHandler.processingInstruction
     RaiseEvent SAXProcessingInstruction(strTarget, strData)
End Sub


' skippedEntity is called when the SAX reader skips an external
' DTD declaration and when it skips an entity. It skips an entity
' when it did not read that entity's declaration, for example
```

```
' if the entitiy was defined in an external declaration.
Overridable Sub CatchSkippedEntity( _
    ByRef strName As String) _
Implements IVBSAXContentHandler.skippedEntity
    RaiseEvent SAXSkippedEntity(strName)
End Sub
End Class
```

SAXErrorEvents

Similarly, the SAXErrorEvents class shown in the following code implements the IVB-SAXErrorHandler interface. When the SAX reader calls one of the SAXErrorEvents subroutines, the subroutine raises an event to let the main program know what's happening.

```
Imports MSXML2

Public Class SAXErrorEvents
    Implements IVBSAXErrorHandler

    ' Events we reraise for the main program.
    Public Event SAXIgnoreableWarning( _
        ByVal oLocator As MSXML2.IVBSAXLocator, _
        ByRef strErrorMessage As String, _
        ByVal nErrorCode As Integer)
    Public Event SAXError( _
        ByVal oLocator As MSXML2.IVBSAXLocator, _
        ByRef strErrorMessage As String, _
        ByVal nErrorCode As Integer)
    Public Event SAXFatalError( _
        ByVal oLocator As MSXML2.IVBSAXLocator, _
        ByRef strErrorMessage As String, _
        ByVal nErrorCode As Integer)

        ' This method is called when the SAX reader encounters
        ' an igorable warning.
        '
        ' Note: SAX2 doesn't call this method.
    Overridable Sub CatchIgnorableWarning( _
        ByVal oLocator As MSXML2.IVBSAXLocator, _
        ByRef strErrorMessage As String, _
        ByVal nErrorCode As Integer) _
    Implements IVBSAXErrorHandler.ignorableWarning
        RaiseEvent SAXIgnoreableWarning( _
            oLocator, _
            strErrorMessage, _
            nErrorCode)
    End Sub

    ' This method is called when the SAX reader encounters
```

```
' a nonfatal error.
'
' Note: SAX2 doesn't call this method.
Overridable Sub CatchError( _
    ByVal oLocator As MSXML2.IVBSAXLocator, _
    ByRef strErrorMessage As String, _
    ByVal nErrorCode As Integer) _
Implements IVBSAXErrorHandler.error
    RaiseEvent SAXError( _
        oLocator, _
        strErrorMessage, _
        nErrorCode)
End Sub

' This method is called when the SAX reader encounters
' a fatal error.
Overridable Sub CatchFatalError( _
    ByVal oLocator As MSXML2.IVBSAXLocator, _
    ByRef strErrorMessage As String, _
    ByVal nErrorCode As Integer) _
Implements IVBSAXErrorHandler.fatalError
    RaiseEvent SAXFatalError( _
        oLocator, _
        strErrorMessage, _
        nErrorCode)
End Sub
End Class
```

Program SAXEvents

Example program SAXEvents uses these classes to calculate order totals much as the program SAXOrder described in the previous section does. Using the SAXContent-Events and SAXErrorEvents classes lets this version of the program move the application logic into the main program. In program SAXOrders, the OrderContentHandler class contains the code that totals the costs of the items in an order. When it sees the end of an order, this class raises an event so the main program can add the order total to its output.

Program SAXEvents performs exactly the same steps, but the processing occurs in the main program. When the SAX reader encounters an Item node, the SAXContent-Events class raises an event to tell the main program. The main program calculates the Item's cost and keeps track of it. When the SAX reader reaches an </Order> closing tag, the SAXContentEvents class raises an event. The main program catches the event and adds the Order's total cost to its output.

The following code fragment shows the SAXEvents program's most interesting code. The program declares the m_ErrorHandler and m_ContentHandler objects using the WithEvents keyword so that it can use their events easily. After they have been declared WithEvents, you can select these objects in the code window's left combo box. Then you can select one of the selected object's event handlers in the right combo box.

The program begins by initializing these two objects and attaching them to the SAX reader. It makes the SAX reader parse the XML document and then displays summary information. The most interesting processing happens when the SAX reader calls the SAXContentEvents object's subroutines and that object raises an event telling the main program what is happening.

When the main program receives the SAXStartElement event, it checks the name of the node SAX is reading to see what kind of element is starting. If this is an Order element, the program resets its total order cost to zero. If the new element is an Item, the program calculates the item's total cost and adds it to the current order's total.

When the main program receives the SAXEndElement event, it again checks the name of the node SAX is reading. If an Order element is ending, the program outputs the order's total cost and adds it to the program's grand total.

After the SAX reader finishes processing the XML file, the call to parseURL returns and the program's main btnTotalOrders_Click event handler displays the grand total.

```
' The SAX XML Reader.
Private m_SaxReader As New SAXXMLReader()


' The SAX reader's error handler.
Private WithEvents m_ErrorHandler As New SAXErrorEvents()


' The SAX reader's content handler.
Private WithEvents m_ContentHandler As New SAXContentEvents()


' The current Order's total price so far.
Private m_OrderTotal As Double


' The grand total of all orders.
Private m_GrandTotal As Double


' Process the XML file.
Private Sub btnTotalOrders_Click( _
  ByVal sender As System.Object, _
  ByVal e As System.EventArgs) Handles btnTotalOrders.Click

    ' Set the SAX XML Reader's content handler.
    m_SaxReader.contentHandler = m_ContentHandler

    ' Set the SAX XML Reader's error handler.
    m_SaxReader.errorHandler = m_ErrorHandler

    ' Clear out any previous results.
    Me.Cursor = Cursors.WaitCursor
    m_GrandTotal = 0
    txtOrders.Text = ""
    Refresh()

    ' Make the SAX reader parse the document.
    Try
        m_SaxReader.parseURL(DataSubdirectory() & "\Orders.xml")
```

```
      Catch exc As Exception
          MsgBox("Error parsing file " & DataSubdirectory() & _
              "\Orders.xml" & vbCrLf & exc.Message, _
              MsgBoxStyle.Exclamation Or MsgBoxStyle.OKOnly, _
              "Parse Error")
      End Try

      ' Display the grand total.
      txtOrders.Text = txtOrders.Text & _
          "--------------------" & vbCrLf & _
          "Grand Total: " & Format(m_GrandTotal, "$#,##0.00")
      txtOrders.Focus()
      txtOrders.Select(txtOrders.Text.Length, 0)
      txtOrders.ScrollToCaret()
      Me.Cursor = Cursors.Default
  End Sub

  ' If this is an Order, start a new total.
  ' If this is an Item, add to the new total.
  Private Sub m_ContentHandler_SAXStartElement( _
    ByRef strNamespaceURI As String, _
    ByRef strLocalName As String, _
    ByRef strQName As String, _
    ByVal oAttributes As MSXML2.IVBSAXAttributes) _
    Handles m_ContentHandler.SAXStartElement

      ' See what kind of element this is.
      If strLocalName = "Order" Then
          ' Order.
          ' Start a new total.
          m_OrderTotal = 0
      ElseIf strLocalName = "Item" Then
          ' Item element.
          ' Add to the current total.
          m_OrderTotal = m_OrderTotal + _
              CDbl(oAttributes.getValueFromName("", "UnitPrice")) * _
              CDbl(oAttributes.getValueFromName("", "Quantity"))
      End If
  End Sub

  ' If this is the end of an Order, add its
  ' total to the output.
  Private Sub m_ContentHandler_SAXEndElement( _
    ByRef strNamespaceURI As String, _
    ByRef strLocalName As String, _
    ByRef strQName As String) Handles m_ContentHandler.SAXEndElement

      ' See if this is the end of an Order element.
      If strLocalName = "Order" Then
          ' Add the order total to the output text.
          txtOrders.Text = txtOrders.Text & _
```

```
            Format(m_OrderTotal, "$#,##0.00") & vbCrLf

        ' Add the order total to the grand total.
        m_GrandTotal = m_GrandTotal + m_OrderTotal
    End If
End Sub
```

Using the generic SAXContentEvents and SAXErrorEvents classes makes working with the SAX events easier. It lets the program define event handlers for only those events that are interesting. It also lets you keep all of the program's interesting code in the main program instead of putting it in a custom-built content handling class.

Conclusion

The XmlTextWriter and XmlTextReader classes provide fast, forward-only methods for writing and reading XML documents. Both of these classes use a proactive approach to processing XML. The classes provide methods the main program uses to explicitly move through the XML file, visiting the nodes it finds interesting.

SAX provides an alternative forward-only method for processing an XML file. As the SAX reader parses the XML document, it raises events telling the main program what kinds of XML nodes it is reading. For example, it raises events when it reads the beginning of an element, the end of an element, a processing instruction, and so forth. The program can then react to those events and take appropriate action.

The SAX wrapper created by Visual Basic translates these events into subroutines defined by the IVBSAXContentHandler and IVBSAXErrorHandler interfaces, but it's not hard to build generic classes that implement these interfaces and translate the subroutine calls back into events.

Both the active approach provided by XmlTextWriter and XmlTextReader and the reactive approach implemented by SAX let a program quickly process XML documents. Either method will work. The approach you should use depends on your preferences and those of any other developers working with you.

Serialization

Serialization is the process of translating a collection of data into a stream of information. Deserialization is the reverse: translating a stream of information back into the data that originally produced it. Sometimes these processes are called dehydration and rehydration.

Serialization is useful for transporting or storing complex data in a simple format. For example, an application might build a complicated data structure consisting of dozens of objects and serialize it into a text string. It could then transmit the string to another program across the network. The receiving program would deserialize the text to create a duplicate of the original data structure.

Serialization need not translate objects into text. It could represent the objects as a stream of binary data. It also need not transmit the data across a network. For example, it could copy the serialization into a file or database for later re-creation. The thing all of these uses of serialization have in common is they convert a possibly complex data structure into a simple serial representation and then translate it back again.

Because XML is a data storage language, it makes sense to use it to serialize information. In fact, the DOM itself provides easy serialization and deserialization for XML document hierarchies. A program can build a document hierarchy using the DOM objects provided by Visual Basic and save it into a file using the XmlDocument object's Save method. Another program can then create a new XmlDocument and use its Load method to read the file and re-create the hierarchy.

To transmit a document directly, a program can use the XmlDocument's OuterXml property to get a text string representing the document hierarchy. It can send the string to another application that can create a new XmlDocument and set its OuterXml property to the serialization string's value.

Using the Save and Load methods or the OuterXml property, you can write programs that serialize and deserialize other data structures by converting them to and from XML documents. In fact, Visual Basic provides tools that make serialization and deserialization using XML even easier.

This chapter describes the tools you can use to make a Visual Basic program serialize and deserialize complex data structures quickly and easily.

Serialization Basics

The XmlSerializer class provides methods for serializing and deserializing objects. When a program instantiates an XmlSerializer object, it passes the constructor a reflection class describing the class it will serialize. A GetType expression creates the reflection class from the class the program will serialize. For example, the following code creates an XmlSerializer object that is prepared to serialize an object of the type OrderedItem.

```
Dim xml_serializer As XmlSerializer

xml_serializer = New XmlSerializer(GetType(OrderedItem))
```

After it has created an XmlSerializer object, the program can use its Serialize and Deserialize methods to read and write an object into a stream. For example, the following code serializes an OrderedItem object named ordered_item into an XML file.

```
' Create a FileStream to write with.
Dim file_stream As New FileStream("C:\Xml\Order.xml", FileMode.Create)

' Serialize the object
xml_serializer.Serialize(file_stream, ordered_item)

' Close the FileStream.
file_stream.Close()
```

When a program serializes an object in this way, the XmlSerializer saves the values of the object's public variables and properties into the XML file.

Deserializing an object is almost as simple. The XmlSerializer's Deserialize method returns a reference to a new generic Object containing the data that was serialized. The program can use CType to convert the object into the appropriate type. The following code shows how a program might deserialize the object saved by the previous code.

```
' Create an XmlSerializer.
Dim xml_serializer As New _
    XmlSerializer(GetType(OrderedItem))

' Create a FileStream to read with.
Dim file_stream As New FileStream("C:\Xml\Order.xml", FileMode.Open)
```

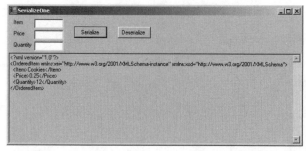

Figure 4.1 Program SerializeOne serializes and deserializes a single OrderedItem object.

```
' Read the item from the serialization.
Dim ordered_item As OrderedItem

ordered_item = CType( _
    xml_serializer.Deserialize(file_stream), OrderedItem)

' Close the file stream.
file_stream.Close()
```

Example program SerializeOne, shown in Figure 4.1, uses the following code to serialize and deserialize an OrderedItem object. When you enter values in the Item, Price, and Quantity text boxes and click the Serialize button, the program copies those values into an OrderedItem object and serializes the object into a text file. When you click the Deserialize button, the program recreates the OrderedItem object from the serialization and displays the Item, Price, and Quantity in its text boxes.

The OrderedItem class used by program SerializeOne contains two public variables, Item and Price, and one private variable, Quantity. The class includes public property procedures to give access to the Quantity value. The XmlSerializer class serializes and deserializes all three of these values.

The btnSerialize_Click event handler copies the values in the Item, Price, and Quantity text boxes into an OrderedItem object. It then uses an XmlSerializer to serialize that object into an XML file.

The btnDeserialize_Click event handler uses an XmlSerializer to reload an Ordered-Item object with the value saved in the serialization. It then displays those values in the Item, Price, and Quantity text boxes.

```
Public Class OrderedItem
    Public Item As String
    Public Price As Decimal
    Private m_Quantity As Integer
```

```vb
    Public Property Quantity() As Integer
        Get
            Quantity = m_Quantity
        End Get
        Set(ByVal Value As Integer)
            m_Quantity = Value
        End Set
    End Property

    Public Sub New()
    End Sub

    Public Sub New( _
      ByVal new_item As String, _
      ByVal new_price As Decimal, _
      ByVal new_quantity As Integer)

        Item = new_item
        Price = new_price
        m_Quantity = new_quantity
    End Sub
End Class

' Serialize the data in the TextBoxes.
Private Sub btnSerialize_Click( _
  ByVal sender As System.Object, _
  ByVal e As System.EventArgs) Handles btnSerialize.Click

    Cursor = Cursors.WaitCursor
    txtSerialization.Text = ""
    Refresh()

    ' Copy the data into an OrderedItem object.
    Dim ordered_item As New OrderedItem( _
        txtItem.Text, _
        CDec(txtPrice.Text), _
        CInt(txtQuantity.Text))

    ' Create an XmlSerializer.
    Dim xml_serializer As New _
        XmlSerializer(GetType(OrderedItem))

    ' Create a FileStream to write with.
    Dim file_stream As New FileStream(m_XMLFile, FileMode.Create)

    ' Serialize the object
    xml_serializer.Serialize(file_stream, ordered_item)

    ' Close the FileStream.
    file_stream.Close()
```

```
        ' Display the results.
        txtSerialization.Text = GetFileContents(m_XMLFile)

        ' Clear the TextBoxes.
        txtItem.Text = ""
        txtPrice.Text = ""
        txtQuantity.Text = ""

        Cursor = Cursors.Default
    End Sub

' Deserialize the data in the TextBoxes.
Private Sub btnDeserialize_Click( _
  ByVal sender As System.Object, _
  ByVal e As System.EventArgs) Handles btnDeserialize.Click

        Cursor = Cursors.WaitCursor
        txtItem.Text = ""
        txtPrice.Text = ""
        txtQuantity.Text = ""
        Refresh()

        ' Create an XmlSerializer.
        Dim xml_serializer As New _
            XmlSerializer(GetType(OrderedItem))

        ' Create an XmlTextReader to read with.
        Dim file_stream As New FileStream(m_XMLFile, FileMode.Open)

        ' Read the item from the serialization.
        Dim ordered_item As OrderedItem
        ordered_item = CType( _
            xml_serializer.Deserialize(file_stream), OrderedItem)
        file_stream.Close()

        ' Copy the data into the TextBoxes.
        With ordered_item
            txtItem.Text = .Item
            txtPrice.Text = .Price
            txtQuantity.Text = .Quantity
        End With

        ' Clear the serialization.
        txtSerialization.Text = ""

        Cursor = Cursors.Default
    End Sub
```

The following code shows the XML file generated by program SerializeOne. It is easy to see the Item, Price, and Quantity values embedded in this file. Notice that there is no difference between the way the Item, Price, and Quantity are stored. Although the

OrderedItem class stores Item and Price as public variables and Quantity using property procedures, the XML serialization doesn't differentiate the types of values.

```
<?xml version="1.0"?>
<OrderedItem xmlns:xsi="http://www.w3.org/2001/XMLSchema-instance"
xmlns:xsd="http://www.w3.org/2001/XMLSchema">
  <Item>Cookies</Item>
  <Price>0.25</Price>
  <Quantity>12</Quantity>
</OrderedItem>
```

If a program invokes an XmlSerializer's Serialize method more than once with the same file stream, it can write multiple objects into the same XML file. Unfortunately, the serializer places those objects at the document's root level so each defines its own document root. Because each object defines its own root, the XML document is not well formed. The following sections explain ways a program can store multiple objects in a single well-formed XML file.

Arrays

One way to store multiple objects in the same XML file is to serialize an array that contains the objects. When the program instantiates the XmlSerializer object, it should use GetType to pass the constructor a reflection class describing an array of objects. The following code shows how a program might serialize an array of OrderedItem objects.

```
' Create an XmlSerializer.
Dim xml_serializer As New _
    XmlSerializer(GetType(OrderedItem()))

' Create a FileStream to write with.
Dim file_stream As New FileStream(m_XMLFile, FileMode.Create)

' Serialize the array.
xml_serializer.Serialize(file_stream, ordered_items)

' Close the FileStream.
file_stream.Close()
```

Example program SerializeArray, shown in Figure 4.2, uses the following code to serialize and deserialize an array of OrderedItem objects. Enter values in the text boxes and click the Serialize button to serialize the data into an XML file. Click the Deserialize button to make the program deserialize the data using the values in the file.

The btnSerialize_Click event handler make an array of three OrderedItem objects and initializes them using the values in the program's text boxes. It then creates a new XmlSerializer object, telling the object that it will serialize an array of OrderedItem objects. The event handler creates a file stream, uses the XmlSerializer to serialize the data into the stream, closes the stream, and displays the resulting XML file much as the code used by program SerializeOne does.

Figure 4.2 Program SerializeArray serializes and deserializes an array of OrderedItem objects.

The btnDeserialize_Click subroutine reverses the process. It creates a new XmlSerializer, opens a file stream, makes the XmlSerializer deserialize the data in the file, and closes the file stream.

```
' Serialize the data in the TextBoxes.
Private Sub btnSerialize_Click( _
  ByVal sender As System.Object, _
  ByVal e As System.EventArgs) Handles btnSerialize.Click

    Cursor = Cursors.WaitCursor
    txtSerialization.Text = ""
    Refresh()

    ' Make an array of OrderedItems.
    Dim ordered_items(2) As OrderedItem

    ' Copy the data into OrderedItem objects.
    ordered_items(0) = New OrderedItem( _
        txtItem0.Text, _
        CDec(txtPrice0.Text), _
        CInt(txtQuantity0.Text))
    ordered_items(1) = New OrderedItem( _
        txtItem1.Text, _
        CDec(txtPrice1.Text), _
        CInt(txtQuantity1.Text))
    ordered_items(2) = New OrderedItem( _
        txtItem2.Text, _
        CDec(txtPrice2.Text), _
        CInt(txtQuantity2.Text))

    ' Create an XmlSerializer.
    Dim xml_serializer As New _
        XmlSerializer(GetType(OrderedItem()))
```

```
    ' Create a FileStream to write with.
    Dim file_stream As New FileStream(m_XMLFile, FileMode.Create)

    ' Serialize the array.
    xml_serializer.Serialize(file_stream, ordered_items)

    ' Close the FileStream.
    file_stream.Close()

    ' Display the results.
    txtSerialization.Text = GetFileContents(m_XMLFile)

    ' Clear the TextBoxes.
    txtItem0.Text = ""
    txtPrice0.Text = ""
    txtQuantity0.Text = ""
    txtItem1.Text = ""
    txtPrice1.Text = ""
    txtQuantity1.Text = ""
    txtItem2.Text = ""
    txtPrice2.Text = ""
    txtQuantity2.Text = ""

    Cursor = Cursors.Default
End Sub

' Deserialize the data in the TextBoxes.
Private Sub btnDeserialize_Click( _
  ByVal sender As System.Object, _
  ByVal e As System.EventArgs) Handles btnDeserialize.Click

    Dim ctl As Control
    For Each ctl In Controls
        If (TypeOf ctl Is TextBox) And _
            (Not (ctl Is txtSerialization)) _
        Then
            ctl.Text = ""
        End If
    Next ctl
    Cursor = Cursors.WaitCursor
    Refresh()

    ' Create an XmlSerializer.
    Dim xml_serializer As New _
        XmlSerializer(GetType(OrderedItem()))

    ' Create an XmlTextReader to read with.
    Dim file_stream As New FileStream(m_XMLFile, FileMode.Open)

    ' Read the items from the serialization.
```

```
        Dim ordered_items() As OrderedItem
        ordered_items = CType( _
            xml_serializer.Deserialize(file_stream), OrderedItem())
        file_stream.Close()

        ' Copy the data into the TextBoxes.
        With ordered_items(0)
            txtItem0.Text = .Item
            txtPrice0.Text = .Price
            txtQuantity0.Text = .Quantity
        End With
        With ordered_items(1)
            txtItem1.Text = .Item
            txtPrice1.Text = .Price
            txtQuantity1.Text = .Quantity
        End With
        With ordered_items(2)
            txtItem2.Text = .Item
            txtPrice2.Text = .Price
            txtQuantity2.Text = .Quantity
        End With

        ' Clear the serialization.
        txtSerialization.Text = ""

        Cursor = Cursors.Default
    End Sub
```

The following code shows the XML produced by program SerializeArray. The
XmlSerializer created a root element named ArrayOfOrderedItem. Within that element, the XmlSerializer used separate OrderedItem tags to store the data for each of
the items in the array.

```
<?xml version="1.0"?>
<ArrayOfOrderedItem xmlns:xsi="http://www.w3.org/2001/XMLSchema-
instance"
xmlns:xsd="http://www.w3.org/2001/XMLSchema">
  <OrderedItem>
    <Item>Brownies</Item>
    <Price>1.25</Price>
    <Quantity>3</Quantity>
  </OrderedItem>
  <OrderedItem>
    <Item>Cookies</Item>
    <Price>0.25</Price>
    <Quantity>12</Quantity>
  </OrderedItem>
  <OrderedItem>
    <Item>Cupcakes</Item>
    <Price>0.5</Price>
    <Quantity>6</Quantity>
  </OrderedItem>
</ArrayOfOrderedItem>
```

The method used by SerializeArray works well with a simple array of objects, but it does not work as well with complex data structures. Later sections in this chapter show how a program can serialize much more complicated data constructs just as easily.

Attributes

The XML document produced by example programs SerializeOne and SerializeArray use separate XML tags to store each value that defines every object. The following code shows the serialization for a single OrderedItem object produced by program SerializeArray.

```
<OrderedItem>
  <Item>Cookies</Item>
  <Price>0.25</Price>
  <Quantity>12</Quantity>
</OrderedItem>
```

In some cases, it might be more appropriate for the object's values to be stored as attributes of the main object's tag. In many cases, particularly when the serialization is of an array, the resulting XML file is smaller and easier to read if the values are stored as attributes. The following example shows the previous object's values stored as attributes.

```
<OrderedItem Item="Cookies" Price="0.25" Quantity="12" />
```

By modifying the definitions of the public variables and property procedures in the OrderedItem class, you can tell the XmlSerializer to store some or all of the object's values as attributes. In the following code, XmlAttributeAttribute statements indicate that the public variable Item should be stored as an attribute called Name, the public variable Price should be stored as an attribute called Cost, and the value of the public property procedures Quantity should be stored as an attribute called Number.

```
Public Class OrderedItem
    <XmlAttributeAttribute(AttributeName:="Name")> _
        Public Item As String
    <XmlAttributeAttribute(AttributeName:="Cost")> _
        Public Price As Decimal
    Private m_Quantity As Integer

    <XmlAttributeAttribute(AttributeName:="Number")> _
    Public Property Quantity() As Integer
        Get
            Quantity = m_Quantity
        End Get
        Set(ByVal Value As Integer)
            m_Quantity = Value
```

```
        End Set
    End Property

    Public Sub New()
    End Sub

    Public Sub New( _
      ByVal new_item As String, _
      ByVal new_price As Decimal, _
      ByVal new_quantity As Integer)

        Item = new_item
        Price = new_price
        Quantity = new_quantity
    End Sub
End Class
```

The example program SerializeWithAttributes, shown in Figure 4.3, serializes an array of this kind of OrderedItem object. The code that serializes and deserializes the array is exactly the same as the code used by program SerializeArray. The only difference is in the declaration of the public variables and property procedures supplied by the OrderedItem class.

Example program SerializeWithAttributes produces the following XML serialization. This is easier to read and much more concise than the file produced by program SerializeArray described in the previous section.

```
<?xml version="1.0"?>
<ArrayOfOrderedItem xmlns:xsi="http://www.w3.org/2001/XMLSchema-
instance"
xmlns:xsd="http://www.w3.org/2001/XMLSchema">
  <OrderedItem Name="Brownies" Cost="1.25" Number="3" />
  <OrderedItem Name="Cookies" Cost="0.25" Number="12" />
  <OrderedItem Name="Cupcakes" Cost="0.5" Number="6" />
</ArrayOfOrderedItem>
```

A program does not need to change the names of the items it is storing as attributes. The following code shows how a program might indicate that the Item value should be stored as an attribute with its default name Item.

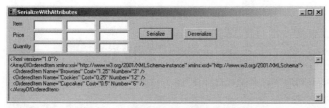

Figure 4.3 Program SerializeWithAttributes serializes and deserializes an array of OrderedItem objects storing data values in tag attributes.

```
<XmlAttributeAttribute()> _
    Public Item As String
```

A program can also save some values as attributes and others in separate tags. The following code indicates that the Item value should be stored in its own tag, and Price and Quantity should be stored in attributes with their default names Price and Quantity.

```
Public Class OrderedItem
    Public Item As String
    <XmlAttributeAttribute()> _
        Public Price As Decimal
    Private m_Quantity As Integer

    <XmlAttributeAttribute()> _
    Public Property Quantity() As Integer
        Get
            Quantity = m_Quantity
        End Get
        Set(ByVal Value As Integer)
            m_Quantity = Value
        End Set
    End Property

    Public Sub New()
    End Sub

    Public Sub New( _
      ByVal new_item As String, _
      ByVal new_price As Decimal, _
      ByVal new_quantity As Integer)

        Item = new_item
        Price = new_price
        Quantity = new_quantity
    End Sub
End Class
```

With these changes, example program SerializeWithAttributes generates the following serialization file.

```
<?xml version="1.0"?>
<ArrayOfOrderedItem xmlns:xsi="http://www.w3.org/2001/XMLSchema-
instance" xmlns:xsd="http://www.w3.org/2001/XMLSchema">
  <OrderedItem Price="1.25" Quantity="3">
    <Item>Brownies</Item>
  </OrderedItem>
  <OrderedItem Price="0.25" Quantity="12">
    <Item>Cookies</Item>
```

```
    </OrderedItem>
    <OrderedItem Price="0.5" Quantity="6">
      <Item>Cupcakes</Item>
    </OrderedItem>
  </ArrayOfOrderedItem>
```

Using XmlAttributeAttribute flags, you can greatly change the way the XmlSerializer object serializes and deserializes objects. It doesn't particularly care which way it does its work. The only thing that really matters is that the programs that serialize and deserialize the objects declare the class being serialized in the same way. If one program creates an XML serialization with values stored in attributes, another program cannot deserialize the file assuming the values are stored in separate tags.

To avoid possible mismatches, you can put the class definition in a separate file and let the serializing and deserializing applications share that file. Then if you make changes to the serialized class, both programs will still have the same view of the class. You might need to write some translation programs to convert any old serializations so they agree with the new format, but at least the programs will stay synchronized in the future.

Subitems

The examples presented so far in this chapter create relatively shallow XML hierarchies. The XmlSerializer class, however, is flexible enough to build deeper hierarchies if it must to represent more complex object arrangements. For example, suppose one class contains a reference to another. If a program serializes the first class, the XmlSerializer will automatically store the subobject's serialization within the main object's serialization.

Example program SerializeSubitem, shown in Figure 4.4, serializes an Order object. The Order class contains a public array of OrderItem objects named Items. When SerializeSubitem tells the XmlSerializer object to serialize the Order object, it automatically serializes the Items array and all of the OrderItems it contains.

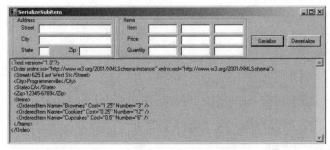

Figure 4.4 Program SerializeSubitem serializes and deserializes an object that contains an array of other objects.

Program SerializeSubitem uses the following class declarations.

```
Public Class Order
    Public Street As String
    Public City As String
    Public State As String
    Public Zip As String
    Public Items() As OrderedItem

    Public Sub New()

    End Sub

    Public Sub New( _
      ByVal new_street As String, _
      ByVal new_city As String, _
      ByVal new_state As String, _
      ByVal new_zip As String)

        Street = new_street
        City = new_city
        State = new_state
        Zip = new_zip
    End Sub
End Class

Public Class OrderedItem
    <XmlAttributeAttribute(AttributeName:="Name")> _
        Public Item As String
    <XmlAttributeAttribute(AttributeName:="Cost")> _
        Public Price As Decimal
    Private m_Quantity As Integer

    <XmlAttributeAttribute(AttributeName:="Number")> _
    Public Property Quantity() As Integer
        Get
            Quantity = m_Quantity
        End Get
        Set(ByVal Value As Integer)
            m_Quantity = Value
        End Set
    End Property

    Public Sub New()
    End Sub

    Public Sub New( _
      ByVal new_item As String, _
      ByVal new_price As Decimal, _
      ByVal new_quantity As Integer)
```

```
        Item = new_item
        Price = new_price
        Quantity = new_quantity
    End Sub
End Class
```

The code program SerializeSubitem uses to serialize and deserialize data is almost identical to the code used by the previous examples. The only difference is in the declaration of the classes it serializes.

Program SerializeSubitem generates the following XML serialization for an Order object containing three OrderedItem objects.

```
<?xml version="1.0"?>
<Order xmlns:xsi="http://www.w3.org/2001/XMLSchema-instance"
xmlns:xsd="http://www.w3.org/2001/XMLSchema">
  <Street>625 East West St</Street>
  <City>Programmerville</City>
  <State>CA</State>
  <Zip>12345-6789</Zip>
  <Items>
    <OrderedItem Name="Brownies" Cost="1.25" Number="3" />
    <OrderedItem Name="Cookies" Cost="0.25" Number="12" />
    <OrderedItem Name="Cupcakes" Cost="0.5" Number="6" />
  </Items>
</Order>
```

Using arrays of objects and objects that contain other objects, an application can serialize and deserialize extremely complicated data hierarchies almost effortlessly. The program just defines the object classes, and the XmlSerializer does the hard part.

Binary Serialization

While normal XML files are textual, Visual Basic's BinaryFormatter class can read and write binary XML files. Binary XML files do not provide all of the features that make XML files useful. In particular, they are not plain text so you cannot view and modify them in a text editor. That makes it harder to debug an application if there is a problem with a binary XML file it must read or write.

On the other hand, binary XML files are smaller than normal XML files so they can be useful when space or transmission bandwidth is at a premium.

Modifying a program that reads or writes normal XML serializations so that it uses binary XML files instead is straightforward. The main change is in creating the object that reads or writes the serialization. Instead of creating an XmlSerializer object, the program creates a BinaryFormatter object. It then attaches the BinaryFormatter object to a stream and calls its Serialize method exactly as it would with an XmlSerializer.

The other change to the code is in the declaration of the classes that the BinaryFormatter will serialize. Those classes must be marked as serializable with a <Serializable()> directive.

Example program SerializeSubitemBinary works exactly as program Serialize-Subitem does except it uses BinaryFormatter objects instead of XmlSerializer objects. The following code shows how program SerializeSubitemBinary declares the Order and OrderedItem classes it serializes. The only change to this code is the addition of the <Serializable()> directive before each class declaration.

```
<Serializable()> _
Public Class Order
    Public Street As String
    Public City As String
    Public State As String
    Public Zip As String
    Public Items() As OrderedItem

    Public Sub New()

    End Sub

    Public Sub New(ByVal new_street As String, ByVal new_city As String,
ByVal new_state As String, ByVal new_zip As String)
        Street = new_street
        City = new_city
        State = new_state
        Zip = new_zip
    End Sub
End Class

<Serializable()> _
Public Class OrderedItem
    <XmlAttributeAttribute(AttributeName:="Name")> _
        Public Item As String
    <XmlAttributeAttribute(AttributeName:="Cost")> _
        Public Price As Decimal
    Private m_Quantity As Integer

    <XmlAttributeAttribute(AttributeName:="Number")> _
    Public Property Quantity() As Integer
        Get
            Quantity = m_Quantity
        End Get
        Set(ByVal Value As Integer)
            m_Quantity = Value
        End Set
    End Property

    Public Sub New()
    End Sub

    Public Sub New(ByVal new_item As String, ByVal new_price As Decimal,
ByVal new_quantity As Integer)
        Item = new_item
```

```
        Price = new_price
        Quantity = new_quantity
    End Sub
End Class
```

The following code shows how program SerializeSubitemBinary serializes and deserializes its data. This is very similar to the code used by program SerializeSubitem except it uses BinaryFormatter objects instead of XmlSerializer objects.

```
' Serialize the data in the TextBoxes.
Private Sub btnSerialize_Click( _
  ByVal sender As System.Object, _
  ByVal e As System.EventArgs) Handles btnSerialize.Click

    Cursor = Cursors.WaitCursor
    txtSerialization.Text = ""
    Refresh()

    ' Make an Order item and load it with the
    ' address information.
    Dim order_info As New Order( _
        txtStreet.Text, txtCity.Text, txtState.Text, txtZip.Text)

    ' Copy the data into OrderedItem objects.
    ReDim order_info.Items(2)
    order_info.Items(0) = New OrderedItem( _
        txtItem0.Text, _
        CDec(txtPrice0.Text), _
        CInt(txtQuantity0.Text))
    order_info.Items(1) = New OrderedItem( _
        txtItem1.Text, _
        CDec(txtPrice1.Text), _
        CInt(txtQuantity1.Text))
    order_info.Items(2) = New OrderedItem( _
        txtItem2.Text, _
        CDec(txtPrice2.Text), _
        CInt(txtQuantity2.Text))

    ' Create a BinaryFormatter.
    Dim binary_formatter As New BinaryFormatter()

    ' Create a FileStream to write with.
    Dim file_stream As New FileStream(m_XMLFile, FileMode.Create)

    ' Serialize the array.
    binary_formatter.Serialize(file_stream, order_info)

    ' Close the FileStream.
    file_stream.Close()

    ' Display the results.
```

```vb
        txtSerialization.Text = "<Binary file>"

        ' Clear the TextBoxes.
        txtStreet.Text = ""
        txtCity.Text = ""
        txtState.Text = ""
        txtZip.Text = ""
        txtItem0.Text = ""
        txtPrice0.Text = ""
        txtQuantity0.Text = ""
        txtItem1.Text = ""
        txtPrice1.Text = ""
        txtQuantity1.Text = ""
        txtItem2.Text = ""
        txtPrice2.Text = ""
        txtQuantity2.Text = ""

        Cursor = Cursors.Default
End Sub

' Deserialize the data in the TextBoxes.
Private Sub btnDeserialize_Click( _
  ByVal sender As System.Object, _
  ByVal e As System.EventArgs) Handles btnDeserialize.Click

        Dim ctl As Control
        For Each ctl In Controls
            If (TypeOf ctl Is TextBox) And _
                (Not (ctl Is txtSerialization)) _
            Then
                 ctl.Text = ""
            End If
        Next ctl
        Cursor = Cursors.WaitCursor
        Refresh()

        ' Create a BinaryFormatter.
        Dim binary_formatter As New BinaryFormatter()

        ' Create an XmlTextReader to read with.
        Dim file_stream As New FileStream(m_XMLFile, FileMode.Open)

        ' Read the item from the serialization.
        Dim order_info As Order
        order_info = CType(binary_formatter.Deserialize(file_stream), Order)
        file_stream.Close()

        ' Copy the data into the TextBoxes.
        With order_info
            txtStreet.Text = .Street
            txtCity.Text = .City
```

```
            txtState.Text = .State
            txtZip.Text = .Zip
        End With
        With order_info.Items(0)
            txtItem0.Text = .Item
            txtPrice0.Text = .Price
            txtQuantity0.Text = .Quantity
        End With
        With order_info.Items(1)
            txtItem1.Text = .Item
            txtPrice1.Text = .Price
            txtQuantity1.Text = .Quantity
        End With
        With order_info.Items(2)
            txtItem2.Text = .Item
            txtPrice2.Text = .Price
            txtQuantity2.Text = .Quantity
        End With

        ' Clear the serialization.
        txtSerialization.Text = ""

        Cursor = Cursors.Default
    End Sub
```

If you open the serialization file in a text editor, you can pick out some readable text, but much of the file is unreadable.

Binary Data

Normal XML files are textual, and they can easily hold textual values such as strings and numbers converted into strings. They do not naturally hold binary data, however. For example, you normally don't store images in a textual XML file.

The BinaryFormatter class introduced in the previous section serializes and deserializes data in a binary XML file, and the data it manipulates can be either text or binary.

Example program SerializeImage, shown in Figure 4.5, uses BinaryFormatter objects to serialize and deserialize an image in a binary XML file.

Figure 4.5 Program SerializeImage serializes and deserializes an image in a binary XML file.

The following code shows how program SerializeImage serializes and deserializes its image.

```vb
Private Sub btnSerialize_Click( _
  ByVal sender As System.Object, _
  ByVal e As System.EventArgs) Handles btnSerialize.Click

    Cursor = Cursors.WaitCursor
    txtSerialization.Text = ""
    Refresh()

    ' Create a BinaryFormatter.
    Dim binary_formatter As New BinaryFormatter()

    ' Create a FileStream to write with.
    Dim file_stream As New FileStream(m_XMLFile, FileMode.Create)

    ' Serialize picImage.
    binary_formatter.Serialize(file_stream, picImage.Image)

    ' Close the FileStream.
    file_stream.Close()

    ' Display the results.
    txtSerialization.Text = "<Binary file>"

    ' Clear the image.
    picImage.Image = Nothing
    picImage.SetBounds(0, 0, m_ImageWid, m_ImageHgt)

    Cursor = Cursors.Default
End Sub

Private Sub btnDeserialize_Click( _
  ByVal sender As System.Object, _
  ByVal e As System.EventArgs) Handles btnDeserialize.Click

    Cursor = Cursors.WaitCursor
    Refresh()

    ' Create a BinaryFormatter.
    Dim binary_formatter As New BinaryFormatter()

    ' Create an XmlTextReader to read with.
    Dim file_stream As New FileStream(m_XMLFile, FileMode.Open)

    ' Read the item from the serialization.
    picImage.Image = CType( _
        binary_formatter.Deserialize(file_stream), Image)
    picImage.SetBounds(0, 0, m_ImageWid, m_ImageHgt)
    file_stream.Close()

    ' Clear the serialization text.
    txtSerialization.Text = ""

    Cursor = Cursors.Default
End Sub
```

This program serializes a single Image object. You could modify the techniques described in the previous sections to serialize arrays or objects that contain images, values, and other objects.

SOAP Serialization

Previous examples have built normal XML files and binary XML files. A third type of XML file is a file formatted for SOAP (Simple Object Access Protocol) applications. SOAP uses a normal, though somewhat elaborate, XML file packaged inside a SOAP envelope. Web Services use SOAP to package requests and responses within an XML package. For more information, see Chapter 8, "Web Services."

Creating a SOAP serialization is just as easy as creating a binary serialization. Instead of using an XmlSerializer or BinaryFormatter object to serialize and deserialize objects, the program uses a SoapFormatter object. Otherwise, the program serializes and deserializes objects just as it would for a binary serialization.

One catch to this method is that the program must import the System.Runtime.Serialization.Formatters.Soap namespace. Normally that namespace is not available to the program so you need to add a reference to the DLL that defines the namespace. Right-click on the References entry in the Solution Explorer and select Add Reference. Locate the System.Runtime.Serialization.Formatters.Soap.dll entry, double-click it, and click the OK button. Now you can successfully add the following line to the beginning of the program's code.

```
Imports System.Runtime.Serialization.Formatters.Soap
```

At this point, the program can create and use SoapFormatter objects.

Example program SerializeSubitemSoap, shown in Figure 4.6, serializes an object that contains an array of other objects. It is very similar to the SerializeSubitem and SerializeSubitemBinary programs except it uses a SOAP serialization instead of a normal text or binary serialization. Note that the class definitions must be marked serializable just as they must be for a binary serialization. See the *Binary Serialization* section earlier in this chapter for more information on marking classes as serializable.

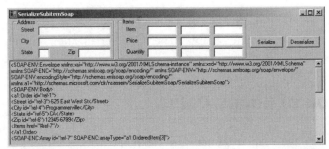

Figure 4.6 Program SerializeSubitemSoap uses SOAP serializations for an object containing an array of other objects.

The following code shows a SOAP serialization produced by program Serialize-SubitemSoap. The indentation was added to make the document's structure more obvious and is not normally added by the SoapFormatter.

```
<SOAP-ENV:Envelope xmlns:xsi="http://www.w3.org/2001/XMLSchema-instance"
xmlns:xsd="http://www.w3.org/2001/XMLSchema"
xmlns:SOAP-ENC="http://schemas.xmlsoap.org/soap/encoding/"
xmlns:SOAP-ENV="http://schemas.xmlsoap.org/soap/envelope/"
SOAP-ENV:encodingStyle="http://schemas.xmlsoap.org/soap/encoding/"
xmlns:a1="http://schemas.microsoft.com/clr/nsassem/SerializeSubitemSoap
/SerializeSubitemSoap">
  <SOAP-ENV:Body>
    <a1:Order id="ref-1">
      <Street id="ref-3">625 East West St</Street>
      <City id="ref-4">Programmerville</City>
      <State id="ref-5">CA</State>
      <Zip id="ref-6">12345-6789</Zip>
      <Items href="#ref-7"/>
    </a1:Order>
    <SOAP-ENC:Array id="ref-7" SOAP-ENC:arrayType="a1:OrderedItem[3]">
      <item href="#ref-8"/>
      <item href="#ref-9"/>
      <item href="#ref-10"/>
    </SOAP-ENC:Array>
    <a1:OrderedItem id="ref-8">
      <Item id="ref-11">Brownies</Item>
      <Price>1.25</Price>
      <m_Quantity>3</m_Quantity>
    </a1:OrderedItem>
    <a1:OrderedItem id="ref-9">
      <Item id="ref-12">Cookies</Item>
      <Price>0.25</Price>
      <m_Quantity>12</m_Quantity>
    </a1:OrderedItem>
    <a1:OrderedItem id="ref-10">
      <Item id="ref-13">Cupcakes</Item>
      <Price>0.5</Price>
      <m_Quantity>6</m_Quantity>
    </a1:OrderedItem>
  </SOAP-ENV:Body>
</SOAP-ENV:Envelope>
```

Compare this document to the output produced by program SerializeSubitem described in the *Subitems* section earlier in this chapter. The SOAP serialization is much more verbose.

SOAP Serialization of Binary Data

Like the BinaryFormatter class, the SoapFormatter class can make a serialization that includes binary data such as images. Unlike the BinaryFormatter, however, the Soap-Formatter produces a textual serialization.

Example program SerializeImageSoap uses the following code fragment to serialize the image displayed by the picImage PictureBox control.

```
' Create a SoapFormatter.
Dim soap_formatter As New SoapFormatter()

' Create a FileStream to write with.
Dim file_stream As New FileStream(m_XMLFile, FileMode.Create)

' Serialize picImage.
soap_formatter.Serialize(file_stream, picImage.Image)

' Close the FileStream.
file_stream.Close()
```

The program uses the following code fragment to deserialize the XML file to restore the PictureBox's image.

```
' Create a SoapFormatter.
Dim soap_formatter As New SoapFormatter()

' Create an XmlTextReader to read with.
Dim file_stream As New FileStream(m_XMLFile, FileMode.Open)

' Read the item from the serialization.
picImage.Image = CType(soap_formatter.Deserialize(file_stream), Image)
picImage.SetBounds(0, 0, m_ImageWid, m_ImageHgt)
file_stream.Close()
```

The following code shows the SOAP serialization generated by program SerializeImageSoap. A huge amount of data has been removed from inside the SOAP-ENC:Array tag. That data contains the textual encoding of the image.

```
<SOAP-ENV:Envelope
xmlns:xsi="http://www.w3.org/2001/XMLSchema-instance"
xmlns:xsd="http://www.w3.org/2001/XMLSchema"
xmlns:SOAP-ENC="http://schemas.xmlsoap.org/soap/encoding/"
xmlns:SOAP-ENV="http://schemas.xmlsoap.org/soap/envelope/"
SOAP-ENV:encodingStyle="http://schemas.xmlsoap.org/soap/encoding/"
xmlns:a1="http://schemas.microsoft.com/clr/nsassem/System.Drawing
/System.Drawing">
<SOAP-ENV:Body>
  <a1:Bitmap id="ref-1">
    <Data href="#ref-3"/>
  </a1:Bitmap>
  <SOAP-ENC:Array id="ref-3" xsi:type="SOAP-ENC:Base64">Qk02wAAAAAAADY
    ... Lots of data deleted ...
    //+A//+A//+A//+A//+A//+A//+A//+A//+A//+A</SOAP-ENC:Array>
</SOAP-ENV:Body>
</SOAP-ENV:Envelope>
```

The SOAP serialization of binary data such as images is all text, but it contains a series of incomprehensible gibberish that's not very meaningful until you deserialize it and convert it back into an image. Because the data is unreadable, you lose one of the main benefits of a text-based XML file: the fact that you can read and understand it.

As long as you won't be able to understand the file anyway, you might consider using a binary serialization like the ones described in the section *Binary Data* earlier in this chapter. Those serializations are even less readable, but they are smaller and BinaryFormatter objects seem to be faster than SoapFormatter objects.

Networks

XML files have a tree-like hierarchical structure. That makes it easy to store hierarchical data in them. Tables containing records made up of fields fit naturally in XML files. Deeper hierarchies such as corporate organization charts and inheritance hierarchies also fit naturally in XML files.

It is less obvious, though, how to fit network data into an XML document tree. In a network, there are no clear parent-child relationships, and the network probably doesn't have a single root node. It is easy to map the tree-like data on the left in Figure 4.7 into an XML file. It is less obvious how to store the data in the network on the right.

The example shown in Figure 4.7 is a graphical network, but any data structure that contains links that form cycles would raise the same issues. For example, suppose a program has Department objects that each contain a list of references to Employee objects representing the employees in the department. Suppose each Employee object contains a reference to the Department object that contains it. The circular reference loop from Department to Employee and back to Department ensures that the data structure is not a tree.

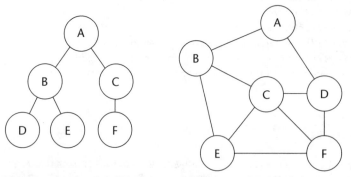

Figure 4.7 The tree-like data on the left maps intuitively into an XML document while the network data on the right does not.

The key to serializing this kind of network data is to assign an index to each of the nodes. Then store the nodes separately, giving each a list of the indexes of the nodes to which it should be attached. The following XML code shows how you might store the network on the right in Figure 4.7.

```
<AllNodes>
  <Node Index="A">
    <Neighbor Index="B" />
    <Neighbor Index="D" />
  </Node>
  <Node Index="B">
    <Neighbor Index="A" />
    <Neighbor Index="C" />
    <Neighbor Index="E" />
  </Node>
  <Node Index="C">
    <Neighbor Index="B" />
    <Neighbor Index="D" />
    <Neighbor Index="E" />
    <Neighbor Index="F" />
  </Node>
  <Node Index="D">
    <Neighbor Index="A" />
    <Neighbor Index="C" />
    <Neighbor Index="F" />
  </Node>
  <Node Index="E">
    <Neighbor Index="B" />
    <Neighbor Index="C" />
    <Neighbor Index="F" />
  </Node>
  <Node Index="F">
    <Neighbor Index="C" />
    <Neighbor Index="D" />
    <Neighbor Index="E" />
  </Node>
</AllNodes>
```

To deserialize this data, a program creates new objects for the individual Node entries. It then uses the Neighbor information to create references connecting the node objects.

BinaryFormatter

The idea for serializing and deserializing networks is relatively straightforward, but it is too complicated for the XmlSerializer class to handle for you. Fortunately, the Binary-Formatter and SoapFormatter classes can serialize and deserialize this kind of data automatically.

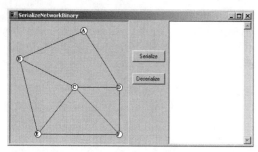

Figure 4.8　Program SerializeNetworkBinary serializes and deserializes network data.

Example program SerializeNetworkBinary, shown in Figure 4.8, serializes and deserializes network data. This program has no network editing features; its data is hard-coded into its Form_Load event handler.

Program SerializeNetworkBinary uses the following code to serialize and deserialize its network data. The variable m_RootNode contains a reference to the node A, but it could refer to any node in the network. As long as the BinaryFormatter object can follow object references from this node to every other node in the network, it will be able to save all of the network data.

```
Private Sub btnSerialize_Click( _
  ByVal sender As System.Object, _
  ByVal e As System.EventArgs) Handles btnSerialize.Click

    Cursor = Cursors.WaitCursor
    txtSerialization.Text = ""
    Refresh()

    ' Create a new BinaryFormatter.
    Dim binary_formatter As New BinaryFormatter()

    ' Create a FileStream to write with.
    Dim file_stream As New FileStream(m_XMLFile, FileMode.Create)

    ' Serialize m_RootNode.
    binary_formatter.Serialize(file_stream, m_RootNode)

    ' Close the FileStream.
    file_stream.Close()

    ' Display the results.
    txtSerialization.Text = "<Binary file>"

    ' Clear the network.
    m_RootNode = Nothing
    DrawNetwork(picNetwork.CreateGraphics())

    Cursor = Cursors.Default
```

```
End Sub

Private Sub btnDeserialize_Click( _
  ByVal sender As System.Object, _
  ByVal e As System.EventArgs) Handles btnDeserialize.Click

    Cursor = Cursors.WaitCursor
    picNetwork.CreateGraphics.Clear(picNetwork.BackColor)
    Refresh()

    ' Create a new BinaryFormatter.
    Dim binary_formatter As New BinaryFormatter()

    ' Create a FileStream to read with.
    Dim file_stream As New FileStream(m_XMLFile, FileMode.Open)

    ' Read the item from the serialization.
    m_RootNode = CType(binary_formatter.Deserialize(file_stream), Node)
    file_stream.Close()

    ' Display the network.
    DrawNetwork(picNetwork.CreateGraphics())

    ' Clear the serialization text.
    txtSerialization.Text = ""

    Cursor = Cursors.Default
End Sub
```

This code works only if the BinaryFormatter object can follow links from the node it serializes, in this case m_RootNode, to all of the other links in the network. If it cannot find some of the nodes, they will not be serialized. Figure 4.9 shows three networks that may not be serialized properly. The network on the left is disconnected so there is no node from which the BinaryFormatter object can reach every other node.

The middle network looks connected, but due to the directions of the links, there is no node from which the BinaryFormatter can reach every other node.

In the right network, no node has a link that leads to node C, so the BinaryFormatter cannot reach node C if it starts serializing from node A, B, D, E, or F. It can reach all of the nodes if it starts at node C, however, so this network is serializable.

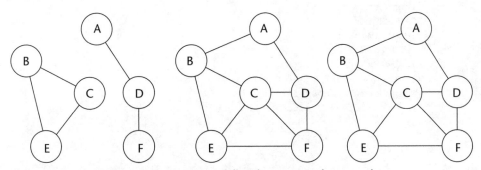

Figure 4.9   BinaryFormatter may not serialize these networks correctly.

If you cannot easily tell whether a BinaryFormatter will be able to reach every node in the network from a given node, create a new dummy root node and connect it to all of the other nodes. Then you can serialize the network using that node as the Binary-Formatter's starting point because you know it contains links to all of the other nodes.

SoapFormatter

Like the BinaryFormatter, the SoapFormatter can also serialize networks. Example program SerializeNetworkSoap works exactly as program SerializeNetworkBinary does except it uses a SoapFormatter instead of a BinaryFormatter.

Because the XML serialization produced by the SoapFormatter object is a SOAP XML file, it is plain text that you can read. The following code shows the XML file produced by program SerializeNetworkSoap.

If you study the file, you will see that it follows the strategy for serializing networks described earlier. Each network node is represented by an a1:Node tag and has an id attribute. Each node's Neighbors entry contains a reference to an id value that identifies a SOAP-ENC:Array tag.

A SOAP-ENC:Array tag contains the id attribute values of the nodes that are contained in the corresponding Neighbors array in the original network.

```
<SOAP-ENV:Envelope xmlns:xsi="http://www.w3.org/2001/XMLSchema-instance"
xmlns:xsd="http://www.w3.org/2001/XMLSchema"
xmlns:SOAP-ENC="http://schemas.xmlsoap.org/soap/encoding/"
xmlns:SOAP-ENV="http://schemas.xmlsoap.org/soap/envelope/"
SOAP-ENV:encodingStyle="http://schemas.xmlsoap.org/soap/encoding/"
xmlns:a1="http://schemas.microsoft.com/clr/nsassem/SerializeNetworkSoap
/SerializeNetworkSoap">
  <SOAP-ENV:Body>
    <a1:Node id="ref-1">
      <X>160</X>
      <Y>20</Y>
      <Caption id="ref-3">A</Caption>
      <Neighbors href="#ref-4"/>
      <Visited>false</Visited>
    </a1:Node>
    <SOAP-ENC:Array id="ref-4" SOAP-ENC:arrayType="a1:Node[2]">
      <item href="#ref-5"/>
      <item href="#ref-6"/>
    </SOAP-ENC:Array>
    <a1:Node id="ref-5">
      <X>20</X>
      <Y>80</Y>
      <Caption id="ref-7">B</Caption>
      <Neighbors href="#ref-8"/>
      <Visited>false</Visited>
    </a1:Node>
    <a1:Node id="ref-6">
      <X>240</X>
      <Y>140</Y>
      <Caption id="ref-9">D</Caption>
```

```
      <Neighbors href="#ref-10"/>
      <Visited>false</Visited>
    </a1:Node>
    <SOAP-ENC:Array id="ref-8" SOAP-ENC:arrayType="a1:Node[3]">
      <item href="#ref-1"/>
      <item href="#ref-11"/>
      <item href="#ref-12"/>
    </SOAP-ENC:Array>
    <SOAP-ENC:Array id="ref-10" SOAP-ENC:arrayType="a1:Node[3]">
      <item href="#ref-1"/>
      <item href="#ref-11"/>
      <item href="#ref-13"/>
    </SOAP-ENC:Array>
    <a1:Node id="ref-11">
      <X>140</X>
      <Y>140</Y>
      <Caption id="ref-14">C</Caption>
      <Neighbors href="#ref-15"/>
      <Visited>false</Visited>
    </a1:Node>
    <a1:Node id="ref-12">
      <X>60</X>
      <Y>240</Y>
      <Caption id="ref-16">E</Caption>
      <Neighbors href="#ref-17"/>
      <Visited>false</Visited>
    </a1:Node>
    <a1:Node id="ref-13">
      <X>240</X>
      <Y>240</Y>
      <Caption id="ref-18">F</Caption>
      <Neighbors href="#ref-19"/>
      <Visited>false</Visited>
    </a1:Node>
    <SOAP-ENC:Array id="ref-15" SOAP-ENC:arrayType="a1:Node[4]">
      <item href="#ref-5"/>
      <item href="#ref-6"/>
      <item href="#ref-12"/>
    <item href="#ref-13"/>
    </SOAP-ENC:Array>
    <SOAP-ENC:Array id="ref-17" SOAP-ENC:arrayType="a1:Node[3]">
      <item href="#ref-5"/>
      <item href="#ref-11"/>
      <item href="#ref-13"/>
    </SOAP-ENC:Array>
    <SOAP-ENC:Array id="ref-19" SOAP-ENC:arrayType="a1:Node[3]">
      <item href="#ref-11"/>
      <item href="#ref-6"/>
      <item href="#ref-12"/>
    </SOAP-ENC:Array>
  </SOAP-ENV:Body>
</SOAP-ENV:Envelope>
```

The SOAP result is a little less concise than the previously described strategy, but it is just as effective.

Improved Control

The XmlSerializer, BinaryFormatter, and SoapFormatter classes allow you to serialize and deserialize complex data structures with practically no effort. Sometimes, however, the default serializations don't give you quite enough control. For example, consider the following Temperature class.

```
' Stores a temperature and returns it in Celsius or Fahrenheit.
Public Class Temperature
    ' Constructors.
    Public Sub New()
        m_TemperatureCelsius = 0
    End Sub

    Public Sub New(ByVal temperature_celsius As Double)
        m_TemperatureCelsius = temperature_celsius
    End Sub

    ' Store the temperature in degrees Celsius.
    Private m_TemperatureCelsius As Double

    ' Get/set the temperature in degrees Fahrenheit.
    Public Property TemperatureFahrenheit() As Double
        Get
            TemperatureFahrenheit = m_TemperatureCelsius * 9 / 5 + 32
        End Get
        Set(ByVal Value As Double)
            m_TemperatureCelsius = (Value - 32) / 9 * 5
        End Set
    End Property

    ' Get/set the temperature in degrees Celsius.
    Public Property TemperatureCelsius() As Double
        Get
            TemperatureCelsius = m_TemperatureCelsius
        End Get
        Set(ByVal Value As Double)
            m_TemperatureCelsius = Value
        End Set
    End Property
End Class
```

This class has two sets of public property procedures: TemperatureFahrenheit and TemperatureCelsius. If you use the XmlSerializer, BinaryFormatter, or SoapFormatter classes to serialize an instance of this class, the serializer adds both public procedure values to the serialization so the resulting XML file includes both TemperatureFahrenheit and TemperatureCelsius values.

Example program ISerializableDuplicate uses an XmlFormatter to serialize a Temperature object and produce the following XML serialization.

```
<?xml version="1.0"?>
<Temperature xmlns:xsi="http://www.w3.org/2001/XMLSchema-instance"
xmlns:xsd="http://www.w3.org/2001/XMLSchema">
   <TemperatureCelsius>0</TemperatureCelsius>
   <TemperatureFahrenheit>32</TemperatureFahrenheit>
</Temperature>
```

What the serializer cannot tell is that the two temperature values are both derived from the single private variable m_TemperatureCelsius so there is no reason to save both values. Ideally, the program would save m_TemperatureCelsius instead of the values produced by the public property procedures.

The BinaryFormatter and SoapFormatter classes provide features that let you control an object's serialization and deserialization completely. In this example, they let you specify that the Temperature object's serialization should store the private value m_TemperatureCelsius and not its public property procedure values.

The following code shows how the new Temperature class manages its own serialization. The BinaryFormatter and SoapFormatter classes work as usual.

The new version of the Temperature class is marked serializable with the <Serializable()> attribute. The class uses the Implements statement to indicate that it provides the routines defined by the ISerializable interface.

One of the methods defined by the ISerializable interface is GetObjectData. When the formatter builds the object's serialization, it calls this method passing it a SerializationInfo object to hold the serialization data. The Temperature object's GetObjectData routine calls the SerializationInfo object's AddValue method to save its m_TemperatureCelsius value. It names this value Temp in the serialization.

Notice how the GetObjectData routine is declared. It is declared Overridable. Its declaration also uses the Implements keyword to indicate that it implements the GetObjectData routine defined by the ISerializable interface.

When it deserializes the Temperature object, the formatter calls a special deserialization constructor. The constructor takes two parameters: a SerializationInfo object and a StreamingContext object. The constructor can use the SerializationInfo object's GetString, GetDouble, GetInteger, and other methods to retrieve the values that were stored in the serialization by GetObjectData.

The rest of the Temperature class is the same as in the previous version.

```
' Stores a temperature and returns it in Celsius or Fahrenheit.
<Serializable()> _
Public Class Temperature
    Implements System.Runtime.Serialization.ISerializable

    ' Save the object's serialization information.
    Overridable Sub GetObjectData(ByVal info As SerializationInfo, _
        ByVal context As StreamingContext) _
```

```vb
Implements System.Runtime.Serialization.ISerializable.GetObjectData
    info.AddValue("Temp", m_TemperatureCelsius)
End Sub


' Constructors.
Public Sub New()
    m_TemperatureCelsius = 0
End Sub


Public Sub New(ByVal temperature_celsius As Double)
    m_TemperatureCelsius = temperature_celsius
End Sub


' Deserialization constructor.
Protected Sub New(ByVal info As SerializationInfo, _
  ByVal context As StreamingContext)

    m_TemperatureCelsius = info.GetDouble("Temp")
End Sub


' Store the temperature in degrees Celsius.
Private m_TemperatureCelsius As Double

' Get/set the temperature in degrees Fahrenheit.
Public Property TemperatureFahrenheit() As Double
    Get
        TemperatureFahrenheit = m_TemperatureCelsius * 9 / 5 + 32
    End Get
    Set(ByVal Value As Double)
        m_TemperatureCelsius = (Value - 32) / 9 * 5
    End Set
End Property


' Get/set the temperature in degrees Celsius.
Public Property TemperatureCelsius() As Double
    Get
        TemperatureCelsius = m_TemperatureCelsius
    End Get
    Set(ByVal Value As Double)
        m_TemperatureCelsius = Value
    End Set
End Property
End Class
```

When a class takes over its serialization by implementing the ISerializable interface, the formatter no longer tries to figure out how to serialize the object itself. It relies completely on the GetObjectData method and the deserialization constructor. In this example, that means the application no longer stores the public TemperatureCelsius and TemperatureFahrenheit values in the serialization.

Example program ISerializableBinary uses a BinaryFormatter to serialize and dese-rialize this new Temperature class. Because the result is a binary XML file, you cannot easily verify that the serialization contains a single value named Temp. If you open the file in WordPad, you will see the text Temp in the file, but that's not complete proof that the file is correct.

Example program ISerializableSoap uses a SoapFormatter instead of a BinaryFor-matter. This program produces the following textual XML file. Here you can clearly see that the Temperature object is stored with a single Temp value.

```
<SOAP-ENV:Envelope xmlns:xsi="http://www.w3.org/2001/XMLSchema-instance"
xmlns:xsd="http://www.w3.org/2001/XMLSchema"
xmlns:SOAP-ENC="http://schemas.xmlsoap.org/soap/encoding/"
xmlns:SOAP-ENV="http://schemas.xmlsoap.org/soap/envelope/"
SOAP-ENV:encodingStyle="http://schemas.xmlsoap.org/soap/encoding/"
xmlns:a1="http://schemas.microsoft.com/clr/nsassem/ISerializableSoap
/ISerializableSoap">
  <SOAP-ENV:Body>
    <a1:Temperature id="ref-1">
      <Temp>24</Temp>
    </a1:Temperature>
  </SOAP-ENV:Body>
</SOAP-ENV:Envelope>
```

Interprogram Communication

All of the examples discussed so far in this chapter have made an important implicit assumption: They assume that the program reading a serialization is the same pro-gram that originally wrote it. For programs that use the XmlDocument object to read and write serializations, this isn't an issue. For programs that use the SoapFormatter or BinaryFormatter classes, however, only the program that wrote the serialization is able to read it.

Example program SerializeOne described near the beginning of this chapter uses an XmlDocument object to produce the following XML file.

```
<?xml version="1.0"?>
<OrderedItem xmlns:xsi="http://www.w3.org/2001/XMLSchema-instance"
xmlns:xsd="http://www.w3.org/2001/XMLSchema">
  <Item>Cookies</Item>
  <Price>0.25</Price>
  <Quantity>12</Quantity>
</OrderedItem>
```

If you look closely at this file, you will see nothing that ties the XML document to this particular program. This is a simple XML file that any program can read.

On the other hand, take a look at the following output produced by program Serial-izeSubitemSoap.

```
<SOAP-ENV:Envelope xmlns:xsi="http://www.w3.org/2001/XMLSchema-instance"
xmlns:xsd="http://www.w3.org/2001/XMLSchema"
xmlns:SOAP-ENC="http://schemas.xmlsoap.org/soap/encoding/"
xmlns:SOAP-ENV="http://schemas.xmlsoap.org/soap/envelope/"
SOAP-ENV:encodingStyle="http://schemas.xmlsoap.org/soap/encoding/"
xmlns:a1="http://schemas.microsoft.com/clr/nsassem/SerializeSubitemSoap
/SerializeSubitemSoap">
  <SOAP-ENV:Body>
    <a1:Order id="ref-1">
      <Street id="ref-3">625 East West St</Street>
      <City id="ref-4">Programmerville</City>
      <State id="ref-5">CA</State>
      <Zip id="ref-6">12345-6789</Zip>
      <Items href="#ref-7"/>
    </a1:Order>
    <SOAP-ENC:Array id="ref-7" SOAP-ENC:arrayType="a1:OrderedItem[3]">
      <item href="#ref-8"/>
      <item href="#ref-9"/>
      <item href="#ref-10"/>
    </SOAP-ENC:Array>
    <a1:OrderedItem id="ref-8">
      <Item id="ref-11">Brownies</Item>
      <Price>1.25</Price>
      <m_Quantity>3</m_Quantity>
    </a1:OrderedItem>
    <a1:OrderedItem id="ref-9">
      <Item id="ref-12">Cookies</Item>
      <Price>0.25</Price>
      <m_Quantity>12</m_Quantity>
    </a1:OrderedItem>
    <a1:OrderedItem id="ref-10">
      <Item id="ref-13">Cupcakes</Item>
      <Price>0.5</Price>
      <m_Quantity>6</m_Quantity>
    </a1:OrderedItem>
  </SOAP-ENV:Body>
</SOAP-ENV:Envelope>
```

This file places all of its data object references in the a1 namespace. For example, the file represents an Order object with the tag a1:Order. The file defines the a1 namespace with the following statement.

```
xmlns:a1="http://schemas.microsoft.com/clr/nsassem/SerializeSubitemSoap
/SerializeSubitemSoap"
```

The end of this statement includes the program's assembly name and root namespace. In this case, these are both SerializeSubitemSoap.

If another program tries to load this file using a SoapFormatter but it has a different assembly name or root namespace, it will fail with the following error.

```
Soap Parser Error System.Runtime.Serialization.SerializationException:
Parse Error, no assembly associated with Xml key a1 DataClass
```

What this is trying to say is that the program doesn't contain the SerializeSubitem-Soap assembly it needs to properly define the a1 namespace as specified in the XML document.

Similarly, if a program tries to read a binary XML file produced by a BinaryFormatter in a program with a different assembly name or root namespace, the program will fail with this error.

```
File or assembly name Writer, or one of its dependencies, was not found.
```

Shared Namespaces

One way to solve this problem is to make the programs that read and write the XML document use the same assembly name and root namespace. To assign the assembly name and root namespace, right-click on the project in the Solution Explorer and select properties. Be sure you right-click the project and not the solution, which probably has the same name. You should see the properties dialog shown in Figure 4.10.

Enter the assembly name and root namespace you want the program to use and click OK.

Repeat these steps for both the program that writes the XML document and the program that reads it. As long as the two programs use the same assembly name and root namespace, they can work with the same SOAP or Binary XML serializations.

Example programs SoapWriter and SoapReader demonstrate this approach. Both use the assembly name SoapWriterAssembly and the root namespace SoapWriterNamespace. They both use the same DataClass and SubClass objects shown in the following code to serialize and deserialize data.

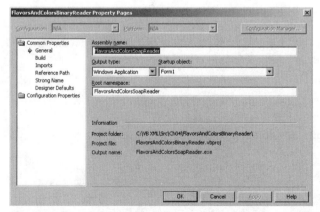

Figure 4.10 The project property dialog lets you specify the program's assembly name and root namespace.

A DataClass object contains two public string variables and a public array containing two SubClass objects. Each SubClass object contains two public string values.

```
<Serializable()> _
Public Class DataClass
    Public Value1 As String
    Public Value2 As String
    Public SubData() As SubClass = {New SubClass(), New SubClass()}

    Public Sub New( _
      ByVal value_1 As String, _
      ByVal value_2 As String, _
      ByVal subvalue_11 As String, _
      ByVal subvalue_12 As String, _
      ByVal subvalue_21 As String, _
      ByVal subvalue_22 As String)
        Value1 = value_1
        Value2 = value_2
        SubData(0).SubData1 = subvalue_11
        SubData(0).SubData2 = subvalue_12
        SubData(1).SubData1 = subvalue_21
        SubData(1).SubData2 = subvalue_22
    End Sub
End Class

<Serializable()> _
Public Class SubClass
    Public SubData1 As String
    Public SubData2 As String
End Class
```

Run the SoapWriter program and enter values in its text boxes. When you click the Serialize button, the program copies the text box values into a DataClass object and its SubClass child objects. It then uses a SoapFormatter object to serialize the DataClass object and its subobjects. The following code shows the resulting XML document. Notice that the document uses the program's namespace and assembly name in the definition of the a1 namespace.

```
<SOAP-ENV:Envelope
xmlns:xsi="http://www.w3.org/2001/XMLSchema-instance"
xmlns:xsd="http://www.w3.org/2001/XMLSchema"
xmlns:SOAP-ENC="http://schemas.xmlsoap.org/soap/encoding/"
xmlns:SOAP-ENV="http://schemas.xmlsoap.org/soap/envelope/"
SOAP-ENV:encodingStyle="http://schemas.xmlsoap.org/soap/encoding/"
xmlns:a1="http://schemas.microsoft.com/clr/nsassem/SoapWriterNamespace
/SoapWriterAssembly">
<SOAP-ENV:Body>
<a1:DataClass id="ref-1">
<Value1 id="ref-3">Pie</Value1>
<Value2 id="ref-4">Cake</Value2>
```

```
<SubData href="#ref-5"/>
</a1:DataClass>
<SOAP-ENC:Array id="ref-5" SOAP-ENC:arrayType="a1:SubClass[2]">
<item href="#ref-6"/>
<item href="#ref-7"/>
</SOAP-ENC:Array>
<a1:SubClass id="ref-6">
<SubData1 id="ref-8">Apple</SubData1>
<SubData2 id="ref-9">Peach</SubData2>
</a1:SubClass>
<a1:SubClass id="ref-7">
<SubData1 id="ref-10">Chocolate</SubData1>
<SubData2 id="ref-11">Lemon</SubData2>
</a1:SubClass>
</SOAP-ENV:Body>
</SOAP-ENV:Envelope>
```

Copy the data file into the SoapReader program's Data directory and run that program. When you click the Deserialize button, the program uses a SoapFormatter to load the XML document into a DataClass object. Because this program uses the same assembly name and root namespace as the SoapWriter program, it can load this file correctly. After it loads the file, the program displays the deserialized values in its text boxes.

Example programs BinaryWriter and BinaryReader demonstrate the same approach for binary XML files. These programs use the exact same code as the SoapWriter and SoapReader program except they use BinaryFormatter objects instead of SoapFormatter objects.

Shared Class Libraries

Making the serialization writer and reader programs use the same assembly name and root namespace works, but it has some limitations. First, it doesn't really obey the spirit of assembly names and root namespaces. Those values should uniquely describe the object to which they are assigned. Giving two different programs the same values is similar to giving them the same name. In the sense that they read and write the same kinds of serializations, that is reasonable. In every other sense, that's a bit confusing.

A more important problem with this method is that it prevents a program from reading two serializations written by two other different programs. If the two writer applications have root namespaces Namespace1 and Namespace2, the reader program cannot have both namespaces at the same time.

Finally, programs SoapReader and SoapWriter contain duplicate code. They both contain the DataClass and SubClass classes. If the code defining these classes changes in either program, the two programs will not work together until the same change is made to the other program. While the two programs and their serialization files are out of synch, they will not work properly. This issue may initially seem unrelated to the problem at hand. In fact, it points the way to a solution.

To solve these problems, make a new class library project and copy the data class definitions into it. Assign the class library an assembly name and root namespace as described in the previous section. Select the Build menu's Build command to make Visual Basic compile the library and create a DLL file.

Next, remove the data class definitions from the XML document writer program. In the Solution Explorer, right-click on References and select Add Reference. Click the Browse button and find the DLL you just created. Select it and click OK. Now the program can use the data class in its code, but the class is still defined in its own DLL.

Repeat these steps for the program that deserializes the data. The serialization and deserialization programs both refer to the same DLL. The DLL has its own assembly name and root namespace so the SoapFormatter used by the two programs uses the same assembly name and root namespace when serializing or deserializing.

The example programs DataClassSoapWriter and DataClassSoapReader demonstrate this approach. The DataClass library defines the data structure they serialize and deserialize.

The following code shows the most interesting parts of the DataClassSoapWriter program. Note that the program imports the DataClassNamespace. This is the namespace defined by the DataClass library. Importing it lets the program create a new Data-Class object without referring to it as DataClassNamespace.DataClass.

```
Imports System.IO
Imports System.Runtime.Serialization.Formatters.Soap
Imports DataClassNamespace

Public Class Form1
    Inherits System.Windows.Forms.Form

    Private Sub btnSerialize_Click( _
      ByVal sender As System.Object, _
      ByVal e As System.EventArgs) Handles btnSerialize.Click

        Cursor = Cursors.WaitCursor
        Refresh()

        ' Load the values into a DataClass object.
        Dim data_object As New DataClass()
        With data_object
            .Value1 = txtValue1.Text
            .Value2 = txtValue2.Text
            .Value3 = txtValue3.Text
        End With

        ' Create an SoapFormatter.
        Dim soap_formatter As New SoapFormatter()

        ' Create a FileStream to write with.
        Dim file_name As String = DataSubdirectory() & "\Flavors.xml"
        Dim file_stream As New FileStream(file_name, FileMode.Create)

        ' Serialize the DataClass object.
        soap_formatter.Serialize(file_stream, data_object)

        ' Close the FileStream.
```

```
            file_stream.Close()

            ' Display the results.
            txtSerialization.Text = GetFileContents(file_name)

            ' Clear the TextBoxes.
            txtValue1.Text = ""
            txtValue2.Text = ""
            txtValue3.Text = ""
            Cursor = Cursors.Default
        End Sub
End Class
```

The following code shows the most interesting pieces of the DataClassSoapReader program. This program also imports the DataClassNamespace.

```
Imports System.IO
Imports System.Runtime.Serialization.Formatters.Soap
Imports DataClassNamespace

Public Class Form1
    Inherits System.Windows.Forms.Form

    Private Sub btnDeserialize_Click( _
      ByVal sender As System.Object, _
      ByVal e As System.EventArgs) Handles btnDeserialize.Click

        Cursor = Cursors.WaitCursor
        Refresh()

        ' Create a SoapFormatter.
        Dim soap_formatter As New SoapFormatter()

        ' Create a FileStream to read with.
        Dim file_name As String = DataSubdirectory() & "\Flavors.xml"
        Dim file_stream As New FileStream(file_name, FileMode.Open)

        ' Read the item from the serialization.
        Dim data_object As DataClass
        data_object = CType(soap_formatter.Deserialize(file_stream), _
            DataClass)
        file_stream.Close()

        ' Copy the data into the TextBoxes.
        With data_object
            txtValue1.Text = .Value1
            txtValue2.Text = .Value2
            txtValue3.Text = .Value3
        End With

        Cursor = Cursors.Default
    End Sub
End Class
```

Example programs FlavorsAndColorsSoapWriter and FlavorsAndColorsSoap-Reader use a similar technique to serialize and deserialize two different XML documents. Flavors.xml contains a serialization for a FlavorsClass object defined in the FlavorsClass library. The file Colors.xml contains a serialization for a ColorsClass object defined in the ColorsClass library. Because these two objects are defined in different class libraries, they can have separate assembly names and root namespaces. That lets the programs read and write two different SOAP serializations without namespace conflicts.

Example programs FlavorsAndColorsBinaryWriter and FlavorsAndColorsBinary-Reader use the exact same code as programs FlavorsAndColorsSoapWriter and Flavors-AndColorsSoapReader except they use BinaryFormatters instead of SoapFormatters. These programs even use the same FlavorsClass and ColorsClass object libraries to define their data objects. The SoapFormatter and BinaryFormatter objects define the object serializations, not the objects themselves, so these programs can all share the same object libraries.

Conclusion

The XmlSerializer class allows you to easily serialize and deserialize classes, arrays, and hierarchical data structures built from linked objects. The XML serialization is plain text and is relatively easy to understand. By placing attributes on an object's public variables and property procedures, a program can map values into XML attributes and change their names.

SoapFormatter and BinaryFormatter provide alternative methods for serializing and deserializing data structures. As their names imply, SoapFormatter creates serializations in SOAP (Simple Object Access Protocol) format, and BinaryFormatter builds compact binary serializations. While the XmlSerializer cannot serialize data structures that contain circular references, SoapFormatter and BinaryFormatter can.

Using these three classes, an application can save and restore complex data structures almost effortlessly. The program defines the data structure's classes, and the XmlSerializer, SoapFormatter, and BinaryFormatter do the rest.

Schemas

XML allows you to store data in a partially self-describing format. For example, by placing the text Rod between two tags named FirstName, you give the reader the hint that the value represents a first name, not a stick, a fast car, or an old-fashioned unit of distance.

This information is handy, but it's not formal enough to help a program. Unless the program has some a priori knowledge of what a FirstName field should look like, it cannot tell that the following XML code is probably incorrect.

```
<FirstName>303-555-6526</FirstName>
```

There have been a couple of attempts to build schema languages that tell an application what kinds of data an XML file should contain. This chapter explains some of the ways a Visual Basic program can use schemas to validate XML documents.

The following section explains what schemas are and why you should care. The section after that discusses some of the different kinds of schemas in use. Microsoft focuses on XSD (XML Schema Definition) schemas so the rest of the chapter deals primarily with XSD schemas.

The Purpose of Schemas

A schema defines the data that an XML file contains. It specifies the ordering of tags in the document, indicates fields that are mandatory or that may occur different numbers of times, gives the data types of the fields, and so forth. A well-constructed schema will let a program know something is wrong if a LastName field contains the value 303-555-6526 or if a PhoneNumber field contains the value 303-555-652.

Many applications perform a huge amount of error checking and data validation. It is common for a program to use thousands of lines of code validating its data and then use only a few hundred lines of code to process the data. If a schema can ensure that the data values in the XML file are valid, the program can skip the validation.

Schemas are also useful when developers in different companies or even in different parts of the same company read and write an XML document. The schema acts as a contract specifying exactly what one program must write into the XML file and what another program can expect to be there. Without a schema, if two applications that read and write an XML file have a format mismatch, the developers may get into arguments about which format is correct. The schema unambiguously says which application is correct. If the XML file satisfies the schema, then the program writing the file has followed the terms of the contract.

Using schemas can also reduce network traffic and minimize unnecessary communication between data producers and data users. For example, suppose your application writes a purchase order using XML and sends it to a vendor. The vendor's application loads the file and discovers a formatting error so it rejects the order and returns it to you. Now you need to figure out what is wrong, possibly phoning the vendor to ask if you cannot figure it out, rebuild the order, and send it again. If you make another mistake, you may need to repeat the processes.

On the other hand, suppose the vendor has published a schema that all orders must satisfy. Your application builds the order and tries to validate it against the schema. When this fails, you can try to figure out what is wrong right away without wasting the time needed to send messages back and forth with the vendor.

A *well-formed* XML document is one that satisfies the usual rules of XML. For example, in a well-formed document there is exactly one data root node, all opening tags have corresponding closing tags, tag names do not contain spaces, the names in opening and closing tags are spelled in exactly the same way, tags are properly nested, and so forth.

A *valid* document is one that is well formed and that satisfies a schema. For example, if a document's schema indicates the FirstName field must contain only letters but a document has a FirstName field that contains a number, the document is invalid.

Visual Basic provides several methods for validating an XML document against a schema. Those methods are described later in this chapter. First, the following sections explain three common types of schemas: DTD, XDR, and XSD schemas.

DTD and XDR

While XML is a relatively new technology, several different schema languages have already been created. Microsoft focuses heavily on the most recent version, XSD schemas, so Visual Basic provides the most tools for working with them, and they are the ones you will probably use the most.

If you work with files created or used by other companies, however, you may need to work with other kinds of schemas. While Visual Basic has few tools for building other types of schemas, it can validate XML data using DTD and XDR.

In XML version 1.0, documents were defined using DTD (Document Type Definition) schemas. DTD schemas have a couple of drawbacks. First, they use a syntax that is different from XML syntax so to use DTD you need to learn yet another language. If you're new to XML, XSL, and XPath, you're probably tired of learning new languages.

To see how different DTD code is from XML, take a look at the following XML file. This file includes a DTD schema within a DOCTYPE tag. Notice how the DTD tags include the ! symbol, don't have closing tags (neither does the DOCTYPE tag), and contain a non-XML-like series of values defining the fields.

This schema defines the People element as containing one or more Person elements. The Person element contains exactly one FirstName, LastName, Email, and Phone field in exactly that order. Each of those fields contains text.

```
<?xml version="1.0" encoding="utf-8" ?>
<!DOCTYPE People [
    <!-- The top-level People element. -->
    <!ELEMENT People    (Person+)>

    <!-- A Person entry. -->
    <!ELEMENT Person    (FirstName, LastName, Email, Phone)>

    <!-- In this example, all fields allow only text. -->
    <!ELEMENT FirstName (#PCDATA)>
    <!ELEMENT LastName  (#PCDATA)>
    <!ELEMENT Email     (#PCDATA)>
    <!ELEMENT Phone     (#PCDATA)>
]>
<People>
    <Person>
        <FirstName>Rod</FirstName>
        <LastName>Stephens</LastName>
        <Email>RodStephens@vb-helper.com</Email>
        <Phone>123-456-7890</Phone>
    </Person>
</People>
```

In addition to the fact that DTD syntax is a bit odd, developers also found DTDs lacked the power and flexibility they needed to completely define all of the data types developers were using in XML. A schema is far less useful if it can validate only some of the data's requirements. If your application needs to perform its own validation anyway, the schema isn't saving you as much work as it should.

XDR (XML Data Reduced) is another schema language. Unlike DTD schemas, XDR schemas follow standard XML syntax. XDR functionality is a superset of the functionality of DTD so an XDR schema lets you specify everything a DTD schema does and more.

Don't confuse XDR (XML Data Reduced) with the Sun Microsystems XDR (External Data Representation) standard. Like XML Data Reduced, External Data Representation is a language for describing data formats. While these two XDRs have similar overall purposes, they have very different focuses. External Data Representation concentrates on the physical representation of data rather than the logical representation provided by XML. External Data Representation is designed to help transfer data from one kind of database to another. While these have the same abbreviation and general purpose, External Data Representation has nothing to do with XML schemas.

Most of Visual Basic's schema tools are designed for working with XSD schemas so the rest of this chapter focuses on XSD schemas. While you will probably build your own schemas using XSD, Visual Basic does provide tools for validating an XML document against DTD and XDR schemas. The section *Validating XML* later in this chapter provides more details.

XSD

Microsoft has selected XSD (XML Schema Definition) schemas as those it will fully support. Visual Basic provides some tools for validating XML documents against DTD and XDR schemas, but it has tools only for building XSD schemas. Because Visual Basic gives preference to XSD schemas, whenever this book says "schema" it means "XSD schema" unless noted otherwise.

The following sections explain the basics of XSD schemas. Like many other topics related to XML, the XSD specification is extremely complicated and quickly evolving. The following sections cover the basics of XSD so you can construct some useful schemas that work with your XML applications. They are not intended to cover everything there is to know about XSD. For more complete or up-to-date information, see a book on XSD or the W3C specifications.

Visual Basic includes an XSD editor that makes generating schemas relatively painless. Unless you understand the rules of XSD, however, the editor can be very confusing. The editor's drop-down commands automatically adjust to provide only the options that are legal at any given moment. If you don't understand which commands are available at different times, finding the command you want can be frustrating.

Types and Elements

XSD schemas contain type definitions and elements. A type definition describes an allowed XML data type. For example, if your XML file contains Customer records, you could create a type named CustomerRecordType that specifies that CustomerRecord-Type objects must have FirstName, LastName, Street, City, State, and Zip fields.

An element represents an item created in the XML file. If the XML file contains Customer tags, then the XSD file will contain a corresponding element named Customer. The data type of the Customer element indicates the type of data allowed in the XML file's Customer tag.

You can think of this process as analogous to defining a new class and declaring a variable using that class in Visual Basic. Consider the following code fragment. The code defines a new class named CustomerClass. It then creates an instance of the class named Customer. Defining the class tells the system what fields are contained in a CustomerClass object. The Customer object declaration makes a reference to an object that has the fields described by the class definition.

```
' Define the Customer class.
Public Class CustomerClass
    Public FirstName As String
    Public LastName As String
    Public Street As String
    Public City As String
    Public State As String
    Public Zip As Integer
End Class
...
' Create a Customer object.
Private Customer As CustomerClass
```

Similarly, an XSD file can define a CustomerType that includes the fields FirstName, LastName, and so forth. The file can then create an element named Customer of type CustomerType. That would mean a Customer tag in the corresponding XML file must correctly satisfy the CustomerType specification.

To see this example more concretely, consider the following XML file. It contains a single Customer record containing information about a customer.

```
<?xml version="1.0" encoding="utf-8" ?>
<Customer xmlns="http://tempuri.org/Customer.xsd">
    <FirstName>Rod</FirstName>
    <LastName>Stephens</LastName>
    <Street>1234 Programmer Way</Street>
    <City>Bugsville</City>
    <State>CO</State>
    <Zip>87654</Zip>
    <Phone>987-654-3210</Phone>
    <Email>RodStephens@vb-helper.com</Email>
</Customer>
```

The following XSD file validates this XML data. Don't worry too much about the details just yet. Later sections explain how to construct complex type definitions and use them to build elements. For now, notice that the file defines a type named CustomerType. This type is defined by an xsd:complexType tag with the name attribute set to CustomerType. The xsd:complexType tag contains an xsd:sequence tag. The xsd:sequence tag means the object must contain the included objects in their given order. In this case, a CustomerType object must contain the fields FirstName, Last-Name, Street, and so forth, in that order.

Each of the items FirstName, LastName, and so on is defined with an xsd:element tag. Because these are elements, they correspond to items in the XML file. In this case that means an object of type CustomerType must contain XML items named First-Name, LastName, and so forth.

In this example, all of these element tags have type attributes set to xsd:string so the XML items must be simple strings. For example, the LastName field cannot be a collection of nested XML tags.

After it has defined CustomerType, the XSD file creates a single element named Customer of type CustomerType. Because this is an element, it corresponds to an item of the same name in the XML file. The definition of CustomerType specifies the format this item must have.

What this essentially means is that the XML file's root item is named Customer and it obeys the restrictions of the CustomerType. The definition of CustomerType indicates that this element must contain FirstName, LastName, Street, City, State, Zip, Phone, and Email fields in that order, and each of the fields must be a simple string.

```
<xsd:schema id="Customers"
    targetNamespace="http://tempuri.org/Customer.xsd"
    xmlns="http://tempuri.org/Customer.xsd"
    xmlns:xsd="http://www.w3.org/2001/XMLSchema"
    xmlns:msdata="urn:schemas-microsoft-com:xml-msdata"
    attributeFormDefault="qualified" elementFormDefault="qualified">
    <!-- CustomerType
        Includes FirstName, LastName, Street, City, State
        Zip, Phone, and Email. -->
    <xsd:complexType name="CustomerType">
        <xsd:sequence>
            <xsd:element name="FirstName" type="xsd:string" />
            <xsd:element name="LastName" type="xsd:string" />
            <xsd:element name="Street" type="xsd:string" />
            <xsd:element name="City" type="xsd:string" />
            <xsd:element name="State" type="xsd:string" />
            <xsd:element name="Zip" type="xsd:string" />
            <xsd:element name="Phone" type="xsd:string" />
            <xsd:element name="Email" type="xsd:string" />
        </xsd:sequence>
    </xsd:complexType>
    <!-- Customer
        The XML file's data root.
        Contains one Customer elements. -->
    <xsd:element name="Customer" type="CustomerType">
</xsd:schema>
```

This format is quite powerful. It first defines the data types it will need. Then it creates elements using those data types. By breaking the definition of an element such as Customer into manageable type definitions, you can keep the XSD file comprehensible.

In a more complicated example, the file might include several layers of type and element definition. For example, an XML file containing customer data might contain a Customers element holding any number of Customer elements. The Customer elements would contain FirstName, LastName, and other elements similar to those used in the previous example. Instead of using simple strings, however, some of the fields might have further restrictions. For example, you can add the following conditions to the fields:

- State should contain a valid state abbreviation.
- Zip should have format XXXXX or XXXXX-XXXX where X is a digit from 0 to 9.

- Phone should have format NXX-XXXX or NXX-NXX-XXXX where N is a digit from 2 to 9 and X is a digit from 0 to 9.

- Email should have the format A@B.C where the strings A, B, and C can contain any characters except the @ symbol.

In this case, you could define the types StateType, ZipType, PhoneType, and EmailType to enforce those restrictions. Then you would use those types to build CustomerType. You would define CustomersType to hold one or more CustomerType objects. Finally, the XSD file would define an element of the type CustomersType to represent the XML file's root data element.

The following sections explain the rules for producing XSD code in more detail.

Elements

An element defines an entity in an XML file. For example, the following element declaration means the FirstName tag in the XML file contains a string.

```
<xsd:element name="FirstName" type="xsd:string" />
```

Remember that XSD is a special form of XML. This element declaration is a well-formed XML construct. It is an empty tag with name xsd:string. The tag's name and type attributes define the element's name and data type. An element tag can have several other attributes that modify the element's behavior.

The following sections describe the most commonly used element attributes.

minOccurs, maxOccurs

Without question the most common of these attributes are minOccurs and maxOccurs. These attributes give the minimum and maximum allowed number of times an element can occur within a complex type. To make an element optional, set minOccurs to 0. To allow an unlimited number of copies of the element, set maxOccurs to "unbounded."

The following code defines the CompanyType complex type. The CompanyType begins with an xsd:string named CompanyName. minOccurs and maxOccurs are both one so the XML data must have exactly one CompanyName element.

Next, the CompanyType includes a PersonType element named Contact. Another part of the XSD file should declare this type to include a person's name, title, address, phone number, and so forth. In CompanyType, this element's minOccurs attribute is set to 1, and maxOccurs is set to "unbounded" so the XML data can include as many Contact elements as necessary as long as it includes at least one.

```
<xsd:complexType name="CompanyType">
    <xsd:sequence>
        <xsd:element name="CompanyName" type="xsd:string"
            minOccurs="1" maxOccurs="1" />
        <xsd:element name="Contact" type="PersonType"
            minOccurs="1" maxOccurs="unbounded" />
```

```
            ... Other elements ...
      </xsd:sequence>
  </xsd:complexType>
```

Note that the xsd:sequence tag requires that the corresponding XML data contain items in the exact order they are listed. In this example, a CompanyType entry must begin with CompanyName, followed by one or more Contact items, followed by whatever other fields are defined by CompanyType.

ref

The ref attribute makes the element a copy of another element defined in the schema. For example, the following schema defines a PhoneNumber element of type xsd:string. Later it defines PersonType. This type includes an element that uses the ref attribute to refer to the previously created PhoneNumber element. This is equivalent to making a new PhoneNumber element within PersonType.

```
<xsd:element name="PhoneNumber" type="xsd:string" />
...
<xsd:complexType name="PersonType">
    <xsd:sequence>
        ...
        <xsd:element ref="PhoneNumber"
            minOccurs="1" maxOccurs="unbounded" />
        ...
    </xsd:sequence>
</xsd:complexType>
```

The ref attribute essentially uses an element defined elsewhere as a type for a new element. This can be confusing, however. Not only does this treat an element almost as if it is a type, but if you later change the original element definition you automatically change all of the elements that reference it. That may or may not be what you intended, depending on whether you remember that the element is a template for others.

To avoid this possible confusion, you can make a new type and then derive all of the PhoneNumber fields from this type, as shown in the following code.

```
<xsd:simpleType name="PhoneNumberType">
    <xsd:restriction base="xsd:string" />
</xsd:simpleType>
<xsd:element name="PhoneNumber" type="PhoneNumberType" />
...
<xsd:complexType name="PersonType">
    <xsd:sequence>
        ...
        <xsd:element name="PhoneNumber" type="PhoneNumberType"
            minOccurs="1" maxOccurs="unbounded" />
        ...
    </xsd:sequence>
</xsd:complexType>
```

This may be a little less confusing than using the ref attribute. One drawback to this method is that the elements created using the new type may not be exactly the same. For example, you may misspell the name in one and create a PhonNumber element. When you use the ref attribute, all of the new elements take their names from the original template element so this sort of thing cannot happen.

This still seems like a minor issue, however. If you misspell an element's name, you will probably discover it the first time you try to validate an XML file with the schema. Overall, using types instead of the ref attribute seems like a less confusing approach.

default

The default attribute assigns a default value to the element. If the XML document omits the corresponding field, it should be assumed to have this value.

An element that has a default value should have minOccurs set to 0 so the XML document can omit it.

Unfortunately, the MSDN documentation is a bit inconsistent about the default and fixed attributes. In some places, it says these attributes exist and do what you would expect. In other places, it says that elements do not have default or fixed attributes. While the textual schema editor allows you to enter these attributes, they don't seem to work properly.

fixed

The fixed attribute gives the element an unchangeable value. The corresponding XML element cannot have any other value, although it may be omitted if minOccurs is 0.

The fixed attribute is useful if you want to ensure that an XML data field has the same value throughout the document. For instance, you might want to add a new Country field to an existing XML document and ensure that its value is US for every record.

Types

Type definitions have two goals. The first is to describe the data allowed in a simple field. For example, PhoneType would require that its contents be text in the format NXX-XXXX or NXX-NXX-XXXX. Simple types satisfy this goal. A simple type determines what data is allowed for a particular purpose.

The second goal of type definitions is to describe relationships among different fields. For example, CustomerType would insist that Customer objects include the fields FirstName, LastName, Street, and so forth. Complex types satisfy this goal. A complex type groups other types to define a more elaborate data structure.

To accomplish these two goals, XSD provides three basic objects: built-in types, simple types, and complex types. Built-in types and simple types specify the data that a field can contain. For instance, using the xsd:gYear type, you can make a field that must contain a valid year number between 1995 and 2002. Using a simple type, you can require a field to contain a valid phone number format.

A complex type can contain elements and other tags. Complex types define relationships among other elements. For instance, the complex type CustomerType can require that the XML tag Customer contain the fields FirstName, LastName, Street, and so forth.

In a more involved situation, a CustomerType might contain basic fields such as CompanyName and BillingAddress. It could then include zero or more objects of type ContactType, each of which contains FirstName, LastName, Phone, and other fields describing a company contact.

Primitive Built-In Types

The simplest element definitions specify an element's name and give its type as a primitive built-in type. For example, the following code says that the Street element is a string.

```
<xsd:element name="Street" type="xsd:string" />
```

Built-in types such as xsd:string are defined by the World Wide Web Consortium's XML schema specification.

A *facet* is a characteristic of a data type that you can use to restrict the values allowed by the type. In a sense, a facet is an attribute of the data type. For example, the string data type has a maxLength facet. Using this facet you can set a maximum allowed length for a string element. For a complete list of the built-in data types and their facets, check the W3C documentation or the MSDN help files. Table 5.1 lists some of the most important built-in data types and their most useful facets.

You use facets to build simple types by restricting another data type. For example, the following code defines a type named AreaStatesType that allows only the values CO, WY, and KS. The type definition begins with an xsd:simpleType tag. That tag contains an xsd:restriction tag indicating the type is a restriction of the built-in xsd:string type. The xsd:restriction tag includes a series of tags that use the xsd:string data type's enumeration facet to impose restrictions on the data type. In this case, the xsd:enumeration tags list the type's allowed values.

```
<xsd:simpleType name="AreaStatesType">
    <xsd:restriction base="xsd:string">
        <xsd:enumeration value="CO" />
        <xsd:enumeration value="WY" />
        <xsd:enumeration value="KS" />
    </xsd:restriction>
</xsd:simpleType>
```

The following sections describe the facets listed in Table 5.1 in more detail.

Table 5.1 Useful Primitive Built-In Data Types

TYPE	FACETS	DESCRIPTION
Boolean	pattern	A Boolean value.
date	enumeration, pattern, minInclusive, minExclusive, maxInclusive, maxExclusive	A date.
dateTime	enumeration, pattern, minInclusive, minExclusive, maxInclusive, maxExclusive	A date and time.
decimal	enumeration, pattern, totalDigits, fractionDigits, minInclusive, minExclusive, maxInclusive, maxExclusive	An arbitrary precision number. Use this to make integers.
double	enumeration, pattern, fractionDigits, minInclusive, minExclusive, maxInclusive, maxExclusive	A 64-bit double-precision floating-point value.
float	enumeration, pattern, fractionDigits, minInclusive, minExclusive, maxInclusive, maxExclusive	A 32-bit single-precision floating-point value.
gDay	enumeration, pattern, minInclusive, minExclusive, maxInclusive, maxExclusive	A day of the month.
gMonth	enumeration, pattern, minInclusive, minExclusive, maxInclusive, maxExclusive	A month of the year.
gMonthDay	enumeration, pattern, minInclusive, minExclusive, maxInclusive, maxExclusive	A month and day.
gYear	enumeration, pattern, minInclusive, minExclusive, maxInclusive, maxExclusive	A year.
string	length, pattern, maxLength, minLength, enumeration	A character string.
time	enumeration, pattern, minInclusive, minExclusive, maxInclusive, maxExclusive	A time of day.

enumeration

The enumeration facet specifies a list of values that the type can have. The AreaStates-Type example in the previous section shows how you can use this facet to make an enumerated type.

The file XSDPeople.xsd contained in example project Schema includes the USStates-Type. This type is a simple but long enumeration of all of the United States state abbreviations plus DC.

```
<!-- USStatesType
     Valid US State abbreviations. -->
<xsd:simpleType name="USStatesType">
    <xsd:restriction base="xsd:string">
        <xsd:enumeration value="AK" />
        <xsd:enumeration value="AL" />
        <xsd:enumeration value="AR" />
        ... Lots of entries omitted ...
        <xsd:enumeration value="WY" />
    </xsd:restriction>
</xsd:simpleType>
```

pattern

The pattern facet specifies a regular expression that the input data must patch. Regular expressions have a complex language of their own, and an expression can be extremely complicated. For a complete discussion of regular expressions, consult the MSDN help. This section explains enough information to get you started using regular expressions in pattern facets.

A regular expression specifies a pattern that the regular expression engine should try to match against an input string. For example, the pattern ABC matches the exact string ABC and nothing else. The following code shows how you could define a type that allowed only the value ABC.

```
<xsd:simpleType name="MatchABCType">
    <xsd:restriction base="xsd:string">
        <xsd:pattern value="ABC" />
    </xsd:restriction>
</xsd:simpleType>
```

This example isn't very useful, but regular expressions can provide much more sophisticated matches. Table 5.2 lists the basic elements of a regular expression. Using these symbols, you can build many useful patterns.

Regular expressions also define escape sequences for matching special characters and common sets of characters. For example, the sequence \t matches the tab character and \d matches a digit 0 through 9. Table 5.3 lists the most useful escape sequences.

Table 5.2 Regular Expression Elements

SYMBOLS	PURPOSE	EXAMPLE	MEANING
literal letters	Matches the letters exactly	ABC	Matches the string ABC
.	Matches any single character	A.C	Matches three-letter strings beginning with A and ending with C
[...]	Matches any of the characters inside the brackets	[aeiouAEIOU]	Matches one vowel
[^...]	Matches any character not inside the brackets	[^aeiouAEIOU]	Matches any character except vowels
x-y	Matches letters within the range *x* to *y*	[a-z]	Matches one lowercase letter
		[a-zA-z]	Matches one upper-case or lowercase letter
+	Matches one or more occur-rences of the previous element	[a-z]+	Matches one or more lowercase letters
*	Matches zero or more occur-rences of the previous element	[a-z]*	Matches zero or more lowercase letters
?	Matches zero or one occur-rences of the previous element	[a-z]?	Matches zero or one lowercase letter
{*m*}	Matches exactly *m* occurrences of the previous element	[0-9]{3}	Matches three digits
{*m,*}	Matches at least *m* occurrences of the previous element	[0-9]{3,}	Matches three or more digits
{*m,n*}	Matches *m* through *n* occur-rences of the previous element	[0-9]{2,5}	Matches two, three, four, or five digits
X|Y	Matches regular expression *X* or *Y*	[a-z]|[0-9]	Matches one lowercase letter or a digit
( )	Groups the enclosed elements	([0-9][a-z]){2}	Matches a digit plus a letter twice

Table 5.3 Special Regular Expression Escape Sequences

SYMBOLS	PURPOSE	EQUIVALENT
\s	Matches any whitespace character	
\S	Matches any non-white space character	
\w	Matches word characters	[a-zA-Z0-9]
\W	Matches non-word characters	[^a-zA-Z0-9]
\d	Matches any decimal digit	[0-9]
\D	Matches any decimal non-digit	[^0-9]
\t	Matches the tab character	\x09
\r	Matches the carriage return character	\x0D
\n	Matches the new-line character	\x0A
\040	Matches a character by ASCII value in octal (040 is octal for 32, which is the ASCII code for the space character)	
\x20	Matches a character by ASCII value in hexadecimal (x20 is hexadecimal for 32, which is the ASCII code for the space character)	
\u0020	Matches a character by Unicode value in hexadecimal (0020 is hexadecimal for 32, which is the Unicode value for the space character)	

The backslash character \ is also useful for matching symbols that usually have a special meaning. For example, the asterisk character * normally makes the expression match zero or more occurrences of the previous regular expression element. The sequence * deactivates this function and makes the expression match the asterisk character itself. This is called *escaping* the character. Similarly, the sequence \\ matches the backslash character, \- matches the dash character, \[matches the open bracket, and so forth.

Using these basic elements and escape sequences, you can build all sorts of useful regular expressions for pattern facets. The following XSD code includes definitions for several handy types constructed using facets of built-in types.

ZipCodeType allows United States Zip codes of the form XXXXX or XXXXX-XXXX where X represents any digit 0 through 9. The pattern "\d{5}(\-\d{4})?" means match a digit five times. Then match a group containing a dash followed by a digit repeated four times. The group must be repeated zero or one times.

EmailType matches an email address of the form A@B.C where A, B, and C are any strings that do not contain the @ symbol. The pattern "[^@]+@[^@]+\.[^@]+" means match any character other than the @ symbol one or more times (that's string A). Then match an @ symbol. Again match any character other than the @ symbol one or more times (that's string B). Next match a period and, one last time, match any character other than the @ symbol one or more times (that's string C).

USPhone7Type matches a phone number of the form NXX-XXXX where N represents a digit from 2 through 9 and X represents a digit from 0 through 9. Its pattern "[2-9]\d{2}\-\d{4}" means match a digit from 2 through 9. Then match any digit exactly two times. Match a dash character and then any digit repeated exactly four times.

Similarly, USPhone10Type matches a phone number of the form NXX-NXX-XXXX. Its pattern "([2-9]\d{2}\-){2}\d{4}" means match a group containing a digit from 2 through 9 followed by any digit two times followed by a dash. Match this group two times. Then match any digit four times.

USPhoneType combines both of the previous types to match phone numbers of the form NXX-XXXX and NXX-NXX-XXXX. This type's pattern "([2-9]\d{2}\-){1,2}\d{4}" means match a group containing a digit from 2 through 9 followed by any two digits followed by a dash. Match this group one or two times. Then match any digit four times.

SSNType matches Social Security Numbers of the form XXX-XX-XXXX where X represents any digit. This type's pattern "\d{3}\-\d{2}\-\d{4}" means match any digit three times, a dash, any digit twice, another dash, and any digit four times.

FEINType is similar to SSNType. It matches FEINs (Federal Employer Identification Numbers), which are similar to Social Security Numbers for corporations. An FEIN has the format XX-XXXXXXX where X represents any digit. The FEINType's pattern "\d{2}\-\d{7}" means match any digit twice times, a dash, and any digit seven times.

```
<!-- ZipCodeType
     A Zip code of the form XXXXX or XXXXX-XXXX. -->
<xsd:simpleType name="ZipCodeType">
    <xsd:restriction base="xsd:string">
        <xsd:pattern value="\d{5}(\-\d{4})?" />
    </xsd:restriction>
</xsd:simpleType>


<!-- EmailType
     A string of the form A@B.C for any strings
     A, B, and C not containing @. -->
<xsd:simpleType name="EmailType">
    <xsd:restriction base="xsd:string">
        <xsd:pattern value="[^@]+@[^@]+\.[^@]+" />
    </xsd:restriction>
</xsd:simpleType>


<!-- USPhone7Type
     A string of the form NXX-XXXX
     where N = 2-9 and X = 0-9. -->
<xsd:simpleType name="USPhone7Type">
    <xsd:restriction base="xsd:string">
        <xsd:pattern value="[2-9]\d{2}\-\d{4}" />
    </xsd:restriction>
```

```
    </xsd:simpleType>


    <!-- USPhone10Type
         A string of the form NXX-NXX-XXXX
         where N = 2-9 and X = 0-9. -->
    <xsd:simpleType name="USPhone10Type">
        <xsd:restriction base="xsd:string">
            <xsd:pattern value="([2-9]\d{2}\-){2}\d{4}" />
        </xsd:restriction>
    </xsd:simpleType>


    <!-- USPhoneType
         A string of the form NXX-XXXX or NXX-NXX-XXXX
         where N = 2-9 and X = 0-9. -->
    <xsd:simpleType name="USPhoneType">
        <xsd:restriction base="xsd:string">
            <xsd:pattern value="([2-9]\d{2}\-){1,2}\d{4}" />
        </xsd:restriction>
    </xsd:simpleType>


    <!-- SSNType
         A US Social Security number of the form XXX-XX-XXXX
         where X = 0-9. -->
    <xsd:simpleType name="SSNType">
        <xsd:restriction base="xsd:string">
            <xsd:pattern value="\d{3}\-\d{2}\-\d{4}" />
        </xsd:restriction>
    </xsd:simpleType>


    <!-- FEINType
         A US Federal Employer Identification Number (FEIN)
         of the form XX-XXXXXXX
         where X = 0-9. -->
    <xsd:simpleType name="FEINType">
        <xsd:restriction base="xsd:string">
            <xsd:pattern value="\d{2}\-\d{7}" />
        </xsd:restriction>
    </xsd:simpleType>
```

Often you can write several different regular expressions that match the same set of strings. One particularly useful regular expression format contains a series of expressions that match an entire string joined with the | symbol. For example, both of the following two types allow strings that begin with the letter A or B. The AOrBType pattern matches the letter A or B, followed by any character repeated any number of times.

The ATypeOrBType matches strings that start with A followed by any character any number of times, plus strings that start with B followed by any character any number of times. This type's pattern is essentially two patterns that each could match the entire string joined with the | symbol.

```
    <!-- Allow strings starting with A or B. -->
    <xsd:simpleType name="AOrBType">
        <xsd:restriction base="xsd:string">
```

```
            <xsd:pattern value="(A|B).*" />
        </xsd:restriction>
    </xsd:simpleType>
<!-- Allow strings starting with A or B. -->
<xsd:simpleType name="ATypeOrBType">
    <xsd:restriction base="xsd:string">
        <xsd:pattern value="(A.*)|(B.*)" />
    </xsd:restriction>
</xsd:simpleType>
```

When a type definition uses a pattern like this one, which consists of two complete regular expressions joined by the | symbol, you can split the regular expressions into separate xsd:pattern tags, as shown in the following code. This type accepts strings that match either of its two patterns.

```
<!-- Allow strings starting with A or B. -->
<xsd:simpleType name="ATypeOrBType">
    <xsd:restriction base="xsd:string">
        <xsd:pattern value="A.*" />
        <xsd:pattern value="B.*" />
    </xsd:restriction>
</xsd:simpleType>
```

Breaking a complicated regular expression into separate patterns in this way can sometimes make the type definition a lot easier to understand. This example is simple enough that you can probably figure it out no matter which of these three versions you use. In more complex situations, it can be much easier to debug a series of patterns separately and then combine them in their own xsd:pattern tags.

Regular expressions have more uses than just defining patterns for XSD types. Other regular expression syntax lets you clip pieces out of a string and rearrange them or replace them with other strings. For more information on uses that are not related to XML, see the MSDN help.

length, minLength, maxLength

The length facet gives the exact length of the type's data. The following code defines a StateType that requires its input to be a string of exactly two characters.

```
<xsd:simpleType name="StateType">
    <xsd:restriction base="xsd:string">
        <xsd:length value="2" />
    </xsd:restriction>
</xsd:simpleType>
```

This facet is useful for values such as abbreviations where you know exactly how long the value must be. In cases like that, you may get a better result using an enumeration to list all of the allowed values explicitly.

The minLength and maxLength facets are more useful than length when a field's length is bounded but the allowed values do not all need to have exactly the same length. For instance, suppose you will be loading data from a LastName tag in an XML file into a database table where the LastName field that has length 20. The XML values should have lengths between 1 and 20.

```
<xsd:simpleType name="LastNameType">
    <xsd:restriction base="xsd:string">
        <xsd:minLength value="1" />
        <xsd:maxLength value="20" />
    </xsd:restriction>
</xsd:simpleType>
```

Giving the type a minimum length of 1 prevents the data from holding an empty LastName element like either of these two statements:

```
<LastName></LastName>
<LastName/>
```

Usually minLength and maxLength together produce the best result for string fields.

totalDigits, fractionDigits

The totalDigits facet tells how many digits a number can have. This includes digits before and after the decimal point but does not include the decimal point itself.

The fractionDigits facet tells how many digits a number can have after its decimal point.

The following code defines a MoneyType that allows a total of at most seven digits and at most two digits after the decimal place.

```
<xsd:simpleType name="MoneyType">
    <xsd:restriction base="xsd:decimal">
        <xsd:totalDigits value="7" />
        <xsd:fractionDigits value="2" />
    </xsd:restriction>
</xsd:simpleType>
```

Note that the schema does not convert values to try to satisfy this facet. For example, the value 32000.000 does not meet the MoneyType's constraints because it contains three digits after the decimal point. This value is rejected even though it is numerically equivalent to the value 32000.00, which does satisfy the type's requirements.

Note also that these facets are less than ideal for bounding numeric values. For example, the previous type allows the value 32000.00 because it contains seven digits, two of which are after the decimal point. It also allows 320000.0 because this value contains seven digits, only one of which is after the decimal point.

If the intent of this type is to allow a value with up to five digits before the decimal point and two after, this definition is insufficient. In that case, you should use the facets minExclusive and maxExclusive, or minInclusive and maxInclusive, to restrict the field's value. Then use fractionDigits to restrict the number of digits allowed after the decimal point.

minExclusive, maxExclusive, minInclusive, maxInclusive

These facets bound a field's value. The two inclusive facets include their values in the field's allowed range. The two exclusive facets exclude their values from those that are allowed. For example, the following definition of AgeType allows numeric values between 1 and 200 including 1 and 200. The fractionDigits facet prohibits digits after the decimal point so the value must be an integer, though it does allow values such as 10. that have a trailing decimal point.

```
<xsd:simpleType name="AgeType">
    <xsd:restriction base="xsd:decimal">
        <xsd:minInclusive value="1" />
        <xsd:maxInclusive value="200" />
        <xsd:fractionDigits value="0" />
    </xsd:restriction>
</xsd:simpleType>
```

The following type definition is similar to the previous one except it prohibits the values 1 and 200 from the range of allowed values.

```
<xsd:simpleType name="AgeType">
    <xsd:restriction base="xsd:decimal">
        <xsd:minExclusive value="1" />
        <xsd:maxExclusive value="200" />
        <xsd:fractionDigits value="0" />
    </xsd:restriction>
</xsd:simpleType>
```

The following definition of MoneyType allows values up to five digits before the decimal point and up to two digits after.

```
<xsd:simpleType name="MoneyType">
    <xsd:restriction base="xsd:decimal">
        <xsd:minInclusive value="0" />
        <xsd:maxInclusive value="99999.99" />
        <xsd:fractionDigits value="2" />
    </xsd:restriction>
</xsd:simpleType>
```

This definition satisfies the intent of a money data type better than the version shown in the previous section.

Derived Built-In Data Types

In addition to primitive built-in types, XSD supports an assortment of built-in types derived from the primitive types. These types refine the definition of primitive types to create more restrictive types.

You use derived types in the same way you use the primitive types. The difference between the primitive and derived built-in types is negligible as far as an XSD file is concerned.

Derived types are based on two primitive types: string and decimal. String types represent various entities that occur in XML syntax itself. For example, the Name type represents a string that satisfies the form of XML token names. It begins with a letter, underscore, or colon. The rest of the string contains letters and digits.

Types derived from the primitive decimal type represent various kinds of numbers. These types are more useful for validating data than the XML-related types.

Table 5.4 lists the types derived from decimal. Because they all represent numbers, these types have many similarities. In particular, they all have the facets enumeration, pattern, totalDigits, minInclusive, maxInclusive, minExclusive, and maxExclusive. See the previous sections for descriptions of these facets.

Table 5.4   Built-In Data Types Derived from Decimal

TYPE	DESCRIPTION
byte	An 8-bit integer between -128 and 127.
short	A 16-bit integer between -32,768 and 32,767.
int	A 32-bit integer between -2,147,483,648 and 2,147,483,647.
long	A 64-bit integer between -9,223,372,036,854,775,808 and 9,223,372,036,854,775,807.
integer	An integer. The documentation implies an integer can have unbounded length, but Visual Basic's implementation seems to allow values between -79,228,162,514,264,337,593,543,950,335 and 79,228,162,514,264,337,593,543,950,335.
nonNegativeInteger	An integer that is greater than or equal to zero.
positiveInteger	An integer that is greater than zero.
nonPositiveInteger	An integer that is less than or equal to zero.
negativeInteger	An integer that is less than zero.
unsignedByte	An unsigned 8-bit integer between 0 and 255.
unsignedShort	An unsigned 16-bit integer between 0 and 65,535.
unsignedInt	An unsigned 32-bit integer between 0 and 4,294,967,295.
unsignedLong	An unsigned 64-bit integer between 0 and 18,446,744,073,709,551,615.

Attributes

You use an XSD schema's element entities to define the data that can be contained in the corresponding XML data elements. Similarly you can use attribute entities to define the attributes the XML element can have.

For example, suppose the XML file contains Car elements that can have attributes Make, Model, Year, and Miles. The XSD schema can define the CarType and its attributes, as shown in the following code. The file first defines NameType to be a string with length between 1 and 40 characters, and the CarYearType to be a year between 1980 and 2001. It then defines the complex type named CarType. Note that only complex types, not simple types, can have attributes.

The Make and Model attributes are both of the type NameType, and both are required. The Year attribute is of type CarYearType and is also required.

The Miles attribute is an integer. It is optional and has a default value of 100. If the Miles attribute is not provided by an XML file, a parser that reads the file using the schema will automatically create a Miles attribute with value 100.

```
<xsd:schema id="Validator"
  targetNamespace="http://tempuri.org/Validator.xsd"
  xmlns="http://tempuri.org/Validator.xsd"
  xmlns:xsd="http://www.w3.org/2001/XMLSchema"
  xmlns:msdata="urn:schemas-microsoft-com:xml-msdata"
  attributeFormDefault="qualified"
  elementFormDefault="qualified">
    <!-- NameType
        String with length between 1 and 40. -->
    <xsd:simpleType name="NameType">
        <xsd:restriction base="xsd:string">
            <xsd:minLength value="1" />
            <xsd:maxLength value="40" />
        </xsd:restriction>
    </xsd:simpleType>
    <!-- CarYearType
        A year between 1980 and 2001. -->
    <xsd:simpleType name="CarYearType">
        <xsd:restriction base="xsd:gYear">
            <xsd:minInclusive value="1980" />
            <xsd:maxInclusive value="2001" />
        </xsd:restriction>
    </xsd:simpleType>
    <!-- CarType
        Has Manufacturer, Model, Year, and Miles attributes. -->
    <xsd:complexType name="CarType">
        <xsd:attribute name="Make" type="NameType" use="required"
            form="unqualified" />
        <xsd:attribute name="Model" type="NameType" use="required"
            form="unqualified" />
```

```
            <xsd:attribute name="Year" type="CarYearType" use="required"
                form="unqualified" />
            <xsd:attribute name="Miles" type="xsd:integer" use="optional"
                form="unqualified" default="100" />
        </xsd:complexType>
        ... More code omitted ...
    </xsd:schema>
```

All of the attributes in this example have their form attributes set to "unqualified." That means the attributes in the XML file do not need to be qualified with the schema's namespace. The following code shows an XML document that satisfies the Car tag defined by this schema.

```
<?xml version="1.0" encoding="utf-8" ?>
<People xmlns="http://tempuri.org/Validator.xsd">
    <Person>
        <FirstName>Rod</FirstName>
        <LastName>Stephens</LastName>
        ... Data omitted ...
        <Car Make="PMC" Model="Narf" Year="1998" Miles="37250" />
    </Person>
</People>
```

On the other hand, suppose the attributes in the schema were marked form="qualified." Or assume the attributes have no form element. Because the schema tag at the beginning of the XSD file contains the statement attributeFormDefault="qualified," the attributes are qualified by default for this schema.

In these cases, the XML file would need to qualify the attributes with the schema's target namespace http://tempuri.org/Validator.xsd, as shown in the following XML code. This file's People tag defines the ns namespace to have the value http://tempuri.org/Validator.xsd. It then qualifies each of the Car tag's attributes using that namespace abbreviation.

```
<?xml version="1.0" encoding="utf-8" ?>
<People xmlns="http://tempuri.org/Validator.xsd"
    xmlns:ns="http://tempuri.org/Validator.xsd">
    <Person>
        <FirstName>Rod</FirstName>
        <LastName>Stephens</LastName>
        ... Data omitted ...
        <Car ns:Make="Pinkie" ns:Model="Narf" ns:Year="2001"
            ns:Miles="69" />
    </Person>
</People>
```

In the current release of Visual Basic, this method, combined with the default attribute in the schema file, causes a rather odd side effect. When an XmlValidating-Reader object loads the XML data, the Car node receives a Miles attribute with the default value 100. The Car node also receives an ns:Miles attribute containing the value shown in the XML file if the file contains that attribute. The XmlValidatingReader finds two different Miles attributes in different namespaces.

If you set the attributes' form values to "unqualified" in the schema, everything is much simpler. The XmlValidatingReader sees one copy of each attribute with no namespace prefix. If the XML data includes a Miles attribute, that is the value the XmlValidatingReader sees. If the XML data omits the Miles attribute, the XmlValidatingReader sees the default value.

Attributes versus Elements

Elements and attributes are often interchangeable. The following XML code fragment shows one method for storing address data using elements.

```
<Address>
    <AddressType>Home</AddressType>
    <Street>1324 Bug Manor</Street>
    <City>Hacker City</City>
    <State>CA</State>
    <Zip>92308</Zip>
</Address>
```

The following code shows another way to store address data where the AddressType value is stored in an attribute and the rest of the address data is stored in elements.

```
<Address AddressType="Home">
    <Street>1324 Bug Manor</Street>
    <City>Hacker City</City>
    <State>CA</State>
    <Zip>92308</Zip>
</Address>
```

The next fragment takes a more extreme approach, storing all of the address data in the Address tag's attributes.

```
<Address AddressType="Home" "Street"=1324 Bug Manor"
    City="Hacker City" State="CA" Zip="92308" />
```

Whether you should make a value an element or an attribute is largely a matter of taste. Generally, elements contain data, and attributes contain information that describes the data. In the previous examples, the Street, City, State, and Zip fields contain information about a physical address while the AddressType field contains information about the data. That indicates AddressType should be stored as an attribute while the other fields should be stored in separate elements.

While this makes sense logically, there are a few practical considerations. First, some applications use more attributes than they probably should to save space. The second "correct" version of this data uses 142 characters while the all-attribute version uses only 100.

Second, attributes can specify default values while elements generally do not. The MSDN documentation is a bit inconsistent about the default and fixed element attributes. In some places, it says these attributes exist and do what you would expect. In other places, it says elements cannot have defaults or fixed values. While the textual schema editor allows you to enter these attributes, they don't seem to work properly. Unless things change in a future version of Visual Basic, you should use attributes if you want to provide default or fixed values.

A sequence element defines the order allowed for its contents but attributes can appear in any order. If you want to require a particular ordering for data, use elements, not attributes.

Elements can occur more than once in a complex type, but an attribute can occur only once. For example, suppose you want to allow an Address element to contain several PhoneNumber values. An Address element cannot have more than one Phone-Number attribute. You could make separate HomePhoneNumber, WorkPhoneNumber, and other phone number attributes but that would spoil the intent and make programming harder. It would be better to use multiple PhoneNumber elements with a Type attribute indicating the type of the phone number.

Table 5.5 summarizes these reasons for using elements versus attributes.

Complex Types

A simple type determines the kinds of data a simple text field can hold. A complex type defines relationships among other types. For instance, an XML file's Person record might include fields to store FirstName, LastName, Street, and so forth. Simple types define the allowed values in each field. A complex type determines the fields that make up the Person record.

Complex types are also useful for defining XML elements that can have attributes. Because a simple type cannot have attributes, you need to use a complex type if you want to define an XML element's attributes.

A complex type can contain only one of a small number of elements. The elements within those elements define the relationship the complex type represents. The most common elements contained in a complex type are simpleContent, sequence, choice, and all. The following sections describe these elements and give examples of them.

Table 5.5   Reasons to Use Elements versus Attributes

USE AN ELEMENT IF...	USE AN ATTRIBUTE IF...
The item is data, not information about data	The item describes the data
The item does not need a default or fixed value	The item needs a default or fixed value
You want to specify the order of the items	The order of the items doesn't matter
You want to allow more than one instance of an item	You want the item to appear only once

simpleContent

A complex type that contains a simpleContent element must contain only character data or a simple type. It may seem a little odd creating a complex type just so that it can contain a simple type, but this technique is useful for adding attributes to a simple type. Remember that a simple type cannot have attributes of its own, but a complex type that contains a simple type can.

The following example defines PhoneType. The type is basically a simple string with the added Boolean attribute Home.

```
<xsd:complexType name="PhoneType">
    <xsd:simpleContent>
        <xsd:extension base="xsd:string">
            <xsd:attribute name="Home" type="xsd:boolean"
                form="unqualified" />
        </xsd:extension>
    </xsd:simpleContent>
</xsd:complexType>
```

sequence

The sequence element indicates that the complex type must contain the included elements in order. In the following example, a PersonType object must contain FirstName, LastName, Street, City, State, Zip, Email, and Phone fields in that order.

```
<xsd:complexType name="PersonType">
    <xsd:sequence>
        <xsd:element name="FirstName" type="NameType"
            minOccurs="1" maxOccurs="1" />
        <xsd:element name="LastName" type="NameType"
            minOccurs="1" maxOccurs="1" />
        <xsd:element name="Street" type="NameType"
            minOccurs="1" maxOccurs="1" />
        <xsd:element name="City" type="NameType"
            minOccurs="1" maxOccurs="1" />
        <xsd:element name="State" type="USStatesType"
            minOccurs="1" maxOccurs="1" />
        <xsd:element name="Zip" type="ZipCodeType"
            minOccurs="1" maxOccurs="1" />
        <xsd:element name="Email" type="EmailType"
            minOccurs="0" maxOccurs="1" />
        <xsd:element name="Phone" type="USPhoneType"
            minOccurs="0" maxOccurs="1" />
    </xsd:sequence>
</xsd:complexType>
```

Note that in this example the Email and Phone elements have minOccurs set to zero so those fields are not required. If they are present, however, these fields must appear in the order given by this sequence.

choice

When a complex type contains a choice element, the corresponding XML data must include exactly one of the elements listed inside the choice. For instance, suppose you are building an account balance system. A Transaction element of type Transaction-Type can be a Payment, a Debit, or a BalanceInquiry. The following code shows how you might define TransactionType.

```
<xsd:complexType name="TransactionType">
    <xsd:choice>
        <xsd:element name="Payment" type="PaymentType" />
        <xsd:element name="Debit" type="DebitType" />
        <xsd:element name="BalanceInquiry" type="BalanceInquiryType" />
    </xsd:choice>
</xsd:complexType>
```

The following XML code shows three data records that satisfy this definition. The kinds of information that must be present inside the Payment, Debit, and Balance-Inquiry tags depend on the definitions of the types PaymentType, DebitType, and BalanceInquiryType.

```
<Transaction>
    <Payment>
        ... Payment information ...
    </Payment>
</Transaction>
<Transaction>
    <Debit>
        ... Debit information ...
    </Debit>
</Transaction>
<Transaction>
    <BalanceInquiry>
        ... Balance inquiry information ...
    </BalanceInquiry>
</Transaction>
```

Don't confuse the choice element with an element that allows a fixed set of values. The choice element allows the complex type to contain one of several *types*. The intent is to allow an element to take on the role of one or more different kinds of data. In the previous example, the Transaction element can represent a payment, debit, or balance inquiry. The choice element is not intended to represent a choice between several simple values such as strings.

To make a type that allows only one of a list of values, use a simple type containing a restriction that uses enumerations to list the allowed choices. The following code shows a type that requires the data to contain one of the strings red, green, or blue.

```
<xsd:simpleType name="FavoriteColorType">
    <xsd:restriction base="xsd:string">
        <xsd:enumeration value="red" />
```

```
            <xsd:enumeration value="green" />
            <xsd:enumeration value="blue" />
        </xsd:restriction>
    </xsd:simpleType>
```

If the FavoriteColor element is of type FavoriteColorType, then the following code shows how XML data can satisfy these definitions.

```
<FavoriteColor>red</FavoriteColor>
```

all

When a complex type includes the all element, the corresponding XML data can include some or all of the listed elements in any order. The following code shows how you might define the type PetsType. It allows the corresponding XML data to include any number of instances of Cat, Dog, and Fish elements in any order.

```
<xsd:complexType name="PetsType">
    <xsd:all>
        <xsd:element name="Cat" type="xsd:string"
            minOccurs="0" maxOccurs="unbounded" />
        <xsd:element name="Dog" type="xsd:string"
            minOccurs="0" maxOccurs="unbounded" />
        <xsd:element name="Fish" type="xsd:string"
            minOccurs="0" maxOccurs="unbounded" />
    </xsd:all>
</xsd:complexType>
```

Assuming the Pets element is of type PetsType, the following code shows XML data that satisfies the PetsType definition.

```
<Pets>
    </Cat>Merlin</Cat>
    </Dog>Snortimer</Dog>
    </Cat>Cobe</Cat>
</Pets>
```

Note that an element's minOccurs and maxOccurs attributes default to 1. If you do not explicitly set values to these attributes in the element statements inside the all statement, each element must appear exactly once, though the elements can appear in any order. If the previous PetsType definition did not explicitly set minOccurs and maxOccurs, this XML data would be invalid because it contains two Cat elements and no Fish element.

Named and Unnamed Types

Most of the examples presented in this chapter use named types. The XSD code first defines a type using the name attribute to give the type a name. It then uses that type to define elements and other types.

If you will use a type only once, you do not need to give it a name. Instead, you can include the type's definition right in the code that uses it. For example, the following code defines EmailType and then uses it to define EmailContactType.

```
<!-- Require Email to be of the form A@B.C where A, B, and C
     are strings that don't contain the @ symbol. -->
<xsd:simpleType name="EmailType">
    <xsd:restriction base="xsd:string">
        <xsd:pattern value="[^@]+@[^@]+\.[^@]+" />
    </xsd:restriction>
</xsd:simpleType>


<!-- An email correspondent. -->
<xsd:complexType name="EmailContactType">
    <xsd:sequence>
        <xsd:element name="Name" type="xsd:string"
            minOccurs="1" maxOccurs="1" />
        <xsd:element name="Email" type="EmailType"
            minOccurs="0" maxOccurs="1" />
    </xsd:sequence>
</xsd:complexType>
```

The following code shows how you can define the EmailContactType without separately defining EmailType.

```
<!-- An email correspondent. -->
<xsd:complexType name="EmailContactType">
    <xsd:sequence>
        <xsd:element name="Name" type="xsd:string"
            minOccurs="1" maxOccurs="1" />
        <xsd:element name="Email"
            minOccurs="0" maxOccurs="1">
            <xsd:simpleType>
                <xsd:restriction base="xsd:string">
                    <xsd:pattern value="[^@]+@[^@]+\.[^@]+" />
                </xsd:restriction>
            </xsd:simpleType>
        </xsd:element>
    </xsd:sequence>
</xsd:complexType>
```

This second form using the unnamed Email type requires a deeper level of nesting and is generally more confusing than the form that uses an explicitly named EmailType. You can reduce the confusion by using lots of comments, but overall the first version seems better.

Editing Schemas in Visual Basic

At its most primitive level, editing XSD schemas is easy. You can open an XSD file in any text editor and type in a complete schema. The rules for XSD are extremely complex, however, so you are very likely to make some mistakes. Fortunately, Visual Basic provides several tools to help in editing schemas. The following sections describe three of Visual Basic's schema tools: the XML menu, the graphical schema editor, and the textual schema editor.

The XML Menu

If you create an XML file and then select it, Visual Basic displays an XML menu. This menu contains two commands: Create Schema and Validate XML Data. The following sections describe these commands in more detail.

Create Schema

If you select the Create Schema command, Visual Basic automatically creates a schema for the XML data. Unfortunately, the schema isn't very intelligently constructed. For example, consider the following simple XML file.

```
<?xml version="1.0" encoding="utf-8" ?>
<People xmlns="http://tempuri.org/Test.xsd">
    <Person>
        <Name>Rod Stephens</Name>
        <Phone>987-654-3210</Phone>
    </Person>
</People>
```

If you enter this code and invoke the XML menu's Create Schema command, Visual Basic produces the following result. Ignoring the various schema header and data options, this schema defines a root element named People. It is a complex type containing a choice element. The choice element contains a single Person element that can occur any number of times in the XML file. Person is a complex type holding a sequence containing Name and Phone elements. These elements are both strings that can occur zero or one times.

```
<xsd:schema
  id="People"
  targetNamespace="http://tempuri.org/Test.xsd"
  xmlns="http://tempuri.org/Test.xsd"
  xmlns:xsd="http://www.w3.org/2001/XMLSchema"
  xmlns:msdata="urn:schemas-microsoft-com:xml-msdata"
```

```
      attributeFormDefault="qualified" elementFormDefault="qualified">
        <xsd:element name="People"
          msdata:IsDataSet="true"
          msdata:EnforceConstraints="False">
            <xsd:complexType>
                <xsd:choice maxOccurs="unbounded">
                    <xsd:element name="Person">
                        <xsd:complexType>
                            <xsd:sequence>
                                <xsd:element name="Name" type="xsd:string"
                                  minOccurs="0" />
                                <xsd:element name="Phone" type="xsd:string"
                                  minOccurs="0" />
                            </xsd:sequence>
                        </xsd:complexType>
                    </xsd:element>
                </xsd:choice>
            </xsd:complexType>
        </xsd:element>
      </xsd:schema>
```

The XML file is valid according to this schema, but there are undoubtedly many improvements you can make to the XSD code. First, Visual Basic gives all of the data elements (Name and Phone in this example) the type xsd:string. To get the most out of a schema, you should make the types of these elements as restrictive as possible. You could restrict Name so that it must contain only letters and spaces and have a length between 1 and 40. You should certainly make a PhoneType that forces data in the Phone field to have a valid telephone number format.

Second, all of the data elements initially have minOccurs set to 0. Because maxOccurs is missing from this schema, it defaults to 1. That means these elements can occur zero or one times in the XML file. While it is possible that this is what you intend, it is just as likely that these elements should be present exactly one time or that they should be allowed any number of times. To make these changes, you should modify the value in the minOccurs clause and you should probably add a maxOccurs value.

Third, this file uses unnamed types so it is deeply nested and unnecessarily confusing. It would be easier to understand if you pull the type definitions out of the main People element, name them, and then use them to build up the People element.

One way to do this is to address the types at the highest level first. The People element contains a complexType element. Pull that element out and give it a name. Then add a corresponding type clause to the People element. As you make these changes, add comments to describe the pieces of the schema, as shown in the following code.

```
<xsd:schema
  id="People"
  targetNamespace="http://tempuri.org/Test.xsd"
  xmlns="http://tempuri.org/Test.xsd"
  xmlns:xsd="http://www.w3.org/2001/XMLSchema"
  xmlns:msdata="urn:schemas-microsoft-com:xml-msdata"
  attributeFormDefault="qualified" elementFormDefault="qualified">
    <!-- PeopleType: Represents a collection of People. -->
```

```
<xsd:complexType name="PeopleType">
    <xsd:choice maxOccurs="unbounded">
        <xsd:element name="Person">
            <xsd:complexType>
                <xsd:sequence>
                    <xsd:element name="Name" type="xsd:string"
                        minOccurs="0" />
                    <xsd:element name="Phone" type="xsd:string"
                        minOccurs="0" />
                </xsd:sequence>
            </xsd:complexType>
        </xsd:element>
    </xsd:choice>
</xsd:complexType>
<!-- People: The XML file's main People element. -->
<xsd:element name="People" type="PeopleType"
    msdata:IsDataSet="true"
    msdata:EnforceConstraints="False">
</xsd:element>
</xsd:schema>
```

Now validate the XML file to make sure it is still valid. If you made no mistakes, Visual Basic's Validate XML Data command, described in the next section, will not find any errors in the XML file. If you did make a mistake, you are better off learning about it now and fixing the problem before you make other changes.

After you have revalidated the XML file, look inside PeopleType to see what it contains. The choice element gives the PeopleType its purpose. It makes PeopleType allow some or all of the things it includes in any order. In this example, you could change the choice to a sequence because PeopleType contains only one kind of object: Person. In an example where the XML file's root element could contain one of several kinds of information, you would probably want to leave this a choice element.

The choice element contains the Person element. Person is of an unnamed complex type. Pull that type out, give it a name, and add a corresponding name clause to the Person element, as shown in the following code.

```
<xsd:schema
  id="People"
  targetNamespace="http://tempuri.org/Test.xsd"
  xmlns="http://tempuri.org/Test.xsd"
  xmlns:xsd="http://www.w3.org/2001/XMLSchema"
  xmlns:msdata="urn:schemas-microsoft-com:xml-msdata"
  attributeFormDefault="qualified" elementFormDefault="qualified">
    <!-- PersonType: Represents a single person. -->
    <xsd:complexType name="PersonType">
        <xsd:sequence>
            <xsd:element name="Name" type="xsd:string"
                minOccurs="0" />
            <xsd:element name="Phone" type="xsd:string"
                minOccurs="0" />
        </xsd:sequence>
```

```
    </xsd:complexType>
    <!-- PeopleType: Represents a collection of People. -->
    <xsd:complexType name="PeopleType">
        <xsd:choice maxOccurs="unbounded">
            <xsd:element name="Person" type="PersonType">
            </xsd:element>
        </xsd:choice>
    </xsd:complexType>
    <!-- People: The XML file's main People element. -->
    <xsd:element name="People" type="PeopleType"
      msdata:IsDataSet="true"
      msdata:EnforceConstraints="False">
    </xsd:element>
</xsd:schema>
```

Once again, validate the XML file to ensure that you haven't made any mistakes.

Repeat these steps as many times as necessary until every type definition has a name. If you like, you can combine tags in the empty elements where you have removed type information. For instance, you can change the Person element's declaration to the following empty tag instead of using a separate closing tag.

```
<xsd:element name="Person" type="PersonType"/>
```

While the Create Schema menu command won't make the perfect schema for you, it will get you started. It builds a schema that is valid and that contains most of the pieces you will need in your final XSD file. Adding comments, stricter type checking on data elements, and named types will go a long way toward making a schema that is useful and understandable.

Validate XML Data

The XML menu's Validate XML Data command validates the current XML file with its selected schema. If the XML menu is not visible, the XML file is not currently selected. Open the XML file and click on it to select it and display the XML menu.

The XML file can become deselected in several ways. If you click on the Solution Explorer, Properties window, or some other window in the development environment, that window is selected and the XML menu disappears. The XML file can also lose focus automatically. If you select the Validate XML Data command and the file is valid, the XML file's window remains selected. If the file is invalid, though, the development environment adds a description of the error to the Task List and sets focus to the Task List window.

After you make the XML menu visible and invoke the Validate XML Data command, Visual Basic displays any errors in the Task list. These error messages are usually too long to fit completely in the list so they are truncated. Float the mouse over the item to see the full message in a popup.

Visual Basic also highlights errors in the XML file using a wiggly line in green or red beneath the element that is confusing the validator. Figure 5.1 shows an XML file with two errors.

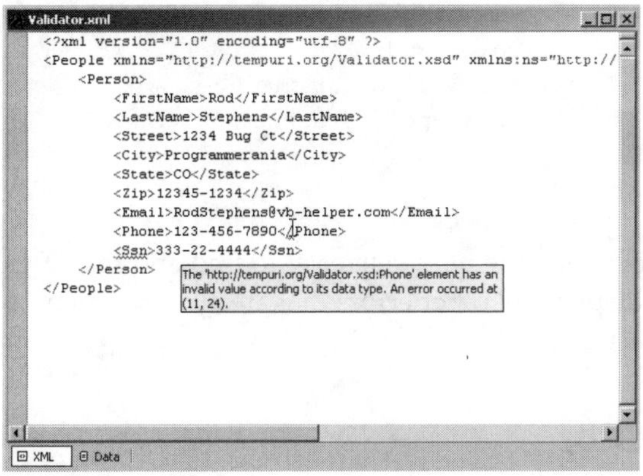

Figure 5.1 Float the mouse over an error in an XML file to see a description of the error.

The mouse is floating over the first error indicator, a green wiggly line beneath the slash in the closing </Phone> tag. The popup indicates that this element's content violates its type definition. In this case, the schema declares the Phone element to be of the type PhoneType, which requires the element to have the format NXX-NXX-XXXX where N represents a digit from 2 through 9 and X represents a digit from 0 through 9. This data's phone number begins with a 1, which violates the PhoneType restrictions so it is an error.

The second error is indicated by a red squiggly line under the <Ssn> opening tag. The schema defines an SSN element but not an Ssn element so this tag is not allowed.

The current beta version of Visual Basic identifies errors in an XML file well but has trouble explaining errors in the XSD schema. If the Visual Basic finds no errors in the XML file, it displays the string "No validation errors were found" in the status bar at the bottom of the development environment. If it finds errors in the XML file, it lists the errors in the Task List window and displays the string "Ready" in the status bar.

If there is an error in the schema, Visual Basic will probably display the string "Ready" in the status bar, but it may not list any errors in the Task list. In cases like this, you may get more information by trying to validate the XML file programmatically.

Example program Validator uses the XmlValidatingReader class to load the XML file Validator.xml, validating it against the schema Validator.xsd. This XML file contains Person elements that hold FirstName, LastName, and several other fields including a Car field. The schema defines the Car field using the following statement.

```
<xsd:element name="Car" type="CarType" minOccurs="0" maxOccurs="1" />
```

If you change the type attribute to Cartype, the schema no longer makes sense because it contains a definition of CarType, not Cartype. This version of Visual Basic cannot validate the XML file, but it doesn't explain what is wrong with the schema.

If you run the Validator program, it displays a series of error messages starting with this one:

```
*** Error loading schema
    Namespace: http://tempuri.org/Validator.xsd
    XSD File: C:\VB XML\Src\Ch13\Validator\Validator.xsd
Type 'http://tempuri.org/Validator.xsd:Cartype' is not declared. An
error occurred at file:///C:/VB
XML/Src/Ch13/Validator/Validator.xsd(138, 5).
```

This error message pinpoints the error so it is relatively easy to find and fix. After this message, the Validator program displays 18 other errors that are all consequences of the first error.

The Graphical Schema Editor

Visual Basic lets you edit schema files using a graphical editor or a textual editor. When you first open a schema, Visual Basic displays the graphical editor shown in Figure 5.2. Note that the DataSet button on the bottom of the editor is selected. If you click on the XML button, Visual Basic lets you edit the schema using the textual editor described in the next section.

Figure 5.2 shows three type definitions. The "ST" in the upper left corner of the EmailType box indicates this is a simple type. The word "string" to the right of the type's name indicates it was derived from the base type xsd:string. The line below this begins with F, indicating the line represents a facet. The facet name is pattern and its value is [^@]+@[^@]+\.[^@]+ so it allows only strings of the form A@B.C where A, B, and C are strings that do not contain the @ symbol.

The "CT" in the upper left corner of the PersonType box indicates this is a complex type. The two lines below the type's name begin with E to indicate they are elements contained by the type. The first line shows that the Name element is of type xsd:string. The second line shows that the Email element is of type EmailType.

The "CT" in the upper left corner of the PeopleType box means this is also a complex type. It contains one element named Person of type PersonType.

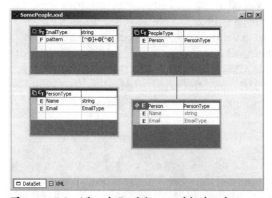

Figure 5.2 Visual Basic's graphical schema editor shows relationships among the schema's types.

The final box, with the "E" in the upper left corner, shows the definition of Person-Type. This box just repeats the definition of the PersonType and is not intended for use in editing that type. This repetition can be useful in a very complex schema where the PersonType might not naturally fit on the screen near the PeopleType object that uses it. This can be particularly helpful if many elements use this type so it cannot fit on the screen with all of them at the same time.

In addition to displaying a schema graphically, you can use the editor to modify the schema. To create a new type, right-click on an empty part of the form, select Add, and pick the appropriate command. For instance, select New complexType to create a new complex type.

In the new box, click on the name area and enter the name you want to assign to the new object. Then use the rows below the name to define the object's components. When you click on the leftmost column, a drop-down arrow appears. Click on the arrow to see a list of the types of objects that are allowed for this type of object. For example, if you create a new complex type, the list includes element, sequence, attribute, and other items that you can add to a complex type.

After you select the new item's type, click on the second entry in the row and give the item a name. Note that some items cannot have names. For instance, if you create a sequence, the editor makes an unnamed sequence so you cannot give it a name. If you want to use a named type containing a sequence, create the named type and then add it to this object as an element.

After you have given a type and name to the new item, click on the third column to make another drop-down arrow appear. Click this arrow to see a list of base types that are allowed for the new item. For example, if the new item is an element, this list includes built-in types such as xsd:float and xsd:string, plus other types defined in the schema. If this item is an attribute, this list includes the built-in types and simple types. It will not include complex types that contain subfields because an attribute in an XML file cannot contain subfields.

When you have finished building a schema using the graphical editor, you will probably need to refine the schema using the textual editor. The graphical editor does not provide tools for setting an element's attributes other than name and type. For example, it does not let you specify minOccurs or maxOccurs. To set these values, you will have to use the textual schema editor.

The Textual Schema Editor

Visual Basic's textual schema editor is a relatively simple text editor with a few enhancements. Its first enhancement is an IntelliSense feature similar to the one provided by the Visual Basic code editor. As you type, the editor tries to predict what you will type next and presents a list of options. For example, Figure 5.3 shows the textual schema editor after typing an open bracket inside an xsd:restriction element. The popup list shows all of the schema objects that are legal at this point.

As you continue to type, the editor highlights the first selection that matches the text you have entered. In this case, if you type xsd:p, the popup list selects the value xsd:pattern because that is the only option that matches the value you typed.

Figure 5.3   The textual schema editor provides valuable IntelliSense features.

When the list highlights the choice you want, you can press Tab to make the editor fill in the rest of the command.

Once you have opened the schema element's tag, IntelliSense can help you fill in the rest. If you press the Space key, the editor displays another popup listing the items that can be attributes of this tag. For the xsd:pattern tag, the only allowed attributes are id and value. After you select one of these attributes and press the = key, the editor adds a matched pair of double quotes and places the cursor between them so you can enter the attribute's value. You can then move past the closing quote and type another space to begin entering the next attribute.

After you have finished entering the tag's attributes and you type the > character to finish the opening tag, the editor automatically adds a closing tag. If you just entered <xsd:complexType name="CarType">, then the editor adds the closing tag </xsd:complexType> and places the cursor between the tags so you can enter the contents of the new complex type.

If you close the new item with />, the editor is smart enough to know that you do not want a separate closing tag. This is common with simple element definitions such as the one shown in the following code.

```
<xsd:element name="Name" type="xsd:string" />
```

You cannot tell from Figure 5.3, but the textual schema editor also provides a rich set of color codes to make different parts of the schema stand apart from each other. By default, comments are green, schema tag names such as <xsd:complexType> and </xsd:schema> are brown, attribute names are red, and attribute values are blue. You can change the color settings by opening the Tools menu, selecting Options, entering the Environment folder, and clicking the Fonts and Colors entry.

One tiny drawback to the textual editor is that it reformats the schema code according to its own conventions whenever you save the schema. That makes all of the tags indent consistently, but it also means you cannot break a long statement across several lines. For example, if you have a very long element definition containing many attributes, you cannot place the attributes on separate lines so you can see them all at once. If you break a line in this manner, the editor will remove your breaks the next time it reformats the file.

Overall, this is a small price to pay in exchange for the editor's IntelliSense features. The rules for building schemas are so complex that it can be quite difficult to remember which items are allowed inside which others. Usually typing an opening bracket < and looking at the popup list is enough to keep you moving.

Validating XML

Loading an XML file takes a significant amount of time and resources. Validating the XML file against a schema as you load takes even longer. To avoid any more overhead than necessary, many of the Visual Basic classes that read and write XML files do not validate XML data. For example, the XmlTextReader class provides fast, forward-only access to an XML document. It doesn't spend extra time validating the file's contents.

On the other hand, the XmlValidatingReader class can validate an XML document as it reads. The XmlValidatingReader's Schemas collection contains a series of schemas the object should validate the XML file against. The ValidationType property tells the reader what kind of schema it is using. This property can take the values listed in Table 5.6.

After you define the XmlValidatingReader's schema(s) and ValidationType, you can use it to read an XML document.

Example program Validator, shown in Figure 5.4, uses an XmlValidatingReader to validate an XML file. Enter the name of the XML file, the XSD schema, and the schema's target namespace in the text boxes. Then click the Validate button to make the program validate the XML file. The program displays the XML elements it encounters, followed by their attributes, together with any error messages it encounters while validating the file. In Figure 5.4, the XML file's Phone element did not satisfy the schema's requirements.

Table 5.6 Schema Validation Types

VALIDATIONTYPE	MEANING
Auto	The XmlValidatingReader determines the schema types from the schema file(s).
Schema	XSD schema.
DTD	DTD schema.
XDR	XDR schema.
None	The XmlValidatingReader does not validate the XML file.

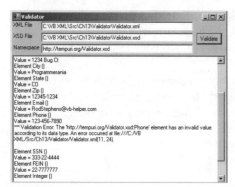

Figure 5.4 Example program Validator uses the XmlValidatingReader class to validate an XML file.

Program Validator uses the following code to validate XML files. When you click the Validate button, the program's btnValidate_Click event handler takes over. This routine creates a new XmlTextReader object attached to the XML file. It passes that object to an XmlValidatingReader's constructor to make a new XmlValidatingReader attached to the file.

The routine then adds the target namespace and schema you entered to the XmlValidatingReader's Schema collection.

Next the routine uses AddHandler to add the ValidationEventHandler subroutine as an event handler for the XmlValidatingReader's ValidationEventHandler event. When the XmlValidatingReader raises this event, Visual Basic invokes the ValidationEventHandler subroutine.

Note that the program could have defined this event handler in a different way. Instead of creating the xml_validating_reader object locally within the btnValidate_Click event handler, it could declare it at the class level using the WithEvents keyword. Then you could select xml_validating_reader from the code editor's left drop-down list and the ValidationEventHandler from the code editor's right drop-down list. In that case, the Windows Form Designer would automatically generate the code to connect the event handler to the event.

After it has defined the XmlValidatingReader's event handler, the program sets its ValidationType property to Schema. It then enters a loop reading from the XML file until the XmlValidatingReader runs out of XML data to read. Each time it encounters an opening element tag in the XML file, the program adds the tag's name to the string m_Results. It then loops through the node's attributes, adding them to m_Results as well. When the program encounters a text node, it adds the text value to m_Results.

Meanwhile, if the XmlValidatingReader encounters a validation error, it invokes the ValidationEventHandler subroutine. That routine adds information about the error to the m_Results string. The error information appears in m_Results at the point where the XmlValidatingReader realized it had encountered an error.

When it has finished reading the XML file, the program displays the results.

```
Private m_Results As String

' Validate the XML file.
Private Sub btnValidate_Click(ByVal sender As System.Object, _
  ByVal e As System.EventArgs) Handles btnValidate.Click
    Dim xml_text_reader As New XmlTextReader(txtXmlFile.Text)
    Dim xml_validating_reader As New
XmlValidatingReader(xml_text_reader)
    Dim i As Integer

    txtResult.Text = ""
    m_Results = ""
    Cursor = Cursors.WaitCursor
    Refresh()

    ' Load the schema.
    Try
        xml_validating_reader.Schemas.Add( _
            txtNamespace.Text, txtXsdFile.Text)
    Catch exc As Exception
        m_Results = m_Results & _
            "*** Error loading schema" & vbCrLf & _
            "    Namespace: " & txtNamespace.Text & vbCrLf & _
            "    XSD File: " & txtXsdFile.Text & vbCrLf & _
            exc.Message() & vbCrLf & vbCrLf
    End Try

    ' Set the validation event handler
    AddHandler xml_validating_reader.ValidationEventHandler, _
        AddressOf Me.ValidationEventHandler

    ' Validate the XML file.
    xml_validating_reader.ValidationType = ValidationType.Schema
    While xml_validating_reader.Read
        ' If this is an element, display its name and attributes.
        If xml_validating_reader.NodeType = XmlNodeType.Element Then
            m_Results = m_Results & "Element " & _
                xml_validating_reader.Name & " ("
            Do While xml_validating_reader.MoveToNextAttribute()
                m_Results = m_Results & xml_validating_reader.Name & _
                    "=" & xml_validating_reader.Value & " "
            Loop
            m_Results = m_Results & ")" & vbCrLf
        End If

        ' If this is a text node, display its value.
        If xml_validating_reader.NodeType = XmlNodeType.Text Then
            m_Results = m_Results & "Value = " & _
                xml_validating_reader.Value & vbCrLf
        End If
```

```
        End While

        xml_validating_reader.Close()
        xml_text_reader.Close()

        m_Results = m_Results & vbCrLf & "Done"
        txtResult.Text = m_Results
        Cursor = Cursors.Default
    End Sub

    ' The event handler called when there is a validation error.
    Public Sub ValidationEventHandler(ByVal sender As Object, _
      ByVal args As ValidationEventArgs)
        m_Results = m_Results & _
            "*** Validation Error: " & _
            args.Message & vbCrLf & vbCrLf
    End Sub
```

The XmlValidatingReader and XmlTextReader classes are both derived from the XmlReader class, and they provide the same methods for manipulating XML files. See Chapter 3, "Forward-Only XML," for more information on the XmlTextReader class and its methods.

Validating the DOM

The XmlDocument class represents XML data using the Document Object Model (DOM). Using XmlDocument methods, you can manipulate the hierarchical structure of an XML document relatively easily.

The XmlDocument class itself does not validate XML data. If you pass an XmlDocument object's Load method the name of an XML file, it will load the file without validating it.

One of the overloaded versions of the Load method takes as a parameter an XmlReader object. Because XmlValidatingReader is derived from XmlReader, an XmlValidatingReader is a special type of XmlReader. That means you can attach an XmlValidatingReader to the XML file, prepare it to validate the file using a schema, and then pass the XmlValidatingReader object to the XmlDocument object's Load method. As the data passes through the XmlValidatingReader on its way to the XmlDocument object, the XmlValidatingReader validates the data.

Example program ValidateDocument uses the following code to validate an XML file while loading it into an XmlDocument object. When you click the program's Validate button, the program's btnValidate_Click event handler takes over. This routine creates a new XmlTextReader object attached to the XML file. It passes that object to an XmlValidatingReader's constructor to make a new XmlValidatingReader attached to the file.

The routine then adds the target namespace and schema you entered to the XmlValidatingReader's Schema collection.

Next the routine uses AddHandler to add the ValidationEventHandler subroutine as an event handler for the XmlValidatingReader's ValidationEventHandler event. When the XmlValidatingReader raises this event, Visual Basic invokes the Validation-EventHandler subroutine.

The program then calls the XmlDocument object's Load event handler, passing it the XmlValidatingReader. As the XmlDocument loads the XML file, the XmlValidating-Reader validates its contents.

After it has finished loading the file, the program displays some information about the file's first data record.

```
' Validate the XML file.
Private Sub btnValidate_Click(ByVal sender As System.Object, _
  ByVal e As System.EventArgs) Handles btnValidate.Click
    Dim xml_text_reader As New XmlTextReader(txtXmlFile.Text)
    Dim xml_validating_reader As New
XmlValidatingReader(xml_text_reader)
    Dim xml_document As New XmlDocument()
    Dim person_node As XmlNode
    Dim child_node As XmlNode

    txtResult.Text = ""
    m_Results = ""
    Cursor = Cursors.WaitCursor
    Refresh()

    ' Load the schema.
    Try
        xml_validating_reader.Schemas.Add( _
            txtNamespace.Text, txtXsdFile.Text)
    Catch exc As Exception
        m_Results = m_Results & _
            "*** Error loading schema" & vbCrLf & _
            "    Namespace: " & txtNamespace.Text & vbCrLf & _
            "    XSD File: " & txtXsdFile.Text & vbCrLf & _
            exc.Message() & vbCrLf & vbCrLf
    End Try

    ' Set the validation event handler
    AddHandler xml_validating_reader.ValidationEventHandler, _
        AddressOf Me.ValidationEventHandler

    ' Load the XmlDocument using the XmlValidatingReader.
    xml_document.Load(xml_validating_reader)
    xml_validating_reader.Close()
    xml_text_reader.Close()

    ' Display the first record's values.
    person_node = xml_document.DocumentElement.ChildNodes.Item(0)
    For Each child_node In person_node.ChildNodes
```

```
        m_Results = m_Results & "   " & child_node.Name & _
            ": " & child_node.InnerText & vbCrLf
    Next child_node

    m_Results = m_Results & vbCrLf & "Done"
    txtResult.Text = m_Results
    Cursor = Cursors.Default
End Sub
```

After a program loads an XmlDocument object with an XML file's data, it can manipulate the data using any of the methods provided by the XmlDocument object. For more information on using the XmlDocument object to manipulate the DOM, see Chapter 2, "DOM."

While an XmlDocument object can validate an XML file when it loads by pulling the data from an XmlValidatingReader object, it does not ensure that the data remains valid afterward. If you use the XmlDocument object's methods to modify the data so that it no longer satisfies the original XML file's schema, the XmlDocument object will not tell you.

Building Schemas Programmatically

XSD schemas are written using XML so they have a hierarchical structure just as any other XML file does. If you wanted, you could open an XSD file using XmlDocument and manipulate its structure using the XmlDocument object's properties and methods. Unless you were careful, however, you could easily damage the file's special structure and make it worthless as an XSD schema.

Fortunately, Visual Basic provides a family of classes to make building and modifying schemas easier. The XmlSchema class lets you read, build, and write a schema. Classes such as XmlSchemaSimpleType, XmlSchemaSimpleTypeRestriction, and XmlSchemaElement help you add types, restrictions, and elements to the schema.

To programmatically build a schema, a program creates a new XmlSchema object. It creates other objects such as XmlSchemaSimpleType and XmlSchemaElement objects and adds them to the XmlSchema object's Items collection.

The properties and methods of the objects contained by the XmlSchema object determine the internal structure of the schema. For instance, an XmlSchemaComplexType object's Particle property indicates the choice or sequence object contained in the complex type.

For a slightly more complicated example, consider a simple type derived from the string type using a restriction. The XmlSchemaSimpleType object's Content property gives a reference to the XmlSchemaSimpleTypeRestriction object representing the restriction. The XmlSchemaSimpleTypeRestriction object's Facets collection contains a series of objects representing the facets that restrict the base type. These facet objects come from the classes XmlSchemaMinLengthFacet, XmlSchemaMaxInclusiveFacet, XmlSchemaTotalDigitsFacet, and so forth.

The result of all these classes is a hierarchical data structure with elements linked using class properties. Unfortunately, the connections between objects in this hierarchy are made in a variety of ways. Objects are linked with such properties as Particle and Content and with Items and Facets collections. This lack of consistency makes it hard to remember how to connect different kinds of objects to others. Using all of these different connection methods doesn't even prevent you from connecting the wrong kinds of objects. For example, you can add an XmlSchemaSimpleType object to a Facets collection even though that doesn't make sense. The XmlSchema object will not compile the schema, but the Visual Basic compiler doesn't have enough type checking information to realize that an XmlSchemaSimpleType doesn't belong in a Facets collection.

Even with all these problems, using the family of XmlSchema classes to build a schema is probably easier than trying to build a schema from scratch.

Example program MakeSchema, shown in Figure 5.5, uses these classes to build the following schema programmatically. If you take a few moments to study the schema now, the program's Visual Basic code presented shortly will make more sense.

The schema begins with an XML declaration and the mandatory schema tag. The schema's attributeFormDefault and elementFormDefault attributes are both set to qualified. That means the attributes and elements referred to in the schema must be explicitly qualified with a namespace. You'll see this in the element declarations shortly.

The schema tag sets the schema's namespace to http://tempuri.org/MakeSchema. xsd. It also sets the namespace for the items inside the schema tag to http://www. w3.org/2001/XMLSchema.

After the schema tag, the file defines a simple type called NameType. The type is defined by restricting the string type with facets minLength and maxLength.

Next the file defines EmailType. This is another simple type based on the built-in string type. EmailType is defined by restriction using the pattern facet to allow only strings of the form A@B.C where A, B, and C are strings that don't contain the @ symbol.

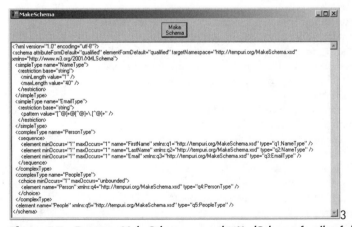

Figure 5.5 Program MakeSchema uses the XmlSchema family of classes to build a schema.

The schema then defines PersonType. This type is a complex type containing a sequence. The sequence defines FirstName, LastName, and Email fields. For each of these fields, minOccurs and maxOccurs is set to 1 so each field is required, can occur only once, and must appear in the order defined by the sequence.

Notice how the schema qualifies each of the fields' types with the namespace http://tempuri.org/MakeSchema.xsd. First it defines an abbreviation for the namespace, and then it uses the abbreviation in the type names.

The schema defines one last type named PeopleType. This is a complex type containing a choice object. The choice contains one or more Person objects of type PersonType. Notice again how the schema qualifies PersonType with the http://tempuri.org/MakeSchema.xsd namespace.

Having finished defining the types it needs, the schema creates an element named People of the type PeopleType. Again, this type is qualified with the namespace.

```xml
<?xml version="1.0" encoding="utf-8"?>
<schema attributeFormDefault="qualified"
  elementFormDefault="qualified"
  targetNamespace="http://tempuri.org/MakeSchema.xsd"
  xmlns="http://www.w3.org/2001/XMLSchema">
  <simpleType name="NameType">
    <restriction base="string">
      <minLength value="1" />
      <maxLength value="40" />
    </restriction>
  </simpleType>
  <simpleType name="EmailType">
    <restriction base="string">
      <pattern value="[^@]+@[^@]+\.[^@]+" />
    </restriction>
  </simpleType>
  <complexType name="PersonType">
    <sequence>
      <element minOccurs="1" maxOccurs="1" name="FirstName"
        xmlns:q1="http://tempuri.org/MakeSchema.xsd"
        type="q1:NameType" />
      <element minOccurs="1" maxOccurs="1" name="LastName"
        xmlns:q2="http://tempuri.org/MakeSchema.xsd"
        type="q2:NameType" />
      <element minOccurs="1" maxOccurs="1" name="Email"
        xmlns:q3="http://tempuri.org/MakeSchema.xsd"
        type="q3:EmailType" />
    </sequence>
  </complexType>
  <complexType name="PeopleType">
    <choice minOccurs="1" maxOccurs="unbounded">
      <element name="Person"
xmlns:q4="http://tempuri.org/MakeSchema.xsd"
        type="q4:PersonType" />
    </choice>
```

```
    </complexType>
    <element name="People" xmlns:q5="http://tempuri.org/MakeSchema.xsd"
      type="q5:PeopleType" />
</schema>
```

The following code shows a small XML file that satisfies this schema. The file defines the data's namespace and includes a single Person record.

```
<?xml version="1.0" encoding="utf-8" ?>
<People xmlns="http://tempuri.org/MakeSchema.xsd">
    <Person>
        <FirstName>Rod</FirstName>
        <LastName>Stephens</LastName>
        <Email>RodStephens@vb-helper.com</Email>
    </Person>
</People>
```

The following code shows how program MakeSchema builds its schema. As you work through the Visual Basic code, refer back to the schema code to see the results.

When you click the Make Schema button, the program's btnMakeSchema_Click event handler takes over. This routine defines some constants and then creates a new XmlSchema object named xml_schema. It sets the schema's target namespace to http://tempuri.org/MakeSchema.xsd. It also sets the schema's attributeFormDefault and elementFormDefault attributes to qualified.

The program then creates a new XmlSchemaSimpleType to represent NameType. This is a top-level object so the program adds it to the xml_schema object's Items collection. It also sets the object's Name property.

The program then defines NameType. It creates a new XmlSchemaSimpleType-Restriction object to represent the type's restriction. It attaches the restriction to the type by setting the NameType object's Content property to the restriction object.

The program sets the restriction object's base type to string and then creates two facet objects to define the restriction. The program makes an XmlSchemaMinLength-Facet object and an XmlSchemaMaxLengthFacet object. It sets the facets' values to 1 and 40, respectively, so NameType values must contain between 1 and 40 characters. The program finishes defining the NameType by adding the facets to the restriction object's Facets collection.

Next the program defines the simple type EmailType. It creates an Xml Schema-SimpleType object as before and sets its Content property to a new XmlSchema-SimpleTypeRestriction object. This time it adds a facet object of type XmlSchema-PatternFacet to the restriction's Facets collection.

Having created the basic field types NameType and EmailType, the program uses them to create the complex type PersonType. It creates the PersonType XmlSchema-ComplexType object, makes a new XmlSchemaSequence object to represent the sequence inside the type, and sets the type's Particle property to this sequence object.

The program then adds elements to the sequence object to define the items that must be present in a PersonType record. It creates a new XmlSchemaElement, adds it to the sequence object's Items collection, and sets the new element's name and type name. It sets the element's MinOccurs and MaxOccurs properties to 1 so the sequence must contain exactly one occurrence of the element. The program repeats these steps for the three elements inside the sequence: FirstName, LastName, and Email.

Next, the program creates the complex type PeopleType that contains a choice object. Building the type and its choice object is similar to building the PersonType. The program creates the XmlSchemaComplexType object. It then makes an XmlSchema-Choice object and assigns it to the type's Particle property. The program creates a new element object and adds it to the choice object's Items collection, much as the previous code added elements to the PersonType's sequence object.

After all of the types are defined, creating the People element that corresponds to the XML data root is practically trivial. The program creates a new XmlSchemaElement object, adds it to the schema's Items collection, sets the element's name to People, and sets its type to PeopleType.

At this point, the program has built the schema. It could use the XmlSchema object's Write method to save the schema information into a file, but the schema may be invalid. If the program saved the schema into a file, the result would not necessarily be a consistent schema.

To test the schema, the program calls the XmlSchema object's Compile method passing it the address of a validation event handler. The Compile method attempts to compile the schema and check it for consistency. If the method has trouble compiling the schema, it calls the validation event handler and that routine can record the error information.

After the program compiles the schema, it saves it into a new XSD file and displays the results in a text box.

```
Private m_Results As String

Private Sub btnMakeSchema_Click(ByVal sender As System.Object, _
   ByVal e As System.EventArgs) Handles btnMakeSchema.Click
    m_Results = ""
    txtResults.Text = ""
    Cursor = Cursors.WaitCursor
    Refresh()

    Try
        Const target_namespace = "http://tempuri.org/MakeSchema.xsd"
        Const xsd_namespace = "http://www.w3.org/2001/XMLSchema"

        ' ******************************
        ' Prepare the schema
        Dim xml_schema As New XmlSchema()
        xml_schema.TargetNamespace = target_namespace
        xml_schema.ElementFormDefault = XmlSchemaForm.Qualified
        xml_schema.AttributeFormDefault = XmlSchemaForm.Qualified

        ' ******************************
        ' NameType
```

```
        Dim name_type As New XmlSchemaSimpleType()
        xml_schema.Items.Add(name_type)
        name_type.Name = "NameType"

        ' NameType/Restriction
        Dim name_type_restriction As New _
XmlSchemaSimpleTypeRestriction()
        name_type.Content = name_type_restriction
        name_type_restriction.BaseTypeName = _
            New XmlQualifiedName("string", xsd_namespace)

        ' NameType/Restriction/minLength
        Dim name_type_min_length As New XmlSchemaMinLengthFacet()
        name_type_min_length.Value = "1"
        name_type_restriction.Facets.Add(name_type_min_length)

        ' NameType/Restriction/minLength
        Dim name_type_max_length As New XmlSchemaMaxLengthFacet()
        name_type_max_length.Value = "40"
        name_type_restriction.Facets.Add(name_type_max_length)

        ' ******************************
        ' EmailType
        Dim email_type As New XmlSchemaSimpleType()
        xml_schema.Items.Add(email_type)
        email_type.Name = "EmailType"

        ' EmailType/Restriction
        Dim email_type_restriction As _
            New XmlSchemaSimpleTypeRestriction()
        email_type.Content = email_type_restriction
        email_type_restriction.BaseTypeName = _
            New XmlQualifiedName("string", xsd_namespace)

        ' EmailType/Restriction/pattern
        Dim email_type_pattern As New XmlSchemaPatternFacet()
        email_type_pattern.Value = "[^@]+@[^@]+\.[^@]+"
        email_type_restriction.Facets.Add(email_type_pattern)

        ' ******************************
        ' Person
        Dim person_type As New XmlSchemaComplexType()
        xml_schema.Items.Add(person_type)
        person_type.Name = "PersonType"

        ' PersonType/Sequence
        Dim person_type_sequence As New XmlSchemaSequence()
        person_type.Particle = person_type_sequence
```

```
' Elements inside PersonType/Sequence
' FirstName
Dim first_name_element As New XmlSchemaElement()
person_type_sequence.Items.Add(first_name_element)
first_name_element.Name = "FirstName"
first_name_element.SchemaTypeName = _
    New XmlQualifiedName("NameType", target_namespace)
first_name_element.MinOccurs = 1
first_name_element.MaxOccurs = 1


' LastName
Dim last_name_element As New XmlSchemaElement()
person_type_sequence.Items.Add(last_name_element)
last_name_element.Name = "LastName"
last_name_element.SchemaTypeName = _
    New XmlQualifiedName("NameType", target_namespace)
last_name_element.MinOccurs = 1
last_name_element.MaxOccurs = 1


' Email
Dim email_element As New XmlSchemaElement()
person_type_sequence.Items.Add(email_element)
email_element.Name = "Email"
email_element.SchemaTypeName = _
    New XmlQualifiedName("EmailType", target_namespace)
email_element.MinOccurs = 1
email_element.MaxOccurs = 1


' *****************************
' PeopleType
Dim people_type As New XmlSchemaComplexType()
xml_schema.Items.Add(people_type)
people_type.Name = "PeopleType"


' PeopleType/Choice
Dim people_type_choice As New XmlSchemaChoice()
people_type.Particle = people_type_choice
people_type_choice.MinOccurs = 1
people_type_choice.MaxOccursString = "unbounded"


' Elements inside PeopleType/Choice
Dim person_element As New XmlSchemaElement()
people_type_choice.Items.Add(person_element)
person_element.Name = "Person"
person_element.SchemaTypeName = _
    New XmlQualifiedName("PersonType", target_namespace)


' *****************************
```

```vb
    ' People
    Dim people_element As New XmlSchemaElement()
    xml_schema.Items.Add(people_element)
    people_element.Name = "People"
    people_element.SchemaTypeName = _
        New XmlQualifiedName("PeopleType", target_namespace)

    ' ********************************
    ' Compile the schema.
    xml_schema.Compile(AddressOf ValidationEventHandler)

    ' Save and display the results.
    Dim file_name As String
    file_name = Application.StartupPath()
    If file_name.EndsWith("\") Then _
        file_name = file_name.Remove(file_name.Length - 1, 1)
    If file_name.EndsWith("\bin") Then _
        file_name = file_name.Remove(file_name.Length - 4, 4)
    file_name = file_name & "\MakeSchema.xsd"

    Dim stream_writer As New StreamWriter(file_name)
    xml_schema.Write(stream_writer)
    stream_writer.Close()

    If m_Results.Length > 0 Then m_Results = m_Results & _
        "**********" & vbCrLf
    m_Results = m_Results & GetFileContents(file_name)
Catch exc As Exception
    MsgBox(exc.Message)
Finally
    txtResults.Text = m_Results
    Cursor = Cursors.Default
End Try
End Sub

' Add errors to m_Results.
Private Sub ValidationEventHandler(ByVal sender As Object, _
  ByVal args As ValidationEventArgs)
    m_Results = m_Results & "*****" & vbCrLf & args.Message & vbCrLf
End Sub
```

Visual Basic provides many other classes for building and manipulating schemas. These classes correspond closely to the types of elements you can create in a schema. Table 5.7 lists some of the most useful of these classes.

Table 5.7   Important Classes for Building Schemas Programmatically

CLASS	CORRESPONDING XSD OBJECT
XmlSchema	The schema as a whole
XmlSchemaElement	element
XmlSchemaSimpleType	simpleType
XmlSchemaComplexType	complexType
XmlSchemaComplexContent	complexContent
XmlSchemaSimpleContent	simpleContent
XmlSchemaComplexContentExtension	extension (inside complexContent)
XmlSchemaComplexContentRestriction	restriction (inside complexContent)
XmlSchemaSimpleContentExtension	extension (inside simpleContent)
XmlSchemaSimpleContentRestriction	restriction (inside simpleContent)
XmlSchemaAll	all
XmlSchemaChoice	choice
XmlSchemaSequence	sequence
XmlSchemaAttribute	attribute

Similarly, Visual Basic provides an assortment of classes representing facets you can use to refine a type's definition. Table 5.8 lists the most useful of these classes. See the section *Primitive Built-In Types* earlier in this chapter for more information on facets.

Building schemas programmatically can be quite difficult. Visual Basic's family of XmlSchema classes is large, objects in a schema hierarchy are connected in inconsistent ways, and the objects do not give you much help remembering which objects must be contained in which others. The IntelliSense features provided by the textual Schema editor give you much more help in constructing schemas. In fact, building a schema in code is much easier if you first construct an example schema using the textual schema editor. Then you can refer to it as you assemble the pieces in code.

Table 5.8   Important Facet Classes for Building Schemas Programmatically

CLASS	CORRESPONDING XSD FACET
XmlSchemaEnumerationFacet	enumeration
XmlSchemaMaxExclusiveFacet	maxExclusive
XmlSchemaMaxInclusiveFacet	maxInclusive

Table 5.8 (Continued)

CLASS	CORRESPONDING XSD FACET
XmlSchemaMinExclusiveFacet	minExclusive
XmlSchemaMinInclusiveFacet	minInclusive
XmlSchemaLength	length
XmlSchemaMaxLength	maxLength
XmlSchemaMinLength	minLength
XmlSchemaFractionDigits	fractionDigits
XmlSchemaTotalDigits	totalDigits
XmlSchemaPatternFacet	pattern

DataSet Schemas

Building a schema from scratch programmatically can be difficult, but building one from a DataSet is simple. The program just loads the DataSet and calls its WriteSchema method.

Example program DataSetSchema, shown in Figure 5.6, loads a DataSet and then writes out the DataSet's XML data and its schema.

Program DataSetSchema uses the following code to generate its XML data and schema. When you click the Make Schema button, the program's btnMakeSchema_Click event handler executes. After some preliminary work, this routine composes a database connect string and uses it to open a connection to the database with an OldDbConnection object.

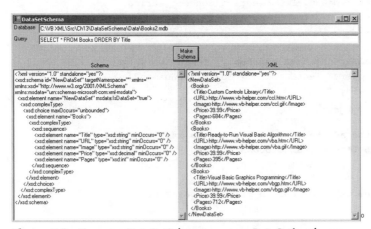

Figure 5.6 Program DataSetSchema saves a DataSet's schema.

Next, the program initializes an OleDbDataAdapter to select the data using the query string entered in the program's text box. The program tells the data adapter to map the automatically created table name Table to the more meaningful name Books and calls the data adapter's Fill method to load the DataSet.

Now all the program needs to do is call the DataSet's WriteXml and WriteXmlSchema methods and display the results.

```
Private Sub btnMakeSchema_Click(ByVal sender As System.Object, _
  ByVal e As System.EventArgs) Handles btnMakeSchema.Click
    Dim connect_string As String
    Dim db_connection As OleDbConnection
    Dim data_adapter As New OleDbDataAdapter()
    Dim data_set As New DataSet()
    Dim db_file As String
    Dim xml_file As String
    Dim xsd_file As String
    Dim file_start As String

    txtXsd.Text = ""
    txtXml.Text = ""
    Cursor = Cursors.WaitCursor
    Refresh()

    db_file = txtDatabase.Text
    file_start = db_file.Remove(db_file.Length - 4, 4)
    xml_file = file_start & ".xml"
    xsd_file = file_start & ".xsd"

    ' Compose the connect string.
    connect_string = _
        "Provider=Microsoft.Jet.OLEDB.4.0;" & _
        "Data Source=" & db_file

    ' Connect to the database.
    db_connection = New OleDbConnection(connect_string)
    db_connection.Open()

    Try
        ' Initialize the data adapter.
        data_adapter.SelectCommand = New OleDbCommand( _
            txtQuery.Text, _
            db_connection)

        ' Tell the adapter to map the Access results Table
        ' to the DataSet table Books.
        data_adapter.TableMappings.Add("Table", "Books")

        ' Use the data adapter to fill the DataSet.
        data_adapter.Fill(data_set)

        ' Write the XML data.
```

```
                data_set.WriteXml(xml_file)

                ' Write the XSD schema.
                data_set.WriteXmlSchema(xsd_file)

                data_adapter.Dispose()

                ' Display the XSD schema.
                txtXsd.Text = GetFileContents(xsd_file)

                ' Display the XML data.
                txtXml.Text = GetFileContents(xml_file)
        Finally
                ' Close the database connection.
                db_connection.Close()
        End Try

        Cursor = Cursors.Default
End Sub
```

The following code shows the XML file created by the DataSet's WriteXml method. This code is very close to what you probably would have created if you had generated the data by hand.

```
<?xml version="1.0" standalone="yes"?>
<NewDataSet>
  <Books>
    <Title>Custom Controls Library</Title>
    <URL>http://www.vb-helper.com/ccl.htm</URL>
    <Image>http://www.vb-helper.com/ccl.gif</Image>
    <Price>39.99</Price>
    <Pages>684</Pages>
  </Books>
  <Books>
    <Title>Ready-to-Run Visual Basic Algorithms</Title>
    <URL>http://www.vb-helper.com/vba.htm</URL>
    <Image>http://www.vb-helper.com/vba.gif</Image>
    <Price>39.99</Price>
    <Pages>395</Pages>
  </Books>
  <Books>
    <Title>Visual Basic Graphics Programming</Title>
    <URL>http://www.vb-helper.com/vbgp.htm</URL>
    <Image>http://www.vb-helper.com/vbgp.gif</Image>
    <Price>39.99</Price>
    <Pages>712</Pages>
  </Books>
</NewDataSet>
```

The following code shows the XSD schema created by the DataSet's WriteXml-Schema method. While the program's XML output is about what you would expect, the schema is less similar to what you would have created yourself. The schema translates the fields' data types more or less correctly but it misses a lot of restrictions placed on the data in the database.

The three string fields should all have minLength and maxLength facets to ensure their data is between 1 and 80 characters long. The Price field should have a fractionDigits facet allowing at most 2 digits after the decimal place. Finally, all of these fields should have minOccurs set to 1 because they are all required in the database.

The URL and Image fields could also have pattern facets to ensure their values look like file paths or URLs, though that is more validation than the original database performs. Similarly, the Pages field could be restricted to reasonable values (perhaps between 100 and 2,000 pages), and the Price field could be restricted to reasonable values ($10 to $100 would probably work).

```xml
<?xml version="1.0" standalone="yes"?>
<xsd:schema id="NewDataSet" targetNamespace="" xmlns=""
 xmlns:xsd="http://www.w3.org/2001/XMLSchema"
 xmlns:msdata="urn:schemas-microsoft-com:xml-msdata">
  <xsd:element name="NewDataSet" msdata:IsDataSet="true">
    <xsd:complexType>
      <xsd:choice maxOccurs="unbounded">
        <xsd:element name="Books">
          <xsd:complexType>
            <xsd:sequence>
              <xsd:element name="Title" type="xsd:string"
                minOccurs="0" />
              <xsd:element name="URL" type="xsd:string"
                minOccurs="0" />
              <xsd:element name="Image" type="xsd:string"
                minOccurs="0" />
              <xsd:element name="Price" type="xsd:decimal"
                minOccurs="0" />
              <xsd:element name="Pages" type="xsd:int"
                minOccurs="0" />
            </xsd:sequence>
          </xsd:complexType>
        </xsd:element>
      </xsd:choice>
    </xsd:complexType>
  </xsd:element>
</xsd:schema>
```

While this schema isn't what you would have come up with by hand, it does work. You would probably want to restructure it to add facets restricting the field values. To make that easier, you might want to break the field element definitions out and give them each their own named types. This file still gives you a starting point, however. In a more complicated example, that can save you some time.

Conclusion

Schemas can be very useful tools for ensuring that data has the right format before an application starts working with it. It is common for a complex application to dedicate a few hundred lines of code to processing data and several thousand to verifying that it meets the program's requirements. If you can move some or all of this data validation into a schema, you can greatly simplify the main program.

Several different schema languages have appeared since XML version 1.0. Currently Visual Basic focuses on XSD (XML Schema Definition) schemas so it provides the most tools for working with them. It provides graphical and textual XSD schema editors that provide context-sensitive cues and IntelliSense to make building schemas easy. The XmlValidatingReader class lets a program validate XML files against DTD, XDR, and XSD schemas. Visual Basic provides classes that help you build schemas programmatically, and the DataSet object's WriteXmlSchema method automatically generates schemas for database data.

You can write tools that manipulate XML without using schemas, but all these tools make building and using schemas easy enough to make schemas worthwhile.

PART

Two

XML on the Web

The most recent versions of Visual Basic have provided tighter integration with the World Wide Web. They have allowed Visual Basic applications to provide functionality more easily than ever before. Using ASP.NET, client-side controls, and Web Services, you can provide Web content using Visual Basic itself.

The chapters in Part Two explain ways you can use XML and Visual Basic .NET to provide Web content. They show how to write Visual Basic applications that use XSL to transform XML data into new formats such as HTML suitable for display on the Web. They tell how to use ASP.NET to build data islands that display XML content on a Web page and how to use XML and Visual Basic to build Web Services that provide responsive Web-based functionality.

CHAPTER 6

XSL (eXtensible Stylesheet Language) is one of the most important XML accessories. It lets you quickly and easily transform an XML document into another language such as HTML, a differently formatted XML file, special XML-based languages such as VoiceXML, or even a plain text file.

XML is a data description language. It provides syntax for describing data, but it is not intended to provide a nicely formatted data display. Using XSL, you can transform the data in an XML file into formatted output suitable for display on Web browsers, hand-held devices, voice hardware, word processors, and more.

Figure 6.1 shows this process graphically. A transformation engine uses the instructions in an XSL style sheet to transform an XML source document into an output document. A formatting application can then display the output document.

Different XSL style sheets can transform the same source document in different ways to produce different kinds of output documents such as HTML, XML, or text files. Different formatting applications can then display the documents. In one common scenario, the transformation engine transforms XML code into an HTML file, which is then viewable by a Web browser.

XSL is a huge topic, and several other books have been written about it. This chapter doesn't try to cover all of XSL in detail. Its purpose is to explain the basics of XSL so you can convert your XML documents into HTML and other similar formats. It also shows how your Visual Basic applications can play the role of the transformation engine shown in Figure 6.1.

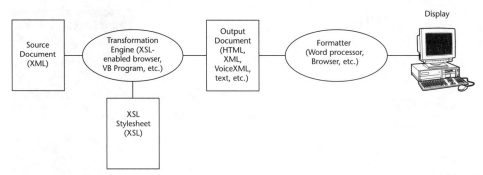

Figure 6.1 XSL transforms XML documents into HTML, XML, text, and other kinds of documents.

For a more complete explanation of XSL, see the World Wide Web Consortium's (W3C) documentation at www.w3.org/Style/XSL or consult a book on XSL such as *XSL Essentials* by Michael Fitzgerald (Wiley, 2001).

The first sections in this chapter introduce the general concepts of XSL and show the results of some simple transformations. The sections that follow describe XSL in greater detail. The final sections in this chapter explain some examples that illustrate the richness of XSL as a programming language and show how to build Visual Basic .NET applications that perform XSL transformations.

Some of the sections that follow appear a bit out of order. For example, it's hard to give good examples using XPath expressions until you understand how to use XSL elements such as xsl:for-each and xsl:value-of to process the nodes selected by the expression. At the same time, it's hard to give good examples using xsl:for-each and xsl:value-of until you understand XPath statements.

As you read the early parts of this chapter, try to focus on the topic at hand. If you don't understand part of an example, skip it. Chances are it will all make sense later when you read the section describing the example's other elements.

The Pieces of XSL

XSL is made up of three components: XSL Transformation Language (XSLT), XML Path Language (XPath), and XSL Formatting Objects (FO).

XSLT is a language for transforming XML documents. It specifies patterns in an XML document and the corresponding results XSL should add to the output file.

XPath is a language used by XSLT to refer to parts of an XML document. For example, the expression //Item refers to any tag named Item in the XML document. The following sections show how flexible XPath is at specifying nodes in an XML document.

XSL Formatting Objects are the entities that make up the result document. Often the formatting objects are hidden by the XSL style sheet's code so you don't need to think about them explicitly. The style sheet tells how to create formatting objects that represent the pieces of the output document. It's really the output you think about, not the objects that produce it.

One of the more confusing aspects of XSL is its relation to XSLT. Many Web developers use the two terms interchangeably. Technically, XSLT is just one part of XSL. In practice, however, XSL and XSLT usually mean the code in an XSL style sheet. Most of the time, you can ignore the difference between these two terms and concentrate on the code.

Using XPath within XSL

While the XSL standard was in development, it became apparent that XSL needed the ability to specify particular nodes in an XML document so that it could associate transformation code with those nodes. XPath fills this need.

XPath is a language for identifying nodes in an XML file's hierarchy. It is similar to the syntax you use to specify a file's path on a hard disk except it specifies nodes instead of files and directories. The XPath standard also contains functions that make searching nodes and manipulating their data easier.

The following section describes some examples that show how XPath fits into XSL processing. The sections that follow explain XPath in greater detail.

A Quick XPath Example

Consider the following snippet of XSL code.

```
<xsl:template match="/">
    <!-- Formatting instructions go here. -->
</xsl:template>
```

The XPath expression / in the match statement means "the document's root node" so this XSL code begins processing the XML file at the root node. Formatting instructions for the specified node belong between the xsl:template tags. You'll see how to add those instructions in later sections.

If you want to begin processing on some other specific node, you can specify the complete path to that node. Consider this simple XML file.

```
<?xml version="1.0"?>
<Contacts>
    <Author>
        <PhoneNumbers>
            <Phone type="home">3035551133</Phone>
        </PhoneNumbers>
    </Author>
</Contacts>
```

To begin processing at the Phone element, the xsl:template code might look like this.

```
<xsl:template match="/Contacts/Author/PhoneNumbers/Phone"/>
    <!-- Formatting instructions go here. -->
</xsl:template>
```

This example shows the importance of XPath to XSL. XPath allows an XSL style sheet to specify which particular nodes receive the formatting instructions within a particular piece of XSL code.

This example also highlights the difference between the XPath expressions used to select nodes (/ or /Contacts/Author/PhoneNumbers) and the XSLT code that processes them (everything else except formatting objects). The examples throughout the rest of the chapter use XPath extensively so understanding the distinction now is important.

Specifying Node Locations

An XML document's root node is represented by a slash (/). This is a little different from the data root node, which is the element containing all of the other data nodes in the document. For example, consider the following XML document.

```
<?xml version="1.0"?>
<Contacts>
    <Author>
        <PhoneNumbers>
            <Phone type="home">3035551133</Phone>
            <Phone type="work">3035559392</Phone>
            <Phone type="fax">3035559393</Phone>
        </PhoneNumbers>
    </Author>
</Contacts>
```

In this file, the data root node Contacts contains all of the other data nodes. The document's root, represented in XPath by /, contains the Contacts node as well as the XML declaration and any processing instructions and comments the file might contain outside of the Contacts node.

An XPath expression can specify an absolute path starting from the root as in:

```
/Contacts/Author
```

This expression matches an Author node that is a direct child of the Contacts node. The Contacts node is a direct child of the document's root node /.

The node the XSL engine is currently processing is called the *context node*. An XPath expression can specify a path relative to the context node. For example, suppose the XSL engine is processing the Contacts node in the previous XML document. Then the XPath expression Author/PhoneNumbers matches the PhoneNumbers node that is a direct child of the Authors node that is a direct child of the current node Contacts.

It is a very common mistake to omit the / when you want to use an absolute path or to use / when you want to use a relative path. The difference between Author/PhoneNumbers and /Author/PhoneNumbers is small but important. Usually the difference is so large that the XPath expression does not select any nodes and the formatting code you have written is never applied.

XPath allows two kinds of wild cards. The * character matches a single node. For example, the XPath expression /Food/*/SideDish matches SideDish nodes that are grandchildren of the Food node. The SideDish node's parent can be any node as long as it is a child of the Food node.

The second wildcard is specified by //. The // wildcard matches any number of nodes in direct descent. For example, the XPath expression /Books//Pages matches all Pages nodes that are descendants of the Books node. Note that the Books node must be a direct child of the document root node. Because the document can have only one root data node, that means /Books is the document's root data node. In that case, all of the nodes in the document must be descendents of /Books so /Books//Pages is practically equivalent to //Pages.

In an XPath expression, the . symbol means the current node. For example, ./Fish matches the current node's Fish children. The statement ./Fish is similar to the statement Fish but is very different from /Fish, which matches a Fish node that is a direct child of the document's root.

Finally, XPath expressions can include .. to mean a node's parent in the document hierarchy. For example, ../Car means the Car child of the current node's parent. In other words, ../Car means the current node's Car sibling.

The .. expression can also be useful in absolute expressions. For example, //Item/.. matches any node that is the direct parent of an Item node.

Using the /, *, //, ., and .. operators, you can specify extremely complex node selections. While you can easily cook up examples that are so elaborate that you will never need to use them, those examples show the power of XPath. You may never need to find nodes that are the parents of nodes that have siblings that are Car nodes, but you could if you found it necessary.

Table 6.1 summarizes XPath symbols that you can use to select nodes.

Table 6.1   XPath Symbols for Selecting Nodes

SYMBOL	DESCRIPTION
/	The document's XmlDocument root node. This contains the data's root node.
.	The current node.
*	Matches a single node. For example, /Food/*/SideDish matches all nodes named SideDish that are grandchildren of the node Food, which is a direct child of the document root.
//	Matches any number of intermediate nodes. For example, //Item//Price matches any Price node that is a descendant of any Item node.
..	The current node's parent node. For example, ../.. is the current node's grandparent.

Navigation Directions

Most XPath expressions specify a node's position starting from the root and working downward into the document hierarchy. For example, /Books/2001/Titles starts at the document root, looks for the Books child, looks for that node's 2001 child, and finally looks for that node's Titles child.

XPath provides several methods for moving through the document hierarchy in different directions. For instance, the .. symbol listed in Table 6.1 moves to a node's parent.

XSL also provides other methods for moving through an XML document's node hierarchy in other directions. One of these different navigation directions is called an *axis*. Some of the most useful axes are described in the following sections.

The axis methods do not work in the match statements shown in the previous examples, although some of them are comparable to the symbols listed in Table 6.1. For example, the descendent axis is in some ways similar to the // symbol in a match statement.

The axis methods are used in select statements, which are described a little later in this chapter. They are most commonly used in the for-each or value-of statements. For example, the following code iterates over a node's children.

```
<xsl:for-each select="child::*">
    <!-- Formatting instructions go here. -->
</xsl:for-each>
```

The section *XSL Elements* later in this chapter describes statements such as for-each in detail.

The following sections describe some of the most useful axis functions. Examples in these sections refer to the following XML document.

```
<?xml version="1.0"?>
<Orders>
    <Order Index="1">
        <Item Quantity="2">Cookie</Item>
        <Item Quantity="1" Size="Medium">Coffee</Item>
    </Order>
    <Order Index="2">
        <Item Quantity="10">Banana</Item>
        <Item Quantity="24">Donut</Item>
        <Drink>Milkshake</Drink>
    </Order>
    <Order Index="3">
        <Order Index="3a">
            <Item Quantity="1">Soda</Item>
            <Item Quantity="1">Sandwich</Item>
            <Item Quantity="1">Apple</Item>
        </Order>
        <Order Index="3b">
            <Item Quantity="1">Water</Item>
```

```
                    <Item Quantity="1">Salad</Item>
                    <Item Quantity="1">Peach</Item>
                </Order>
            </Order>
        </Orders>
```

The examples that follow use this XML file to illustrate the nodes selected by different axis statements.

ancestor

The ancestor axis selects the context node's ancestors. For example, ancestor::* selects all of the context's node's ancestors. If context node is the Item node with value Donut in the previous XML document, then the ancestor nodes are the Order node with Index attribute equal to 2 and the Orders node.

The statement ancestor::Order selects the ancestors of the context node named Order. If the context node is the Item node with value Peach in the previous XML document, then ancestor::Order selects the Order nodes with Index attributes 3b and 3, and the Orders node.

attribute

The attribute axis selects the context node's attributes. In the previous XML document, if the context node is the Item node with value Coffee, the statement attribute::* selects all of the node's attributes Quantity and Size. The statement attribute::Size selects only the node's Size attribute.

child

The child axis selects the context node's child nodes. If context node is the Order node with Index attribute 3 in the previous XML document, then the statement child::* selects the Order nodes with Index 3a and 3b.

If the context node is the Order with Index 2, the statement child::Item selects the Items with values Banana and Donut. It doesn't select the context node's third child because it is a Drink node, not an Item node.

descendant

The descendant axis selects the context node's descendants. If context node is the Order node with Index attribute 3 in the previous XML document, then descendant::* selects the Order node with Index 3a, the three Items that node contains, the Order node with Index 3B, and the three Items that Order contains.

For the same content node, the statement descendant::Order selects only the two Order nodes with Indexes 3a and 3b.

following

The following axis selects the nodes that occur in the document hierarchy after the context node. They do not include the nodes in the subtree rooted at the context node. For example, suppose the context node in the previous XML document is the Order node with Index 3a. Then following::* selects the Order node with Index 3b and the three Items that Order contains. The statement does not select the items with values Soda, Sandwich, or Apple because they are part of the context node's subtree.

For the same context node, the statement following::Item selects only the Item nodes that come after the context node's subtree. In this example, those are the Item nodes with values Water, Salad, and Peach.

following-sibling

The following-sibling axis selects the nodes that follow the context node and that have the same parent as the context node. In other words, they are the context node's following siblings.

If the context node in the previous XML document is the Order with Index 2, then the statement following-sibling::* selects the Order node with Index 3. The Order with Index 1 is also a sibling of the context node, but it doesn't follow the context node.

If the context node is the Item with value Banana, the statement following-sibling::Item selects the Item node with value Donut. This statement does not select the Drink node because it is not an Item.

parent

The parent axis selects the context node's parent. If the context node is the root data element, this axis selects nothing.

preceding

The preceding axis selects nodes that come before the context node in the XML document's hierarchy. The nodes do not include the context node's ancestors or any nodes in the document subtree rooted at the context node. For example, if the context node is the Order with Index 3 in the previous XML document, then the statement preceding::* selects the nodes Drink Milkshake, Item Donut, Item Banana, Order 2, Item Coffee, Item Cookie, and Order 1.

With the same context node, the statement preceding::Item selects the preceding nodes that are Item nodes. In this example, those are Item Donut, Item Banana, Item Coffee, and Item Cookie.

preceding-sibling

The preceding-sibling axis selects the nodes that precede the context node and that have the same parent as the context node. In other words, they are the context node's preceding siblings.

For example, if the context node is the Order with Index 2 in the previous XML document, then the statement preceding-sibling::* selects the Order node with Index 1.

For the same context node, the statement preceding-sibling::Item selects no nodes because the context node has no siblings named Item.

Axis Summary

Table 6.2 summarizes these useful axes.

Constraining Selections

In addition to using the symbols listed in Table 6.1 to specify nodes, you can add conditions to an XPath expression to constrain the selection. To add a constraint, place the condition in square brackets after the node selection expression. For example, the expression //Part[Quantity=1] selects all nodes named Part that have a child node named Quantity with value 1.

XPath expressions allow many kinds of constraints. The previous example shows how to select nodes that have a specific value. The expression //Part[1] selects Part nodes that are their parents' first children (note that indexing starts with 1, not 0).

In an XPath expression, the @ symbol indicates a node's attribute. In an XSL style sheet, the @ symbol is usually used to constrain a node selection or to display an attribute's value in the result document. For example, //Phone[@Type='Work'] selects Phone nodes that have a Type attribute with value Work.

Table 6.2   Useful Axes

AXIS	DESCRIPTION
ancestor	Selects the context node's ancestors
attribute	Selects the context node's attributes
child	Selects the context node's children
descendant	Selects the context node's descendants
following	Selects nodes that occur after the context node in the document hierarchy, excluding the context node's subtree
following-sibling	Selects nodes that occur after the context node in the document hierarchy and that have the same parent as the context node
parent	Selects the context node's parent
preceding	Selects nodes that occur before the context node in the document hierarchy, excluding the context node's subtree
preceding-sibling	Selects nodes that occur before the context node in the document hierarchy and that have the same parent as the context node

A Visual Basic program can also use the XmlDocument object's SelectNodes method to select nodes representing the attributes themselves. For example, //Phone/@Type selects the nodes representing the Type attributes of Phone nodes.

You can combine the @ symbol with wildcards. For example, //Item[@*='Missing'] selects all Item nodes that have any attribute with value Missing. A Visual Basic program could use the XmlDocument's SelectNodes method and the XPath expression //Phone/@* to select the nodes representing the attributes of any Phone node.

XPath Functions

XPath includes several functions that help you test for certain conditions and to display calculated values in the result document. For example, the following value-of statement adds the context node's name to the output.

```
<xsl:value-of select="name()"/>
```

The following sections describe the most useful XPath functions in detail.

boolean

The boolean function returns true or false depending on its parameter's value. For example, the function returns true in the following code fragment if the context node has a child named address.

```
boolean(child::address)
```

Usually the value returned by boolean is used in an xsl:if statement.

In keeping with its fondness for lowercase, XSL uses the values true and false rather than True and False.

ceiling

The ceiling function returns the smallest integer that is at least as large as the input parameter. For example:

- ceiling(2.0001) = 3
- ceiling(2.9999) = 3
- ceiling(3) = 3

Remember that small negative numbers are greater than big negative numbers so ceiling moves negative numbers closer to zero. For example, ceiling(-2.1) returns -2.

concat

The concat function concatenates two or more strings. For example, the statement concat("Sub", "cla", "ss") returns the value Subclass.

contains

The contains function determines whether a string contains a substring. For example, the following XPath statement selects Part nodes that have a child node named Item with a value containing the substring Right.

```
//Part[contains(Item, "Right")]
```

Note that contains performs a case-sensitive comparison.

count

The count function returns a count of whatever is its argument. For instance:

- count(child::*) returns the context node's number of children.
- count(ancestor::*) returns the context node's number of ancestors, which is equal to its depth in the document hierarchy.
- count(descendant::Item) returns the number of the context node's descendants that are Item nodes.

format-number

The format-number function returns a number formatted as a string. The function's format specifier is somewhat similar to the one used by Visual Basic's Format function. Some of the more useful format characters are listed in Table 6.3.

Table 6.3 Format Specifiers for format-number

SPECIFIER	MEANING
0	A digit or zero if the value does not have a digit at this position.
#	A digit or nothing if the value does not have a digit at this position.
,	A group separator (a thousands separator in American English).
.	A decimal separator.
E or e	An exponent separator.
%	Percent. The value is multiplied by 100 and followed by a percent sign.

Table 6.4   Examples Produced by format-number

VALUE	FORMAT SPECIFIER	RESULT
1234.567	0.0	1234.6
1234.567	#,##0.00	1,234.57
1234.5	0.00	1234.50
1234	0.00e00	.12e04
1234	00.00e00	12.34e02
0.123	0%	12%
0.123	0.00%	12.30%

Table 6.4 shows some examples produced by the format-number function.

Note that in at least some combinations of software versions, a bug makes format-number(1234.567, '0.00e00') return .12e04 instead of 1.23e03 as it should.

floor

The floor function returns the largest integer that is less than or equal to the input parameter. For example:

- floor(2.0001) = 2
- floor(2.9999) = 2
- floor(3) = 3

Remember that small negative numbers are greater than big negative numbers so floor moves negative numbers farther from zero. For example, floor(-2.1) returns -3.

last

The last function returns the position of the last element in the document. For example, if the context node has three children, then the statement last() returns 3. Remember that nodes are numbered starting with 1, not 0.

name

The name function returns the name of either the context node or an attribute. The following example adds the names of the context node's attributes to the output.

```
<xsl:for-each select="attribute::*">
    <xsl:value-of select="name()"/>
</xsl:for-each>
```

namespace-uri

The namespace-uri function returns the namespace URI of the node sent as an argument. For example, the statement namespace-uri(.) returns the namespace URI for the context node. This is a value similar to http://www.vb-helper.com/XML/Chapter6.

If no namespace is defined for the node, namespace-uri returns an empty string.

normalize-space

The normalize-space function removes leading and trailing white space from a string. For example, the statement normalize-space(Rod Stephens   ) returns Rod Stephens.

This function is similar in principle to Visual Basic's Trim function except the Trim function removes only spaces; it does not remove carriage returns, linefeeds, and other white space characters.

position

The position function returns a node's position among its children. For example, if a node is its parent's third child, the position function returns 3 for that node.

Note that the document's root data element is not necessarily the first child of the document root. For example, consider the following XML document.

```
<?xml version="1.0"?>
<xml-stylesheet type="text/xsl" href="Test.xsl"?>
<!-- Sales data for August, 2001 -->
<AllOrders>
    :
</AllOrders>
```

This document's root contains three child nodes: an xml-style sheet node, a comment, and the AllOrders element. In this case, when the context node reaches the AllOrders element, position returns 3 because AllOrders is the document's third child.

You can use position to constrain a selection. For example, the XPath expression //Part[position()=2] selects Part nodes that are their parents' second Part children. Consider the following XML document.

```
<Orders>
    <Order1>
        <Part>Monitor</Part>
        <Part>CPU</Part>
        <Part>Cabinet</Part>
    </Order1>
    <Order2>
        <Book>Manual</Book>
        <Part>Wheels</Part>
        <Warranty>1yr</Warranty>
        <Part>Seat</Part>
    </Order2>
</Orders>
```

For this document, the expression //Path[position()=2] matches the Part node with value CPU because it is the second Part child or Order1.

The expression also matches the Part node with value Seat. While this is the fourth child node in Order2, it is the second node named Part.

round

The round function rounds a number to the nearest integer. For example, round(2.4) returns 2 and round(2.6) returns 3.

If the input is exactly an integer plus 0.5, round returns the next larger integer. For example, round(2.4999) returns 2, but round(2.5) returns 3.

string-length

The string-length function returns the length of a string. For example, the following code adds the length of the context node's name to the output.

```
<xsl:value-of select="string-length(name())"/>
```

You can also use string-length to constrain node selection. For example, the following XPath statement selects text nodes with a value longer than three characters.

```
//text()[string-length(.)>3]
```

substring

The substring function returns part of a string. Its parameters give the string, the substring's start position, and the substring's length. For example, the statement substring("ABCDE", 2, 3) returns the string BCD.

substring-after

The substring-after function returns the part of a string that comes after a specific substring. For example, the statement substring-after("ABCDE", "C") returns the string DE.

substring-before

The substring-before function returns the part of a string that comes before a specific substring. For example, the statement substring-before("ABCDE", "C") returns the string AB.

text

The text function selects text nodes. For example, //Part//text() selects all text nodes that are descendants of a Part node.

translate

The translate function searches a string for characters in another string and replaces them with the corresponding characters in a third. For example, translate("clever", "abcdef", "ABCDEF") replaces a with A, b with B, and so forth to return ClEvEr.

XSL Elements

XSL provides many elements that tell the style sheet's transformation engine how to produce output. Some of these elements provide program control much as the statements in a Visual Basic program do. These elements let the engine create variables (similar to Visual Basic's Dim statement), loop over nodes (similar to Visual Basic's For Each statement), and execute conditional code (similar to Visual Basic's If Then statement). Other elements create formatting objects that place text, attributes, comments, and other values into the output file.

The following sections show some of the most useful elements in converting XML into HTML. The section *XSL Examples* that follows shows how some of these elements work in practice.

Keep in mind that XSL has more elements than those shown here. For a complete listing, see the World Wide Web Consortium's Web site, www.w3c.org.

xsl:attribute

The xsl:attribute command creates attributes in the resulting document. For example, consider the following piece of XSL code.

```
<xsl:attribute name="City">
    Boulder
</xsl:attribute>
```

This code creates the following output.

```
City="Boulder"
```

The xsl:attribute statement is very useful when you are building XML or HTML documents, particularly when the resulting XML or HTML elements have a lot of attributes.

xsl:call-template

The xsl:call-template element lets XSL code explicitly call a template by name. For example, the following code invokes the template named ShowItem.

```
<xsl:call-template name="ShowItem">
```

See also xsl:template, xsl:param, and xsl:with-param.

xsl:choose

The xsl:choose statement is roughly analogous to Visual Basic's Select statement. It lets a style sheet execute one of several pieces of code depending on a series of tests. For example, consider the following code fragment.

```
<xsl:choose>
    <xsl:when test="position()='CEO'">Chief Executive Officer</xsl:when>
    <xsl:when test="position()='CFO'">Chief Financial Officer</xsl:when>
    <xsl:when test="position()='COO'">Chief Operating Officer</xsl:when>
    <xsl:otherwise>Slave</xsl:otherwise>
</xsl:choose>
```

The transformation engine looks through the xsl:when statements until it finds one with a test that evaluates to true. It then executes the code inside that statement. If none of the xsl:when statements has a test that evaluates to true, the engine executes the XSL code in the xsl:otherwise statement.

xsl:comment

The xsl:comment element creates a comment in the output file. These comments have the <!-- ... --> format so they work only in languages that use these comment symbols. For example, this format works in XML, HTML, and Javascript.

For an example, consider the following XSL code.

```
<xsl:comment>Naughty and nice list, December 2002</xsl:comment>
```

This code places the following code in the output file.

```
<!--Naughty and nice list, December 2002-->
```

Each comment appears on a separate line in the output file. Use this command often to document your output file.

xsl:for-each

The xsl:for-each statement works just as a For Each loop does in Visual Basic. For example, the following code loops through each of the context node's children displaying the value of each node's type attribute and each node's value.

```
<xsl:for-each select="child::*">
    <!-- Display the node's name. -->
    <xsl:value-of select="@type"/>

    <!-- Display the node's value. -->
    <xsl:value-of select="."/>
</xsl:for-each>
```

Consider the following XML file.

```
<?xml version="1.0"?>
<Contacts>
    <PhoneNumbers>
        <Phone type="home">3035551133</Phone>
        <Phone type="work">3035556372</Phone>
        <Phone type="fax">3035556373</Phone>
    </PhoneNumbers>
</Contacts>
```

This example contains no formatting instructions so the output is run together without any spaces or carriage returns. When the context node is the PhoneNumbers element shown in this document, the transformation engine adds the following string to the output file.

```
home3035551133work3035556372fax3035556373
```

The XPath expression in this example, child::*, is only one of many expressions you could use for the for-each statement. Another useful expression is attribute::*, which loops through the context node's attributes.

The xsl:value-of statement used in this example is described in a later section.

xsl:if

The xsl:if statement is similar to Visual Basic's If statement. The following code examines the string variable SomeVar and executes the value-of statement only if the length SomeVar is greater than 8.

```
<xsl:if test="string-length($SomeVar)>8">
    <!-- Display the node. -->
    <xsl:value-of select="."/>
</xsl:if>
```

Note that you can use any XPath function as part of the xsl:if statement's test. For example, the following code displays information for nodes with names that contain the string error.

```
<xsl:if test="contains(name(), 'error')">
    <!-- Display the node. -->
    <xsl:value-of select="."/>
</xsl:if>
```

XSL does not have an Else statement. If you want to perform two different actions based on one condition, you need to use two different xsl:if statements, as shown in the following code.

```
<xsl:if test="contains(name(), 'error')">
    <!-- Do something. -->
        ...
</xsl:if>
<xsl:if test="not(contains(name(), 'error'))">
    <!-- Do something else. -->
        ...
</xsl:if>
```

You can use the xsl:choose statement described earlier to make a series of choices easier to read.

xsl:import and xsl:include

These two elements allow you to import a style sheet into the current document. The commands are similar except for the way they handle the precedence of the commands in the calling style sheet and the imported style sheet. With xsl:include, the two style sheets have the same precedence. With xsl:import, the XSL commands in the calling style sheet have precedence over the ones in the imported style sheet.

For example, the following statement imports a style sheet over the Internet. The second statement includes a style sheet using a relative URL.

```
<xsl:import href="http://www.vb-helper.com/XML/Chapter6/rules.xsl"/>
<xsl:include href="/XML/Chapter6/more_rules.xsl"/>
```

The imported or included page must be complete and valid. Both xsl:import and xsl:include must be top-level elements in the XSL file. In other words, they must be children of the xsl:stylesheet element.

These two commands are good ways to promote code reuse.

xsl:number

The xsl:number element is quite complicated, but its main purpose is to generate a sequence of numbers. Its format property indicates the types of symbols xsl:number uses in the sequence. Table 6.5 lists the most common format specifiers and their meanings.

Table 6.5 Format Specifiers for xsl:number

FORMAT SPECIFIER	RESULTING SEQUENCE	EXAMPLE
1	Numbers	1, 2, 3, ...
01	Numbers with leading zeros	01, 02, 03, ..., 10, ...
a	Lowercase letters	a, b, c, ...
A	Uppercase letters	A, B, C, ...
i	Lowercase Roman numerals	i, ii, iii, iv, v, ...
I	Uppercase Roman numerals	I, II, III, IV, V, ...

For example, consider the following XML document.

```
<?xml version="1.0"?>
<Contacts>
    <Author>
        <PhoneNumbers>
            <Phone type="home">303-555-1133</Phone>
            <Phone type="work">303-555-9392</Phone>
            <Phone type="fax">303-555-9393</Phone>
        </PhoneNumbers>
    </Author>
</Contacts>
```

Now look at the following XSL code.

```
<xsl:template match="//Phone">
Number <xsl:number format="A"/>: <xsl:value-of select="."/>
</xsl:template>
```

When a transformation engine applies this XSL file to the previous XML document, the output looks like this:

```
Number A: 303-555-1133
Number B: 303-555-9392
Number C: 303-555-9393
```

The xsl:number element can also generate multilevel hierarchical values such as 3.12.2 or A(2). Generating this kind of number is fairly involved, however, so it is not described here. For more information, see the W3C documentation or a book that covers XSL in more detail.

xsl:output

The xsl:output element tells the transformation engine the general kinds of spacing and indentation that should appear in the output file. This element's method parameter can take one of three values: text, html, and xml.

The xsl:output element can also take an indent parameter that tells the transformation engine whether it should generate indentation to make the resulting HTML or XML code more readable. For example, the following code tells the engine to generate indenting that makes HTML readable.

```
<xsl:output method="html" indent="yes"/>
```

If the xsl:output element specifies a method of html, the transformation engine automatically adds a Content-Type META tag after the HEAD tag in the resulting HTML file. This tag looks like the following.

```
<META http-equiv="Content-Type" content="text/html; charset="UTF-16">
```

If the xsl:output element's method is xml, the transformation engine automatically adds an XML declaration statement to the output file similar to this one.

```
<?xml version="1.0" encoding="UTF-8"?>
```

If the xsl:output elements method is text, the transformation does not add any declaration.

Note that the XslTransform object does not always add these statements. If the XslTransform object is writing output into a Stream or TextWriter object, it automatically generates the HTML META tag or the XML declaration when it encounters an xsl:output element. If the XslTransform object is sending output to an XmlReader or XmlWriter object, it ignores the xsl:output statement. This includes the XmlTextWriter class that inherits from XmlWriter.

For more information on the XslTransform class, see the section *A Visual Basic Transformation Engine* later in this chapter.

xsl:param

The xsl:param element creates a parameter for a template. Its select clause specifies the parameter's default value. When another part of the XSL style sheet invokes the template using the xsl:call-template element, it can override this default by including the xsl:with-param element.

For example, in the following code the ShowBook template displays a book's title. It also displays the value of its Length parameter. The xsl:param element defines this parameter and sets its default value to short.

The Book template checks the current book's number of pages. If the book has more than 500 pages, this template calls the ShowBook template, setting its Length parameter to long. If the book does not have more than 500 pages, the Book template calls ShowBook without overriding its Length parameter.

```
<?xml version="1.0"?>
<xsl:stylesheet version="1.0"
xmlns:xsl="http://www.w3.org/1999/XSL/Transform">
<xsl:output method="text" />

    <!-- Books. -->
    <xsl:template match="/">
        <xsl:apply-templates/>
    </xsl:template>

    <!-- Book. -->
    <xsl:template match="Book">
        <!-- See if the title has the word XML in it. -->
        <xsl:if test="@Pages > 500">
            <xsl:call-template name="ShowBook">
                <xsl:with-param name="Length" select="'long'"/>
            </xsl:call-template>
```

```
        </xsl:if>

        <xsl:if test="not(@Pages > 500)">
            <xsl:call-template name="ShowBook"/>
        </xsl:if>
    </xsl:template>

    <xsl:template name="ShowBook">
        <xsl:param name="Length" select="'short'"/>

        <xsl:value-of select="Title"/> (<xsl:value-of
select="$Length"/>)<xsl:text>
</xsl:text>
    </xsl:template>

</xsl:stylesheet>
```

The following shows the result of this style sheet for a small XML file.

```
Ready-to-Run Visual Basic Algorithms (short)
Custom Controls Library (long)
Visual Basic Graphics Programming (long)
```

See also xsl:template, xsl:call-template, and xsl:with-param.

xsl:preserve-space

The xsl:preserve-space element tells the transformation engine to preserve white space found in the source document. The following statement tells the engine to preserve white space for all elements found in the source document.

```
<xsl:preserve-space elements="*"/>
```

The following example makes the transformation engine preserve white space inside Author elements.

```
<xsl:preserve-space elements="Author"/>
```

xsl:processing-instruction

The xsl:processing-instruction element adds an XML processing instruction to the output file. Because processing instructions apply only to XML files, xsl:processing-instruction makes sense only when the output file is an XML file.

Place the processing instruction's text inside the xsl:processing-instruction. For example, consider the following code.

```
<xsl:processing-instruction name="xml-stylesheet">
    type="text/xsl"
    href="Test.xsl"
</xsl:processing-instruction>
```

This XSL code produces the following output.

```
<xml-stylesheet
    type="text/xsl"
    href="Test.xsl"
?>
```

Usually when you write an XML file by hand, you put each XML processing instruction on a single line, but this multiline format is allowed and makes the XSL style sheet code easier to read than one very long line.

The previous example is actually an abbreviated form of the following XSL code.

```
<xsl:processing-instruction name="xml-stylesheet">
<xsl:text>type="text/xsl" href="Test.xsl"</xsl:text>
</xsl:processing-instruction>
```

This code produces the following single-line version of the processing instruction.

```
<xml-stylesheet type="text/xsl" href="Test.xsl"?>
```

You should use whichever form you think is easier to read.

xsl:sort

The xsl:sort element specifies the order in which the transformation engine processes nodes selected by an xsl:apply-templates or xsl:for-each element. The xsl:sort element should be placed inside the statement selecting the nodes.

For example, consider the following XML document.

```
<?xml version="1.0"?>
<?xml-stylesheet type="text/xsl" href="Test.xsl" ?>

<Books>
    <Book Price="$49.99" Pages="395">
        <Title>Ready-to-Run Visual Basic Algorithms</Title>
        <URL>http://www.vb-helper.com/vba.htm</URL>
        <Image>http://www.vb-helper.com/vba.gif</Image>
    </Book>
    <Book Price="$49.99" Pages="684">
        <Title>Custom Controls Library</Title>
        <URL>http://www.vb-helper.com/ccl.htm</URL>
        <Image>http://www.vb-helper.com/ccl.gif</Image>
    </Book>
    <Book Price="$49.99" Pages="712">
```

```
        <Title>Visual Basic Graphics Programming</Title>
        <URL>http://www.vb-helper.com/vbgp.htm</URL>
        <Image>http://www.vb-helper.com/vbgp.gif</Image>
    </Book>
</Books>
```

When the XSL transformation engine reaches the Books tag, the following fragment of XSL code executes. The xsl:for-each element executes its code for each Book element contained in the context node Books. The xsl:sort element makes the xsl:for-each loop process the Book tags ordered by their Title subtags. The result is a list of the books ordered by their titles.

```
<xsl:template match="Books">
    <xsl:for-each select="Book">
        <xsl:sort select="./Title"/>
        <TR><TD><xsl:value-of select="./Title" /></TD></TR>
    </xsl:for-each>
</xsl:template>
```

In the following XSL code fragment, the first template executes when the XSL transformation engine reaches the document's root node. The xsl:apply-templates element selects all Book nodes and applies the file's templates to them. The xsl:sort statement makes the engine visit the Book nodes ordered by their Pages attributes in descending order.

The second template executes when the transformation engine processes a Book tag. This template displays the Book's Title subelement and Pages attribute.

The result is a list of books sorted in descending order by page length.

```
<xsl:template match="/">
    <xsl:apply-templates select="//Book">
        <xsl:sort select="@Pages" order="descending" />
    </xsl:apply-templates>
</xsl:template>

<xsl:template match="Book">
    <TR>
        <TD><xsl:value-of select="Title"/></TD>
        <TD ALIGN="Right"><xsl:value-of select="@Price"/></TD>
    </TR>
</xsl:template>
```

The xsl:sort element's optional case-order attribute determines whether the engine sorts uppercase letters before or after lowercase letters. This attribute can take the values upper-first or lower-first.

The optional data-type attribute determines whether the engine sorts values numerically or alphabetically. If data-type is text, the engine sorts values alphabetically. If data-type is number, the engine sorts values as numbers. For example, the values 5, 10, 15, 20 belong in the order 5, 10, 15, 20 when sorted as numbers, but they belong in the order 10, 15, 20, 5 when sorted alphabetically.

xsl:strip-space

The xsl:strip-space element usually appears right after the style sheet declaration. This element determines in which other elements white space is considered insignificant. For example, the following code indicates that white space is insignificant in all elements in the source XML document.

```
<xsl:strip-space elements="*"/>
```

The following example indicates that white space is insignificant in all elements named FirstName.

```
<xsl:strip-space elements="//FirstName"/>
```

The transformation engine removes insignificant white space when it finds all white space text elements.

xsl:stylesheet

The xsl:stylesheet element defines the root element of the XSL style sheet and sets up the namespace xsl. All XSL style sheets must contain this root element in order for the transformation to occur.

```
<xsl:stylesheet xmlns:xsl="http://www.w3.org/TR/WD-xsl">
    <!-- All XSL commands must occur between these tags. -->
        :
</xsl:stylesheet>
```

All XSL commands between the xsl:stylesheet tags must be prefixed with xsl.

xsl:template

The xsl:template element defines a series of statements to execute when the context node matches the specified XPath expression. For example, consider the following XSL code.

```
<xsl:template match="Data/WebPage/Title">
    <!-- Execute these XSL commands. -->
        :
</xsl:template>
```

The XSL commands between the xsl:template tags execute when the context node matches the XPath statement Data/WebPage/Title.

The xsl:template element can take an optional name parameter that defines the template's name for use by the xsl:call-template element. For example:

```
<xsl:template match="//Book" name="ShowBook">
    <!-- Describe the book. -->
        :
</xsl:template>
```

See also xsl:call-template, xsl:param, and xsl:with-param.

xsl:text

The xsl:text element adds text to the output. For example, consider the following XSL code.

```
<xsl:template match="Play">
    <H1>
    <xsl:text>Title: </xsl:text>
    <xsl:value-of select="Title">
    </H1>
</xsl:template>
```

For Play elements, this code displays Title: followed by the value of the Play's Title child element, as shown in the following output.

```
<H1>
Title: A Midsummer Night's Scream
</H1>
```

Often, you can omit the xsl:text element and include the text you want displayed directly in the XSL code. For example, the following XSL code is roughly equivalent to the previous version.

```
<xsl:template match="Play">
    <H1>
    Title:
    <xsl:value-of select="Title">
    </H1>
</xsl:template>
```

The xsl:text element can give you greater control over white space in the result document. For example, the following code inserts a space between the FirstName and LastName values in the output.

```
<xsl:value-of select="FirstName"/>
<xsl:text> </xsl:text>
<xsl:value-of select="LastName"/>
```

Without the xsl:text element, the transformation engine would display the First-Name and LastName elements run together.

Note that the XslTransform object may become confused if the value inside the xsl:text element contains text that looks like XML. For instance, consider the following XSL code. When it encounters the first xsl:text element, the XslTransform object gets confused trying to figure out the name of the new tag it thinks is starting with the less-than symbol. The second statement works, presumably because the XslTransform object can figure out that the greater-than symbol does not close an open tag.

The third statement uses the standard character entities for the less-than and greater-than symbols. This version always works and is a bit safer.

```
<xsl:text>1 < 2</xsl:text>        <!-- This doesn't work. -->
<xsl:text>2 > 1</xsl:text>        <!-- This works. -->
<xsl:text>1 &lt;&gt; 2</xsl:text>  <!-- This works. -->
```

The XslTransform object also places more faith in the xsl:output statement than on xsl:text's ability to include unusual characters. Normally, the xsl:text element can take an attribute disable-output-escaping that, when set equal to yes, prevents the transformation engine from replacing characters such as < and > with their character entities :lt; and >. XslTransform, however, determines whether it should translate these characters based on the xsl:output element. If the xsl:output element specifies xsl or html output, XslTransform replaces these characters with their entities. If the xsl:output element specifies text output, XslTransform leaves these characters as they are. In fact, it even translates character entity references into their character equivalents.

In some cases, you can use a CDATA section to make these translations easier to understand. For more information, see the section *xsl:value-of* that follows.

For more information on the XslTransform class, see the section *A Visual Basic Transformation Engine* later in this chapter.

xsl:value-of

The xsl:value-of element outputs a value specified by its select argument. The select statement can specify a node value or an attribute value using a normal XPath expression.

For example, consider the following snippet of XML code.

```
<Product ReorderLevel="3">Kringle</Product>
```

When the XSL transformation engine considers the Product element, the following XSL statements display the node's value (Kringle) followed by the value of the ReorderLevel attribute (3).

```
<xsl:value-of select="."/>
<xsl:value-of select="@ReorderLevel"/>
```

To display the name of the context node, use the name function within the xsl:value-of statement like this:

```
<xsl:value-of select="name(.)"/>
```

If the context node contains a CDATA section including XML or HTML tags, the results may not be what you expect. Normally a CDATA section prevents an application from parsing the data it contains. When the XSL transformation engine outputs the CDATA contents, however, it replaces special characters such as < and > with their XML entities < and >. This prevents the output file from containing improperly formed XML code.

For instance, consider the following XML code.

```
<BodyText><![CDATA[<a href="http://www.xml.com">]]></BodyText>
```

Suppose the XSL style sheet uses the following code to display the CDATA.

```
<xsl:template match="BodyText">
    <xsl:value-of select="."/>
</xsl:template>
```

In that case, the transformation engine produces the following output.

```
&lt;a href="http://www.xml.com"&gt;
```

If you want to preserve the CDATA value exactly, you can add the disable-output-escaping attribute to the xsl:value-of element, as shown in the following XSL code.

```
<xsl:template match="BodyText">
    <xsl:value-of disable-output-escaping="yes" select="."/>
</xsl:template>
```

This results in the following output when BodyText is the context element.

```
<a href="http://www.xml.com">
```

Note that the XslTransform object does not always honor the disable-output-escaping attribute. If the XslTransform object is sending output to an XmlReader or XmlWriter object, it translates CDATA characters such as < and > into their character entities < and >.

If the XslTransform object is writing output into a Stream or TextWriter object and the xsl:output element indicates that the result is xml or html, then the XslTransform object translates these CDATA characters into their character entities as before. If the XslTransform object is writing output into a Stream or TextWriter object and the xsl:output element indicates that the result is text, the XslTransform leaves these CDATA characters as they are. In this case, it does not translate character entities such as < and > into their character equivalents because they are contained in a CDATA section.

For more information on the XslTransform class, see the section *A Visual Basic Transformation Engine* later in this chapter.

The xsl:value-of element is one of the most important XSL elements because it transforms XML data into output text. Many of the examples in this chapter use xsl:value-of to generate output.

xsl:variable

The xsl:variable element creates a constant value that the XSL style sheet can later output using an xsl:value-of element. For example, the following code defines several variables containing pieces of a return address. It then creates a ReturnAddress variable that combines the others into a value that contains the entire return address. Its main xsl:template element uses an xsl:value-of element to display the return address.

```
<!-- Make variables for the pieces of a return address. -->
<xsl:variable name="DeptName"
    select="'State of Confusion, Department of Disorder'"/>
<xsl:variable name="DeptStreet"
    select="'1425 Lost Way'"/>
<xsl:variable name="DeptCityStateZip"
    select="'Whereami  FL  12345'"/>

<!-- Combine these to make a return address. -->
<xsl:variable name="ReturnAddress">
<xsl:value-of select="$DeptName"/>
<xsl:text>
</xsl:text>
<xsl:value-of select="$DeptStreet"/>
<xsl:text>
</xsl:text>
<xsl:value-of select="$DeptCityStateZip"/>
<xsl:text>
</xsl:text>
</xsl:variable>

        <!-- Execute this code for the root element. -->
        <xsl:template match="/">

            <!-- Display the return address. -->
            <xsl:value-of select="$ReturnAddress"/>

            <!-- Do other stuff. -->
                :
        </xsl:template>
```

This example could have included the return address information directly in the main xsl:template element. Using variables makes the code easier to read. If the style sheet needed to use the return address several other times, using the variable would save a lot of typing. It also keeps the return address definition localized. If you needed to change the address, you could make the change once where the return address is defined instead of needing to find all of the places the return address is used and modifying them all.

xsl:with-param

The xsl:with-param element specifies parameters for a call to a template made using xsl:call-template. For example, the following code calls the ShowBook template. It uses the xsl:with-param element to make the OutputText parameter in the ShowBook template have the value LONG.

```
<xsl:call-template name="ShowBook">
    <xsl:with-param name="OutputText" select="'LONG'"/>
</xsl:call-template>
```

The xsl:call-template element can contain more than one xsl:with-param statement to define several parameters for the called template.

See also xsl:template, xsl:param, and xsl:call-template.

Summary of XSL Elements

Table 6.6 provides a quick reference to the commands listed in the previous sections.

Table 6.6 Summary of Commonly Used XSLT Elements

ELEMENT	DESCRIPTION

`<xsl:attribute name="City">`
`Boulder`
`</xsl:attribute>`
	Creates an attribute in the result file.

`<xsl:choose>`
`  <xsl:when test="test1">`
`    Value1`
`  </xsl:when>`
`  <xsl:when test="test2">`
`    Value2`
`  </xsl:when>`
`    :`
`  <xsl:otherwise>`
`    ValueOtherwise`
`  </xsl:otherwise>`
`</xsl:choose>`
	Evaluates a series of expressions and executes code for the first it finds that is true. Similar to Visual Basic's Select Case statement. See also xsl:if.

`<xsl:comment>Just a comment.` `</xsl:comment>`	Adds a comment to the result file.

`<xsl:for-each select="child::*">`
`    <!-- Process the children. -->`
`      :`
`</xsl:for-each>`
	Loops through the selected nodes or attributes much as a For loop in Visual Basic does.

`<xsl:if test="string-length`
`($SomeVar)>8">`
`    <!-- Do something. -->`
`      :`
`</xsl:if>`
	Conditionally performs actions much as a Visual Basic If statement does. There is no XSL equivalent of Visual Basic's ElseIf or Else statements. See also xsl:choose.

`<xsl:import href="http://www.` `vb-helper.com/XML/Chapter7/rules.xsl"/>`	Includes a style sheet in the current one. The rules in the current style sheet take precedence over the imported one.
`<xsl:include href="http://www.` `vb-helper.com/XML/Chapter7/rules.xsl"/>`	Includes a style sheet in the current one. Rules in both style sheets have the same precedence.

continues

Table 6.6 (Continued)

ELEMENT	DESCRIPTION
`<xsl:number format="A"/>`	Generates and displays the number of times a particular piece of XSL code executes for a particular node.
`<xsl:output method="html" indent="yes"/>`	Tells XSLT that the spacing and indenting used to display data should be for HTML. Can also specify text and XML for method to ensure that the appropriate spacing is provided.
`<xsl:param name="OutputText" select="."/>`	Defines a parameter. Similar to xsl:variable.
`<xsl:preserve-space elements="*"/>`	Preserves white space found in the source document within the specified elements.

`<xsl:processing-instruction`
  `name="xml-stylesheet">`
    `type="text/xsl"`
    `href="Test.xsl"`
`</xsl:processing-instruction>`
	Adds an XML processing instruction to the result document.

`<xsl:sort select="./Title"/>`	Makes the transformation engine visit the nodes in an xsl:apply-templates or xsl:for-each element in a specific order.
`<xsl:strip-space elements="*"/>`	Removes text elements that contain only white space within the specified elements.

`<xsl:stylesheet`
  `xmlns:xsl="http://www.w3.org/`
`TR/WD-xsl">`
    `:`
`</xsl:stylesheet>`
	Defines the XSLT document and sets up the xsl namespace. Note that all tags that are part of the XSLT standard have the xsl prefix in the document.

`<xsl:template match="Data/WebPage/`
`title">`
    `:`
`</xsl:template>`
	Conditional code section that executes when the context node matches the XPath expression in the match statement.

`<xsl:text>    </xsl:text>`	Adds text to the result document.
`<xsl:value-of select="$ReturnAddress"/>`	Adds the value of the variable ReturnAddress to the result document.
`<xsl:value-of select="."/>`	Adds the value of the context node to the result document.

Table 6.6 (Continued)

ELEMENT	DESCRIPTION
`<xsl:value-of select="@ReorderLevel"/>`	Adds the value of the context node's ReorderLevel attribute to the result document.
`<xsl:value-of select="City"/>`	Adds the value of the context node's City child element to the result document.
`<xsl:value-of select="name(.)"/>`	Adds the value of the context node's name to the result document.

`<xsl:variable`
`  name="OutputText"`
`  select="."/>`
	Defines a variable. Similar to xsl:param.

Use Table 6.6 to refresh your memory when you write XSL style sheets. If you need more information on a particular command, refer to the earlier, more detailed sections, the W3C documentation, or your favorite XSL book.

XSL Flow of Control

Earlier sections in this chapter describe the functions and elements you can use to build an XSL style sheet. Using those language elements, you can build xsl:template elements that add text and data taken from the XML source document to the result document.

This section explains how an XSL transformation engine uses the XSL templates. It tells how the engine decides which templates to use and how control passes from one template to another.

For the following examples, consider the following XML document.

```
<?xml version="1.0"?>
<?xml-stylesheet type="text/xsl" href="Test5.xsl" ?>

<Books>
    <Book Price="$39.99" Pages="395">
        <Title>Ready-to-Run Visual Basic Algorithms</Title>
    </Book>
    <Book Price="$39.99" Pages="684">
        <Title>Custom Controls Library</Title>
    </Book>
    <Book Price="$39.99" Pages="712">
        <Title>Visual Basic Graphics Programming</Title>
    </Book>
</Books>
```

The sections that follow present example XSL style sheets that modify this XML document in different ways.

A First Match

Ignoring declarations and possibly some xsl:param or xsl:variable statements, an XSL file contains a series of templates that tell the transformation engine what to do with different kinds of nodes in the XML document.

The transformation engine begins processing with the XML document's root node so it sets the context node to the root node.

Then, as long as a context node is defined, the engine compares the context node to the templates, looking for one that matches the node. If it finds a match, the transformation engine executes the template for the context node. The engine is then done processing that node and its entire subtree in the XML document hierarchy. This is a fairly subtle idea that bears a little more thought.

If the engine cannot find a template that matches the context node, it examines the node's children. It continues this process, comparing the context node to the templates, looking for a match and examining the context node's children if it doesn't find one, until it finds a template to run or it runs out of XML nodes to examine.

Execution begins with the XML document's root node selected as the context node. If the style sheet contains a template that matches the root node, the transformation engine executes that template. When that template finishes, the engine is done with that node and its subtree. This node is the XML document's root node, however, so every other node is in its subtree. That means the engine is finished processing the entire XML document. If that template did not do something with all of the nodes in the XML document, they are not processed even if other templates might match them.

For example, consider the following XSL code. This style sheet contains templates that match the XML document's root, Books, Book, and Title elements. Each template displays a value indicating the type of node it is processing.

```
<?xml version="1.0"?>
<xsl:stylesheet version="1.0"
    xmlns:xsl="http://www.w3.org/1999/XSL/Transform">
<xsl:output method="text" />

    <!-- Root. -->
    <xsl:template match="/">
        <xsl:text>Root
</xsl:text>
    </xsl:template>

    <!-- Books. -->
    <xsl:template match="Books">
        <xsl:text>  Books
</xsl:text>
    </xsl:template>

    <!-- Book. -->
    <xsl:template match="Book">
        <xsl:text>    Book
</xsl:text>
    </xsl:template>
```

```
    <!-- Title. -->
    <xsl:template match="Title">
        <xsl:text>      Title
</xsl:text>
    </xsl:template>

</xsl:stylesheet>
```

Because this style sheet looks a bit like a Select statement in Visual Basic, you might assume the templates are applied repeatedly to every node in the XML document. That is understandable, but it is not true.

Instead, the transformation engine begins with the context node set to the XML document's root node. It searches for a template that matches that node and discovers that the first template matches it. It adds the text Root to the output document and then stops. Nothing else happens. The first template doesn't contain any code that processes the rest of this node's subtree so, when this template stops executing, the transformation engine is finished.

Moving into Subtrees

A template processes other nodes using the xsl:apply-templates element. This element makes the transformation engine apply all of its templates to the selected nodes. By default, the selected nodes are the context node's children. You can give the xsl:apply-templates element a select attribute to tell the engine which other nodes to process.

Consider the following style sheet. This example is very similar to the previous one except several of the templates include an xsl:apply-templates element.

```
<?xml version="1.0"?>
<xsl:stylesheet version="1.0"
    xmlns:xsl="http://www.w3.org/1999/XSL/Transform">
<xsl:output method="text" />

    <!-- Root. -->
    <xsl:template match="/">
        <xsl:text>Root
</xsl:text>
        <xsl:apply-templates/>
    </xsl:template>

    <!-- Books. -->
    <xsl:template match="Books">
        <xsl:text>  Books
</xsl:text>
        <xsl:apply-templates/>
    </xsl:template>

    <!-- Book. -->
    <xsl:template match="Book">
```

```
        <xsl:text>     Book
</xsl:text>
        <xsl:apply-templates select="Title"/>
    </xsl:template>

    <!-- Title. -->
    <xsl:template match="Title">
        <xsl:text>       Title
</xsl:text>
    </xsl:template>

</xsl:stylesheet>
```

As before, the transformation engine starts with the context node set to the XML document's root node. The first template matches that node so the transformation engine executes that template's code. It adds the text Root to the output document. Then the xsl:apply-templates element makes the transformation engine apply the style sheet's templates to the context node's children. The document root has a single child: Books.

With the Books element as the new context node, the transformation engine examines its templates searching for a match. The second template matches so the engine executes its code. The template adds the text Books to the output document and again uses the xsl:apply-templates element. This makes the transformation engine consider the Books node's children: the Book nodes.

For each Book node, the engine looks through its templates for a match. The third template matches the Book nodes so for each of the Book nodes, the transformation engine executes that template's code. That template adds the string Book to the output document and again calls xsl:apply-templates. This time, the template adds the statement select="Title" to the xsl:apply-templates element. That tells the transformation engine to apply its templates only to the context node's Title children.

Once again, the transformation engine compares its templates to the context node, in this case a Title node, looking for a match. The last template matches the node so the engine executes its code and adds the text Title to the output document. This template does not contain the xsl:apply-templates element so when it finishes, the engine returns to the Book template that invoked it. The Book template is also finished so the engine returns to the Books template that sent it to the Book template.

After it has gotten to this point in processing the first Book node, the engine moves on to the next Book element. It processes this Book exactly as it did the previous one. When it again returns to the Books template, the engine processes the last Book element. This time when it returns the to the Books template, the engine is done processing Book nodes so it returns to the root template that started the whole process. That template is also done so the transformation engine is finished. The following text shows the result.

```
Root
  Books
    Book
      Title
    Book
      Title
    Book
      Title
```

If you think this is a lot of work for little result, you're right. This example illustrates the flow of control from one template to another as the xsl:apply-templates elements work their way through the XML document's hierarchy. Examples that produce more useful results can be much harder to understand.

More Complete Processing

For a more interesting result, consider the following style sheet.

```
<?xml version="1.0"?>
<xsl:stylesheet version="1.0"
xmlns:xsl="http://www.w3.org/1999/XSL/Transform">
<xsl:output method="text" />

    <!-- Root. -->
    <xsl:template match="/">
        <xsl:text>Root
</xsl:text>
        <xsl:apply-templates/>
    </xsl:template>

    <!-- Books. -->
    <xsl:template match="Books">
        <xsl:text>  Books
</xsl:text>
        <xsl:apply-templates/>
    </xsl:template>

    <!-- Book. -->
    <xsl:template match="Book">
        <xsl:text>    Title: </xsl:text>
        <xsl:value-of select="Title"/>
        <xsl:text>
</xsl:text>
        <xsl:text>    Price: </xsl:text>
        <xsl:value-of select="@Price"/>
        <xsl:text>
</xsl:text>
        <xsl:text>    Pages: </xsl:text>
        <xsl:value-of select="@Pages"/>
        <xsl:text>

</xsl:text>
    </xsl:template>
</xsl:stylesheet>
```

This style sheet produces the following result.

```
Root
  Books
    Title: Ready-to-Run Visual Basic Algorithms
```

```
Price: $39.99
Pages: 395

Title: Custom Controls Library
Price: $39.99
Pages: 684

Title: Visual Basic Graphics Programming
Price: $39.99
Pages: 712
```

This result document might actually be useful.

HTML Output

The previous style sheets produce text files. A style sheet that builds an HTML document can follow exactly the same format. The only real difference is that this style sheet surrounds the data taken from the XML document with HTML tags.

The following XSL style sheet transforms the same XML document and produces an HTML document. The root template outputs some tags to start the document. Because the style sheet contains the xsl:output element with method set to html, the transformation engine automatically adds a META tag after the <HEAD> tag.

The root template starts an HTML table and then uses xsl:apply-templates to make the transformation engine apply templates to the root's child nodes. When the engine returns from processing the child nodes, the root template finishes the HTML table and the HTML document.

This style sheet's only other template matches Book nodes. That template displays the Book node's Title child, and its Price and Pages attributes as cells in the HTML table.

```
<?xml version="1.0"?>
<xsl:stylesheet version="1.0"
xmlns:xsl="http://www.w3.org/1999/XSL/Transform">
<xsl:output method="html" />

    <!-- Root. -->
    <xsl:template match="/">
        <!-- Start the HTML page -->
        <HTML>
        <HEAD>
        <!-- Note that the transformation engine automatically
            inserts a META tag here because we have the
            xsl:output element above with method="html". -->
        <TITLE>Books</TITLE>
        </HEAD>
        <BODY>

        <!-- Start a table for the results. -->
        <TABLE BORDER="1" CELLPADDING="5" CELLSPACING="1"
```

```
                BGCOLOR="#E0E0E0">
          <THEAD>
              <TH>Title</TH>
              <TH>Price</TH>
              <TH>Pages</TH>
          </THEAD>

          <!-- Apply templates to this node's children. -->
          <xsl:apply-templates/>

          <!-- Finish the table and the HTML document. -->
          </TABLE>
          </BODY>
          </HTML>
      </xsl:template>


      <!-- Book. -->
      <xsl:template match="Book">
          <TR>
              <TD><xsl:value-of select="Title"/></TD>
              <TD ALIGN="Right"><xsl:value-of select="@Price"/></TD>
              <TD ALIGN="Right"><xsl:value-of select="@Pages"/></TD>
          </TR>
      </xsl:template>

  </xsl:stylesheet>
```

The following code shows the result. Notice the automatically generated META tag in the document's HEAD section.

```
<HTML>
  <HEAD>
    <META http-equiv="Content-Type" content="text/html; charset=utf-16">
    <TITLE>Books</TITLE>
  </HEAD>
  <BODY>
    <TABLE BORDER="1" CELLPADDING="5" CELLSPACING="1" BGCOLOR="#E0E0E0">
      <THEAD>
        <TH>Title</TH>
        <TH>Price</TH>
        <TH>Pages</TH>
      </THEAD>
      <TR>
        <TD>Ready-to-Run Visual Basic Algorithms</TD>
        <TD>$39.99</TD>
        <TD>395</TD>
      </TR>
      <TR>
        <TD>Custom Controls Library</TD>
        <TD>$39.99</TD>
```

```
        <TD>684</TD>
      </TR>
      <TR>
        <TD>Visual Basic Graphics Programming</TD>
        <TD>$39.99</TD>
        <TD>712</TD>
      </TR>
    </TABLE>
  </BODY>
</HTML>
```

Figure 6.2 shows Internet Explorer displaying this HTML document.

Rootless Style Sheets

The previous examples include a template that matches the XML document's root node so the transformation engine begins processing with the root node. That template contains xsl:apply-templates elements to make processing move into the root node's subtree. This is probably the most common approach in XSL style sheets, but a style sheet does not need to start by matching the XML document's root node.

Suppose the transformation engine searches for a template that matches the context node but it doesn't find one. In that case, the engine moves to the context node's children and tries to find templates to match them. If it fails again, the engine considers those nodes' children. The engine continues in this way, moving further down into the XML document's hierarchy, until it finds a template that matches a node or until it runs out of nodes.

If you need a style sheet to process only one type of XML node, there's no need for the style sheet to start at the root node and work its way down into the XML document. Instead, it can include only a template for that specific type of node. The transformation engine searches the XML document until it reaches the nodes that match this template, and it applies the template.

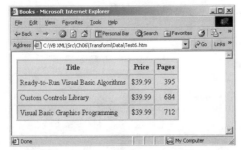

Figure 6.2   A style sheet can transform an XML document into HTML containing a table.

The following style sheet is similar to the previous text-producing style sheet except it doesn't start by matching the XML document's root node. It contains a single template that matches nodes named Book. When it finds a Book node, the transformation engine displays the books' Title, Price, and Pages.

```
<?xml version="1.0"?>
<xsl:stylesheet version="1.0"
xmlns:xsl="http://www.w3.org/1999/XSL/Transform">
<xsl:output method="text" />

    <!-- Book. -->
    <xsl:template match="Book">
        <xsl:text>Title: </xsl:text>
        <xsl:value-of select="Title"/>
        <xsl:text>
</xsl:text>
        <xsl:text>Price: </xsl:text>
        <xsl:value-of select="@Price"/>
        <xsl:text>
</xsl:text>
        <xsl:text>Pages: </xsl:text>
        <xsl:value-of select="@Pages"/>
        <xsl:text>

</xsl:text>
    </xsl:template>
</xsl:stylesheet>
```

The following text shows the output of this style sheet.

```
Title: Ready-to-Run Visual Basic Algorithms
Price: $39.99
Pages: 395

Title: Custom Controls Library
Price: $39.99
Pages: 684

Title: Visual Basic Graphics Programming
Price: $39.99
Pages: 712
```

This style sheet's flat structure can be a bit misleading. It seems as if the transformation engine matches every node against the style sheet's single template looking for matches. That's almost but not quite what happens. The engine searches the XML document's nodes looking for matches until it finds one. It executes the template for that node and then stops processing that node and its subtree. It will not process any of the node's children unless the template contains an appropriate xsl:apply-templates element.

In this example, this distinction makes little difference. On the other hand, suppose the XML document's Book nodes contained other book nodes (perhaps a trilogy is represented by a Book node that contains three other Book nodes). After it executes the template for the first Book node, the engine doesn't consider the child nodes. Although the template matches the Book child nodes, they are never considered.

Flow Summary

It is important to understand how a transformation engine processes the nodes in an XML document. It does not simply apply each template to every node in the document. Instead it starts at the document's root and looks for a matching template. If it finds a template that matches, the engine executes its code. The processing ends there unless the template includes an xsl:apply-templates element.

Study the examples in this section until you understand this flow of control. When you understand how the style sheet controls the transformation engine, you can move on to the more realistic examples described in the next section.

XSL Examples

Most of the earlier sections in this chapter describe the pieces of XSL. They explain XPath expressions, functions that manipulate XML data, expressions that control program flow through a style sheet, and expressions that generate output. The previous section presented some examples to demonstrate the flow of control through a style sheet.

The following sections show more complete examples that use the concepts described earlier to produce useful results.

HTML Paragraphs

The section *HTML Output* earlier in this chapter shows how to display information in an HTML table. Using similar techniques, you can produce output that uses other HTML elements. Consider the following XML document.

```
<?xml version="1.0"?>
<?xml-stylesheet type="text/xsl" href="Authors.xsl" ?>

<Authors>
    <Author>
        <LastName>Stephens</LastName>
        <FirstName>Rod</FirstName>
        <Email>RodStephens@vb-helper.com</Email>
        <WebSite>http://www.vb-helper.com</WebSite>
        <PictureRef>rod.jpg</PictureRef>
        <Bio>
            Rod has been an application developer for more than 14
            ... text deleted ...
```

```
        </Bio>
    </Author>
    <Author>
        <LastName>Hochgurtel</LastName>
        <FirstName>Brian</FirstName>
        <Email>brian@advocatemedia.com</Email>
        <WebSite>http://advocatemedia.com</WebSite>
        <PictureRef>brian.jpg</PictureRef>
        <Bio>
            Brian has been a Web developer for than six years. He has
            ... text deleted ...
        </Bio>
    </Author>
</Authors>
```

The following XSL style sheet transforms this document into an HTML biography page. Its xsl:output element indicates that the result should be indented HTML code.

The style sheet's first template matches the XML document's root node. That template starts the HTML document by creating the <HTML> and <HEAD> tags. Because the style sheet's xsl:output element has a method attribute of html, the transformation engine automatically creates an appropriate META tag after the <HEAD> tag.

Next the root template gives the HTML a TITLE, closes the HEAD section with the </HEAD> tag, and starts the document's BODY section. It then uses the xsl:apply-templates element to process the root node's subtree. When the transformation engine returns from the subtree, the root template finishes the HTML document by generating the </BODY> and </HTML> tags.

The style sheet's second template matches Author nodes. This template begins by creating an HTML paragraph tag <P>. Note that the transformation engine gets confused if the style sheet contains unclosed tags. While an HTML document can include a series of <P> tags, the style sheet must have corresponding closing tags </P>. If you skip to the bottom of this template, you will see those tags.

Next the Author template uses the xsl:number element to get the number of this Author node in the XML document. It uses the xsl:variable element to make a variable named AuthorNumber that holds the value generated by the xsl:number element. Later the template will use this variable to determine whether this is an odd- or even-numbered node.

The template then adds code to the resulting HTML document to display the picture that it defined for this Author node. It starts with an HTML anchor with the <A> tag. Next it uses the xsl:attribute element to define an attribute named HREF for the anchor. It uses the xsl:value-of element to give the attribute the value defined by the Author node's WebSite child.

The template then inserts an image inside the anchor. It adds an <IMG> tag to the output to start the image. It uses the xsl:attribute element to set the image's SRC attribute to the value defined by the Author node's PictureRef child.

The template then uses xsl:if to determine whether the Author node number is odd. If the number is odd, the template uses the xsl:attribute to set the image's ALIGN property to Left. The template uses xsl:if again to determine whether the Author node number is even. If the number is even, the template uses the xsl:attribute to set the image's ALIGN property to Right. These two xsl:if elements make the images alternate between left and right alignment in the resulting HTML code.

Next, the template uses the xsl:attribute element to give the image an ALT attribute. It sets the value of this attribute to the values of the Author node's FirstName and Last-Name children separated by a space. When a Web browser displays the resulting HTML document and the user hovers the mouse over the image, a tooltip appears displaying the value in the ALT attribute.

The template finishes the image with the </IMG> tag and closes the anchor with the </A> tag.

Finally, the template uses xsl:value-of to display the contents of the Author node's Bio child. It finishes by outputting a paragraph close tag </P> to close the paragraph it opened when it started displaying the Author node's information.

```xml
<?xml version="1.0"?>
<xsl:stylesheet version="1.0"
  xmlns:xsl="http://www.w3.org/1999/XSL/Transform">
<xsl:output method="html" indent="yes"/>


    <!-- Root. -->
    <xsl:template match="/">
        <HTML>
        <HEAD>
        <TITLE>Authors</TITLE>
        </HEAD>
        <BODY>


        <!-- Process Author nodes. -->
        <xsl:apply-templates/>


        </BODY>
        </HTML>
    </xsl:template>


    <!-- Author. -->
    <xsl:template match="Author">
        <P>
            <!-- Get the Author node number. -->
            <xsl:variable name="AuthorNumber">
                <xsl:number/>
            </xsl:variable>


            <!-- Show the picture. -->
            <A>
                <xsl:attribute name="HREF">
                    <xsl:value-of select="WebSite"/>
                </xsl:attribute>
                <IMG>
                    <xsl:attribute name="SRC">
                        <xsl:value-of select="PictureRef"/>
```

```
            </xsl:attribute>

            <!-- Alternate placement of pictures. -->
            <xsl:if test="$AuthorNumber mod 2 = 1">
              <xsl:attribute name="ALIGN">Left</xsl:attribute>
            </xsl:if>
            <xsl:if test="$AuthorNumber mod 2 = 0">
              <xsl:attribute name="ALIGN">Right</xsl:attribute>
            </xsl:if>

            <xsl:attribute name="ALT">
                <xsl:value-of select="FirstName"/>
                <xsl:text> </xsl:text>
                <xsl:value-of select="LastName"/>
            </xsl:attribute>
          </IMG>
        </A>

        <!-- Show the biographical text. -->
        <xsl:value-of select="Bio"/>
      </P>
    </xsl:template>

</xsl:stylesheet>
```

This style sheet generates the following HTML code. Notice the automatically generated META tag and the way the IMG tags' ALIGN attributes alternate between Left and Right.

```
<HTML>
  <HEAD>
    <META http-equiv="Content-Type" content="text/html; charset=utf-16">
    <TITLE>Authors</TITLE>
  </HEAD>
  <BODY>
    <P>
      <A HREF="http://www.vb-helper.com">
        <IMG SRC="rod.jpg" ALIGN="Left" ALT="Rod Stephens">
      </A>
          Rod has been an application developer for more than 14
          ... text deleted ...
</P>
    <P>
      <A HREF="http://advocatemedia.com">
        <IMG SRC="brian.jpg" ALIGN="Right" ALT="Brian Hochgurtel">
      </A>
          Brian has been a Web developer for than six years. He has
          ... text deleted ...
      </P>
  </BODY>
</HTML>
```

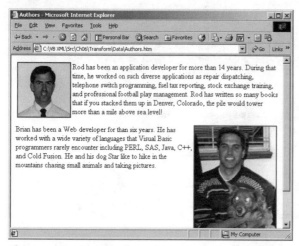

Figure 6.3 A style sheet can transform an XML document into HTML that displays information in paragraphs.

This example demonstrates a few techniques that are shared by many style sheets that generate HTML output. The first template matches the XML document's root node. This template starts the HTML document by creating the <HTML>. It creates the document's HEAD section in its entirety and opens the document's BODY section. It then includes the xsl:apply-templates element and finishes the document by creating the </BODY> and </HTML> tags.

Other templates match the nodes in the XML document and produce repeating HTML elements. In this example, the other template generates paragraphs for the Author nodes. Each paragraph contains an image and some text.

Figure 6.3 shows Internet Explorer displaying this style sheet's results.

HTML Tables

The previous example generates a series of paragraphs to display information in Author nodes. Other style sheets could place values in a table, ordered list, or unordered list. In those cases, a node containing the content nodes would start the table or list, call xsl:apply-templates to let another template display the repeating elements, and then close the table or list.

For example, consider the following style sheet. This version begins much as the previous version does. Its first template matches the XML document's root, and is the same as the previous version. Its second template matches the Authors node that contains all of the XML document's Author nodes. This template begins a table and includes the xsl:apply-templates element to make the transformation engine process the Author nodes. When the engine finishes, this template closes the table it opened.

The third template matches an Author node and displays that node's information in the table.

```
<?xml version="1.0"?>
<xsl:stylesheet version="1.0"
  xmlns:xsl="http://www.w3.org/1999/XSL/Transform">
<xsl:output method="html" indent="yes"/>

    <!-- Root. -->
    <xsl:template match="/">
        <HTML>
        <HEAD>
        <TITLE>Authors</TITLE>
        </HEAD>
        <BODY>

        <!-- Process the Authors node. -->
        <xsl:apply-templates/>

        </BODY>
        </HTML>
    </xsl:template>

    <!-- Authors. -->
    <xsl:template match="Authors">
        <!-- Start the table. -->
        <TABLE BGCOLOR="#00D0FF" BORDER="1">

        <!-- Process Author nodes. -->
        <xsl:apply-templates/>

        <!-- Close the table. -->
        </TABLE>
    </xsl:template>

    <!-- Author. -->
    <xsl:template match="Author">
        <TR>
            <!-- Show the picture. -->
            <TD>
            <A>
                <xsl:attribute name="HREF">
                    <xsl:value-of select="WebSite"/>
                </xsl:attribute>
                <IMG BORDER="0">
                    <xsl:attribute name="SRC">
                        <xsl:value-of select="PictureRef"/>
                    </xsl:attribute>
                    <xsl:attribute name="ALT">
                        <xsl:value-of select="FirstName"/>
```

```
                        <xsl:text> </xsl:text>
                        <xsl:value-of select="LastName"/>
                    </xsl:attribute>
                </IMG>
            </A>
            </TD>

            <!-- Show the biographical text. -->
            <TD>
                <xsl:value-of select="Bio"/>
            </TD>
        </TR>
    </xsl:template>

</xsl:stylesheet>
```

Figure 6.4 shows the resulting HTML document.

HTML Lists

A style sheet can produce an ordered or unordered HTML list in almost the same way it builds an HTML table. A template matches a higher-level node that contains the node holding the data of interest. The higher-level template starts the list, uses xsl:apply-templates to make the transformation engine process its child nodes, and then closes the list.

The following XSL style sheet displays information in a definition list. This example uses the same root template as before. Instead of starting a table, the Authors template starts a definition list with the <DL> tag. It uses xsl:apply-templates to make the transformation engine process the Author nodes, and then it finishes the list with the </DL> tag.

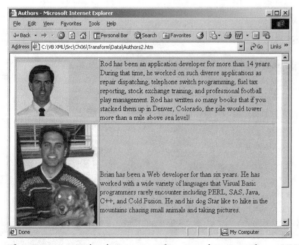

Figure 6.4 Style sheets are often used to transform XML data into HTML tables.

The Author template creates the series of tags <DT><B><FONT COLOR="#FF0000">. This begins a definition text entry and makes the Web browser use a bold red font. The template then outputs the values in the Author node's FirstName and LastName child nodes and closes the tags it opened. The template finishes by displaying the contexts of the Author node's Bio child inside the definition tag <DD>.

```
<?xml version="1.0"?>
<xsl:stylesheet version="1.0"
  xmlns:xsl="http://www.w3.org/1999/XSL/Transform">
<xsl:output method="html" indent="yes"/>

    <!-- Root. -->
    <xsl:template match="/">
        <HTML>
        <HEAD>
        <TITLE>Authors</TITLE>
        </HEAD>
        <BODY>

        <!-- Process the Authors node. -->
        <xsl:apply-templates/>

        </BODY>
        </HTML>
    </xsl:template>

    <!-- Authors. -->
    <xsl:template match="Authors">
        <!-- Start the list. -->
        <DL>

        <!-- Process Author nodes. -->
        <xsl:apply-templates/>

        <!-- Close the list. -->
        </DL>
    </xsl:template>

    <!-- Author. -->
    <xsl:template match="Author">
        <!-- Display the author's name. -->
        <DT><B><FONT COLOR="#FF0000">
            <xsl:value-of select="FirstName"/>
            <xsl:text> </xsl:text>
            <xsl:value-of select="LastName"/>
        </FONT></B></DT>

        <!-- Display the author's bio information. -->
        <DD>
            <xsl:value-of select="Bio"/>
        </DD>
        <P/>
    </xsl:template>

</xsl:stylesheet>
```

Figure 6.5 shows the Internet Explorer displaying the resulting definition list.

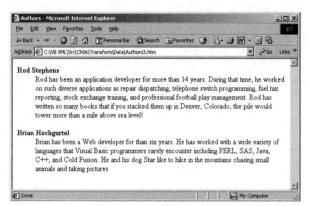

Figure 6.5 Building an HTML list is very similar to building an HTML table.

Building other kinds of HTML lists is very similar to building an HTML definition list. For example, to build an ordered list you would replace the <DL> and </DL> tags in the Authors template with the ordered list tags <OL> and </OL>. In the Author template, you would then include the text you wanted to display for an Author node between <LI> and </LI> tags.

A style sheet that transforms an XML document into an unordered list would be identical to this one except the Authors template would use the <UL> and </UL> tags instead of <OL> and </OL> tags.

A Generic Table

XML documents do a good job of describing data, but they often make finding patterns in the data difficult. While it is easy to view the data representing a particular record in an XML file, it is harder to compare similar fields in different records. A table lets you compare fields between different records much more naturally.

This example shows how to display a simple generic table listing the data in a three-level XML document. The document should have a structure similar to the Authors file used in the previous examples. It should have a single root data node containing any number of record nodes. Each record node should contain field nodes that contain data values. For example, the following XML document contains a data root node (Authors) that contains record nodes (Author), each containing data field nodes (LastName, FirstName, and so forth).

```
<?xml version="1.0"?>
<?xml-stylesheet type="text/xsl" href="GenericTable.xsl" ?>

<Authors>
    <Author>
        <LastName>Stephens</LastName>
        <FirstName>Rod</FirstName>
```

```
        <Email>RodStephens@vb-helper.com</Email>
        <WebSite>http://www.vb-helper.com</WebSite>
        <PictureRef>rod.jpg</PictureRef>
    </Author>
    <Author>
        <LastName>Hochgurtel</LastName>
        <FirstName>Brian</FirstName>
        <Email>brian@advocatemedia.com</Email>
        <WebSite>http://advocatemedia.com</WebSite>
        <PictureRef>brian.jpg</PictureRef>
    </Author>
</Authors>
```

The following style sheet displays a generic table representation of this XML document without using any information about the document's contents. It begins with the customary set of declarations. The root template begins the resulting HTML file with the usual HTML tags.

The root template uses an xsl:value-of element to set the HTML document's TITLE. This element's select attribute selects the name of the node that matches the /* XPath expression. That is the data root node. In the previous XML document, that node is named Authors.

After it gets the HTML document started, the root template includes the xsl:apply-templates element to make the transformation engine parse the document's other nodes.

The style sheet's second template matches the XPath expression /*. This expression specifies the data root node. In the previous XML document, that node is Authors.

This template generates the <TABLE> tag that starts an HTML table. It then outputs a <THEAD> tag to begin the table's header elements. Next the template uses an xsl:for-each element to iterate over the nodes that match the XPath expression *[1]/*. The *[1] part of this expression selects the context node's first child node. The /* part of the expression selects all of that node's children. In the previous XML document, these nodes are the first set of LastName, FirstName, and so forth.

For each of these nodes, the second template generates a <TH> tag to begin a table column header. It then displays the name of the node it is examining and closes the header with the </TH> tag. This loop produces table column headers displaying the names of the data field nodes.

After building the table headers, the second template includes an xsl:apply-templates element to make the transformation engine process the data field nodes.

The final template uses the XPath expression /*/*. This expression matches nodes that are children of the children of the document root node. Those are the data record nodes named Author.

The final template begins by displaying a <TR> tag indicating a row of table data follows. It then uses an xsl:for-each element to iterate over all of the node's children. For each child, the template outputs the child's value surrounded by the <TD> and </TD> tags, indicating it is a table data entry.

```
<?xml version="1.0"?>
<xsl:stylesheet version="1.0"
  xmlns:xsl="http://www.w3.org/1999/XSL/Transform">
```

```
<xsl:output method="html" indent="yes"/>

    <!-- Root. -->
    <xsl:template match="/">
        <HTML>
        <HEAD>
        <TITLE><xsl:value-of select="name(/*)"/></TITLE>
        </HEAD>
        <BODY>

        <!-- Process the data root node. -->
        <xsl:apply-templates/>

        </BODY>
        </HTML>
    </xsl:template>

    <!-- The data root node. -->
    <xsl:template match="/*">
        <!-- Start the table. -->
        <TABLE BORDER="1" CELLPADDING="2">

        <!-- Make column headers. -->
        <THEAD>
            <xsl:for-each select="*[1]/*">
                <TH><xsl:value-of select="name()"/></TH>
            </xsl:for-each>
        </THEAD>

        <!-- Process the data record nodes. -->
        <xsl:apply-templates/>

        <!-- Close the table. -->
        </TABLE>
    </xsl:template>

    <!-- Data record nodes. -->
    <xsl:template match="/*/*">
        <TR>
            <!-- Display the child nodes. -->
            <xsl:for-each select="*">
                <TD>
                    <xsl:value-of select="."/>
                </TD>
            </xsl:for-each>
        </TR>
    </xsl:template>

</xsl:stylesheet>
```

Figure 6.6 shows the result of this style sheet.

Figure 6.6 The GenericTable.xsl style sheet generates this table representation of an XML document without knowing the document's contents.

This style sheet transforms a three-level XML document into an HTML file that displays the document's data in a table. While it uses the fact that the document has three levels (a data root node, record nodes, and field nodes), it doesn't need to know anything else about the file's contents. You can use this style sheet to transform any similarly structured XML document into a table with no modifications.

Attribute Only XML Files

XML files are naturally quite verbose. Even a tag with a one-letter name takes up seven characters in an XML document.

```
<A>value</A>
```

Many XML documents consist of a series of "record" nodes that contain "field" nodes. For example, the following XML code fragment defines an Author record containing eight fields.

```
<Author>
    <FirstName>Brian</FirstName>
    <LastName>Hochgurtel</LastName>
    <Street>"123 Gold Hill Drive</Street>
    <City>Boulder</City>
    <State>CO</State>
    <Zip>80504</Zip>
    <PhoneHome>3035551212</PhoneHome>
    <PhoneWork>3035551213</PhoneWork>
</Author>
```

Some of the overhead in this file is necessary. For example, the <FirstName> is important because it indicates that the data it contains is a FirstName value.

The closing tags, on the other hand, don't add any new information to the file. The </FirstName> closes the FirstName field but doesn't really say anything new. Logically it could be replaced with something like </> to indicate that the previous field is closing. The only purpose of using the text FirstName in this tag is to let an application verify that the tag closes the correct opening tag.

In really large XML documents, some developers save all this "unnecessary" overhead by storing field values in attributes rather than in separate elements. For example, the following code shows how the previous data could be stored in a single element.

```
<Author FirstName="Brian" LastName="Hochgurtel" Address="123 Gold Hill
Drive" City="Boulder" State="CO" Zip="80504" PhoneHome="3035551212"
PhoneWork="3035551213"/>
```

The previous version of this data uses 264 characters; this version uses only 161 characters. For a large file containing many records, this can add up to a significant savings.

The following style sheet transforms a two-level XML document into an HTML table. The XML document should contain a single data root node that contains record nodes. Each record node contains data field values in its attributes.

This style sheet is very similar to the previous one. The only differences are in how the style sheet generates the table's column headers and how it displays the data values.

As before, the second template uses the XPath expression /* to match the data root node. It prepares the table, begins the table header with the <THEAD> tag, and uses an xsl:for-each element to build the table's column headers. The xsl:for-each element selects nodes that match the XPath expression *[1]/attribute::*. The first * in the expression matches the context node's children. The [1] selects the first child. The attribute::* piece selects all of that node's attributes. In total, the expression selects all of the attributes of the context node's first child.

As it iterates over these attributes, the template displays their names in the table's column headers.

As in the previous example, the style sheet's third template uses the XPath expression /*/* to match the data record nodes. In the example XML file, those are the Author nodes.

The template uses an xsl:for-each element with select attribute set to the expression attribute::*. This selects the context node's attributes, which contain the file's real data. As it iterates over the attributes, the template displays each attribute's value as a table entry.

```
<?xml version="1.0"?>
<xsl:stylesheet version="1.0"
  xmlns:xsl="http://www.w3.org/1999/XSL/Transform">
<xsl:output method="html" indent="yes"/>

    <!-- Root. -->
    <xsl:template match="/">
        <HTML>
        <HEAD>
        <TITLE><xsl:value-of select="name(/*)"/></TITLE>
        </HEAD>
        <BODY>
```

```
        <!-- Process the data root node. -->
        <xsl:apply-templates/>

        </BODY>
        </HTML>
    </xsl:template>

    <!-- The data root node. -->
    <xsl:template match="/*">
        <!-- Start the table. -->
        <TABLE BORDER="1" CELLPADDING="2">

        <!-- Make column headers. -->
        <THEAD>
            <xsl:for-each select="*[1]/attribute::*">
                <TH><xsl:value-of select="name()"/></TH>
            </xsl:for-each>
        </THEAD>

        <!-- Process the data record nodes. -->
        <xsl:apply-templates/>

        <!-- Close the table. -->
        </TABLE>
    </xsl:template>

    <!-- Data record nodes. -->
    <xsl:template match="/*/*">
        <TR>
            <!-- Display the attributes. -->
            <xsl:for-each select="attribute::*">
                <TD>
                    <xsl:value-of select="."/>
                </TD>
            </xsl:for-each>
        </TR>
    </xsl:template>

</xsl:stylesheet>
```

The results of this style sheet are identical to those of the previous example, which you can see in Figure 6.6.

CDATA

Some data is difficult to include directly in an XML document. The CDATA element lets you include text that normally would violate XML's rules in an XML file. For example, suppose an XML document needs to contain the statement $|A + B| <= |A| + |B|$. This statement is not valid XML code because it contains the characters <=. When it sees these characters, an XML parser tries to figure out what tag is starting and it gets confused.

An XML document can contain this text if it is included in a CDATA section, as shown in the following code.

```
<?xml version="1.0"?>
<WebPage>
    <Theorem>
        <Title>The Triangle Inequality</Title>
        <BodyText>
            <![CDATA[
For all numbers A and B, |A + B| <= |A| + |B|.
]]>
        </BodyText>
    </Theorem>
</WebPage>
```

The following style sheet transforms this XML document into HTML code using a slightly different approach than the previous examples. Its first template matches the XML document's root node. It generates an <HTML> tag, includes the xsl:apply-templates element to make the transformation engine visit the rest of the nodes, and finishes with the </HTML> tag.

The second template matches the XML document's Title node. It starts the HTML document HEAD section with the <HEAD> tag, sets the document's TITLE to the value of the Title node, and finishes with the </HEAD> tag.

The style sheet's third template matches the XML document's BodyText node. This template starts the HTML document's BODY section with the <BODY> tag. It uses the xsl:value-of element to display the text inside the BodyText element and finishes with the </BODY> tag.

```
<?xml version="1.0"?>
<xsl:stylesheet version="1.0"
  xmlns:xsl="http://www.w3.org/1999/XSL/Transform">
<xsl:output method="html" indent="yes"/>

    <!-- Root. -->
    <!-- Generate the start and end the HTML tags. -->
    <xsl:template match="/">
        <HTML>
        <xsl:apply-templates/>
        </HTML>
    </xsl:template>

    <!-- Title. -->
    <!-- Generate the HEAD section. -->
    <xsl:template match="//Title">
        <HEAD>
        <TITLE><xsl:value-of select="."/></TITLE>
        </HEAD>
```

```
    </xsl:template>

    <!-- BodyText. -->
    <!-- Generate the BODY section. -->
    <xsl:template match="//BodyText">
        <BODY>
        <xsl:value-of select="."/>
        </BODY>
    </xsl:template>

</xsl:stylesheet>
```

This style sheet's templates follow the structure of the HTML document closely. The first template creates the <HTML> and </HTML> tags that surround the document's contents. This template is as simple as possible. It must provide some coordination for the XML document's other nodes because it generates tags surrounding the data from those other nodes. That's all it needs to do, however.

The Title template creates the document's HEAD section, and the BodyText template creates the document's BODY section. These two sections are completely separate in the XML document, and they are separate in the resulting HTML document. Keeping these templates separate and self-contained makes them easier to understand.

The following code shows the resulting HTML text. Notice that the transformation engine automatically translated the < character in the CDATA section into the < entity. Because the style sheet's xsl:output element specified an output method of html, the character was automatically translated into its HTML-safe form.

```
<HTML>
  <HEAD>
    <META http-equiv="Content-Type" content="text/html; charset=utf-16">
    <TITLE>The Triangle Inequality</TITLE>
  </HEAD>
  <BODY>For all numbers A and B, |A + B| &lt;= |A| + |B|.</BODY>
</HTML>
```

Other Transformations

The examples so far in this chapter have shown how to transform an XML document into HTML or text. Transforming documents into HTML and text is probably the most common use for XSL style sheets.

Transforming an XML document into another XML document is just as easy as transforming a document into HTML. You might want to do this to add calculations to the data, remove unnecessary values from the original file, or rearrange the data using the xsl:sort element.

The only difference between a style sheet that transforms XML data into HTML data and one that transforms XML data into XML data is the xsl:output element. The new style sheet should use an xsl:output statement similar to this one:

```
<xsl:output method="xml" indent="yes"/>
```

Text, HTML, and XML are not the only formats into which a style sheet can transform an XML document. A style sheet can generate text files that use all sorts of other tag-based formats such as VoxML, MathML, SMIL (pronounced "smile"), and VoiceXML.

The X in XML stands for eXtensible, and all of these languages extend XML. Because these languages use the underlying XML syntax and structure, you already know quite a bit about them. You already know the basic syntax of these languages. Most of the rest of what you need to learn are the languages' commands. The rest of this section focuses on one of these languages: VoiceXML.

The Tellme Networks Web site at www.tellme.com is a particularly useful place to get information about VoiceXML. At the Tellme Studio subdomain at studio. tellme.com, you can download Web-based development tools for building VoiceXML applications. If you want to try building your own voice-based application, register at the Tellme Studio site.

Consider the following XML document.

```
<?xml version="1.0"?>
<Data>
    <WebPage>
        <Title>VoiceXML is So Cool!</Title>
        <Heading>Is XML The Beginning or the End?</Heading>
        <BodyText>
            You can learn more about XML at:
                http://www.xml.com
                http://www.w3c.org
        </BodyText>
    </WebPage>
</Data>
```

If you were planning to transform this document into HTML, you would probably want to include more information with the two Web links. If you stored the links' names as well as their URLs, you could add nicely formatted anchors to the HTML output. That information won't help a voice application much, however, so it is missing from this file.

The following style sheet transforms this XML document into a VoiceXML file. A VoiceXML application can read this file and generate speech. The file includes special tags that tell the VoiceXML application what to do. To get the tags into the file, the style sheet must generate them.

The style sheet's first template matches the document's root node. This template uses a vxml tag to define the root of the VoiceXML document. The meta tag shown in the example allows you to use the latest version of Voice XML. Without this tag, the functionality will not match what the VXML standard 1.0 specifies. The VXML page will use functionality that was available with a previous version of Tellme.

Next, the template opens a form tag. All of the VoiceXML action must occur within a form tag. This is analogous to the HTML tags that surround the contents of an HTML file.

The template then creates a block tag to contain the code it will execute. The document could have more than one block if it needed to execute several separate blocks of

VXML code. For example, the template might contain several blocks if it contained conditional logic. The block elements would isolate the code for each conditional statement.

The template then includes an xsl:apply-templates element to make the transformation engine process the XML document's other nodes. When the engine finishes, the first template closes the block and form templates it created.

The style sheet's second template matches the XML document's Title tag. It writes a comment into the result file. It then creates an audio tag containing some text. The audio tag tells the VoiceXML application to read the text in the tag. The template uses the pause tag to tell the application to pause briefly. It uses the audio tag again to make the application read more text, this time taken from the XML document by an xsl:value-of element. The template finishes with a slightly longer pause.

The style sheet's third template matches the XML document's Heading node. It is similar to the second template except it makes the VoiceXML application read different text values.

The final template is similar to the previous two. It matches the XML document's BodyText node and makes the VoiceXML application read the appropriate text.

```xsl
<xsl:stylesheet version="1.1"
  xmlns:xsl="http://www.w3.org/1999/XSL/Transform">
<xsl:output method="xml" omit-xml-declaration="yes" indent="yes"/>
<xsl:strip-space elements="*"/>

  <!-- Root. -->
  <xsl:template match="/">
    <!-- Begin the VoiceXML application. -->
    <vxml application="http://resources.tellme.com/lib/universals.vxml">

      <!-- Begin Scope of VXML application. -->
      <meta name="scoping" content="new"/>

      <!-- All the action of a Voice XML application
           occurs within form tags. -->
      <form id="Read Web Page Info">
        <!-- A VXML app may have several blocks where code executes. -->
        <block>
          <!-- Process the other nodes. -->
          <xsl:apply-templates/>
        </block>
      </form>
    </vxml>
  </xsl:template>

  <!-- Title. -->
  <xsl:template match="//Title">
    <xsl:comment>Read the title.</xsl:comment>

    <!-- The audio tag tells the voice app to begin reading.-->
    <audio>
      The title of this XML document is:
```

```
      </audio>

      <!-- Pause briefly between reading things. -->
      <pause>100</pause>

      <audio>
        <xsl:value-of select="."/>
      </audio>

      <pause>1000</pause>
  </xsl:template>

  <!-- Heading. -->
  <xsl:template match="//Heading">
    <xsl:comment>Read the heading.</xsl:comment>
    <audio>
      The heading of this XML document is:
    </audio>
    <pause>100</pause>
    <audio>
      <xsl:value-of select="."/>
    </audio>
    <pause>1000</pause>
  </xsl:template>

  <!-- BodyText. -->
  <xsl:template match="//BodyText">
    <xsl:comment>Read the body text.</xsl:comment>
    <audio>
      The text of this XML document includes:
    </audio>
    <pause>100</pause>
    <audio>
      <xsl:value-of select="."/>
    </audio>
    <pause>1000</pause>
  </xsl:template>
</xsl:stylesheet>
```

The following code shows the resulting VoiceXML file. If you join the Tellme Studio Web site, you can cut and paste this code into its Scratchpad application and save it to its Web site. Then you can call an 800 number and listen to the Tellme system read your VoiceXML document.

```
<vxml application="http://resources.tellme.com/lib/universals.vxml">
  <meta name="scoping" content="new" />
  <form id="Read Web Page Info">
    <block>
      <!--Read the title.-->
```

```
      <audio>
      The title of this XML document is:
  </audio>
      <pause>100</pause>
      <audio>VoiceXML is So Cool!</audio>
      <pause>1000</pause>
      <!--Read the heading.-->
      <audio>
      The heading of this XML document is:
  </audio>
      <pause>100</pause>
      <audio>Is XML The Beginning or the End?</audio>
      <pause>1000</pause>
      <!--Read the body text.-->
      <audio>
      The text of this XML document includes:
  </audio>
      <pause>100</pause>
      <audio>
          You can learn more about XML at:
              http://www.xml.com
              http://www.w3c.org
      </audio>
      <pause>1000</pause>
    </block>
  </form>
</vxml>
```

Transforming an XML file into another language derived from XML is just as easy as converting into HTML or VoiceXML. The most difficult part in these translations is knowing which tags to use to produce language-specific results.

A Visual Basic Transformation Engine

Much as XML does nothing without a parser, XSL does nothing without a transformation engine. A transformation engine often consists of an API within a particular programming language. This section shows how you can use Visual Basic .NET objects to build a transformation engine application.

Example program Transform, shown in Figure 6.7, transforms an XML document using an XSL style sheet. Enter the names of the XML and XSL files in the text boxes or click on the buttons next to the text boxes to select the files using a file selection dialog. After you have entered or selected the files, click the Transform button to make the program perform the transformation and display the results. The program also saves the results in a file with the same name as the XML file but with the .htm extension. For example, if the XML file is C:\Sales.xml, the program saves the result file in C:\Sales.htm.

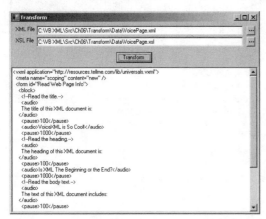

Figure 6.7 Example program Transform uses Visual Basic's XslTransform object to transform an XML document using an XSL style sheet.

The following code shows the most interesting parts of program Transform. When the user clicks the Translate button, the btnTranslate_Click event handler fires. That routine begins by declaring the variables it will use. The routine declares an XslTransform object to represent the XSL style sheet transformation, an XPathDocument object to represent the XML file that it will translate, and a StringWriter to compile the results.

After declaring these variables and setting the application's cursor to an hourglass, the subroutine creates a new XslTransform object. It calls this object's Load method to load the selected XSL file. The program protects itself using a Try Catch statement in case the file doesn't exist or is improperly formatted.

Next the routine creates a new XPathDocument object, passing the object's constructor the name of the XML file it should load. Again, the program protects itself from a missing or invalid file with a Try Catch statement.

The program then calls the XslTransform object's Transform method to translate the XML document using the XSL style sheet, sending the output to the StringWriter. The program displays the results in its txtResults text box and calls the SetFileContents subroutine to save the transformed document into a file.

```
Private Sub btnTransform_Click( _
  ByVal sender As System.Object, _
  ByVal e As System.EventArgs) Handles btnTransform.Click

    Dim xsl_transform As XslTransform
    Dim xpath_document As XPathDocument
    Dim string_writer As New StringWriter()

    txtResults.Text = ""
    Cursor = Cursors.WaitCursor
    Refresh()

    ' Load the XSL file into the XslTransform object.
```

```
xsl_transform = New XslTransform()
Try
    xsl_transform.Load(txtXsl.Text)
Catch exc As Exception
    MsgBox("Error loading XSLT file '" & txtXsl.Text & "'" & _
        vbCrLf & exc.Message, _
        MsgBoxStyle.Exclamation Or MsgBoxStyle.OKOnly, _
        "XSLT Load Error")
    Cursor = Cursors.Default
    Exit Sub
End Try

' Load the XML file into the XPathDocument object.
Try
    xpath_document = New XPathDocument(txtXml.Text)
Catch exc As Exception
    MsgBox("Error loading XML file '" & txtXml.Text & "'" & _
        vbCrLf & exc.Message, _
        MsgBoxStyle.Exclamation Or MsgBoxStyle.OKOnly, _
        "XML Load Error")
    Cursor = Cursors.Default
    Exit Sub
End Try

' Transform xpath_document (the XML), sending the results
' to the string_writer.
Try
    xsl_transform.Transform(xpath_document, Nothing, string_writer)
Catch exc As Exception
    MsgBox(exc.Message)
End Try
string_writer.Flush()

' Display the results.
txtResults.Text = string_writer.ToString()

' Save the resulting file.
SetFileContents(txtXml.Text.Replace(".xml", ".htm"), _
    string_writer.ToString())

Cursor = Cursors.Default
End Sub
```

If the XSL style sheet contains the xsl:output element, the XslTransform object may add appropriate initialization code to the result text. If the xsl:output element's method attribute is xml, the XslTransform object adds an XML declaration, similar to the following one, to the output.

```
<?xml version="1.0" encoding="UTF-8"?>
```

If the xsl:output element's method attribute is html, the XslTransform object adds a META tag to the output document after the <HEAD> tag. If the XSL style sheet does not write a <HEAD> tag into the document, the XslTransform object does not add a META tag. When it is added, the tag looks like this:

```
<META http-equiv="Content-Type" content="text/html; charset="UTF-16">
```

If the xsl:output element's method is text, the XslTransform object adds neither the XML declaration nor the HTML META tag.

To slightly complicate matters, the behavior of the XslTransform object also depends on the kind of object to which it sends the result. If the XslTransform object is sending output to a Stream or TextWriter object, it generates these tags normally. Program Transform sends the XslTranform object's output to a StringWriter, which is derived from TextWriter, so it produces these tags.

On the other hand, if the XslTransform object is sending its output to an XmlReader or XmlWriter object, it ignores the xsl:output element and produces neither of these tags. Table 6.7 summarizes how the XslTransform object treats the xsl:output element.

If you have a style sheet-enabled browser such as Internet Explorer 5, you can add a style sheet reference similar to the following one to an XML file. Then you can open the XML file with the browser. The browser will automatically transform the document and display the results.

```
<xml-stylesheet type="text/xsl" href="Test.xsl"?>
```

This works well if the style sheet produces an HTML document. If it creates a text file or some other format, the browser may not display it correctly. For example, it will compress carriage returns and spaces in a text file.

In cases like this, the Transform example program can be invaluable. It provides a fast and easy way to transform XML documents into any output format using XSL style sheets and view the results.

Table 6.7 Summary of XslTransform Output Behavior

OUTPUT OBJECT	XSL:OUTPUT METHOD	RESULT
Stream or TextWriter	html	META tag
Stream or TextWriter	xml	XML declaration
Stream or TextWriter	text	Nothing
TextReader or TextWriter	html	Nothing
TextReader or TextWriter	xml	Nothing
TextReader or TextWriter	text	Nothing

Conclusion

XSL style sheets let you transform an XML document into another format quickly and easily. XPath expressions determine the nodes matched or selected in XSLT templates. The elements and functions used by the templates create the output document.

Although the focus of this chapter is on transforming XML into HTML, XSL is also useful for generating text, XML, XML-derived languages such as VoiceXML, or practically any other text-based format.

Using multiple XSL files on the same XML document, you can create different versions for display in different contexts. For example, different style sheets might transform the same XML document into a text document, a detailed Web page, and a synopsis to be read by a VoiceXML application.

ASP.NET

Active Server Pages (ASP) allows you to provide dynamic Web content by including VBScript code in an ASP document. A scripting engine on the server executes the code to produce a static HTML result that it sends to the visitor's browser. While this technique is quite powerful, VBScript provides only a subset of the Visual Basic language.

ASP.NET is the next step in the evolution of ASP. While VBScript provides only a subset of the Visual Basic language, ASP.NET gives you access to the complete Visual Basic. NET language. Because ASP.NET includes all of the functionality of Visual Basic. NET, it gives you access to the same XML functionality shown throughout this book. After you master a few ASP.NET basics, you will be able to create XML-enabled Web applications.

This chapter explains how you can use Visual Basic code in ASP.NET to display complex views of XML data on the Web. The following sections cover background you need to understand and use ASP.NET. The sections after that explain specific techniques for displaying and manipulating XML data using ASP.NET.

This chapter doesn't cover everything there is to know about ASP.NET. Its intent is to give you enough information so that you can display XML data in a few useful ways using ASP.NET. For more information, consult a book that concentrates on ASP.NET.

IIS

Microsoft ships the Web server Internet Information Services (IIS) with Windows 2000 Pro and Server. IIS plays an integral part in creating ASP.NET pages. Through its configuration, it directs Web requests to actual files on the system. In order to use

ASP.NET, you must install IIS on your system. Just viewing the files locally on your hard drive won't work because ASP.NET requires that the request go through IIS so that it can broker the ASP.NET request to the .NET Framework SDK.

Microsoft also includes functionality in ASP.NET to improve the reliability of IIS. Previous versions of ASP were notorious for having memory problems and shutting down IIS. Once IIS crashed, the server no longer allowed browsers to visit the ASP page. With the ASP.NET run-time processes are closely monitored, and if a page hangs or doesn't respond, another process can quickly replace it.

In an effort to increase speed and functionality, Microsoft introduced the *common language runtime* with the .NET initiative. The common language runtime provides a means to compile ASP.NET pages (and other applications created in Visual Studio .NET) into an executable image. This allows for greater performance because the compiled image executes rather than the scripting engine when the browser visits the page. This improves the reliability of IIS because it is no longer relying on the scripting engine.

For further information on how to install IIS and learn some more about its XML capabilities, see Chapter 11, "SQL Server 2000."

ASP.NET Basics

ASP.NET uses any of the Visual Studio .NET languages to create dynamic Web pages. These languages include JScript, C# (pronounced "C-sharp"), and Visual Basic.

You can use any text editor such as Notepad or Wordpad to write ASP.NET code; you don't need to use a special editor. If you save the file with a .aspx extension and you've installed the .NET Framework SDK, a Web server such as IIS will know the page contains ASP.NET code.

An ASP.NET page should begin with a statement telling the server the language in which scripts on the page are written. The following command says this page uses Visual Basic .NET.

```
<%@ Page Language="VB" %>
```

The <% and %> symbols denote where script code begins and ends. You can use script code to mix Visual Basic and HTML. For example, the following code fragment adds some HTML text to the resulting document only if the value MyVariable is Nothing.

```
<%
  If (MyVariable = Nothing)
%>
  <B>Please Enter A Value</B><BR>
<%
  End If
%>
```

Notice that the pieces of script code do not need to be contiguous. In the previous example, a piece of HTML code sits in the middle of the If and End If statements. While the If and End If statements are not contained in the same block of script code, they are still connected in the flow of the script's execution.

You can also surround script code with SCRIPT tags, as shown in the following code. In this example, the SCRIPT tag overrides the page's scripting language and uses JScript code.

```
<SCRIPT Language="JScript">
    function to_beginning()
    {
        xmlAuthors.recordset.moveFirst();
    }
</SCRIPT>
```

The ASP.NET page Styles.aspx, shown in the following code, displays samples of text in the HTML heading styles H1 through H6. The page begins by stating that it will use Visual Basic .NET code for its scripts. It then uses the SCRIPT tag to define the ShowStyle subroutine. This subroutine uses the Response object's Write method to add text to the page's HTML output that defines a new row in an HTML table.

The page then displays several lines of HTML code just as an HTML Web page would. It creates the document's HEAD section and gives it a TITLE. It starts the document's BODY section, displays a heading, and starts a TABLE.

The ASP.NET page then includes some script code. The code declares the variable i and then uses it to loop from 1 to 6. For each value of i, the code calls the ShowStyle method, passing it the name of an HTML heading style: H1, H2, and so forth.

When the script code finishes, the document closes its TABLE, BODY, and HTML tags.

```
<%@ Page Language="VB" %>

<SCRIPT Language="VB" runat="server">
    Sub ShowStyle(ByVal style_name As String)
        Response.Write("<TR><TD>")
        Response.Write("<" & style_name & _
            ">This line was written in style " & style_name & _
            "</" & style_name & ">")
        Response.Write("</TD></TR>")
    End Sub
</SCRIPT>

<HTML>
  <HEAD>
    <TITLE>Styles</TITLE>
  </HEAD>

  <BODY>
    <CENTER><H1>Styles</H1></CENTER>
    <TABLE BORDER="1" BGCOLOR="#E0E0E0">
      <%
        Dim i As Integer

        For i = 1 To 6
```

```
            ShowStyle("H" & i)
        Next i
    %>
    </TABLE>
  </BODY>
</HTML>
```

Figure 7.1 shows Styles.aspx displayed in Internet Explorer.

ASP.NET Requests

The previous example uses the Response object to add text to the Web document's output. Response is one of the more useful objects available to script code when an ASP.NET file loads. Another useful object is Request. The Request object contains information about the request that invoked the document. In particular, the Request object's QueryString collection provides access to the variables passed to the document in its query string.

For example, the following URL invokes the ASP.NET page Purchase.aspx, passing it the query values ItemId = 1234 and Quantity = 12.

```
http://www.vb-helper.com/Purchase.aspx?ItemId=1234&Quantity=12
```

The following code shows the file Purchase.aspx. This code begins with normal HTML code. In the middle of the HTML, it uses the Request.QueryString collection to display the values of its ItemId and Quantity parameters. The special syntax <%=...%> pulls the value out of a script variable without starting a whole section of code.

```
<%@ Page Language="VB" %>

<HTML>
```

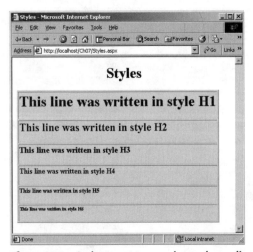

Figure 7.1 Styles.aspx uses script code to display HTML heading styles.

```
<HEAD>
    <TITLE>Purchase</TITLE>
</HEAD>

<BODY>
    <B>
        Item ID:
        <%=Request.QueryString("ItemId")%>
        <BR>
        Quantity:
        <%=Request.QueryString("Quantity")%>
    </B>
</BODY>
</HTML>
```

Figure 7.2 shows Purchase.aspx in Internet Explorer.

Self-Made Requests

A common technique in ASP pages is to use the same Web page to gather data and display the results. When the page initially loads, it checks its query string to see if it has the parameters it needs to do something useful.

If it doesn't have all the data it needs, the page displays text boxes, option buttons, and other controls to let the visitor enter the needed data. Usually the page puts all of these controls inside an HTML form and includes a Submit button. When the visitor clicks this button, the Web browser automatically builds a query string and invokes the page again with that query string.

When the page is displayed with a fully formed query string, it does whatever it is supposed to do.

The file HelloWorld.aspx, shown in the following code, demonstrates this technique. If the form is invoked without a query string, it displays a text box and asks the visitor to enter a numeric value. When the visitor clicks the Submit button, the page invokes itself, passing the entered value in the query string. If the value entered is non-numeric, the page complains. If the value is numeric, the page says Hello World that number of times.

The code begins by using a SCRIPT section to define the Ordinal function. This function returns a number's ordinal representation. For example, on input 12 the function returns the string 12th.

Figure 7.2   Purchase.aspx uses the Response object's QueryString collection to display the values of its parameters.

The page then uses some normal HTML code to get the page started. In its BODY section, the page creates a FORM with ACTION set to the HelloWorld.aspx page. When the visitor clicks the form's Submit button, the form automatically invokes this page.

Next the code checks the value of the Repetitions query string value. If the value is missing, the page displays a prompt and a text box named Repetitions. When it invokes the ASP page, the FORM adds the text box's value to the query string using its name, Repetitions, and the query string value's name. The page also makes a Submit button to make the form automatically send the request to the form.

If the Repetitions query string value is not missing but Visual Basic's IsNumeric function says it is not numeric, the page displays an error message. It then displays a prompt, text box, and Submit button as before.

If the Repetitions value is present and numeric, the page enters a loop and repeatedly prints out a greeting using the Ordinal function to nicely format the number of each line.

```
<%@ Page Language="VB" %>

<SCRIPT runat="server">
    ' Return an ordinal string like 1st, 2nd, etc.
    Function Ordinal(ByVal i As Integer) As String
        Dim ending As String
        Dim two_digits As Integer

        ' Most numbers end with th.
        ending = "th"

        ' See if (i Mod 100) is between 11 and 19.
        ' Those numbers all end with th.
        two_digits = i Mod 100
        If (two_digits < 11) or (two_digits > 19) Then
            ' (i Mod 100) is not between 11 and 19.
            ' Look for special cases 1st, 2nd, 3rd.
            Select Case i Mod 10
                Case "1"
                    ending = "st"
                Case "2"
                    ending = "nd"
                Case "3"
                    ending = "rd"
            End Select
        End If

        Return i & ending
    End Function
</SCRIPT>

<HTML>
  <HEAD>
    <TITLE>Hello World</TITLE>
  </HEAD>
```

```
<BODY>
  <FORM ACTION="./HelloWorld.aspx">
    <% If Request.QueryString("Repetitions") Is Nothing Then %>
      <!-- We have no query string. Prompt the visitor. -->
      Repetitions:
      <INPUT TYPE="Text" NAME="Repetitions">
      <P>
      <INPUT TYPE="Submit" VALUE="Say Hello">
    <% Else If Not IsNumeric(Request.QueryString("Repetitions")) _
    Then %>
      <!-- The value is nonnumeric. Complain. -->
      <FONT COLOR="red">Repetitions must be numeric.</FONT>
      <BR>
      Repetitions:
      <INPUT TYPE="Text" NAME="Repetitions"
        VALUE="<%=Request.QueryString("Repetitions")%>">
      <P>
      <INPUT TYPE="Submit" VALUE="Try Again">
    <% Else %>
      <!-- We have the value we need. Say hello repeatedly. -->
      <%
        Dim i As Integer

        For i = 1 To Request.QueryString("Repetitions")
      %>
          <B>Hello World for the <%=Ordinal(i)%> time!</B>
          <BR>
      <%
        Next i
      %>
    <% End If %>
  </FORM>
</BODY>
</HTML>
```

Figure 7.3 shows HelloWorld.aspx in Internet Explorer.

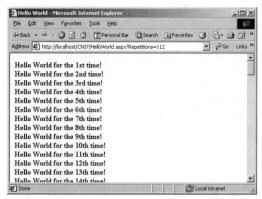

Figure 7.3 HelloWorld.aspx displays a prompt, an error message and prompt, or a repeated greeting, depending on how it is invoked.

This technique of using the same form to gather information and then display the results can be confusing at first, but it is extremely common on ASP pages. After you get used to the idea and mentally separate the page's different modes of operation, this method isn't too hard to understand.

Data Islands

A *data island* is a chunk of XML data embedded in a Web page. It's a little island of XML data surrounded by a sea of HTML and ASP.NET code.

ASP.NET code can transform a data island and display its data in many ways. It can process the data and write directly into the Response object representing the Web page to display text, tables, or anything else HTML can build. It can also use Visual Basic objects to transform the data using XSL and take advantage of all of the features provided by XSL.

The following sections explain several ways ASP.NET can display and manipulate information stored in data islands. It also explains two different types of data islands: client side and server side.

Client-Side Data Islands

In a client-side data island, the ASP.NET page downloads the XML data to the client and transforms the XML into HTML or some other format using the functionality built into the browser. Doing this on the client side can be faster than running a script on the server side because a Web server may have thousands of processes running on it. It could take several seconds for a Web server to execute a piece of ASP.NET code while an ASP.NET page running on the client side may run immediately.

The disadvantage to the client-side approach is that browsers previous to version 5 of Internet Explorer do not have built-in XML functionality. In addition, browsers other than Internet Explorer such as Netscape have minimal XML functionality. Unless you can control which browsers view your Web site, many people won't be able to view your information.

The Web page Table.html, shown in the following code, contains XML information in-line. That means the XML data is written into the same page as the HTML. The page surrounds the data with the XML tag. This tag lets Internet Explorer know that there is XML information in this page.

After the data, the HTML page begins. The HTML table outputs the XML using the <SPAN></SPAN>, <DIV></DIV>, <A></A>, and <IMG> tags. Each of these tags uses its DATAFLD attribute to name the XML field that it needs to display. For example, the <SPAN DATAFLD="FirstName"></SPAN> tag makes the HTML display the FirstName element. The HTML TABLE knows to repeat the row for each record stored in the XML.

Notice that this code contains only HTML tags and no Visual Basic code.

```
<!-- Author XML data. -->
<XML ID="xmlAuthors">
  <Authors>
    <Author>
```

```
          <FirstName>Rod</FirstName>
          <LastName>Stephens</LastName>
          <EmailAddress>RodStephens@vb-helper.com</EmailAddress>
          <HomePageName>VB Helper</HomePageName>
          <HomePageURL>http://www.vb-helper.com</HomePageURL>
          <Image>./rod.jpg</Image>
      </Author>
      <Author>
          <FirstName>Brian</FirstName>
          <LastName>Hochgurtel</LastName>
          <EmailAddress>brian@advocatemedia.com</EmailAddress>
          <HomePageName>Advocate Media</HomePageName>
          <HomePageURL>http://www.advocatemedia.com</HomePageURL>
          <Image>./brian.jpg</Image>
      </Author>
   </Authors>
</XML>

<!-- HTML Code. -->
<HTML>
<HEAD>
  <TITLE>Table</TITLE>
</HEAD>

<BODY>
  <H1><CENTER>Table</CENTER></H1>

  <!-- Create the table. DATASRC tells it where to find data. -->
  <TABLE BORDER="1" BGCOLOR="#E0E0E0" CELLPADDING="5"
  DATASRC="#xmlAuthors">
    <THEAD>
       <TH>Name</TH>
       <TH>Email Address</TH>
       <TH>Home Page</TH>
       <TH>Image</TH>
    </THEAD>
    <TR>
       <!-- Define the row data members.
            DATAFLD tells cells which fields to display. -->
       <TD>
         <SPAN DATAFLD="FirstName"></SPAN>
          
         <SPAN DATAFLD="LastName"></SPAN>
       </TD>
       <TD><DIV DATAFLD="EmailAddress"></DIV></TD>
       <TD><A DATAFLD="HomePageURL">
         <DIV DATAFLD="HomePageName"></DIV></A></TD>
       <TD><IMG DATAFLD="Image"></IMG></TD>
    </TR>
  </TABLE>
</BODY>
</HTML>
```

Figure 7.4 shows Table.html in Internet Explorer.

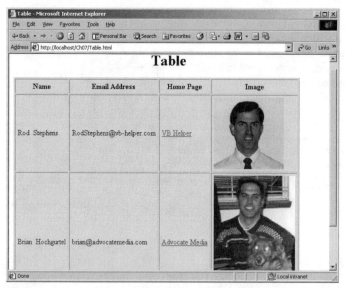

Figure 7.4   A Web page can bind an HTML table to an XML data island.

Table 7.1 lists HTML tags you can use to display XML data. Note that these are HTML tags so they must have the closing element. They cannot be treated as empty XML elements.

Table 7.1   Summary of XML-Specific HTML Tags

TAGS	PURPOSE
<SPAN DATAFLD="FirstName"></SPAN>	Displays the value of the XML tag FirstName without any line breaks.
<DIV DATAFLD="FirstName"></DIV>	Displays the value of the XML tag FirstName with a line break.
<IMG DATAFLD="Image"></IMG>	Creates an HTML image tag assigning the DATAFLD value to the tag's SRC attribute. The results may look like this: <IMG SRC="brian.gif">
<A DATAFLD="HomePageURL">Ok</A>	Creates an HTML anchor assigning the DATAFLD value to the tag's HREF attribute like this: <A HREF="http://www.advocatemedia.com">Ok</A>

Importing XML Data

In addition to including XML data in-line, the <XML> tag allows you to import XML data from either another file or URL.

Web page TableImport.html, shown in the following code, uses the exact same HTML code as Table.html. Instead of including the XML directly in the HTML page, it imports its data from a file. Storing the data in a separate XML file helps you isolate your Web site's content from the presentation details provided by the HTML code. This way the data can change independently of the HTML and vice versa.

```
<!-- Author XML data. -->
<XML ID="xmlAuthors" SRC="./Author.xml"></XML>

<!-- HTML Code. -->
<HTML>
<HEAD>
  <TITLE>Table</TITLE>
</HEAD>

<BODY>
  <H1><CENTER>Table</CENTER></H1>

  <!-- Create the table. DATASRC tells it where to find data. -->
  <TABLE BORDER="1" BGCOLOR="#E0E0E0" CELLPADDING="5"
  DATASRC="#xmlAuthors">
    <THEAD>
      <TH>Name</TH>
      <TH>Email Address</TH>
      <TH>Home Page</TH>
      <TH>Image</TH>
    </THEAD>
    <TR>
      <!-- Define the row data members.
           DATAFLD tells cells which fields to display. -->
      <TD>
        <SPAN DATAFLD="FirstName"></SPAN>
         
        <SPAN DATAFLD="LastName"></SPAN>
      </TD>
      <TD><DIV DATAFLD="EmailAddress"></DIV></TD>
      <TD><A DATAFLD="HomePageURL">
        <DIV DATAFLD="HomePageName"></DIV></A></TD>
      <TD><IMG DATAFLD="Image"></IMG></TD>
    </TR>
  </TABLE>
</BODY>
</HTML>
```

The results of this code look just like the results shown in Figure 7.4.

XSL Transformations

In addition to using HTML tags such as SPAN and DIV to display XML data, you can use an XSL file to transform the XML data into HTML code.

Consider the following XML file, Author.xml, imported in the previous example.

```
<?xml version="1.0"?>
<Authors>
    <Author>
        <FirstName>Rod</FirstName>
        <LastName>Stephens</LastName>
        <EmailAddress>RodStephens@vb-helper.com</EmailAddress>
        <HomePageName>VB Helper</HomePageName>
        <HomePageURL>http://www.vb-helper.com</HomePageURL>
        <Image>./rod.jpg</Image>
    </Author>
    <Author>
        <FirstName>Brian</FirstName>
        <LastName>Hochgurtel</LastName>
        <EmailAddress>brian@advocatemedia.com</EmailAddress>
        <HomePageName>Advocate Media</HomePageName>
        <HomePageURL>http://www.advocatemedia.com</HomePageURL>
        <Image>./brian.jpg</Image>
    </Author>
</Authors>
```

Rather than using Visual Basic .NET code to display this data, you can use XSL to transform it and surround it with static HTML code. The XSL file Author.xsl, shown in the following code, transforms this XML data into an HTML table. For more information on XSL, see Chapter 6, "XSL."

```
<xsl:stylesheet version="1.1"
  xmlns:xsl="http://www.w3.org/1999/XSL/Transform">
<xsl:output method="html" indent="yes"/>
    <!-- Begin matching elements. -->
    <xsl:template match="/">
        <HTML>
            <BODY>
                <xsl:apply-templates/>
            </BODY>
        </HTML>
    </xsl:template>

    <!-- Match on the Author Element. -->
    <xsl:template match="Author">
        <P>
            <!-- Display information in a table format. -->
            <TABLE BORDER ="1" CELLPADDING="1" CELLSPACING="1">
                <xsl:for-each select="child::*">
                    <TR>
                        <TD><xsl:value-of select="name(.)"/></TD>
```

```
                    <TD><xsl:value-of select="."/></TD>
                </TR>
            </xsl:for-each>
        </TABLE>
    </P>
  </xsl:template>
</xsl:stylesheet>
```

The file TransformAuthor.aspx, shown in the following code, transforms the XML file using this XSL code and displays the result. After building the HTML HEAD section, the file creates two XML controls. The first is named xml_data and has SRC attribute set to the XML data file. The second XML control is named xsl_stylesheet, and its SRC attribute is set to the XSL style sheet.

Next, the page begins the HTML BODY section and displays some static HTML code. It then creates a DIV tag named result. This control will display the results of the transformation.

The SCRIPT tag at the end of the file indicates that its code should run when the Web page's window loads. At that point, the script calls the xml_data control's transformNode method, passing it the xsl_stylesheet control's XMLDocument element. This transforms the XML data using the style sheet. The script assigns the result to the result control's innerHTML property to make it display the transformed data.

```
<HTML>
    <HEAD>
        <TITLE>XML Data Island</TITLE>
    </HEAD>

    <!-- Load the XML file. -->
    <XML ID="xml_data" SRC="Author.xml"></XML>

    <!-- Load the XSL file. -->
    <XML ID="xsl_stylesheet" SRC="Author.xsl"></XML>

    <BODY>
        <P>
            <B>This is a data island demo</B><br>
            The following information comes from the XML data.
        </P>

        <!-- Display the transformed XML file -->
        <DIV ID="result"></DIV>
    </BODY>

    <!-- Use some VBScript to call the object in IE that performs
         transformations. -->
    <SCRIPT LANGUAGE="VBScript" FOR="window" EVENT="onload">
        result.innerHTML =
xml_data.transformNode(xsl_stylesheet.XMLDocument)
    </SCRIPT>
</HTML>
```

Figure 7.5 shows TransformAuthor.aspx in Internet Explorer.

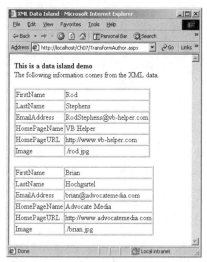

Figure 7.5   A Web page can use client-side XML controls to display transformed XML data.

Server-Side Data Islands

The problem with a client-side data island is that it requires a fairly recent release of Internet Explorer (version 5 and later). If a visitor hasn't upgraded, the browser doesn't have the SPAN, XML, and other controls needed to transformation and display the data properly so it will try to display the XML tags.

Client-side data islands work well if you can set browser requirements—for example, when you are developing an intranet. If you need to ensure that all browsers are able to view this data, however, this approach won't work. The following sections show one way around this problem.

To make your data island browser independent, you need to move the data transformation to the server side. This imposes an extra burden on the server, but it ensures that all browsers can view the data correctly.

Using Visual Basic .NET Code

One option for creating a server-side data island is to use Visual Basic .NET code in an ASP.NET page to explicitly transform the data and produce HTML code displaying the result.

The Web page TranslateHTML.aspx, shown in the following code, transforms an XML file using an XSL style sheet much as the example in the previous section does.

This example performs the transformation on the server, however, and passes HTML code only to the client browser.

This example invokes classes written in Visual Basic .NET and stored in source code files with a .vb extension. To tell the script engine where to find these classes, the page's initial Page tag includes the statement Src="TranslateHTML.vb". The code contained in the file TranslateHTML.vb is described later in this section.

The code adds the attribute statement RUNAT="server" to its SCRIPT and FORM tags, as well as the ASP controls it uses. This is important because it ensures that all of the Visual Basic code on this ASP.NET page executes on the server side. This keeps the code independent of the client and lets the page display the same way regardless of the version of Internet Explorer.

The page's SCRIPT section defines two routines: Page_Load and UrlPath. Page_Load is a standard event handler and works much as normal event handlers in Visual Basic. When the Page object loads, the Page_Load event handler executes.

The Page_Load subroutine begins by creating a new instance of the TranslateHTML class defined in the file TranslateHTML.vb and described later. It then calls function UrlPath to get the path to the current document. It adds the strings Authors.xml and Authors.xsl to this path to get the paths to the XML and XSL files it will use.

Next, Page_Load calls the TranslateHTML object's TranslateFiles method, passing it the locations of the XML and XSL files. The TranslateHTML object returns the transformed XML data, and Page_Load displays the result in the transResult label control.

Function UrlPath gets the Web page's URL from the Request object. It removes the characters following the URL's final / character to remove the file's name. For instance, if the Web page's URL is http://www.vb-helper.com/Authors.aspx, then the UrlPath function returns the value http://www.vb-helper.com/.

After the script code, the Web page displays standard HTML code. The only interesting part to this code is that it creates the asp:label control named transResult used by the Page_Load subroutine to display the result.

```
<%@ Page Language="VB" Src="TranslateHTML.vb"%>
<SCRIPT RUNAT="server">
Sub Page_Load(obj As Object, e As EventArgs)
    Dim path_to_file As String
    Dim xml_file As String
    Dim xsl_file As String
    Dim transformed_file As String
    Dim translate_html As TranslateHTML

    ' Create a TranslateHTML object.
    translate_html = New TranslateHTML

    ' Set a variable to the URL called to activate this page.
    path_to_file = UrlPath()

    ' Set the full path to the XML file.
    xml_file = path_to_file & "Author.xml"
```

```
    ' Set the full path to the XSL file.
    xsl_file = path_to_file & "Author.xsl"
    ' Perform the transformation.
    transformed_file = translate_html.TranslateFiles(xml_file, xsl_file)

    ' Display the transformed XML in the asp:text field named tbLabel.
    transResult.text = transformed_file
End Sub

Private Function UrlPath() As String
    Dim the_url As String
    Dim pos As Integer

    ' Get the URL called to activate this page.
    the_url = Request.Url.ToString

    ' Remove the name of the aspx file so we can append filenames.
    pos = InStrRev(the_url, "/")
    Return the_url.SubString(0, pos)
End Function
</SCRIPT>

<HTML>
    <HEAD>
        <TITLE>Data Island Example</TITLE>
    </HEAD>

    <BODY>
        <H2>Data Island Example</H2>
        <FORM RUNAT="server">
            <HR>
            <!-- This is the label for showing the results. -->
            <asp:label id="transResult" runat="server" text=""/>
        </FORM>
        <P>
            <B>You could put some other HTML here as well</B>
        </P>
    </BODY>
</HTML>
```

The following code shows the file TranslateHTML.vb that defines the Translate-HTML class. This code is very similar to the code shown in Chapter 6, "XSL," for Visual Basic .NET applications that perform the same task.

The TransformHTML class provides a single method TranslateHTML that takes parameters giving the locations of XML and XSL files and returns the transformed result. TranslateHTML begins by creating a new XslTransform object and loading the

XSL style sheet. Next the function loads the indicated XML document into a new XPathDocument object.

The function invokes the XmlTransform object's Transform method, passing it the XPathDocument containing the XML data. An XmlTextWriter processes the result and sends it to its associated StringWriter, which converts the result into a string.

```
' Import needed namespaces.
' Note that this must occur before the class definition.
Imports System.Xml
Imports System.Xml.Xsl
Imports System.Xml.XPath
Imports System.IO


' A simple XSL transformation class.
Public Class TranslateHTML
    ' This is a function because a value returns.
    Public Function TranslateFiles(ByVal xml_file As String, _
      ByVal xsl_file As String) As String
        Dim xsl_transform As XslTransform
        Dim xpath_document As XPathDocument
        Dim string_writer As New StringWriter()
        Dim xml_text_writer As New XmlTextWriter(string_writer)

        ' Load the XSL file into the XslTransform object.
        xsl_transform = New XslTransform()
        xsl_transform.Load(xsl_file)

        ' Load the XML file into the XPathDocument object.
         xpath_document = New XPathDocument(xml_file)

        ' Transform xpath_document (the XML), sending the results
        ' to the xml_text_writer, which sends its results to
        ' string_writer.
        xml_text_writer.Formatting = Formatting.Indented
        xsl_transform.Transform(xpath_document, Nothing, _
 xml_text_writer)
        xml_text_writer.Flush()

        ' Return the results.
        Return string_writer.ToString()
    End Function
End Class
```

Many of the examples described in the rest of this chapter use the TranslateHTML class to perform transformations.

Figure 7.6 shows the TranslateHTML.aspx Web page in Internet Explorer.

Figure 7.6   A Web page can use a Visual Basic .NET class to manipulate XML data.

This example uses a lot of code to perform this translation. The following section shows a simpler method. This example is still useful, however, because it shows the basics of manipulating XML data in a server-side script. Examples later in this chapter elaborate on this technique.

The XML Control

Performing a transformation with XSL is a relatively common task. It makes sense that Microsoft would provide a server control to perform this task. This control is called asp:xml.

The file TranslateHTMLSimple.asp, shown in the following code, uses the asp:xml control to transform and display XML data. The asp:xml control has four attributes. The id attribute gives the control a name on the Web page. DocumentSource and TransformSource give the locations of the XML and XSL files, respectively. The runat attribute has the value server so the control executes on the server rather than the client.

That's all there is to this example. The asp:xml control automatically loads the XML document, transforms it, and adds the result to the Web page.

```
<%@ Page Language="VB" %>
<HTML>
    <HEAD>
        <TITLE>Server Side Data Island</TITLE>
    </HEAD>
    <BODY>
        <asp:xml id="page_content"
```

```
                    DocumentSource="./Author.xml"
                    TransformSource="./Author.xsl"
                    runat="server"/>
        </BODY>
</HTML>
```

Figure 7.7 shows TranslateHTMLSimple.aspx in Internet Explorer.

If you want to display unformatted XML in the browser, simply leave off the TransformSource attribute. The file UnformattedXML, shown in the following code, takes this approach.

```
<%@ Page Language="VB" %>
<HTML>
    <HEAD>
        <TITLE>Server Side Data Island</TITLE>
    </HEAD>
    <BODY>
        <asp:xml id="page_content"
            DocumentSource="./Author.xml"
            runat="server"/>
    </BODY>
</HTML>
```

Figure 7.8 shows the unformatted XML output of UnformattedXML.aspx. Notice how the XML data is run together. The result isn't very appealing, but the code is extremely easy.

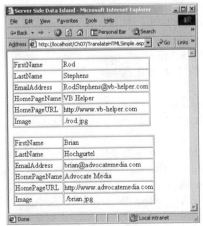

Figure 7.7   A server-side XML control can transform and display XML data.

Figure 7.8   A server-side XML control can display unformatted XML data.

Using XSL in a Web page is convenient, particularly if you already have XSL written to transform an XML document. XSL, though, is not always convenient, and, depending on the transformation you need to make, it may be time consuming. The following sections explain how you can use ASP.NET code to load XML data directly and manipulate it using the techniques described in other parts of this book.

XmlDocument

The following example uses an XmlDocument object to load an XML document. It then uses the XmlDocument object's methods to manipulate the data and add HTML code to the Web results.

The file Table.aspx, shown in the following code, begins by using an XML tag to load data into an XML control named xmlAuthors. In this version of ASP.NET, including the XML data by referring to an external XML file seems to confuse the LoadXml statement used later. Including the data directly in the file, as is shown here, works.

The page then begins a SCRIPT block. Subroutine BuildRows begins by creating a new XmlDocument object and using its LoadXml method to load the XML data stored in the xmlAuthors control. It then uses a For loop to move through each of the root node's child elements. For each child node, the code starts a new table row with the HTML <TR> tag.

The routine then starts a new table cell using the <TD> tag. It calls the child node's SelectSingleNode method to find the child's FirstName child node. If that node exists, the code writes the node's value into the table. The subroutine repeats these steps to add the value of the LastName to the FirstName, and then it closes the cell with the </TD> tag.

Subroutine BuildRows starts a new table cell. It uses SelectSingleNode to find the current node's EmailAddress child. It uses that value to build a mailto link and closes this cell.

The routine then uses SelectSingleNode to find the HomePageName and Home-PageURL child nodes. It uses their values to create another cell containing a link to HomePageURL, giving the link the name HomePageName.

The code uses similar steps to build an image displaying the file given by the Image child node. Finally, BuildRows closes the HTML table.

Compared to the Web page's script code, the HTML code is simple. The file builds the HEAD section, starts the BODY section, and begins an HTML table. It displays the table's column headings and calls subroutine BuildRows to generate the table's rows. The Web page finishes by closing the table.

```
<%@ Page Language="VB" %>
<%@ Import Namespace="System.Xml" %>


<!-- Author data island. -->
<!-- Note that including an XML declaration confuses LoadXml. -->
<XML ID="xmlAuthors" RUNAT="Server">
  <Authors>
    <Author>
      <FirstName>Rod</FirstName>
      <LastName>Stephens</LastName>
      <EmailAddress>RodStephens@vb-helper.com</EmailAddress>
      <HomePageName>VB Helper</HomePageName>
      <HomePageURL>http://www.vb-helper.com</HomePageURL>
      <Image>./rod.jpg</Image>
    </Author>
    <Author>
      <FirstName>Brian</FirstName>
      <LastName>Hochgurtel</LastName>
      <EmailAddress>brian@advocatemedia.com</EmailAddress>
      <HomePageName>Advocate Media</HomePageName>
      <HomePageURL>http://www.advocatemedia.com</HomePageURL>
      <Image>./brian.jpg</Image>
    </Author>
  </Authors>
</XML>


<!-- Create the subroutine that builds the table's rows. -->
<SCRIPT Language="VB" RUNAT="Server">
Sub BuildRows()
    Dim xml_doc As New XmlDocument()
    Dim row_node As XmlNode
    Dim field_node As XmlNode
    Dim home_page_url_node As XmlNode
    Dim row_name As String

    xml_doc.LoadXml(xmlAuthors.InnerHTML)
    For Each row_node In xml_doc.DocumentElement.ChildNodes
        ' Send data to the Response object using the Write method.
        ' Write out the beginning table row tag.
        Response.Write("<TR>")

        ' Begin a table cell.
        Response.Write("<TD>")

        ' Write the value of FirstName.
        field_node = row_node.SelectSingleNode("FirstName")
        If Not (field_node Is Nothing) Then _
```

```
            row_name = field_node.InnerXml

         ' Write the value of LastName and close the cell.
         field_node = row_node.SelectSingleNode("LastName")
         If Not (field_node Is Nothing) Then _
            row_name = row_name & " " & field_node.InnerXml
         Response.Write(row_name)
         Response.Write("</TD>")

         ' Create the Email link.
         Response.Write("<TD>")
         field_node = row_node.SelectSingleNode("EmailAddress")
         If Not (field_node Is Nothing) Then Response.Write( _
            "<A HREF=""mailto:" & field_node.InnerXml & """>" & _
            field_node.InnerXml & "</A>")
         Response.Write("</TD>")

         ' Create the link to each author's home page.
         Response.Write("<TD>")
         field_node = row_node.SelectSingleNode("HomePageName")
         If Not (field_node Is Nothing) Then
            home_page_url_node = row_node.SelectSingleNode("HomePageURL")
            If Not (home_page_url_node Is Nothing) Then
               Response.Write( _
                  "<A HREF=""" & home_page_url_node.InnerXml & """>" & _
                  field_node.InnerXml & "</A>")
            End If
         End If
         Response.Write("</TD>")

         ' Display the Image.
         Response.Write("<TD>")
         field_node = row_node.SelectSingleNode("Image")
         If Not (field_node Is Nothing) Then Response.Write( _
            "<IMG SRC=""" & field_node.InnerXml & """></IMG>")
         Response.Write("</TD>")

         Response.Write("</TR>")
      Next row_node
   End Sub
</SCRIPT>


<!-- HTML Code. -->
<HTML>
    <HEAD>
        <TITLE>Authors</TITLE>
    </HEAD>
```

```
<BODY>
    <H1><CENTER>Authors</CENTER></H1>

    <!-- Create the table. -->
    <TABLE BORDER="1" BGCOLOR="#E0E0E0" CELLPADDING="5">
        <THEAD>
            <TH>Name</TH>
            <TH>Email Address</TH>
            <TH>Home Page</TH>
            <TH>Image</TH>
        </THEAD>

        <!-- Call BuildRows to make the table's rows. -->
        <% BuildRows() %>
    </TABLE>
</BODY>
</HTML>
```

Figure 7.9 shows Table.aspx in Internet Explorer. Compare the result to the table shown in Figure 7.4. The file Table.html, shown in Figure 7.4, uses bound controls to generate the table's contents. Those controls don't provide as much flexibility as the Visual Basic .NET code used by Table.aspx. The file Table.aspx can manipulate the data fields to make HTML mailto links in the table's second column while Table.html cannot.

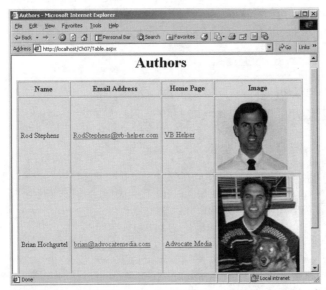

Figure 7.9   ASP.NET code can load XML data and manipulate it directly to build an HTML table.

DataGrid

Figure 7.10 shows the Web page SortedDataGrid.aspx displaying XML data in a DataGrid control. If you click on the Name, Email, of Home Page column header, the control redisplays the information sorted by that column.

The following code shows how this Web page works. Like previous examples, the Web page contains an XML tag including the XML data. It then includes the Visual Basic .NET script code.

The Page_Load event handler calls subroutine MakeDataSource to build a data source for the DataGrid control to use. Page_Load assigns the returned data source to the DataSource property of the DataGrid control named grdAuthors. This control is defined later in the HTML code. After it sets the DataSource property, Page_Load calls the DataGrid control's DataBind method to make it read the data from the data source.

Function MakeDataSource creates a new DataSet object and uses its ReadXml method to make it load the XML data stored in the xmlAuthors XML control. It adds a new column named Name to the DataSet and indicates that the value of the Name column should be the concatenation of the LastName and FirstName columns. Subroutine MakeDataSource then creates a new DataView object that selects all of the data. The routine sets the DataView's Sort property so that it sorts its data by the selected column and returns the DataView.

Subroutine Grid_Sort is invoked when the visitor clicks on one of the DataGrid's column headings. This routine resets the grid's DataSource property using a new data source that sorts on the selected column. It then calls the grid's DataBind method to make it load the newly arranged data.

The HTML code in this example is a little more complex than the code shown in previous examples. After starting the HTML code as usual, the Web page creates an asp:DataGrid control. It sets the control's CellPadding, BorderColor, and BackColor attributes to modify the control's appearance.

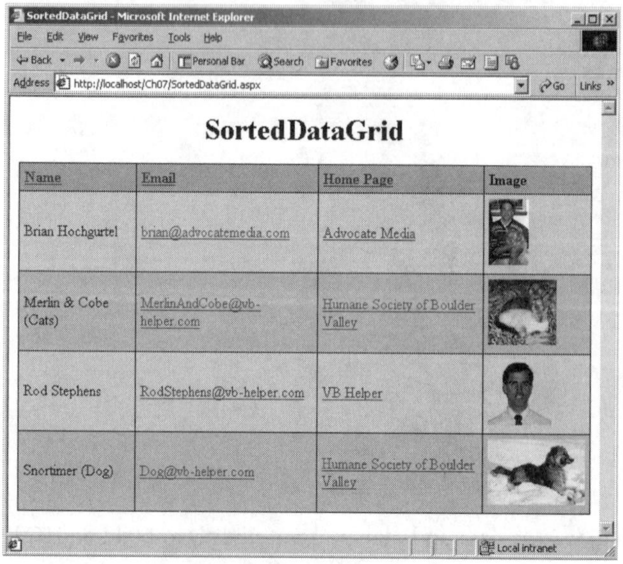

Figure 7.10 An ASP.NET file can use a DataGrid control to easily display a data island.

It sets the AutoGenerateColumns attribute to False so the control doesn't try to figure out what data to display from its data source. This example selects only some of the data source's fields and reformats the data so the control should not try to display all of the fields on its own.

The page sets the AllowSorting property to True so the control will let the visitor click on columns to change the data's ordering. The OnSortCommand attribute tells the control which Visual Basic .NET subroutine to execute when the visitor wants to resort the data.

Inside the asp:DataGrid's tags, other tags refine the control's appearance and determine the data the control displays. The HeaderStyle tag allows the page to define the DataGrid's header style. In this example, the page makes the header's background color dark gray and makes its text bold.

Similarly the AlternatingItemStyle tag lets the code determine how every other grid row is displayed. This example gives every other row a silver background color. The other rows are colored using the background color set in the asp:DataGrid opening tag: light gray.

Next, the Columns tag defines the grid's columns. Inside this tag, asp:BoundColumn tags define the columns the grid displays. The asp:BoundColumn attributes determine the text displayed in the column's header, the data field in the data source used to fill the column, and the column's sort expression. When the visitor clicks on a column's header to sort using that column, the event handler called to sort the data receives a DataGrid-SortEventArgs object as a parameter. That object's SortExpression property tells the event handler which column was clicked. The SortExpression attribute in the asp:BoundColumn tells the system what value to send to the event handler.

When you look at the code, notice that the last column's definition does not specify a SortExpression value. If a column does not have a SortExpression, the control does not call its sorting event handler if the user clicks on that column's heading. Notice that in Figure 7.10 the heading Image over the last column is not underlined. That gives the visitor a visible clue that clicking on this header does nothing. This example does not allow the user to sort on this column because it doesn't make sense to sort using the images shown in the grid's last column.

Notice also that two of the asp:BoundColumn tags contain DataFormatString attributes. This attribute tells the control what data to send to the HTML output for the grid cell. The control replaces the string {0} with the value of the field. This example uses the DataFormatString to produce an HTML mailto link and an HTML IMG tag.

Finally, the Columns tag contains one HyperLinkColumn element. This element's DataNavigationUrlField and DataTextField attributes tell the control which data source fields to use for the link's URL and displayed value.

```
<%@ Page Language="VB" Debug="True" %>
<%@ Import Namespace="System.IO" %>
<%@ Import Namespace="System.Data" %>

<!-- Author XML data. -->
<XML ID="xmlAuthors" RUNAT="server">
  <Authors>
    <Author>
```

```
        <FirstName>Merlin &amp; Cobe</FirstName>
        <LastName>(Cats)</LastName>
        <EmailAddress>MerlinAndCobe@vb-helper.com</EmailAddress>
        <HomePageName>Humane Society of Boulder Valley</HomePageName>
        <HomePageURL>
            http://www.boulderhumane.org/html/animals/pages/cats.htm
        </HomePageURL>
        <Image>./cats.jpg</Image>
      </Author>
      <Author>
        <FirstName>Snortimer</FirstName>
        <LastName>(Dog)</LastName>
        <EmailAddress>Dog@vb-helper.com</EmailAddress>
        <HomePageName>Humane Society of Boulder Valley</HomePageName>
        <HomePageURL>
            http://www.boulderhumane.org/html/animals/pages/dogs.htm
        </HomePageURL>
        <Image>./dog.jpg</Image>
      </Author>
      <Author>
        <FirstName>Rod</FirstName>
        <LastName>Stephens</LastName>
        <EmailAddress>RodStephens@vb-helper.com</EmailAddress>
        <HomePageName>VB Helper</HomePageName>
        <HomePageURL>http://www.vb-helper.com</HomePageURL>
        <Image>./rod.jpg</Image>
      </Author>
      <Author>
        <FirstName>Brian</FirstName>
        <LastName>Hochgurtel</LastName>
        <EmailAddress>brian@advocatemedia.com</EmailAddress>
        <HomePageName>Advocate Media</HomePageName>
        <HomePageURL>http://www.advocatemedia.com</HomePageURL>
        <Image>./brian.jpg</Image>
      </Author>
    </Authors>
</XML>


<!-- Bind the data to the DataGrid control. -->
<SCRIPT Language="VB" RUNAT="Server">
Sub Page_Load(sender As Object, e As EventArgs)
    ' See if this is the first time we have loaded.
    If Not IsPostBack Then
      ' Load the data into the grid.
      grdAuthors.DataSource = MakeDataSource()
      grdAuthors.DataBind()
    End If
End Sub


' Return a data source containing the data.
Function MakeDataSource(Optional ByVal sort_column As String = "Name") _
```

```
        As ICollection
            ' Load the XML data into a DataSet.
            Dim string_reader As New StringReader(xmlAuthors.InnerHTML)
            Dim data_set As New DataSet
            data_set.ReadXml(string_reader)

            ' Add a new Name column combining FirstName and LastName.
            data_set.Tables(0).Columns.Add("Name", _
                System.Type.GetType("System.String"), _
                "FirstName + ' ' + LastName")

            ' Make a DataView that sorts on the right column.
            Dim data_view As New DataView(data_set.Tables(0))
            data_view.Sort = sort_column

            ' Return the DataView.
            Return data_view
        End Function

        ' Rebuild the data sorting on the selected column.
        Sub Grid_Sort(sender As Object, e As DataGridSortCommandEventArgs)
            ' Rebind the data.
            grdAuthors.DataSource = MakeDataSource(e.SortExpression.ToString())
            grdAuthors.DataBind()
        End Sub
    </SCRIPT>

    <!-- HTML Code. -->
    <HTML>
      <HEAD>
        <TITLE>SortedDataGrid</TITLE>
      </HEAD>
      <BODY>
        <H1><CENTER>SortedDataGrid</CENTER></H1>

        <FORM RUNAT="server">
          <!-- Create the data grid. -->
          <asp:DataGrid ID="grdAuthors" RUNAT="Server"
            CellPadding="5"
            BorderColor="black"
            BackColor="lightgray"
            AutoGenerateColumns="False"
            AllowSorting="True"
            OnSortCommand="Grid_Sort"
          >
            <HeaderStyle BackColor="darkgray">
              <FONT BOLD="true" />
            </HeaderStyle>
            <AlternatingItemStyle BackColor="silver" />
            <Columns>
              <asp:BoundColumn HeaderText="Name" DataField="Name"
```

```
                    SortExpression="Name"
                /> 
                <asp:BoundColumn HeaderText="Email" DataField="EmailAddress"
                    DataFormatString="<A HREF='mailto:{0}'>{0}</A>"
                    SortExpression="EmailAddress"
                />
                <asp:HyperLinkColumn HeaderText="Home Page"
                    DataNavigateUrlField="HomePageURL"
                    DataTextField="HomePageName"
                    SortExpression="HomePageName"
                />
                <asp:BoundColumn HeaderText="Image" DataField="Image"
                    DataFormatString="<IMG SRC='{0}' HEIGHT='70'></IMG>"
                />
            </Columns>
        </asp:DataGrid>
    </FORM>
  </BODY>
</HTML>
```

The DataGrid control is quite powerful and contains many features you can use to format and display XML data. See the MSDN help for more information on the Data-Grid control.

Web Forms

Web forms give you the ability to enter information in a Web browser and to click a button to make something happen. This could involve sending your credit card information over the Web to an e-commerce site, banking online, or many other tasks that have become common on the World Wide Web. A form is simply a way to tell the server to do something in response to some information you send through the browser. ASP.NET provides several tools to make sending information with a form easier.

The Web page TransformButtons.aspx, shown in the following code, takes two values entered into server controls and uses them to perform a transformation. The example shows how to use buttons to activate subroutines in ASP.NET code.

The page begins with a SCRIPT section that defines the two subroutines Btn_Click and Click_Clear. Subroutine Btn_Click sets the DocumentSource and TransformSource properties of an asp:xml control to the values stored in the text boxes xml_file_display and xsl_file_display.

The Click_Clear subroutine clears out the entire form including the transformed data by setting the text values of the two asp:textbox server controls to the empty string "" and by clearing the asp:xml control's DocumentSource and TransformSource properties.

The rest of the page's code defines the various server controls and some HTML to provide some formatting. Once the Web form loads in the browser, there are textboxes shown. One is for entering the path of the XML file that needs to be transformed, and the other is for the path to the XSL file that performs the transformation.

```
<%@ Page Language="VB" Debug="True"%>

<SCRIPT Language="VB" runat="server">
Sub Btn_Click(sender As Object, e As EventArgs)
    ' Send the name of the XML file to transform
    ' (DocumentSource) and the name of the XSL file to the
    ' asp:xml server control.
    page_content.DocumentSource =  xml_file_display.text
    page_content.TransformSource = xsl_file_display.text
End Sub

Sub Clear_Click(sender As Object, e As EventArgs)
    ' Clear out the value of the asp:textbox xml_file_display
    ' and xsl_file_display.
    xml_file_display.text = ""
    xsl_file_display.text = ""

    ' Clear out the values of the asp:xml server control.
    ' This removes the transformed text from the ASP.NET page.
    page_content.DocumentSource = ""
    page_content.TransformSource = ""
End Sub
</SCRIPT>

<HTML>
    <HEAD>
        <TITLE>Server Side Data Island</TITLE>
    </HEAD>
    <BODY>
        <FORM RUNAT="server">
            XML file:<asp:textbox id="xml_file_display"
                runat="server"
                columns="50"/>
            <BR>
            XSL file: <asp:textbox id="xsl_file_display"
                runat="server"
                columns="50"/>
            <BR>

            <!-- This button activates the transformation. The OnClick
                 attribute indicates the subroutine to call. -->
            <asp:button id="tbSubmit"
                runat="server"
                text="Transform"
                OnClick="Btn_Click" />

            <!-- This button clears the textbox and
                 xml server controls. -->
            <asp:button id="tbClear"
                runat="server"
                text="Clear"
```

```
                    OnClick="Clear_Click" />
            <HR>

            <!-- The script subroutines set this control's properties
                 to display the transformed data. -->
            <asp:xml id="page_content"
                runat="server"/>
        </FORM>
     </BODY>
</HTML>
```

Figure 7.11 shows TransformButtons.aspx in Internet Explorer.

While this example may not be as spectacular as some of the previous ones, it shows how an ASP.NET page can connect script subroutines to buttons. When the visitor clicks a button, the underlying routines take over and use the form's controls to load and display XML data.

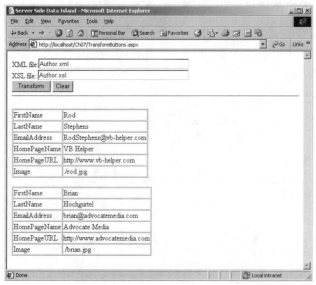

Figure 7.11   TransformButtons.aspx uses script code triggered by buttons to display XML data.

Conclusion

Combining the abilities of Visual Basic .NET, ASP.NET, and XML gives you a broad toolset for creating dynamic Web pages. ASP.NET provides methods for implementing Web applications that are more flexible and responsive than those built using its predecessors. Visual Basic .NET gives the programmer easy access to XML and all of the techniques for manipulating XML data. Special controls such as the XML control make transforming and displaying XML data easy on Web pages.

Client-side data islands let you mix XML and HTML without the overhead of XSL or the cost of spawning a new process on the server. Using XML tags such as SPAN and DIV, you can display XML data on the client side quickly and easily.

Server-side controls and scripting code let you keep your Web pages independent of browser type and version. Even if a visitor's browser knows nothing about XML, it can display ASP.NET pages that use server-side controls to format XML data.

Web Services

As the Web has grown, programmers have started to look at it as a means to accomplish things other than serving HTML pages and doing e-commerce. A next logical step is remote computing: when one computer calls a method or a function on another machine across the Web. Web Services are the next generation in remote computing.

This concept is really nothing new. Common Object Request Brokerage (CORBA), Remote Procedure Calls (RPC), Enterprise Java Beans (EJB), and the Common Object Model (COM) are all implementations of remote computing. The difference is Web Services are far easier to implement than all of the others. By incorporating a simple Web technology such as ASP.NET, Web Services make remote computing easy enough for those without advanced C++ training. In addition, Web browsers can interact with Web Services, allowing a wider audience to consume the service.

Beyond being easier to implement, Web Services also provide greater flexibility than previous methods because Web Services provide more access methods. A Web Service must be able to handle HTTP POST and GET methods along with Simple Object Access Protocol (SOAP) requests and responses. Earlier forms of remote computing used request and response formats specific to their own standards.

SOAP makes Web Services relevant to this book because SOAP uses XML to access remote methods. An application sends a request encoded in XML to a Web Service, and the response returns encoded in XML. Fortunately, all of the encoding and decoding happens under the hood of SOAP, and a user rarely deals with this XML directly.

This chapter contains examples showing how to create Web Services using ASP.NET, how to make clients to consume these Web Services, and how to access a Web Service that was not created by the .NET environment.

Implementing Web Services

Web Services provide you with a way to create middle layers to isolate dynamic or complicated code from day-to-day operations such as those on a Web site. Separating the code in this manner means Web pages and applications don't have to change each time a Web Service does. As long as the kind of information passed in and out of the Web Service remains the same, the code calling the Web Service remains the same. This becomes particularly useful in a large corporate environment where business logic requirements can change on a daily basis. When these changes occur, you have to change only the Web Service, not the possibly thousands of Web pages and applications that call it.

To create a Web Service, you need to install the .NET Framework Software Development Kit (SDK). Using a text editor such as Notepad, you can create the ASP.NET pages, proxies, and Web Services you need. In order to execute the ASP.NET code or the Web Services, you need to have IIS under Windows 2000 running. After you install the Framework SDK, you may want to reboot to ensure that IIS can recognize the changes the SDK installation made.

Creating a Simple Web Service

The following code shows a simple Web Service that returns the number 12. The first line describes the file as a Web Service that uses the Visual Basic language. It also indicates that this Web Services implements the class named VBHelper. The file imports the System and System.Web.Services namespaces so the Web Service can use their functionality.

The file then begins the VBHelper class implementation. The class declaration indicates that the VBHelper class inherits from the WebService class.

The class could implement several functions, but this example defines only the SimpleNumber function. The <WebMethod()> statement means this function is available to a browser or application accessing it over the Web. The SimpleNumber function contains only one line of executable code: Return (12). This statement returns the number 12 to the caller.

```
<%@ WebService Language="VB" Class="VBHelper" %>

<!-- Import the needed namespaces. -->
Imports System
Imports System.Web.Services

<!-- Define the class and its namespace. -->
<WebService(Namespace:=" ")> Public Class VBHelper : Inherits WebService

    <!-- Define the method that returns 12. -->
    <WebMethod()> Public Function SimpleNumber() As Integer
      Return (12)
    End Function
End Class
```

You might assume in this first example that if you point your browser to http://localhost/websvc/VBHelper.asmx, the number 12 returns. Actually, this doesn't happen. The Web Service's response shows the available method and a brief description of what the Web Service does. Figure 8.1 shows this response.

The response in the browser says that this Web Service uses the namespace http://tempuri.org/. This is the default namespace that comes with Visual Studio .NET, and you need to change this namespace to match your application. In this case, the namespace http://www.vb-helper.com/XML/CH08 seems more appropriate. For a brief introduction to namespaces, see Chapter 1, "XML Overview."

The Web Service can add the namespace in its <WebService()> tag. The following code shows the modified class definition. Adding the statement Namespace:=" http://www.vb-helper.com/XML/CH08" within the Web Service definition tag changes the namespace. Note that the namespace definition uses := rather than just =. If you don't use the colon, the browser displays an error with very confusing information.

```
<%@ WebService Language="VB" Class="VBHelper" %>

<!-- Import the needed namespaces. -->
Imports System
Imports System.Web.Services

<!-- Define the class and its namespace. -->
<WebService(Namespace:="http://www.vb-helper.com/XML/CH08")> _
          Public Class VBHelper : Inherits WebService
    <!-- Define the method that returns 12. -->
    <WebMethod()> _
     Public Function SimpleNumber() As Integer
          Return (12)
     End Function
End Class
```

Figure 8.2 shows the Web Service's response in the browser now. This version no longer displays a warning about using the default namespace.

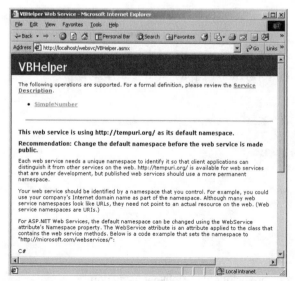

Figure 8.1 The VBHelper Web Service initially returns this response to a browser.

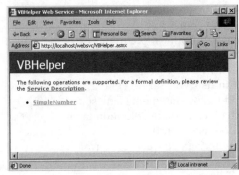

Figure 8.2   This version of the Web Service does not use the default namespace.

The WebService and WebMethod tags allow you to add more information to methods and classes to help identify their functionality. The following code adds Descripton parameters to both of these tags. Note that the comma between the Namespace and the Description parameters in the WebService tag is required.

```
<%@ WebService Language="VB" Class="VBHelper" %>

<!-- Import the needed namespaces. -->
Imports System
Imports System.Web.Services

<!-- Define the class and set the Web Service namespace and
     description. -->
<WebService(Namespace:="http://www.vb-helper.com/XML/CH08", _
            Description:="A simple Web Service to return numbers.")> _
            Public Class VBHelper : Inherits WebService
    <!-- Define the method that returns 12 and give the method a
         description.-->
    <WebMethod(Description:="Returns the Number 12")> _
    Public Function SimpleNumber() As Integer
        Return (12)
    End Function
End Class
```

Figure 8.3 shows how the added information displays in the browser.

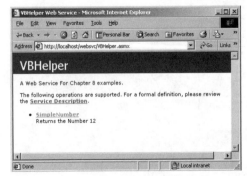

Figure 8.3   The WebService definition can include descriptive information.

You can activate the SimpleNumber Function by entering the following URL in Internet Explorer.

```
http://localhost/websvc/VBHelper.asmx/SimpleNumber
```

The resulting code returned to the browser looks like the following.

```
<?xml version="1.0" encoding="utf-8" ?>
<int xmlns="http://www.vb-helper.com/XML/CH08">12</int>
```

This is only one of the possible responses a Web Service can return. A Web Service in Visual Studio .NET gives a programmer a great deal of flexibility. It responds to a variety of requests and responses including SOAP, POST, and GET. The next section describes each one of the possible requests and responses.

Viewing the Requests and Responses

If you point your browser at http://localhost/websvc/VBHelper.asmx, you'll notice that the page displays two links. One says Service Description, and the other says Simple Number. Ignore the Service Description for now. If you click on SimpleNumber, you'll see more information about the SimpleNumber method. The resulting page contains four sections: Test, SOAP, HTTP GET, and HTTP Post. In Figure 8.4, you can see the Test section and the beginning of the SOAP section.

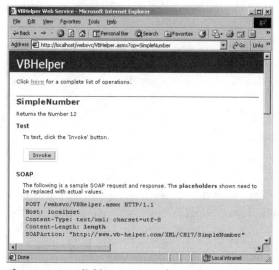

Figure 8.4 Clicking on a Web Service's method presents a description page similar to this one.

Test

The test section gives you quick access to the method itself. If SimpleNumber needed to have values passed to it, this section would include ASP.NET textboxes where you could enter values. You'll see an example later in this chapter that does this. In this case, the only thing needed to test this function is the Invoke button. Once you press this button, you'll see the following response.

```
<?xml version="1.0" encoding="utf-8" ?>
<int xmlns="http://www.vb-helper.com/XML/CH17">12</int>
```

Note that this is the same response that you saw when you pointed the browser at http://localhost/websvc/VBHelper.asmx/SimpleNumber.

SOAP Request

A SOAP request section contains both an HTTP header and an XML document. The header contains information that tells the Web server where to route the request. If you look at the following request from the SimpleNumber method, you'll note that the XML doesn't even begin until the middle of the request.

The first part of the HTTP header is the request method, in this case POST. Then a relative path to the Web Service tells the Web server where to find the code to execute the request. Following that you'll see HTTP/1.1. This indicates that the request uses HTTP version 1.1.

The header shows the host name next. In this case, only Host: localhost shows up in the header. The value localhost indicates that these examples execute locally. If a Web Service executes on a remote machine, a hostname such as www.vb-helper.com appears here.

Content-Type defines the content and the character set that the message uses. Without this information the server wouldn't know what the request contains.

The Content-Length value tells how many characters are in the request. In this case, the message contains 312 characters.

Finally, SOAPAction contains the name of the method and its namespace. In this example, the namespace is http://www.vb-helper.com/XML/CH08/ and the method is SimpleNumber. The following code shows the complete header.

```
POST /VBHelperService1/Service1.asmx HTTP/1.1
Host: localhost
Content-Type: text/xml; charset=utf-8
Content-Length: 312
SOAPAction: "http://www.vb-helper.com/XML/CH08/SimpleNumber"
```

The second part of the SOAP request is the XML document that contains the appropriate information to activate the Web Service. Usually this includes values that the Web Service needs.

The first line of the XML portion of the SOAP request is an XML declaration processing instruction. This statement defines the version of XML used and the character set. Note that the character set information is redundant because the header contains it as well.

Next is the root data element soap:Envelope. This is the root element of all soap messages. The root element's attributes define three namespaces. The first namespace, xsi, represents a schema instance. Next comes the closely related xsd namespace representing schema commands. Last comes the SOAP namespace.

The soap:Envelope tag contains the soap:Body element. This element holds the data needed to call the function SimpleNumber. In this case, all the element contains is the name of the function and its namespace. If this were a more complicated function, it would contain other values.

```
<?xml version="1.0" encoding="utf-8"?>
<soap:Envelope
xmlns:xsi="http://www.w3.org/2001/XMLSchema-instance"
xmlns:xsd="http://www.w3.org/2001/XMLSchema"
xmlns:soap="http://schemas.xmlsoap.org/soap/envelope/">
  <soap:Body>
    <SimpleNumber xmlns="http://www.vb-helper.com/XML/CH08" />
  </soap:Body>
</soap:Envelope>
```

The following code shows the complete SOAP request.

```
POST /websvc/VBHelper.asmx HTTP/1.1
Host: localhost
Content-Type: text/xml; charset=utf-8
Content-Length: 312
SOAPAction: "http://www.vb-helper.com/XML/CH08/SimpleNumber"

<?xml version="1.0" encoding="utf-8"?>
<soap:Envelope xmlns:xsi="http://www.w3.org/2001/XMLSchema-instance"
xmlns:xsd="http://www.w3.org/2001/XMLSchema"
xmlns:soap="http://schemas.xmlsoap.org/soap/envelope/">
  <soap:Body>
    <SimpleNumber xmlns="http://www.vb-helper.com/XML/CH08" />
  </soap:Body>
</soap:Envelope>
```

The next section shows the response, which is very similar.

SOAP Response

The SOAP response is a little simpler than the request because the header needs a little less information. In the request, the server needs to know which Web Service to execute so the request header contains a path to that Service. The response, on the other hand, doesn't need that information.

The first thing that appears in the response header is HTTP/1.1 200 OK. This means that the response uses HTTP version 1.1. The 200 is just the server's code for a complete response. OK indicates that the request did not have an error. If the request fails, this part of the response says FAIL rather than OK.

Next, the header contains the content type of the request. In this case, the message contains text that is in the form of XML. Note that a header on a regular HTML page would be text/html. The content type also defines the character set the response uses. In this case, utf-8 indicates that the contents use the standard ASCII character set.

```
HTTP/1.1 200 OK
Content-Type: text/xml; charset=utf-8
Content-Length: 395
```

The XML portion of the SOAP response is almost identical to that of the request. The soap:Envelope and soap:Body tags are the same. The only difference occurs inside the soap:Body tag. The response includes a SimpleNumberResponse element that contains the Web Service's response value. If the Web Service did not return a value, this would be an empty tag.

The returning value, SimpleNumberResult, is a child elment of SimpleNumberResponse. It has a value of 12, which is the value that the function returns.

```
<?xml version="1.0" encoding="utf-8"?>
<soap:Envelope xmlns:xsi="http://www.w3.org/2001/XMLSchema-instance"
xmlns:xsd="http://www.w3.org/2001/XMLSchema"
xmlns:soap="http://schemas.xmlsoap.org/soap/envelope/">
  <soap:Body>
    <SimpleNumberResponse xmlns="http://www.vb-helper.com/XML/CH08">
      <SimpleNumberResult>12</SimpleNumberResult>
    </SimpleNumberResponse>
  </soap:Body>
</soap:Envelope>
```

The following code shows the complete response.

```
HTTP/1.1 200 OK
Content-Type: text/xml; charset=utf-8
Content-Length: 395

<?xml version="1.0" encoding="utf-8"?>
<soap:Envelope xmlns:xsi="http://www.w3.org/2001/XMLSchema-instance"
xmlns:xsd="http://www.w3.org/2001/XMLSchema"
xmlns:soap="http://schemas.xmlsoap.org/soap/envelope/">
  <soap:Body>
    <SimpleNumberResponse xmlns="http://www.vb-helper.com/XML/CH08">
      <SimpleNumberResult>12</SimpleNumberResult>
    </SimpleNumberResponse>
  </soap:Body>
</soap:Envelope>
```

The SOAP standard is constantly evolving and may change by the time you read this. At some point, the W3C will probably rename SOAP to XMLP for XML Protocol. For the latest information, check the World Wide Web Consortium's Web page, www.w3c.org.

HTTP GET Request

A GET command occurs when a browser calls a flat HTML page. It's a standard way to retrieve data from a Web site. This command also passes data to the Web server in what's called a Query String. Consider the following example.

```
http://www.vbhelper.com/XML/Example.aspx?FirstName=Brian&LastName
=Hochgurtel
```

The Query String is everything that occurs after the question mark. In this case, the variables FirstName and LastName pass the appropriate values to the server.

The request in this example is very simple. The following code shows the GET request for the SimpleNumber function.

```
GET /websvc/VBHelper.asmx/SimpleNumber? HTTP/1.1
Host: localhost
```

The initial GET keyword indicates the request method. The next item is the path to the function you want to execute. HTTP/1.1 indicates the version of HTTP this Web Service uses. The next line gives the Web Service's host. In this case, the host is local-host because the Web Service is running locally. If the Web Service ran on a remote machine, the Host value may look something like Host: www.vb-helper.com.

HTTP GET Response

The header of the GET response is identical to the SOAP response. It contains the HTTP version, a success code, the response's content type and character set, and the message's length.

```
HTTP/1.1 200 OK
Content-Type: text/xml; charset=utf-8
Content-Length: 94
```

The returning XML is different from that of the SOAP response. The only things in the response are the XML declaration processing instruction and an element named int that resides in the http://www.vb-helper.com/XML/CH08 namespace. The value of int is 12, the value returned by the SimpleNumber function.

```
<?xml version="1.0" encoding="utf-8"?>
<int xmlns="http://www.vb-helper.com/XML/CH08">12</int>
```

The complete response looks like this.

```
HTTP/1.1 200 OK
Content-Type: text/xml; charset=utf-8
Content-Length: 94
<?xml version="1.0" encoding="utf-8"?>
<int xmlns="http://www.vb-helper.com/XML/CH08">12</int>
```

Note that the response to the POST command is completely identical.

HTTP POST Request

The POST command may be familiar to you if you have done a lot of work with HTML forms. It is a method of sending information to a Web page or an application that is encoded. The information provides some more security than the GET command because information is not sent as part of the URL.

The POST request is very similar to the GET request in that the first line contains the command, path to the Web Service, and the HTTP protocol version. The Host and the Content-Length are the same as in the previous requests.

The main difference with the POST request is that the Content-Type is different. Here the information is encoded with the value application/x-www-form-urlencoded. This is a format that encodes the data in a request so that special characters and spaces are passed correctly to the Web Service.

```
POST /websvc/VBHelper.asmx/SimpleNumber HTTP/1.1
Host: localhost
Content-Type: application/x-www-form-urlencoded
Content-Length: 94
```

Allowing a Web Service to understand a POST request and response makes it easy to create an HTML form that can send data to the Web Service. This is covered in more detail in the *Creating Clients* section of this chapter.

HTTP POST Response

The HTTP Post response is identical to the GET response. For more details, see the earlier section, *HTTP GET Response*.

Expanding the VBHelper Service

Having a Web Service that returns only the number 12 isn't really all that useful. There are many other, more useful tasks a Web Service could perform such as performing meaningful calculations, analyzing data from different data sources, generating graphics, or translating currencies.

Web Services that perform these kinds of tasks are often middle tiers in multitier applications. They can gather data from different databases, XML repositories, and other sources, and they can return their results. They can even call on each other to perform intermediate calculations. Figure 8.5 shows a small collection of Web Services, clients, and data sources working together to implement multitier business solutions.

Separating client applications from the underlying data in a multitier application enables the clients and data representations to evolve independently. If the data changes, the clients can remain the same as long as the Web Services don't change their public interfaces. Similarly, if a Web Service changes the way it calculates a value or generates a report, the clients don't need to change as long as the way the Web Service presents its data remains unchanged.

The following sections describe some example Web Services that perform potentially useful tasks.

Currency Converter

By adding the following function to the VBHelper.asmx file, you can make the VBHelper Web Service convert dollars into Mexican pesos. In the new function's first line, the WebMethod tag describes what the function does. Then the function declares the ConvertPesos function. This function takes a decimal Dollars parameter and returns a string.

Defining the Pesos variable as decimal allows the function to perform mathematical operations on its value easily. In this case, the function multiplies the value of dollars by 9.10 to get the equivalent number of pesos. This conversion rate changes daily and will almost certainly be different when you read this. If this Web Service were used for a real commercial application, you would need to update its code daily or perhaps even more frequently.

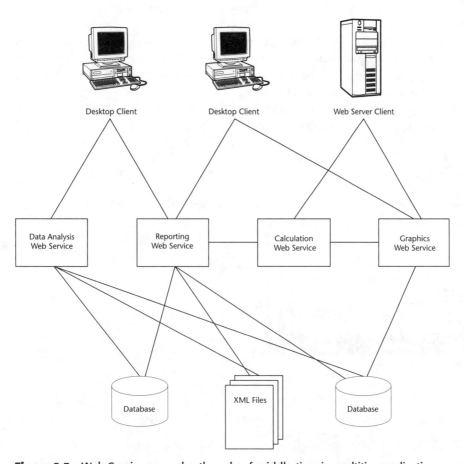

Figure 8.5 Web Services can play the role of middle tiers in multitier applications.

Finally, to return a properly formatted value, the function uses the Peso value's ToString("C") method. The format C makes the result a monetary value with two decimal places. On this server, the default conversion from currency to a string adds a $ symbol to the result, which happens to be the symbol for Mexican pesos as well as American dollars.

```
<WebMethod(Description:="Converts Dollars Into Pesos")>_
Public Function ConvertPesos(Dollars as Decimal) As String
     ' Return Pesos.
     Dim Pesos As Decimal

     ' As of this writing, 1 Dollar converts to 9.10 pesos.
     Pesos = Dollars * 9.10

     Return (Pesos.ToString("C"))
End Function
```

Figure 8.6 shows the new Web Service description in Internet Explorer showing the new ConvertPesos function.

Unlike the SimpleNumber function, ConvertPesos takes an input parameter. If you click on the ConvertPesos link on your browser, you'll come to a page that has an Invoke button as before. This page's Test section contains a textbox where you can enter a dollar amount, as shown in Figure 8.7.

If you enter 100 as the amount of dollars you want to convert to pesos and click the Invoke button, you'll see the following result.

```
<?xml version="1.0" encoding="utf-8" ?>
<string xmlns="http://www.vb-helper.com/XML/CH08">$910.00</string>
```

Here the Web Service has returned the amount $910, the correct value for the conversion factor 9.10.

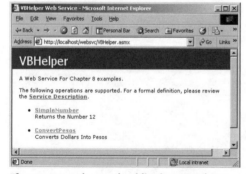

Figure 8.6   The method list for VBHelper.asmx now includes the ConvertPesos function.

Figure 8.7   The ConvertPesos method takes a parameter named Dollars.

Returning Graphics

It is possible to transmit a picture across the Internet in the form of an XML document. To do this, a program takes the image and encodes it in a text string. The program adds the encoded string to an XML document and sends it to another program. The other program decodes it to recover the original image. The following example uses the Base64 encoding to return a picture to its client. For more information on using XML encodings of binary data, see Chapter 3, "Forward-Only XML."

To use the necessary graphic encoding routines, the Web Service imports several system libraries. The Web Service's GetImage function uses the Server object's Map-Path function to get the path to the Web Service's location. It adds the name of the requested file and creates a new Bitmap object attached to that file. The function assigns the Bitmap to a new Image variable to load the picture into the Image.

The function creates a new MemoryStream object and saves the image into the MemoryStream. The function then returns the MemoryStream's bytes in an array. The result is packaged into an XML document for return to the client, but an XML document cannot contain an arbitrary array of bytes so the bytes are automatically converted into a Base64 encoding.

```
... Code omitted ...

Imports System
Imports System.Web.Services
Imports System.Drawing
```

```
Imports System.Drawing.Imaging
Imports System.IO

... Code omitted ...

<WebMethod(Description:="Returns a Base64 encoded image")> _
    Public Function GetImage(ByVal FileName As String) As Byte()
        Dim image_file As Image

        ' Get Full Path to the file passed in and create a new image
        ' to be returned to the caller.
        image_file = New Bitmap(Server.MapPath(".\") & FileName)

        ' A memory stream stores data in memory rather than in a
        ' buffer or on disk. Makes the response faster.
        Dim memory_strm As New MemoryStream()

        ' Save the image_file to a jpeg format in a memory stream.
        image_file.Save(memory_strm, ImageFormat.Jpeg)

        ' Return the encoded jpeg to the caller.
        Return memory_strm.GetBuffer()
    End Function
```

When the browser calls this function, the results look like the following mess.

```
<?xml version="1.0" encoding="utf-8" ?>
<base64Binary xmlns=http://www.vb-helper.com/XML/CH08>
">/9j/4AAQSkZJRgABAQEASABIAAD/2wBDAAUDBAQEAwUEBAQFBQUGBwwIBwcHBw8LCwkM
EQ8SEhEPERETFhwXExQaFRERGCEYGh0dHx8fExciJCIeJBweHx7/2wBDAQUFBQcGCGBw4ICA
4eFBEUHh4eHh4eHh4eHh4eHh4eHh4eHh4eHh4eHh4eHh4eHh4eHh4eHh4eHh4e
... Lots of bytes removed...
</base64Binary>
```

Don't worry; you're not supposed to be able to read this response. This text is just an encoded version of the image that will be decoded by the client. The section *Creating Clients* later in this chapter shows how a client can receive the image.

Transforming an XML Document

To transform an XML file using a specified XSL file, all you need to do is recycle the code used by example program Transform in Chapter 6, "XSL." Just by adding the WebMethod tag before the function declaration and making some minor modifications, you can add the function to the VBHelper Web Service almost instantly.

The following code shows the new Web Service function. The new function needs to use a few of the system's transformation services so the Web Service needs to import a couple of new namespaces.

The function takes as parameters the names of the XML and XSL files. It creates a StringWriter object and an XmlTextWriter object attached to the StringWriter. It then uses the Server object's MapPath method to get the path to the Web Service. It appends the names of the XML and XSL files to get their locations. This assumes that both the XML and XSL file are in the same directory as the Web Service.

Next the function creates a new XslTransform object and loads the XSL file into it. It loads the XML file into an XPathDocument object and calls the XslTransform object's Transform method. This translates the XML document using the XSLstyle sheet, sending the result to the XmlTextWriter and ultimately the StringWriter.

The function then sends the translated file back to the client.

```
... Code omitted ...

Imports System
Imports System.Web.Services
Imports System.Drawing
Imports System.Drawing.Imaging
Imports System.IO
Imports System.Xml
Imports System.Xml.Xsl
Imports System.Xml.XPath


... Code omitted ...

<WebMethod(Description:="Returns a transformed XML file")> _
    Public Function TranslateFiles(ByVal xml_file As String, _
                                   ByVal xsl_file As String) As String
        Dim xsl_transform As XslTransform
        Dim xpath_document As XPathDocument
        Dim string_writer As New StringWriter()
        Dim xml_text_writer As New XmlTextWriter(string_writer)

        'Get the server path to the files so they can be loaded.
        xml_file = Server.MapPath(".\") & xml_file
        xsl_file = Server.MapPath(".\") & xsl_file

        ' Load the XSL file into the XslTransform object.
        xsl_transform = New XslTransform()
        xsl_transform.Load(xsl_file)

        ' Load the XML file into the XPathDocument object.
        xpath_document = New XPathDocument(xml_file)

        ' Transform xpath_document (the XML), sending the results
        ' to the xml_text_writer, which sends its results to
        ' string_writer.
        xml_text_writer.Formatting = Formatting.Indented
        xsl_transform.Transform(xpath_document, Nothing, _
            xml_text_writer)
        xml_text_writer.Flush()

        ' Return the results.
        Return string_writer.ToString()
    End Function
```

If you click the Invoke button on the TranslateFiles function's description page, you'll see the following result.

```
<?xml version="1.0" encoding="utf-8" ?>
<string xmlns="http://www.vb-helper.com/XML/CH08"><html> <head>
<title>Welcome to VBHelper</title> </head> <h2>This is the Default
Page</h2> <body> <p> This is the Default Page for Transform.aspx and
TransformQS.aspx </p> </body> </html></string>
```

Notice that the HTML is still treated as XML. This happens until the client displays the result. See the section *Creating Clients* later in this chapter for more information on displaying these kinds of results in a meaningful way.

The Complete VBHelper Web Service

Now that you've seen each of the VBHelper Web Service's functions up close, you should look at the whole thing. Here is the complete code.

```
Imports System
Imports System.Web.Services
Imports System.Drawing
Imports System.Drawing.Imaging
Imports System.IO
Imports System.Xml
Imports System.Xml.Xsl
Imports System.Xml.XPath

    ' Declare the Web Service.
    <WebService(Namespace:="http://www.vb-helper.com/XML/CH08", _
        Description:="A Web Service For Chapter 8 examples.")> _
        Public Class VBHelper : Inherits WebService

    ' Define the method that returns 12 and give the method a
    ' description.
    <WebMethod(Description:="Returns the Number 12")> _
    Public Function SimpleNumber() As Integer
        Return (12)
    End Function

    <WebMethod(Description:="Converts Dollars Into Pesos")>_
    Public Function ConvertPesos(Dollars as Decimal) As String
        ' Return Pesos
        Dim Pesos As Decimal

        ' As of this writing, 1 Dollar converts to 9.10 pesos
        Pesos = Dollars * 9.10

        Return (Pesos.ToString("C"))
    End Function
```

```
<WebMethod(Description:="Returns a base-64 encoded image")> _
Public Function GetImage(ByVal FileName As String) As Byte()
    Dim image_file As Image

        ' Get Full Path to the file passed in and create a new image
        ' to be returned to the caller.
        image_file = New Bitmap(Server.MapPath(".\") & FileName)

        ' A memory stream stores data in memory rather than in a
        ' buffer or on disk. Makes the response faster.
        Dim memory_strm As New MemoryStream()

        ' Save the image_file to a jpeg format in a memory stream.
        image_file.Save(memory_strm, ImageFormat.Jpeg)

        ' Return the encoded jpeg to the caller.
        Return memory_strm.GetBuffer()
End Function

<WebMethod(Description:="Returns a transformed XML file")> _
Public Function TranslateFiles(ByVal xml_file As String, _
                               ByVal xsl_file As String) As String
    Dim xsl_transform As XslTransform
    Dim xpath_document As XPathDocument
    Dim string_writer As New StringWriter()
    Dim xml_text_writer As New XmlTextWriter(string_writer)

    'Get the server path to the files so they can be loaded.
    xml_file = Server.MapPath(".\") & xml_file
    xsl_file = Server.MapPath(".\") & xsl_file

    ' Load the XSL file into the XslTransform object.
    xsl_transform = New XslTransform()
    xsl_transform.Load(xsl_file)

    ' Load the XML file into the XPathDocument object.
    xpath_document = New XPathDocument(xml_file)

    ' Transform xpath_document (the XML), sending the results
    ' to the xml_text_writer, which sends its results to
    ' string_writer.
    xml_text_writer.Formatting = Formatting.Indented
    xsl_transform.Transform(xpath_document, Nothing, _
        xml_text_writer)
    xml_text_writer.Flush()

    ' Return the results.
    Return string_writer.ToString()
    End Function
End Class
```

Now that you have a handful of Web Service examples, you can move on to the next section to learn how to create clients for each of these functions.

Creating Clients

Using a Web Service from a client is called consuming the Web Service. The fact that a Web Service handles POST, GET, and SOAP requests and responses gives you a great deal of flexibility in how you consume a Web Service.

The examples in the following sections show how to consume a Web Service using HTML, ASP.NET, and Visual Basic .NET. Although this book focuses on Visual Basic .NET, you can also consume a Web Service from other languages including C#, C++, Java, PERL, and many more.

HTML Clients

Because a Web Service can send a GET or a POST command, a simple Web form can act as a client for each one of the methods of the VBHelper Web Service. Consider the following HTML example.

Because the SimpleNumber function has no input, this HTML code doesn't need any text fields. All it needs is a form with an ACTION attribute that points to the correct Web Service and function and a Submit button. That's all the following HTML contains.

```
<HTML>
  <HEAD>
    <TITLE>Call GetSimpleNumber</TITLE>
  </HEAD>
  <BODY>
    <H2>
      Call GetSimpleNumber from the VBHelper Web Service
    </H2>
    <FORM ACTION="http://localhost/websvc/VBhelper.asmx/SimpleNumber"
          METHOD="GET">
      <INPUT TYPE="Submit" NAME="Get Number 12">
    </FORM>
  </BODY>
</HTML>
```

Figure 8.8 shows the form in a browser window.

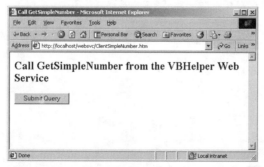

Figure 8.8 This Web page invokes the SimpleNumber function of the VBHelper Web Service.

When you click on the "Get Number 12" button, you get the following result.

```
<?xml version="1.0" encoding="utf-8" ?>
<int xmlns="http://www.vb-helper.com/XML/CH08">12</int>
```

Taking the HTML example one step further to invoke the ConvertPesos function is relatively easy. In this example, the HTML form needs to have one text field for the number of dollars you want to convert to pesos.

The text field in the following HTML code must have the same name as the function's parameter. In this case, the field must be named Dollars because the ConvertPesos function takes a single parameter named Dollars.

```
<HTML>
  <HEAD>
    <TITLE>Convert Dollars to Pesos</TITLE>
  </HEAD>
  <BODY>
    <H2>
      Enter the number of dollars you want converted to pesos
    </H2>

    <FORM ACTION="http://localhost/websvc/VBhelper.asmx/ConvertPesos"
        METHOD="GET">
      <P>
        Dollars: <INPUT TYPE="text" NAME="Dollars" SIZE="20"><BR>
        <INPUT TYPE="Submit">
      </P>
    </FORM>
  </BODY>
</HTML>
```

Figure 8.9 shows the form in Internet Explorer.

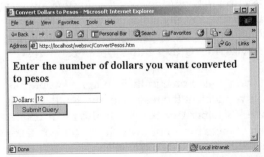

Figure 8.9   This form invokes the VBHelper Web Service's ConvertPesos function.

Enter 12 and click the button. The following code shows the results.

```
<?xml version="1.0" encoding="utf-8" ?>
<string xmlns="http://www.vb-helper.com/XML/CH08">$109.20</string>
```

When a form uses the GET method in this way, it passes the value of the Dollars text field as part of the URL. The browser shows the following URL at the same time it shows the result.

```
http://localhost/websvc/VBhelper.asmx/ConvertPesos?Dollars=12
```

Every value after the question mark with a GET method is part of the query string. The GET method passes all of the form's information in the URL while POST hides these values from the user. When the form uses the POST request method, the URL looks like this.

```
http://localhost/websvc/VBhelper.asmx/ConvertPesos
```

When a Web form sends POST and GET commands to a Web Service, getting results back in XML is rarely useful. With an HTML client, your user expects to get HTML results. In these two cases, the results were simple enough that a user could probably use the results. If the Web Service returns many variables buried in a pile of XML, the user is likely to become frustrated.

Probably the best method for creating clients for Web Services is using ASP.NET. The rest of the chapter covers this method in detail.

wsdl.exe

To use a Web Service with ASP.NET or Visual Basic .NET on a remote machine, you must first create a proxy class DLL (dynamic link library) on the client computer. The proxy tells the .NET environment about the Web Service. It includes such information as the Web Service's location and the methods it provides.

Visual Basic .NET comes with a tool called wsdl.exe that creates Visual Basic source code to implement the proxy class. This tool is a command program found in the directory C:\Program Files\Microsoft.Net\SDK\bin. If you installed .NET in a directory other than the standard one, search for wsdl.exe using Windows Explorer.

The wsdl.exe tool takes as input a document that describes the Web Service written in a flavor of XML called Web Service Description Language (WSDL). Fortunately, you don't need to build this file. A Web Service automatically generates this file whenever a client accesses the Web Service's URL, followed by a query string containing the value WSDL. For the VBHelper Web Service, this URL is http://localhost/websvc/VBhelper.asmx?WSDL.

If you point your browser at this URL, you'll see a practically incomprehensible pile of XML that describes the Web Service. If you look at the result closely, you'll see that it includes entries for each function in the VBHelper Web Service. It also regulates the types of values that get passed in and out of these functions. Later in the file you'll see entries for the POST, GET, and SOAP methods. Don't look too closely at this document or worry too much about what it does.

You don't need to do anything with this file; you just need to tell the wsdl.exe tool where to find it. You do that by entering the following command all on one line in a DOS window.

```
wsdl /l:VB /n:VBHelper /out:VBHelper.VB
http://localhost/websvc/VBHelper.asmx?wsdl
```

The /l option tells wsdl.exe to produce its result using Visual Basic code. The /n option tells wsdl.exe what to name the proxy class.

The /out option lets you tell wsdl.exe where to place the resulting source code. This can be a fully qualified path or a relative path, as in this example. If you are installing the proxy on a remote client computer, you may want to specify a complete URL that puts this file on the remote computer.

The final parameter to the tool is the URL that makes the Web Service return its WSDL description document. The tool invokes this URL and uses the response to build the proxy class code.

The resulting file contains Visual Basic source code for the proxy class. It is a bit easier to understand than the WSDL description document, but you don't really need to look at it if you don't want to. You just need to compile it.

Compile the proxy DLL using the Visual Basic command-line compiler vbc by entering the following command all on one line in a DOS window.

```
vbc /t:library /out:VBHelper.dll /r:system.dll
/r:system.web.services.dll
/r:system.xml.dll VBHelper.vb
```

The /t option tells the compiler the type of output file it should produce. In this case, the output should be a DLL library. Other possible values include exe to create a console application and winexe to create a Windows executable.

The /out option tells the compiler what to name the resulting DLL. The /r options tell the compiler which libraries it will need to use to make the DLL.

After you compile the proxy class DLL, copy it into the Web root's /bin directory. The examples shown in this chapter were made in a Web root directory at the path C:\inetpub\wwwroot. In order for ASP.NET pages to find the dll, make a bin directory inside the Web root and put the Web proxy dll in that directory. The full path in this case is C:\inetpub\wwwroot\bin.

ASP.NET Clients

ASP.NET is one of many possible consumers of a Web Service. A common use of a Web Service or middle tier is to encapsulate an application's most complicated and dynamic code. If this central code base must change, only the Web Service changes. The many ASP.NET pages that call the Web Service remain the same, making your code base much more manageable. In the following examples, ASP.NET is used as the client for each one of the methods in the VBHelper Web Service.

When you use Web Services, it is easy to forget that XML is working behind the scenes. Each of the Web client examples shown in the following sections is sending and receiving SOAP messages. SOAP, as mentioned in the previous sections, encodes requests and responses in XML. Microsoft made all the functionality in these Web Services at a high enough level that you never need to worry about the XML being used.

SimpleNumber ASP.NET Client

The following code shows an ASP.NET client that calls the VBHelper Web Service's SimpleNumber function. The code begins by importing the VBHelper namespace. This statement makes the functionality in the proxy dll created in the previous section available to the ASP.NET page.

Then a script tag defines the language used here as Visual Basic. The subroutine Submit_Click defines the action that takes place when you click the Submit button.

The first line of the subroutine creates a new VBHelper object named my_service. It invokes the my_service object's SimpleNumber function, uses ToString to convert the numeric value into a string, and assigns the result to the asp:Label control named Result.

```
<%@ Import Namespace="VBHelper" %>

<HTML>
<script language="VB" runat="server">
    Public Sub Submit_Click(Sender As Object, E As EventArgs)
        ' Create the VBHelper object.
        Dim my_service As New VBHelper
        ' Send the results to the asp:Label named Result.
        ' Notice that the results of SimpleNumber() are converted
        ' to a string with the ToString()function.
        Result.Text = "<B>the function returns</B> = " & _
        my_service.SimpleNumber().ToString()
    End Sub
</script>

<BODY>
    <H4>Get Simple Number (always returns 12)</H4>
    <FORM RUNAT="server">
        <!-- There is only a button here to call the function -->
        <!-- because the function accepts no arguments.       -->
        <INPUT TYPE="submit" id="GetSimpleNumber"
               VALUE="Get Simple Number"
               OnServerClick="Submit_Click"
               RUNAT="server">
        <P>
            <!-- This is the label the results is sent to. -->
            <B><asp:Label id="Result" runat="server"/></B>
        </P>
    </FORM>
</BODY>
</HTML>
```

Figure 8.10 shows this example as it appears in Internet Explorer.

Just returning a number to a text field on a Web form really isn't all that interesting, but it does demonstrate all of the basic elements needed to access a Web Service. The ConvertPesos example shown in the next section is more interesting because it both sends and receives a value.

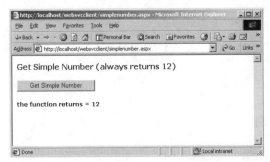

Figure 8.10　This ASP.NET page invokes the VBHelper Web Service's SimpleNumber function.

ConvertPesos ASP.NET Client

This example is quite similar to the SimpleNumber example shown in the previous section. The main difference is that this example passes a value, the number of dollars, to the Web Service's method.

The following code begins by importing the VBHelper namespace. Again the meta information about the VBHelper Web Service comes from the proxy dll created earlier.

The Submit_Click subroutine creates a new VBHelper object named my_service. It assigns the my_money variable the value of the Money text box. It then calls the VBHelper object's ConvertPesos method, passing it the value in my_money, and assigning the result to the asp:Label control named Result.

```
<%@ Import Namespace="VBHelper" %>

<HTML>
<script language="VB" runat="server">
    Public Sub Submit_Click(Sender As Object, E As EventArgs)
        ' Declare a variable for the dollar amount to convert
        ' to pesos.
        Dim my_money As Decimal

        ' my_service is a new instance of the VBHelper object.
        Dim my_service As New VBHelper

        ' Get the value of the asp:textbox Money.
        my_money=Money.Text

        ' Send the results of the method call to the asp:label Results.
        ' Notice the use of the ToString() method at the end of the
        ' VBHelper method call.
```

```
        Result.Text = _
            "<B>Here is the appropriate amount of pesos:</B> = " & _
            my_service.ConvertPesos(my_money).ToString()
    End Sub
</script>

<BODY STYLE="font: 10pt verdana">
    <H4>Convert Dollars to Pesos</H4>
    <FORM RUNAT="server">
        <!-- Button that calls the Submit_Click sub. -->
        <INPUT TYPE="submit" ID="Button"
                VALUE="Perform Conversion"
                OnServerClick="Submit_Click"
                RUNAT="server">
        <P>
            <BR>
            Enter the amount in US Dollars you want to convert to pesos:
            <asp:TextBox id="Money" Text="" runat="server"/><BR>
            <B>
                <!-- Label that displays the number of pesos. -->
                <asp:Label id="Result" runat="server"/>
            </B>
        </P>
    </FORM>
</BODY>
</HTML>
```

Figure 8.11 shows how this example appears in Internet Explorer.

In this example, the ASP.NET code sent a value to the Web Service and received a result. This is common for any method call, not just for a Web Service. The next section shows how to pass a value to a method and receive an image in return, a slightly more unusual process.

Figure 8.11 This ASP.NET page invokes the VBHelper Web Service's ConvertPesos function.

GetImage ASP.NET Client

This example calls the VBHelper Web Service's GetImage method, passing it the name of an image file. The Web Service loads the image and sends it back to the client using a Base64 encoding as text in part of a SOAP response.

The code begins by importing several namespaces it will need. In addition to the VBHelper namespace, the program needs namespaces for manipulating the image.

Note that this page contains only one Visual Basic subroutine: Page_Load. This page loads its images and immediately displays them using the Response object. Because it displays the images when it loads, the page doesn't need any HTML controls or any other subroutines.

Page_Load uses the Request object's QueryString method to find the value of the imagefile variable in the URL's query string. It clears the Response object and invokes its VBHelper object's GetImage method to fetch the image. It copies the image into a MemoryStream and uses the MemoryStream to initialize a bitmap.

The routine then sets the Response object's content type to image/jpeg, indicating the page will hold only an image. It saves the bitmap into the Response object's output stream and calls the Response object's End method to make the page appear.

```
<%@ Import Namespace="VBHelper" %>
<%@ Import Namespace="System.IO" %>
<%@ Import Namespace="System.Drawing" %>
<%@ Import Namespace="System.Drawing.Imaging" %>
<%@ Import Namespace="System.Web.Services.Protocols" %>
<%@ Import Namespace="System.Runtime.Remoting.Messaging" %>
<!-- Notice all the new imports. They are present for the image
     the example reads and then decodes. -->

<script language="VB" runat="server" debug="true">
    ' Using a page load because all that is happening is the display
    ' of an image.
    Sub Page_Load (obj As Object, e As EventArgs)
        ' Declare the need variables and objects.
        Dim image_content As Byte()
        Dim memory_stream As MemoryStream
        Dim return_image As String
        Dim remote_service As New VBHelper

        ' Get the name of the image to request from the query string.
        return_image = Request.QueryString("imagefile")

        ' All ASP.NET pages have static Requests and Response objects
        ' available. The response object is cleared here so that
        ' information from previous forms doesn't interfere.
        Response.Clear()

        ' Get the image from the Web Service. Note that the image gets
        ' converted from binary into Base64 encryption, which is text.
        ' This way the Web Service sends the data as part of a SOAP
        ' response.
        image_content = remote_service.GetImage(return_image)
        memory_stream = New MemoryStream(image_content)
```

```
          ' Create the image to display and send the memory stream to it.
          Dim bitmap_stream As New Bitmap(memory_stream)
          ' This sets the response type for the browser. Being set to
          ' image/jpeg means that only an image displays on this page.
          ' There can't be any HTML.
          Response.ContentType= "image/jpeg"

          ' Save the bitmap out to the OutputStream of the Response object.
          bitmap_stream.Save(Response.OutputStream, ImageFormat.Jpeg)

          ' Call the end function of the response object so the browser
          ' quits rendering.
          Response.End()
      End Sub
</script>
```

The following HTML code calls the previous ASP.NET page. Note how the name of the image is sent as part of the query string variable imagefile.

```
<HTML>
   <HEAD>
      <TITLE>Image Test For ReturnImage Function</TITLE>
   </HEAD>

   <BODY>
      <H2>Image Test</H2>
      <IMG SRC=".\ReturnImage3.aspx?imagefile=brian.jpg"
         alt="brian.jpg">
      <P>
      <IMG SRC=".\ReturnImage3.aspx?imagefile=rod.jpg"
         alt="rod.jpg">
   </BODY>
</HTML>
```

Figure 8.12 HTML code can invoke an ASP.NET page that fetches an image from a Web Service.

Figure 8.12 shows this Web page in Internet Explorer. The second image is scrolled off the bottom of the page.

TranslateFiles ASP.NET Client

If you put the proper reference to an XSL file in an XML document, an XML-enabled browser such as Internet Explorer can transform the document automatically. ASP.NET's asp:xml control can also transform an XML document using XSL. The following code shows how easy it is to transform an XML file using the asp:xml control.

```
<asp:xml id="DisplayXML"
    DocumentSource="SalesData.xml"
    TransformSource="SalesChart.xsl"
    Runat="server">
```

Given how easy it is to transform XML files, why would anyone use a Web Service to perform the same task?

The asp:xml control works just fine if the XML and XSL files reside on the Web server. In today's distributed environment, however, it is quite possible that the Web server may reside at an Internet Service Provider off-site while corporate information such as sales data, pricing, and inventory reside on-site. Publishing data like this on a Web server could take hours, especially if there is a lot of data. If you have load-balanced systems, you could end up moving the data many times. If you create a Web Service, the Web servers or applications can access the data from one central repository.

The following code demonstrates the VBHelper Web Service's TransformHTML method. The Submit_Click subroutine copies the values entered in the form's two text boxes into the variables xml_file and xsl_file. It then invokes its VBHelper object's TranslateFiles method and assigns the result to the asp:Label control named Result.

```
<%@ Import Namespace="VBHelper" %>

<HTML>
<script language="VB" runat="server">
    Public Sub Submit_Click(Sender As Object, E As EventArgs)
        ' Declare the variables and the VBHelper object.
        Dim xml_file As String
        Dim xsl_file As String
        Dim my_service As New VBHelper

        ' Get the XML and XSL files.
        xml_file = file_to_transform.text
        xsl_file = file_that_transforms.text

        ' Display the results of the TranslateFiles function in the
        ' asp:label Results.
        Results.Text = my_service.TranslateFiles(xml_file,xsl_file)
    End Sub
</script>
```

```
<BODY STYLE="font: 10pt verdana">
   <H4>Convert Dollars to Pesos</H4>
   <FORM RUNAT="server">
      <P>
         <br>Enter the name of the xml file:
         <!-- The name of the XML file to transform. -->
         <asp:TextBox id="file_to_transform" runat="server"/><BR>

         <BR>
         Enter the name of the xsl file:
         <!-- The name of the XSL file to transform. -->
         <asp:TextBox id="file_that_transforms" runat="server"/><BR>
         <INPUT TYPE="submit" ID="Button"
             VALUE="Perform Conversion"
             OnServerClick="Submit_Click"
             RUNAT="server">
      </P>
      <asp:Label id="Results" runat="server"/>
   </FORM>
</BODY>
</HTML>
```

Figure 8.13 shows how this example displays the transformed XML.

All of the clients described so far use ASP.NET and the proxy dll made earlier in this chapter. All of these examples can be made with the Framework SDK distributed by Microsoft. The following section shows how to build a client in Visual Studio .NET, a slightly easier process.

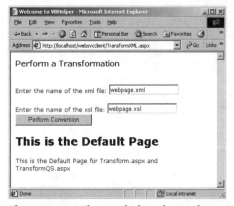

Figure 8.13   The text below the Perform Conversion button is an XML file transformed by the VBHelper Web Service's TranslateFiles function.

Visual Basic .NET Clients

This section shows how to create a Visual Basic .NET client for a Web Service within Visual Studio .NET. Visual Studio .NET provides some tools that make creating the proxy much easier than the wsdl.exe tool and vbc compiler do. Other than that, the code really isn't terribly different from the code used in the previous examples. The example described in this section creates a Visual Basic client that displays an image using the VBHelper Web Service's GetImage function. You can modify the previous examples to make similar clients using Visual Basic.

Open a Visual Basic form in design mode and add a PictureBox, a ComboBox, and a Button. Name the PictureBox ImageResults, the ComboBox image_name, and the Button GetImage. Give the ComboBox the three choices: brian.jpg, rod.jpg, and beta.jpg.

Before you add any code, you need to create a reference to the VBHelper Web Service. On the project menu select Add Web Reference to display the dialog box shown in Figure 8.14.

In the Address box, enter the URL http://localhost/websvc/VBHelper.asmx?wsdl. This is the path to the Web Services description of the VBHelper Web Service. It tells Visual Studio what methods the Service provides. Figure 8.15 shows the Web Service's wsdl on the left. Click the Add Reference button.

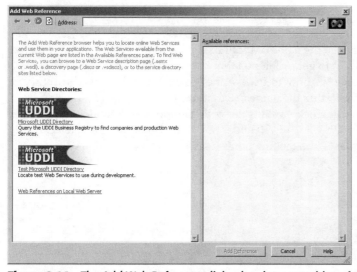

Figure 8.14   The Add Web Reference dialog box lets you add a reference to a Web Service.

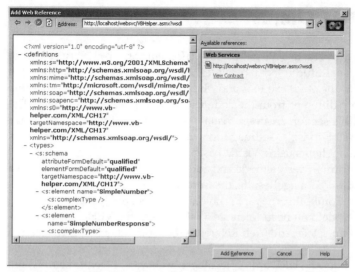

Figure 8.15 The Add Web Reference dialogue displays the Web Service's WSDL information.

If you look at the Solution Explorer under Web references, you'll see that there is now an entry for localhost. Figure 8.16 shows Solution Explorer after creating the Web reference. Click the localhost entry to display the vbhelper.wsdl entry it contains. You now have access to all of the methods provided by the VBHelper Web Service.

The program can now create a new VBHelper object, as shown in the following code.

```
Dim remote_service As New localhost.VBHelper()
```

Note that you can change the name of localhost in the Solution Explorer. Right-click your mouse over localhost to get a dialogue that has a Rename option.

The following code shows how to invoke the VBHelper Web Service's GetImage function. It begins by importing the namespaces it needs.

The subroutine Button1_Click handles the code behind the GetImage button. The subroutine begins by creating a new VBHelper object. It also declares a byte array and a string to manipulate the GetImage function's results.

Figure 8.16 The localhost Web reference contains the vbhelper.wsdl reference.

The subroutine gets the image name from the image_name ComboBox and calls the VBHelper object's GetImage function. It copies the result into a MemoryStream, uses the MemoryStream to initialize a new Bitmap object, and displays the Bitmap in the PictureBox ImageResults.

```
Imports System.IO
Imports System.Drawing
Imports System.Drawing.Imaging
Imports System.Web.Services.Protocols
Imports System.Runtime.Remoting.Messaging

Public Class Form1
    Inherits System.Windows.Forms.Form

    +Windows Form Designer generated code

    Private Sub Button1_Click(ByVal sender As System.Object, _
    ByVal e As System.EventArgs) Handles GetImage.Click
        ' Create a new VBHelper instance.
        Dim remote_service As New localhost.VBHelper()

        ' Create image_content as byte. This is the type that
        ' VBHelper returns.
        Dim image_content As Byte()

        ' Create a memory stream to send to the Bitmap object.
        Dim memory_stream As MemoryStream

        ' Name of the image to get.
        Dim return_image As String

        ' Get the name of the image from the drop-down.
        return_image = image_name.Text

        ' Get the image from VBHelper.
        image_content = remote_service.GetImage(return_image)

        ' Create a memory stream to pass to the bitmap object.
        memory_stream = New MemoryStream(image_content)

        ' Create the bitmap object with the memory_stream.
        Dim bitmap_stream As New Bitmap(memory_stream)

        ' Make the Picture Box not visible.
        ImageResults.Visible = False

        ' Send the picture box the contents of the bitmap object.
        ImageResults.Image = bitmap_stream

        ' Center the image in the picture box.
        ImageResults.SizeMode = PictureBoxSizeMode.CenterImage

        ' Display the results.
        ImageResults.Visible = True
    End Sub
End Class
```

Figure 8.17 shows the Windows program displaying an image returned by the VBHelper Web Service.

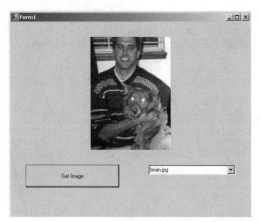

Figure 8.17 This program displays an image returned by the VBHelper Web Service's GetImage function.

One of the most remarkable features of Web Services is that they cross platforms and programming languages. A client written in Visual Basic .NET can access a Web Service written in Java or vice versa. The next section explains how to take advantage of this fact in Visual Basic.

Not .NET Web Services

One of the most exciting things about Web Services is that they are not limited to a particular platform or Web server. As long as the Web Service produces correct wsdl information, it doesn't matter to Visual Basic how the Web Service is coded or how it runs. The trick is finding available Web Services. Using discovery techniques described later in this chapter and searching the Web are two techniques for locating useful Web Services.

The Web site www.xmethods.com is one of many sites dedicated to promoting publicly accessible Web Services. This site lists many Web Services including the Zip code temperature Service used in this section. You can find information about the Web Service at www.xmethods.com/detail.html?id=8.

To consume this Web Service, create a new Visual Basic Windows Application in Visual Studio. On the default form that displays, add a Button, a TextBox, and two Labels. Name the Button SendInformation, the TextBox EnterZipCode, and one of the Labels ShowReplay. It doesn't matter what you name the second label. Set that Label's Text property to "Enter Zip Code" and place it next to the TextBox.

The Web page describing this Service gives the URL for the Service's WSDL file. You'll need that for creating the Web reference. That page also states that there is one available method, getTemp, which returns the temperature of the Zip code sent to it.

Create the Web reference by going to the Project menu and selecting Add Web Reference. Enter the URL for the WSDL file of this Web Service and click Add Reference. The name of the Web reference is net.xmethods.www. By right-clicking on this name and selecting Rename, you can name it something easier to remember. These examples refer to this Service as xmethods.

The following code shows how the program invokes the Web Service. The program retrieves the Zip code from its TextBox. It creates a new xmethods.TemperatureService object and calls its getTemp method to get the temperature at the given Zip code. The program displays the result in the ShowReply Label.

```
Private Sub Button1_Click(ByVal sender As System.Object, _
    ByVal e As System.EventArgs) Handles SendInformation.Click
        'Create the vars needed. Temperature is the returning value.
        'Zipcode is the value passed to the method.
        Dim Temperature As Decimal
        Dim Zipcode As String

        'Get the Zipcode value from the text box.
        Zipcode = EnterZipCode.Text

        'Create the remote_service object from the xmethods
        'Web reference.
        Dim remote_service As New xmethods.TemperatureService()

        'Get the temperature at the specified zip code.
        Temperature = remote_service.getTemp(Zipcode)

        'Put the response in a text box.
        ShowReply.Text = "The temperature at " & Zipcode & _
            " is " & Temperature
End Sub
```

Figure 8.18 shows the Get Temperature program displaying the temperature for the 80504 Zip code.

Figure 8.18   The xmethods.TemperatureService Web Service returns the temperature at a given Zip code.

Note that if a Web Service doesn't have the right version of WSDL, you may be able to create the Web reference, but you may not be able to use it. If the WSDL information is incorrect, your program will be unable to correctly invoke the Web Service's methods. While writing this chapter, Brian tried many different non-.NET Web Services. Adding the Web reference was always possible, but Visual Basic was not always able to use the Web Service.

Discovery

Previous versions of remote computing required a programmer or administrator to somehow learn about the routines the program was going to call. The Web Services technology, on the other hand, promises to have tools that help discover Web Service methods on the Web. Microsoft's disco.exe tool helps discover other .NET resources on the Web.

Universal Description, Discovery, and Integration (UDDI) is another method that helps discover Web Services. The following sections describe these two tools.

disco.exe

The .NET Framework SDK includes a simple Web Services discovery tool named disco.exe. This tool looks for .disco files that may exist on the remote URL. Suppose you enter the following command in a DOS window.

```
Disco http://localhost
```

This command reveals the Web Services that are available on your computer. On the computer used to develop this book, this command produced the following results.

```
Disco found documents at the following URLs:
http://localhost/WebService1/Service1.asmx?wsdl
http://localhost/VBHelper/HelloWorld/HelloWorld.vsdisco
http://localhost/VBHelperService1/VBHelperService1.vsdisco
http://localhost/VBHelperService/VBHelperService.vsdisco
http://localhost/TempConvertClient1/TempConvertClient1.vsdisco
http://localhost/Default.vsdisco
http://localhost/WebService1/WebService1.vsdisco
http://localhost/VBHelper/ParseXML/ParseXML.vsdisco
http://localhost/VBHelper/VBHelper.vsdisco
http://localhost/WebApplication1/WebApplication1.vsdisco
```

```
http://localhost/VBHelperService1/Service1.asmx?wsdl
http://localhost/VBHelper/Service1.asmx?wsdl
```

When you execute the disco tool, it downloads all the .disco documents to your system. For example, the VBHelper.disco file looks like this.

```
<?xml version="1.0" encoding="utf-8"?>
<discovery
xmlns:xsi="http://www.w3.org/2001/XMLSchema-instance"
xmlns:xsd="http://www.w3.org/2001/XMLSchema"
xmlns="http://schemas.xmlsoap.org/disco/">
  <contractRef ref="http://localhost/VBHelper/Service1.asmx?wsdl"
    docRef="http://localhost/VBHelper/Service1.asmx"
    xmlns="http://schemas.xmlsoap.org/disco/scl/" />
  <discoveryRef
    ref="http://localhost/VBHelper/HelloWorld/HelloWorld.vsdisco" />
  <discoveryRef
    ref="http://localhost/VBHelper/ParseXML/ParseXML.vsdisco" />
</discovery>
```

The information shown in this response would help create a proxy because it reveals where the wsdl file is for VBHelper.

The flaw with disco is that it assumes that you know where a Web Service resides. Or at least that you know that a Web site uses .NET and responds to a disco request. UDDI is a repository of Web Services made available to the public.

UDDI

UDDI is a Web Services repository that lets you search for company names. By going to uddi.microsoft.com or www-3.ibm.com/services/uddi/find, you can search by company name for Web Services. You may also add any Web Service that you create. Figure 8.19 shows the results of a search for Sun Microsystems at uddi.microsoft.com. This page shows that Sun provides several public Web Services related to its products and services.

You can also access UDDI through Visual Studio .NET. Open a project and select the Project menu's Add Web Reference command to make the dialog box shown earlier in Figure 8.14 appear. If you click on the link labeled Microsoft UDDI Directory, the search dialog box shown in Figure 8.20 appears. You can use this dialog box to search UDDI for company names.

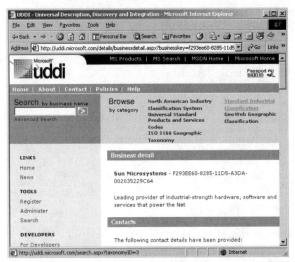

Figure 8.19 UDDI lets you search for company names to locate Web Services.

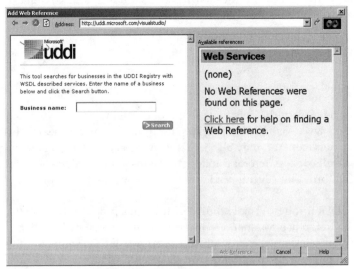

Figure 8.20 The Add Web Reference dialog provides a link to a UDDI search interface.

Conclusion

Web Services promise to make remote computing easier and more common. Previous versions of remote computing, such as CORBA and COM+, involved complicated implementations together with copious documentation so users could access the functionality. Now with Web Services, many of these problems are solved.

Web Services are not hard to implement or program. Using standard Visual Basic .NET code, you can easily create a Web Service. All you need to do to invoke the Service is to point a browser at it using its URL. By creating a proxy, you can let your Visual Basic .NET applications and ASP.NET Web pages access the Service.

To provide information to your users, Microsoft added parameters to the WebServices() and WebMethod() tags that allow you to describe your Web Service. Users access this information simply by pointing their browsers at the Service. Discovery tools such as UDDI and disco can also help users get information about your Service.

Implementations of CORBA and COM+ are far more complicated. These technologies don't have discovery methods, and a browser will not tell you what methods they make available. In addition, CORBA requires that you purchase an Object Request Broker (ORB) in order to broker requests between a Web server and server objects. COM+, on the other hand, requires modifications to each client machine's registry.

Finally, Web Services use a common data standard, XML, to transmit information. That makes it easy to write applications in languages and platforms that may have support for XML but not necessarily for .NET. That gives some hope for cross-platform support.

Years ago, remote computing technologies promised a new level of interoperability among applications scattered all over the Internet. With such ease of implementation, Web Services in Visual Basic .NET have the potential to make good on that promise.

XML in Other Applications

One of XML's most important features is its position as a neutral data description language. Applications written in Visual Basic, C#, C++, Fortran, Cobol, or any other language can share information through XML documents. By avoiding close ties to any specific programming language, XML has positioned itself to become the lingua franca of data exchange.

Of course, the ability to exchange data with applications written in other languages does little good if you have no such applications. The chapters in Part Three explain some of the ways Visual Basic applications can use XML to interact with other applications. They show how to move data to and from several Microsoft Office 2000 applications including Word, Excel, and Access. They tell how to use XML with Internet Explorer and SQL Server 2000.

CHAPTER 9

Microsoft Office 2000

XML is a data representation language. By providing an application-neutral format for data, XML can play a central role in data distribution and processing. One application can generate data in XML format. Then any number of other applications can load and manipulate that data.

A large portion of Visual Basic developers use Microsoft Office products such as Word and Excel to manipulate and display data. Unfortunately, support for XML in these applications lags somewhat behind support for XML in Visual Basic .NET. Microsoft Office 2000 uses Visual Basic for Applications (VBA) as its back-end macro language. VBA is an almost complete subset of Visual Basic 6, but Visual Basic 6 does not provide integrated support for XML. It is likely that future versions of these products will use Visual Basic .NET as a back-end language, and using XML with them will be easy. Until then, you need to do a little work to move XML data in and out of these applications.

All of the Microsoft Office applications use VBA for their back-end macro languages so once you know how to manipulate XML files using one Office application, you know a lot about how to manipulate them in other Office applications. The differences lie in how the VBA code interacts with the particular application. For example, how a Word macro reads and writes data in a Word document is different from how an Excel macro reads and writes data in a spreadsheet. The way they access an XML document is the same, however.

This chapter explains how to move data in and out of Microsoft Office applications. The chapter focuses mostly on Word and Excel because Visual Basic developers use them to analyze and display data more than they use other Office applications. The end of the chapter also gives a few examples using Access and Outlook.

This chapter is not intended to cover everything there is to know about programming Microsoft Office 2000. It contains just enough to let you import and export XML documents in a reasonably straightforward manner. It also provides examples you can use as starting points for more elaborate programs of your own. It does not explain all of the specifics of working with each individual application. For more information on Office programming, see an Office programming book such as *Developing Solutions with Office 2000 Components and VBA* by Peter Aitken (Prentice Hall, 2000).

Approaches

There are two basic approaches to moving data in and out of an Office application: push and pull. In a push approach, an application loads data in its native format and then writes it in a different format. For example, a Microsoft Word application can load a Word document and then write its data into an XML file.

In a pull approach, an application loads data in a foreign format and translates it into data in its native format. For example, a Word application might load an XML document and transform its data into a Word document.

Pushing and pulling give four possible scenarios for each Office application. Using Microsoft Word as an example those scenarios are as follows:

- A Word application pulls data from XML into a Word document.

- A Word application pushes data from a Word document into an XML file.

- A Visual Basic application pulls data from a Word document into an XML file.

- A Visual Basic application pushes data from an XML file into a Word document.

You may not need to use all of these approaches in your applications. For example, if you write a Visual Basic application that translates data between XML and Word documents, you don't really need to write VBA macros to do the same thing. When you need to incorporate XML data in your Word document, you can translate the XML data into a table in a new Word document, open the document, and copy and paste the table into your document.

That translation requires an extra manual step, however. Many developers use Word and Excel to generate integrated reports, and performing this kind of extra step can slow the process greatly. A complex Office application should be able to start a Word document, enter some overview information, pull XML data into a table, provide more textual information, pull in another table from a different XML source, and so forth. While you may not strictly need every combination of routines, loading and saving XML data from VBA and Visual Basic, having them all is convenient.

Word

Using different XSL stylesheets, you can transform the same XML document into several different output formats. For example, one stylesheet could format a table of data for display in an HTML table on a Web page. Another stylesheet could format the data in a text document. A third stylesheet might extract only some of the data and build an executive summary using HTML.

It might also be nice to display this kind of data in a Microsoft Word document. Corporate reports are often written in Word so it is natural to want to include information from a central XML repository in a Word report.

Microsoft Word 2000 does not provide direct support for XML, but you can use Microsoft's MSXML library, described in Chapter 3, "Forward-Only XML," to load and save XML documents within Word. For information on installing this library, see the section *Installing SAX* in Chapter 3.

After you have installed the MSXML library, you can use the DOM objects it contains to read and write XML documents. Start the Microsoft Word application. Open the Tools menu, select the Macro submenu, and pick Visual Basic Editor. That opens Word's Visual Basic editing environment.

Open the Tools menu and select the References command. Find the entry labeled Microsoft XML, v4.0 (your version number may differ), check the box next to it, and click OK. Now your Word macros can use the objects provided by this library.

In the Project Explorer, you will see entries for different Word documents you have open plus an entry named Normal. Open the entry where you want to create the XML macros. For example, if you want the macros to be available to all documents, open the Normal entry.

If the project you selected does not already have a Modules entry, right-click on the project, select Insert, and invoke the Module command. Now you can add macro code to the module.

Example program XmlWord, shown in Figure 9.1, pulls and pushes data between Word and XML documents. Enter or select the names of the files and click a button to make the program translate the data. The buttons on the left move table-like data from a Word document to an XML file and vice versa. The buttons on the right move hierarchical data between Word and XML files.

The following sections describe the code that the XmlWord program uses. The sections after that explain VBA code that performs the same translations. The VBA code is contained in the file XmlWord.bas in the XmlWord program's project directory.

Figure 9.1 Program XmlWord pulls and pushes data between Word and XML documents.

Word Servers

The XmlWord example program is a Visual Basic application that uses a Word server to manipulate Microsoft Word documents. Before a Visual Basic application can use a Word server, it needs a reference to the Word object library. Start a new project. In the Solution Explorer, right-click on the References entry and select Add Reference. Move to the COM tab and find the entry labeled Microsoft Word 9.0 Object Library. Double-click that entry to select it and then click OK. The environment will display a dialog box that says:

> *Could not find a primary interop assembly for the COM component 'Microsoft Word 9.0 Object Library'. A primary interop assembly is not registered for this type library. Would you like to have a wrapper generated for you?*

Click Yes to make the environment build .NET classes that support the library. Now you can use the library's objects and their methods in your application.

The XmlWord program declares a private Word application server outside of its subroutines so all of the subroutines can use the same server object. When the program starts, the main form's Load event handler initializes the Word server, as shown in the following code. This may take a few seconds now but saves time later. When the program's subroutines need to use the server, it is already running so the program doesn't need to wait at that point.

```
' The Word server we use to manipulate Word.
Private m_WordServer As Word.Application

Private Sub Form1_Load( _
  ByVal sender As System.Object, _
  ByVal e As System.EventArgs) Handles MyBase.Load

    ' Prepare the default data filenames.
    cboXmlFiles.Items.Add(DataSubdirectory() & "\Article.xml")
    cboXmlFiles.Items.Add(DataSubdirectory() & "\Table.xml")

    cboWordFiles.Items.Add(DataSubdirectory() & "\Article.doc")
    cboWordFiles.Items.Add(DataSubdirectory() & "\Table.doc")

    cboXmlFiles.Text = DataSubdirectory() & "\Article.xml"

    ' Open the Word server now so we don't have to wait
    ' to open it when the user clicks a button.
    m_WordServer = New Word.Application()
End Sub
```

When the program closes, the form's Closing event handler closes the Word server, as shown in the following code.

```
' Close the Word server.
Private Sub Form1_Closing( _
  ByVal sender As Object, _
```

```
        ByVal e As System.ComponentModel.CancelEventArgs) _
        Handles MyBase.Closing

        m_WordServer.Quit()
        m_WordServer = Nothing
    End Sub
```

Note that the server must close normally using its Quit method. If you are debugging the program and you halt the application prematurely, the server may keep a lock on any Word file it has open. When you later try to open the file, the system will give you a warning and prevent you from opening the file for editing.

If you need to halt the program early, go to the development environment's Command Window and execute the m_WordServer.Quit() command manually before you stop the program.

Table-Like Data

The examples in this chapter show how to manipulate data for two types of example data: table-like data and hierarchical data. The table-like data is stored in rows and columns similar to an HTML table. The following code shows the structure of the XML document. The data root node is a Books element. That element contains any number of Book tags representing table rows. Each row contains one or more BookInfo tags representing table data.

```
<?xml version="1.0"?>
<Books>
  <Book>
    <BookInfo>Title</BookInfo>
    <BookInfo>Price</BookInfo>
    <BookInfo>Pages</BookInfo>
    <BookInfo>URL</BookInfo>
    <BookInfo>Image</BookInfo>
  </Book>
  <Book>
    <BookInfo>Ready-to-Run Visual Basic Algorithms</BookInfo>
    <BookInfo>$39.99</BookInfo>
    <BookInfo>395</BookInfo>
    <BookInfo>http://www.vb-helper.com/vba.htm</BookInfo>
    <BookInfo>http://www.vb-helper.com/vba.gif</BookInfo>
  </Book>
  ... More rows ...
</Books>
```

These examples assume each row in the table contains the same number of elements. The code does not create a special row for the table's column headers. If you want column headers, either create a row of data holding the column header values or modify the code to make it create the headers.

The section *Hierarchical Data* later in this chapter tells how to move hierarchical data between Word and XML documents.

Visual Basic: Pulling Table Data

Program XmlWord uses the TableWordToXml subroutine, shown in the following code, to load a Microsoft Word document and copy the data in its first table into an XML document. The routine starts by creating an XmlTextWriter, configuring it to generate indented XML output, writing the XML declaration, and writing the <Books> start tag.

The subroutine then uses the Word server to open the Word document and find its first Table object. For each row in the table, the subroutine makes the XmlTextWriter create a <Book> start tag. Then for each column in the row, the subroutine makes the XmlTextWriter create a <BookInfo> start tag. It uses the XmlTextWriter's WriteString method to save the table entry's text. It then calls the WriteEndElement method to write the </BookInfo> column closing tag.

When it finishes writing a table row, the subroutine calls the WriteEndElement method again to write the </Book> row closing tag. When it finishes writing every row in the table, the subroutine calls the WriteEndElement method one last time to write the </Books> closing tag.

The subroutine finishes by calling WriteEndDocument to close the XML document and by calling the XmlTextWriter's Close method to close it and flush its text buffer.

```vb
Private m_WhitespaceCharacters() As Char = _
    {" ", vbTab, vbCr, vbLf, vbCrLf, vbVerticalTab, _
     vbBack, vbFormFeed, vbNewLine, Chr(7)}

' Copy table-like Word data into an XML file.
Private Sub TableWordToXml( _
  ByVal word_file As String, _
  ByVal xml_file As String)

    Dim word_table As Word.Table
    Dim xml_text_writer As XmlTextWriter
    Dim r As Integer
    Dim c As Integer

    ' Create the XmlTextWriter.
    xml_text_writer = New XmlTextWriter( _
        xml_file, Encoding.UTF8)
    xml_text_writer.Formatting = Formatting.Indented
    xml_text_writer.Indentation = 2
    xml_text_writer.IndentChar = " "

    ' Start the document.
    xml_text_writer.WriteStartDocument(True)

    ' Start the Books element.
    xml_text_writer.WriteStartElement("Books")

    With m_WordServer
        ' Open the Word document.
```

```
        .Documents.Open( _
            FileName:=word_file, _
            ConfirmConversions:=False, _
            ReadOnly:=True, _
            AddToRecentFiles:=False, _
            PasswordDocument:="", _
            PasswordTemplate:="", _
            Revert:=False, _
            WritePasswordDocument:="", _
            WritePasswordTemplate:="", _
            Format:=wdOpenFormatAuto)

    ' Find the table.
    word_table = .ActiveDocument.Tables.Item(1)

    ' Write the rows.
    For r = 1 To word_table.Rows.Count
        ' Start the Book element.
        xml_text_writer.WriteStartElement("Book")

        ' Write this row's columns.
        For c = 1 To word_table.Columns.Count
            ' Start the BookInfo element.
            xml_text_writer.WriteStartElement("BookInfo")

            ' Add the cell's text.
            xml_text_writer.WriteString( _
                word_table.Cell(r, c).Range.Text.Trim( _
                    m_WhitespaceCharacters))

            ' End the BookInfo element.
            xml_text_writer.WriteEndElement()
        Next c

        ' End the Book element.
        xml_text_writer.WriteEndElement()
    Next r
End With

' End the Books element.
xml_text_writer.WriteEndElement()

' Save the XML document.
xml_text_writer.WriteEndDocument()
xml_text_writer.Close()
End Sub
```

This subroutine relies on the fact that every row in the Word table contains the same number of columns. If you use Word's Merge Cell capabilities to make a cell span more than one column, the subroutine will crash when it tries to access more cells in that row than the table contains.

Visual Basic: Pushing Table Data

Program XmlWord uses the TableXmlToWord subroutine, shown in the following code, to copy table-like XML data into a new Word file.

The TableWordToXml subroutine described in the previous section uses an XmlText-Writer to write a new XML document. When subroutine TableXmlToWord converts XML data into a Word table, it is easier to read the data using an XmlDocument object rather than the corresponding XmlTextReader object.

Subroutine TableXmlToWord starts by opening the XML document in an XmlDocument object and finding the data root node <Books>. It uses this node's number of children as the number of rows in the new Word table. The number of children in the first row node gives the number of columns in the new table.

The subroutine creates a new Word document and adds a table to it with the correct number of rows and columns. Next the routine loops through the children of the Books node. Those children are the Book row elements in the XML document.

For each row element, the subroutine loops through the row's child nodes. These nodes are the BookInfo table data nodes that contain the cell text. For each BookInfo node, the routine copies the node's text into the new Word table.

When it has finished copying all of the XML document's data into the Word table, the subroutine saves the Word document and closes it.

```
' Copy table-like XML data into a Word file.
Private Sub TableXmlToWord( _
  ByVal xml_file As String, _
  ByVal word_file As String)

    Const wdAutoFitContent As Integer = 1
    Const wdWord9TableBehavior As Integer = 1

    Dim xml_document As XmlDocument
    Dim table_node As XmlNode
    Dim row_node As XmlNode
    Dim column_node As XmlNode
    Dim num_rows As Integer
    Dim num_cols As Integer
    Dim word_table As Word.Table
    Dim r As Integer
    Dim c As Integer

    ' Open the XML document.
    xml_document = New XmlDocument()
    xml_document.Load(xml_file)

    ' See how many rows and columns we need.
    table_node = xml_document.DocumentElement
    num_rows = table_node.ChildNodes.Count
    row_node = table_node.ChildNodes(0)
    num_cols = row_node.ChildNodes.Count
```

```
With m_WordServer
    ' Open a new Word document.
    .Documents.Add(DocumentType:=wdNewBlankDocument)

    ' Create the new table.
    word_table = .ActiveDocument.Tables.Add( _
        Range:=.Selection.Range, _
        NumRows:=num_rows, _
        NumColumns:=num_cols, _
        DefaultTableBehavior:=wdWord9TableBehavior, _
        AutoFitBehavior:=wdAutoFitContent)

    ' Enter the data.
    r = 1
    For Each row_node In table_node.ChildNodes
        c = 1
        For Each column_node In row_node.ChildNodes
            word_table.Cell(r, c).Range.Text = column_node.InnerText
            c = c + 1
        Next column_node
        r = r + 1
    Next row_node

    ' Save the document.
    .ActiveDocument.SaveAs( _
        FileName:=word_file, _
        FileFormat:=wdFormatDocument, _
        LockComments:=False, _
        Password:="", _
        AddToRecentFiles:=True, _
        WritePassword:="", _
        ReadOnlyRecommended:=False, _
        EmbedTrueTypeFonts:=False, _
        SaveNativePictureFormat:=False, _
        SaveFormsData:=False, _
        SaveAsAOCELetter:=False)

    ' Close the document.
    .ActiveDocument.Close()
End With
End Sub
```

This subroutine relies on the fact that every Book element has the same number of
BookInfo elements as children. It uses the number of children in the first row to determine the number of columns the table needs. If any of the rows contain more children,
the subroutine will crash when it tries to access a table cell that does not exist.

Figure 9.2 shows a Word table created by subroutine TableXmlToWord.

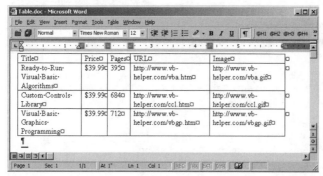

Figure 9.2 Program XmlWord creates Word tables like this one from XML documents.

Word: Pulling Table Data

VBA subroutine LoadXmlTable, shown in the following code, loads table data from an XML file and uses its data to create a table in Word. The subroutine creates a new DOMDocument object from the MSXML library. It uses the DOMDocument's Load method to load the XML file and finds the XML document's Books node. The number of the Books node's children gives the number of rows in the table. The number of the first row's children gives the number of columns in the table. After determining the number of rows and columns in the table, the routine uses the Word document's Tables collection to add a new table to the document.

Next LoadXmlTable loops through the Books node's children. For each Book node, the subroutine loops through that node's children. For each of its BookInfo nodes, the subroutine copies the node's text value into the corresponding Word table cell.

```
' Load the data in the XML document into a Word table
' in the currently active document.
Sub LoadXmlTable(ByVal xml_file_name As String)
    Dim word_table As Table
    Dim dom_document As DOMDocument
    Dim table_node As IXMLDOMNode
    Dim row_node As IXMLDOMNode
    Dim column_node As IXMLDOMNode
    Dim num_rows As Integer
    Dim num_cols As Integer
    Dim r As Integer
    Dim c As Integer

    ' Load the XML file into a DOM representation.
    Set dom_document = New DOMDocument
    dom_document.Load xml_file_name

    ' Get the Books node.
```

```
Set table_node = dom_document.documentElement

' See how many rows there are.
num_rows = table_node.childNodes.Length

' See how many columns there are.
Set row_node = table_node.childNodes(0)
num_cols = row_node.childNodes.Length

' Create the new table.
Set word_table = ActiveDocument.Tables.Add( _
    Range:=Selection.Range, _
    NumRows:=num_rows, _
    NumColumns:=num_cols, _
    DefaultTableBehavior:=wdWord9TableBehavior, _
    AutoFitBehavior:=wdAutoFitContent)

' Enter the data.
r = 1
For Each row_node In table_node.childNodes
    c = 1
    For Each column_node In row_node.childNodes
        word_table.Cell(r, c).Range.Text = column_node.Text
        c = c + 1
    Next column_node
    r = r + 1
Next row_node
End Sub
```

Subroutine LoadXmlTable contains no error checking so the XML document's table structure must be correct. In particular, if one of the rows has more BookInfo entries than the first row, the subroutine fails with the error, "The requested member of the collection does not exist." It would not be hard to use an On Error statement to protect the routine and make it ignore any extra entries in a row, but handling this sort of error more intelligently would be hard.

For example, you could define an XML format to let you build tables with cells that span multiple columns. This would make both the XML document and the code more complicated, and you would probably need to tailor it to your specific application, so this example sticks to the simplest possible case.

Word: Pushing Table Data

VBA subroutine SaveXmlTable, shown in the following code, creates an XML document that holds the data in the Word document's currently selected table. The subroutine begins by creating a new DOMDocument and giving it an XML declaration processing instruction. It locates the selected table and starts the Books element.

For each row in the table, the routine starts a Book element. For each column in the row, the code creates a BookInfo element and adds the Word table's cell contents inside that element.

When it has visited every cell in the document, the subroutine calls the DOMDocument's Save method to write the XML file.

```vba
' Save the currently selected table in an XML file.
Sub SaveXmlTable(ByVal xml_file_name As String)
    Dim word_table As Table
    Dim dom_document As DOMDocument
    Dim processing_instruction As IXMLDOMProcessingInstruction
    Dim table_element As IXMLDOMElement
    Dim row_element As IXMLDOMElement
    Dim cell_element As IXMLDOMElement
    Dim r As Integer
    Dim c As Integer

    ' Create the new DOM document.
    Set dom_document = New DOMDocument
    Set processing_instruction = _
        dom_document.createProcessingInstruction("xml", "version='1.0'")
    dom_document.appendChild processing_instruction

    ' Find the table.
    Set word_table = Selection.Tables.Item(1)

    ' Write the Books element.
    Set table_element = dom_document.createElement("Books")
    dom_document.appendChild table_element

    ' Write the rows.
    For r = 1 To word_table.Rows.Count
        ' Indent.
        table_element.appendChild _
            dom_document.createTextNode(vbCrLf & "   ")

        ' Create the Book element.
        Set row_element = dom_document.createElement("Book")
        table_element.appendChild row_element

        ' Write this row's columns.
        For c = 1 To word_table.Columns.Count
            ' Indent.
            row_element.appendChild _
                dom_document.createTextNode(vbCrLf & "      ")

            ' Create the BookInfo element.
            Set cell_element = dom_document.createElement("BookInfo")
            row_element.appendChild cell_element

            ' Add the cell's text.
            cell_element.appendChild _
                dom_document.createTextNode( _
                    StripWhitespace(word_table.Cell(r, c).Range.Text))
```

```
        Next c

          ' Indent before the </Book> tag.
          row_element.appendChild _
              dom_document.createTextNode(vbCrLf & "    ")
      Next r

          ' New line before the </Books> tag.
          table_element.appendChild dom_document.createTextNode(vbCrLf)

          ' Save the DOM document.
          dom_document.Save xml_file_name
          Set dom_document = Nothing
    End Sub
```

The simple flat structure of the table makes this subroutine much simpler than the routines that read and write hierarchical article data.

Note that this routine relies on the fact that each row in the Word table contains the same number of cells. Using Word's Merge Cells capability, you can build a table where a cell spans two or more columns. If the subroutine encounters such a row, it crashes when it tries to access missing cells.

Hierarchical Data

Tables are relatively easy to work with in Microsoft Word, but hierarchical data is probably more common. A typical document contains sections that contain text and possibly subsections. It may also contain blocks of text formatted in special styles. For example, in this book source code is displayed differently from normal text.

The following sections show how to move data between Word and an XML file with a hierarchical magazine article-like structure. The document's data root node is an Article element with a Title property giving the article's title. This element contains any number of Section elements with Title attributes giving each section's title. Each Section element contains paragraph elements indicated by <P> and </P> tags. The paragraph tags contain paragraph text.

```
<?xml version="1.0" standalone="yes"?>
<Article Title="Building VB Games">
  <Section Title="">
    <P>
      This section has no title. It holds the article's introduction...
    </P>
  </Section>
  <Section Title="Getting Started">
    <P>
      This is the first paragraph in the second section...
    </P>
    <P>
      This is the second paragraph in the second section...
    </P>
```

```
    </Section>
    ... More sections ...
  </Article>
```

These examples work only with three levels: Article, Section, and paragraph text. They map these elements into Word styles Heading 1, Heading 2, and Normal. You could easily extend these examples to allow other XML elements defining other Word styles.

Visual Basic: Pulling Hierarchical Data

Program XmlWord uses the ArticleWordToXml subroutine, shown in the following code, to load a Microsoft Word document and copy its hierarchical article-like data into an XML document. The routine starts by creating an XmlTextWriter, configuring it to generate indented XML output, writing the XML declaration, and writing the <Article> start tag.

The subroutine uses the Word server to open the Word document. It then loops through each of the document's paragraphs. If a paragraph has nonzero length, the routine examines its Style to see what style the text has. If the Style is Heading 1, the subroutine starts the Article element.

If the Style is Heading 2, the routine checks its section_open variable to see if a Section element is open and, if one is, the routine closes it. The subroutine then starts a new Section element.

If the paragraph's Style is Normal, the subroutine again checks its section_open variable. If no Section is currently open, the subroutine creates a new Section with a blank Title attribute. It then opens a new paragraph element <P>, writes the paragraph's text, and closes the paragraph element.

When the subroutine has finished processing all of the Word document's paragraphs, it once again checks its section_open variable. If a Section element is open, the routine closes it. It finishes by closing the Article element and the XmlTextWriter.

```
' Copy article-like hierarchical Word data into an XML file.
Private Sub ArticleWordToXml( _
  ByVal word_file As String, _
  ByVal xml_file As String)

    Dim word_paragraph As Word.Paragraph
    Dim xml_text_writer As XmlTextWriter
    Dim section_open As Boolean
    Dim paragraph_text As String

    ' Create the XmlTextWriter.
    xml_text_writer = New XmlTextWriter( _
        xml_file, Encoding.UTF8)
    xml_text_writer.Formatting = Formatting.Indented
    xml_text_writer.Indentation = 2
    xml_text_writer.IndentChar = " "

    ' Start the document.
    xml_text_writer.WriteStartDocument(True)
```

```
With m_WordServer
    ' Open the Word document.
    .Documents.Open( _
        FileName:=word_file, _
        ConfirmConversions:=False, _
        ReadOnly:=True, _
        AddToRecentFiles:=False, _
        PasswordDocument:="", _
        PasswordTemplate:="", _
        Revert:=False, _
        WritePasswordDocument:="", _
        WritePasswordTemplate:="", _
        Format:=wdOpenFormatAuto)

    ' Process the document's paragraphs.
    For Each word_paragraph In .ActiveDocument.Paragraphs
        ' Process this paragraph.
        paragraph_text = _
            word_paragraph.Range.Text.Trim(m_WhitespaceCharacters)
        If paragraph_text.Length > 0 Then
            Select Case word_paragraph.Style.NameLocal
                Case "Heading 1"
                    ' Start the Article element.
                    xml_text_writer.WriteStartElement("Article")
                    xml_text_writer.WriteAttributeString( _
                        "Title", paragraph_text)

                Case "Heading 2"
                    ' If there is an open Section, close it.
                    If section_open Then
                        xml_text_writer.WriteEndElement()
                    End If

                    ' Start a new Section element.
                    xml_text_writer.WriteStartElement("Section")
                    xml_text_writer.WriteAttributeString( _
                        "Title", paragraph_text)
                    section_open = True

                Case "Normal"
                    ' If there's no Section yet,
                    ' make one with a blank Title.
                    If Not section_open Then
                        ' Start a new Section element.
                        xml_text_writer.WriteStartElement("Section")
                        section_open = True
                    End If

                    ' Make a new Paragraph element.
                    xml_text_writer.WriteStartElement("P")
                    xml_text_writer.WriteString(paragraph_text)
                    xml_text_writer.WriteEndElement()
            End Select
```

```
            End If
        Next word_paragraph
    End With


    ' Close the final Section.
    If section_open Then xml_text_writer.WriteEndElement()


    ' Close the Article.
    xml_text_writer.WriteEndElement()


    ' Save the XML document.
    xml_text_writer.WriteEndDocument()
    xml_text_writer.Close()
End Sub
```

Subroutine ArticleWordToXml handles only three Word styles: Heading 1, Heading 2, and Normal. A real article might have many other customized styles such as ByLine, Code, and FigureCaption. This example sticks to standard styles defined by Word itself, but you could modify it to handle other styles needed by your particular application.

Visual Basic: Pushing Hierarchical Data

Program XmlWord uses the ArticleXmlToWord subroutine, shown in the following code, to load an article-like hierarchical XML document and convert it into a Word document. The subroutine begins by opening the XML document with an XmlTextReader object and setting its WhitespaceHandling property to None so that it can ignore extraneous white space.

The routine then creates a new Word document and starts reading the XML data. For each element start node, the routine examines the element's name. If the node is named Article, the subroutine selects the Word style Heading 1 and writes the node's Title attribute into the Word document.

If the node is named Section, the subroutine checks the node's Title attribute. If the title is not blank, the routine selects the Word style Heading 2 and writes the node's Title attribute into the Word document. If the node has no Title attribute, it represents a section with no title. In that case, the subroutine doesn't need to do anything yet.

If the node is named P, the subroutine selects the Word style Normal and writes the node's text into the Word document.

After it has processed all of the XML document's nodes, the routine saves the new Word document and closes it and the XmlTextReader.

```
' Copy hierarchical article-like XML data into a Word file.
Private Sub ArticleXmlToWord( _
  ByVal xml_file As String, _
  ByVal word_file As String)

    Dim xml_text_reader As XmlTextReader
    Dim section_title As String

    ' Open the XML document.
    xml_text_reader = New XmlTextReader(xml_file)
    xml_text_reader.WhitespaceHandling = WhitespaceHandling.None
    With m_WordServer
```

```
      ' Open a new Word document.
      .Documents.Add(DocumentType:=wdNewBlankDocument)

      ' Process the XML document.
      Do While xml_text_reader.Read()
          If xml_text_reader.NodeType = XmlNodeType.Element Then
              Select Case xml_text_reader.Name
                  Case "Article"
                      .Selection.Style = _
                          .ActiveDocument.Styles.Item("Heading 1")
                      .Selection.TypeText( _
                          xml_text_reader.GetAttribute( _
                              "Title").Trim(m_WhitespaceCharacters))
                      .Selection.TypeParagraph()
                  Case "Section"
                      section_title = _
                          xml_text_reader.GetAttribute( -
                              "Title").Trim(m_WhitespaceCharacters)
                      If section_title.Length > 0 Then
                          .Selection.Style = _
                              .ActiveDocument.Styles.Item("Heading 2")
                          .Selection.TypeText(section_title)
                          .Selection.TypeParagraph()
                      End If
                  Case "P"
                      .Selection.Style = _
                          .ActiveDocument.Styles.Item("Normal")
                      .Selection.TypeText(vbTab & _
                          xml_text_reader.ReadString.Trim( _
                              m_WhitespaceCharacters))
                      .Selection.TypeParagraph()
              End Select
          End If
      Loop

      ' Save the document.
      .ActiveDocument.SaveAs( _
          FileName:=word_file, _
          FileFormat:=wdFormatDocument, _
          LockComments:=False, _
          Password:="", AddToRecentFiles:=True, _
          WritePassword:="", _
          ReadOnlyRecommended:=False, _
          EmbedTrueTypeFonts:=False, _
          SaveNativePictureFormat:=False, _
          SaveFormsData:=False, _
          SaveAsAOCELetter:=False)

      ' Close the document.
      .ActiveDocument.Close()
    End With
End Sub
```

Figure 9.3 shows a Word document created by subroutine ArticleXmlToWord.

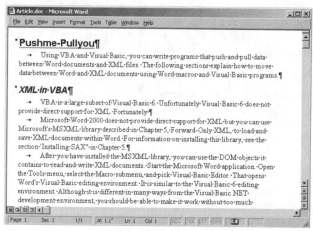

Figure 9.3   Program XmlWord builds hierarchical Word documents like this one from XML documents.

Word: Pulling Hierarchical Data

The LoadXmlArticle VBA subroutine shown in the following code loads an XML document containing an article data hierarchy, as described in the first section in this chapter.

When translated into a Word document, the article's title is displayed in the Heading 1 style, section titles are displayed in the Heading 2 style, and paragraph text is displayed in the Normal style.

Subroutine LoadXmlArticle begins by declaring a DOMDocument and several IXMLDOMNode objects. These are objects from the MSXML library that are roughly equivalent to the DOM objects described in Chapter 2, "DOM."

LoadXmlArticle calls the DOMDocument object's Load method to make it load the XML data file. It selects the Word style Heading 1 and displays the root data element's Title attribute in that style. That adds the article's title to the document.

Next the routine loops through the data root node's children. Because of the document's structure, those are Section elements. For each Section element, the subroutine examines the element's Title attribute. If the element has a nonblank Title, the routine selects the Word style Heading 2 and displays the Title.

After it has displayed the Section's Title attribute, the subroutine loops through the Section's child nodes. Because of the way the XML document is arranged, those are paragraph nodes. For each paragraph node, LoadXmlArticle uses the node's nodeValue method to get the text contained within the paragraph. It selects the Word style Normal and outputs the text.

The StripWhitespace helper routine removes any invisible characters from the front and back of a string. Subroutine LoadXmlArticle uses StripWhitespace to remove XML indentation and carriage returns from the text it displays.

```
' Load the indicated XML file containing an article
' into the currently active document.
Sub LoadXmlArticle(ByVal xml_file_name As String)
    Dim dom_document As DOMDocument
    Dim article_node As IXMLDOMNode
    Dim section_node As IXMLDOMNode
    Dim paragraph_node As IXMLDOMNode
    Dim section_title As String

        ' Load the XML file into a DOM representation.
    Set dom_document = New DOMDocument
    dom_document.Load xml_file_name

    ' Process the Article node.
    Set article_node = dom_document.documentElement
    Selection.Style = ActiveDocument.Styles.Item("Heading 1")
    Selection.TypeText Trim$(article_node.Attributes(0).nodeValue)
    Selection.TypeParagraph

    ' Process the Section nodes.
    For Each section_node In article_node.childNodes
        ' Get the Section Title.
        section_title = Trim$(section_node.Attributes(0).nodeValue)

        ' If the Title is nonblank, display it.
        If Len(section_title) > 0 Then
            Selection.Style = ActiveDocument.Styles.Item("Heading 2")
            Selection.TypeText section_title
            Selection.TypeParagraph
        End If

        ' Process the Section's Paragraph nodes.
        For Each paragraph_node In section_node.childNodes
            Selection.Style = ActiveDocument.Styles.Item("Normal")
            Selection.TypeText vbTab & _
                StripWhitespace(paragraph_node.childNodes(0).nodeValue)
            Selection.TypeParagraph
        Next paragraph_node
    Next section_node
End Sub

' Remove leading and trailing invisible characters from the string.
Private Function StripWhitespace(ByVal txt As String) As String
    Dim ch As String
    Dim pos1 As Integer
    Dim pos2 As Integer

    ' Find the first nonwhite-space character.
    For pos1 = 1 To Len(txt)
        ch = Mid$(txt, pos1, 1)
        If ch > " " And ch <= "~" Then Exit For
```

```
    Next pos1

    ' Find the first nonwhite-space character.
    For pos2 = Len(txt) To pos1 Step -1
        ch = Mid$(txt, pos2, 1)
        If ch > " " And ch <= "~" Then Exit For
    Next pos2

    ' Return the text between pos1 and pos2, inclusive.
    If pos1 > pos2 Then
        StripWhitespace = ""
    Else
        StripWhitespace = Mid$(txt, pos1, pos2 - pos1 + 1)
    End If
End Function
```

When subroutine LoadXmlArticle has finished, the active Word document contains the properly formatted contents of the XML document.

Word: Pushing Hierarchical Data

The SaveXmlArticle VBA subroutine, shown in the following code, builds an XML file from the active Word document. It begins by creating a new DOMDocument object to hold the new XML data. It adds an XML declaration processing instruction and starts processing the Word document.

For each paragraph in the Word document, the routine examines the paragraph's style. If the style is Heading 1, the code adds a new Article element to the XML document. If the paragraph has style Heading 2, the code creates a new Section element.

If the paragraph's style is Normal, the subroutine determines whether it has created a Section element yet. If it has not, the code makes a Section element with a blank Title attribute. That ensures that all paragraph elements are contained in a Section element. Then the subroutine builds a paragraph <P> element containing the text of the current Word paragraph.

After it has finished building the DOMDocument, the routine calls the document's Save method to write the XML data into a file.

The MakeArticle, MakeSection, and MakeParagraph subroutines called by SaveXml-Article are relatively straightforward. Each uses the DOMDocument's createElement method to create a new DOM element to represent the new section in the document. Each then makes the new element a child of the element that should contain it.

These routines also use the DOMDocument's createTextNode method to add white space nodes to the document to nicely indent the result. The calls to createTextNode are not very interesting as far as the structure of the document goes, though they were hard to get just right.

Subroutine MakeParagraphText is similar to these routines except it doesn't create a complex element for the paragraph text. Instead, it uses the DOMDocument's create-TextNode method to add a paragraph's text to the document. The MakeParagraph subroutine that calls MakeParagraphText builds the <P> </P> tags that surround the text.

```
' Save the currently active document in an XML file
' containing an article.
Sub SaveXmlArticle(ByVal xml_file_name As String)
    Dim word_paragraph As Paragraph
    Dim dom_document As DOMDocument
    Dim processing_instruction As IXMLDOMProcessingInstruction
    Dim article_element As IXMLDOMElement
    Dim section_element As IXMLDOMElement
    Dim paragraph_element As IXMLDOMElement

    ' Create the new DOM document.
    Set dom_document = New DOMDocument
    Set processing_instruction = _
        dom_document.createProcessingInstruction("xml", "version='1.0'")
    dom_document.appendChild processing_instruction

    ' Process the active document.
    For Each word_paragraph In ActiveDocument.Paragraphs
        ' Process this paragraph.
        Select Case word_paragraph.Style
            Case "Heading 1"
                ' Make the Article element.
                Set article_element = MakeArticle( _
                    dom_document, _
                    dom_document, _
                    StripWhitespace(word_paragraph.Range.Text))

            Case "Heading 2"
                ' Make a new Section element.
                Set section_element = MakeSection( _
                    dom_document, _
                    article_element, _
                    StripWhitespace(word_paragraph.Range.Text), _
                    2)

            Case "Normal"
                ' If there's no Section yet, make one with a blank Title.
                If section_element Is Nothing Then
                    Set section_element = MakeSection( _
                        dom_document, _
                        article_element, _
                        StripWhitespace(word_paragraph.Range.Text), _
                        2)
                End If

                ' Make a new Paragraph element.
                Set paragraph_element = MakeParagraph( _
                    dom_document, _
                    section_element, _
                    StripWhitespace(word_paragraph.Range.Text), _
```

```
                    4)
            End Select
        Next word_paragraph


        ' Save the DOM document.
        dom_document.Save xml_file_name
        Set dom_document = Nothing
    End Sub


    ' Make an Article with the indicated Title.
    ' Return the new Article element.
    Private Function MakeArticle( _
      ByVal dom_document As DOMDocument, _
      ByVal parent As Object, ByVal title As String) As IXMLDOMElement

        Dim article_element As IXMLDOMElement

        ' Make the Article element.
        Set article_element = dom_document.createElement("Article")
        parent.appendChild article_element
        article_element.setAttribute "Title", title

        ' Start a new line inside the Article element.
        article_element.appendChild dom_document.createTextNode(vbCrLf)

        ' Return the new Article element.
        Set MakeArticle = article_element
    End Function


    ' Make a Section with the indicated Title.
    ' Return the new Section element.
    Private Function MakeSection( _
      ByVal dom_document As DOMDocument, _
      ByVal article_element As IXMLDOMElement, _
      ByVal title As String, ByVal indent_level As Integer) As
    IXMLDOMElement

        Dim section_element As IXMLDOMElement

        ' Indent.
        article_element.appendChild _
            dom_document.createTextNode(Space$(indent_level))

        ' Make a new Section element.
        Set section_element = dom_document.createElement("Section")
        article_element.appendChild section_element
        section_element.setAttribute "Title", StripWhitespace(title)

        ' Start a new line inside the Section element.
        section_element.appendChild dom_document.createTextNode( _
            vbCrLf & Space$(indent_level))
```

```
    ' Add a new line after the </Section>.
    article_element.appendChild dom_document.createTextNode(vbCrLf)

    ' Return the new Section element.
    Set MakeSection = section_element
End Function

' Make a Paragraph with the indicated text.
' Return the new Paragraph element.
Private Function MakeParagraph( _
  ByVal dom_document As DOMDocument, _
  ByVal parent As IXMLDOMElement, _
  ByVal text_value As String, ByVal indent_level As Integer) _
    As IXMLDOMElement

    Dim paragraph_element As IXMLDOMElement

    ' Make sure there's something here.
    If Len(text_value) = 0 Then Exit Function

    ' Indent.
    parent.appendChild dom_document.createTextNode(Space$(2))

    ' Make a new Paragraph element.
    Set paragraph_element = dom_document.createElement("P")
    parent.appendChild paragraph_element

    ' Start a new line inside the Paragraph element.
    paragraph_element.appendChild dom_document.createTextNode(vbCrLf)

    ' Make the paragraph text element.
    MakeParagraphText dom_document, paragraph_element, _
        text_value, indent_level + 2

    ' Indent the </P> tag.
    paragraph_element.appendChild _
        dom_document.createTextNode(Space$(indent_level))

    ' Add a new line after the </P>.
    parent.appendChild dom_document.createTextNode( _
        vbCrLf & Space$(indent_level - 2))

    ' Return the new Paragraph element.
    Set MakeParagraph = paragraph_element
End Function

' Make a new TextNode.
' Return the new node.
Private Function MakeParagraphText( _
  ByVal dom_document As DOMDocument, _
  ByVal parent As IXMLDOMElement, _
```

```
      ByVal text_value As String, ByVal indent_level As Integer) _
        As IXMLDOMElement

      Dim text_node As IXMLDOMText

      ' Indent.
      parent.appendChild dom_document.createTextNode(Space$(indent_level))

      ' Create the TextNode.
      Set text_node = dom_document.createTextNode(text_value)
      parent.appendChild text_node

      ' Add a new line after the text.
      parent.appendChild dom_document.createTextNode(vbCrLf)
  End Function
```

This example provides for only three text styles: Heading 1, Heading 2, and Normal. A real article might include several other customized styles such as ByLine, Code, Figure Caption, Table, and so forth. You can modify the code to handle these and the other custom styles you need for your particular application.

Excel

Because Microsoft Excel displays spreadsheets, it is naturally designed to work with table-like data. That makes it a little easier to move table-like XML data in and out of Excel than Word. The following sections use XML data with the following format.

```
<?xml version="1.0"?>
<Books>
  <Book>
    <BookInfo>Title</BookInfo>
    <BookInfo>Price</BookInfo>
    <BookInfo>Pages</BookInfo>
    <BookInfo>URL</BookInfo>
    <BookInfo>Image</BookInfo>
  </Book>
  <Book>
    <BookInfo>Ready-to-Run Visual Basic Algorithms</BookInfo>
    <BookInfo>$39.99</BookInfo>
    <BookInfo>395</BookInfo>
    <BookInfo>http://www.vb-helper.com/vba.htm</BookInfo>
    <BookInfo>http://www.vb-helper.com/vba.gif</BookInfo>
  </Book>
  ... More rows ...
</Books>
```

Example program XmlExcel, shown in Figure 9.4, pulls and pushes data between Excel and XML documents. Click the left button to make the program copy Excel data into an XML file. Click the right button to make the program copy the data into an Excel worksheet.

Figure 9.4   Program XmlExcel pulls and pushes data between Excel and XML documents.

The next two sections describe the code behind program XmlExcel. The two sections after that explain VBA code that performs the same translations. The VBA code is contained in the file XmlExcel.bas in the XmlExcel program's project directory.

The XmlExcel example program declares a private Excel application server outside of its subroutines so all of the subroutines can use the same server object. When the program starts, the main form's Load event handler initializes the Excel server, as shown in the following code. This may take a few seconds now but saves time later. When the program's subroutines need to use the server, it is already running so the program doesn't need to wait at that point.

```
' The Excel server we use to manipulate Excel.
Private m_ExcelServer As Excel.Application

Private Sub Form1_Load( _
  ByVal sender As System.Object, _
  ByVal e As System.EventArgs) Handles MyBase.Load

    lblXmlFile.Text = DataSubdirectory() & "\Table.xml"
    lblExcelFile.Text = DataSubdirectory() & "\Table.xls"

    ' Open the Excel server now so we don't have to wait
    ' to open it when the user clicks a button.
    m_ExcelServer = New Excel.Application()
End Sub
```

When the program closes, the form's Closing event handler closes the Excel server, as shown in the following code.

```
' Close the Excel server.
Private Sub Form1_Closing( _
  ByVal sender As Object, _
  ByVal e As System.ComponentModel.CancelEventArgs) _
  Handles MyBase.Closing

    m_ExcelServer.Quit()
    m_ExcelServer = Nothing
End Sub
```

The server must close normally using its Quit method. If you are debugging the program and you halt the application prematurely, the server will keep running invisibly.

If you halt the application several times like this, you may end up with several Excel servers running in the background and wasting your system's resources. You can stop these servers using the Task Manager, but it is better to not leave them running in the first place.

If you need to halt the XmlExcel program early, go to the development environment's Command Window and execute the m_ExcelServer.Quit() command manually before you stop the program.

Using Excel Servers

Before a Visual Basic application can use an Excel server, it needs a reference to the Excel object library. Start a new project. In the Solution Explorer, right-click on the References entry and select Add Reference. Move to the COM tab and find the entry labeled Microsoft Excel 9.0 Object Library. Double-click that entry to select it and then click OK. The environment will display a dialog box that says:

Could not find a primary interop assembly for the COM component 'Microsoft Excel 9.0 Object Library'. A primary interop assembly is not registered for this type library. Would you like to have a wrapper generated for you?

Click Yes to make the environment build .NET classes that support the library. Now you can use the library's objects and their methods in your application.

Visual Basic: Pulling Table Data

Program XmlExcel uses the TableExcelToXml subroutine, shown in the following code, to copy data from an Excel worksheet into an XML document. The subroutine starts by creating an XmlTextWriter, setting its Formatting property to produce an indented XML document, and writing the document's XML declaration. It then writes the <Books> start tag.

Next TableExcelToXml opens the Excel worksheet providing the data. It uses the worksheet's properties to find the rows and columns that contain data. It then iterates over each row. For each row, the routine writes a <Book> start tag and then iterates over the row's columns.

For each column, the subroutine writes a <BookInfo> start tag, the appropriate worksheet cell's text value, and a </BookInfo> tag closing the cell entry.

After it finishes writing the data for each cell in the row, the subroutine writes the </Book> tag closing the row. After it finishes writing all of the row data, the subroutine writes the </Books> tag closing the table.

Finally, the subroutine ends the XML document by calling the XmlTextWriter's WriteEndDocument method and closing the XmlTextWriter.

```
' Copy table-like Excel data into an XML file.
Private Sub TableExcelToXml(ByVal excel_file As String, ByVal xml_file
As String)
    Dim xml_text_writer As XmlTextWriter
    Dim cell_text As String
    Dim min_row As Integer
```

```
Dim max_row As Integer
Dim min_col As Integer
Dim max_col As Integer
Dim r As Integer
Dim c As Integer

' Create the XmlTextWriter.
xml_text_writer = New XmlTextWriter( _
    xml_file, Encoding.UTF8)
xml_text_writer.Formatting = Formatting.Indented
xml_text_writer.Indentation = 2
xml_text_writer.IndentChar = " "

' Start the document.
xml_text_writer.WriteStartDocument(True)

' Start the Books element.
xml_text_writer.WriteStartElement("Books")

With m_ExcelServer
    ' Open the Excel document.
    .Workbooks.Open( _
        FileName:=excel_file, _
        ReadOnly:=True, _
        AddToMru:=False)

    ' Find the nonblank rows and columns.
    min_row = .ActiveSheet.UsedRange.Rows.Row
    max_row = min_row + .ActiveSheet.UsedRange.Rows.Count - 1
    min_col = .ActiveSheet.UsedRange.Columns.Column
    max_col = min_col + .ActiveSheet.UsedRange.Columns.Count - 1

    ' Write the rows.
    For r = min_row To max_row
        ' Start the Book element.
        xml_text_writer.WriteStartElement("Book")

        For c = min_row To max_row
            ' Start the BookInfo element.
            xml_text_writer.WriteStartElement("BookInfo")

            ' Add the cell's text.
            xml_text_writer.WriteString( _
                .ActiveSheet.Cells(r, c).Text)

            ' End the BookInfo element.
            xml_text_writer.WriteEndElement()
        Next c

        ' End the Book element.
        xml_text_writer.WriteEndElement()
```

```
        Next r
    End With


    ' End the Books element.
    xml_text_writer.WriteEndElement()

    ' Save the XML document.
    xml_text_writer.WriteEndDocument()
    xml_text_writer.Close()
End Sub
```

Subroutine TableExcelToXml assumes the data stored in the Excel worksheet is arranged in normal rows and columns. If some of the worksheet's cells have been merged, the XML data will translate the merged cells into a single entry in the resulting XML document. It's not worth complicating this simple example to handle such things, but you could modify the code to deal with merged cells, cell formatting, and other issues for a particular application.

Visual Basic: Pushing Table Data

Program XmlExcel uses the TableXmlToExcel subroutine, shown in the following code, to copy XML data into an Excel document. The routine begins by opening the XML document and locating its Books element. It then uses the Excel server to create a new worksheet.

Next, the subroutine iterates over the children of the Books node in the XML document. Those nodes are the Book elements representing the table's rows.

For each row node, the subroutine iterates over the node's children. These nodes are the BookInfo nodes that make up the row's cells. For each of the cell nodes, the subroutine writes the node's InnerText value into the Excel worksheet.

After it has finished writing all of the data into the worksheet, the subroutine selects the newly entered cells. It uses Excel's AutoFit method to make the columns containing the data fit themselves to the new values. The subroutine then puts a thick border around the cells and finishes by saving and closing the Excel workbook.

```
' Copy table-like XML data into a Excel file.
Private Sub TableXmlToExcel(ByVal xml_file As String, ByVal excel_file
As String)
    Dim xml_document As XmlDocument
    Dim table_node As XmlNode
    Dim row_node As XmlNode
    Dim column_node As XmlNode
    Dim r As Integer
    Dim c As Integer

    ' Open the XML document.
    xml_document = New XmlDocument()
    xml_document.Load(xml_file)

    ' Get the Books node.
```

```
table_node = xml_document.DocumentElement

With m_ExcelServer
    ' Open a new worksheet.
    .Workbooks.Add()

    ' Enter the data.
    r = 1
    For Each row_node In table_node.ChildNodes
        c = 1
        For Each column_node In row_node.ChildNodes
            .ActiveSheet.Cells(r, c) = column_node.InnerText
            c = c + 1
        Next column_node
        r = r + 1
    Next row_node

    ' Autofit the new cells.
    .ActiveSheet.Range( _
        .ActiveSheet.Cells(1, 1).Address & ":" & _
        .ActiveSheet.Cells(r - 1, c - 1).Address).Select()
    .Selection.Columns.AutoFit()

    ' Give the new cells a border.
    With .Selection.Borders(xlEdgeLeft)
        .LineStyle = xlContinuous
        .Weight = xlThick
        .ColorIndex = xlAutomatic
    End With
    With .Selection.Borders(xlEdgeTop)
        .LineStyle = xlContinuous
        .Weight = xlThick
        .ColorIndex = xlAutomatic
    End With
    With .Selection.Borders(xlEdgeBottom)
        .LineStyle = xlContinuous
        .Weight = xlThick
        .ColorIndex = xlAutomatic
    End With
    With .Selection.Borders(xlEdgeRight)
        .LineStyle = xlContinuous
        .Weight = xlThick
        .ColorIndex = xlAutomatic
    End With

    ' Save the workbook.
    .ActiveWorkbook.SaveAs( _
        Filename:=excel_file, _
        FileFormat:=xlNormal, _
        Password:="", _
        WriteResPassword:="", _
```

```
                    ReadOnlyRecommended:=False, _
                    CreateBackup:=False)

            ' Close the workbook.
            .ActiveWorkbook.Close()
        End With
    End Sub
```

Subroutine TableXmlToExcel positions the XML data in the upper left corner of the Excel worksheet. You could position the data elsewhere and perform other formatting functions, but the real intent of this routine is to move the XML data into an Excel format that you can then modify using Excel.

Excel: Pulling Table Data

VBA subroutine LoadXmlTable, shown in the following code, loads table data from an XML file into an Excel spreadsheet. The subroutine creates a new DOMDocument object from the MSXML library. It uses the DOMDocument's Load method to load the XML file and finds the XML document's Books node.

The routine then finds the row and column of the current Excel worksheet's active cell. This is the currently selected cell and marks the position where the routine will place the XML data.

The subroutine then loops through each of the Books node's children. Those nodes are the XML document's Book elements representing table rows.

For each table row, the subroutine loops through the row node's children. Those nodes are the BookInfo elements representing table data. The subroutine copies the BookInfo node's text into the correct Excel cell.

After it has finished copying the XML data into the worksheet, the subroutine performs two formatting tasks. First, it selects the newly entered cells and calls the AutoFit method for their columns. That makes Excel resize their columns to fit the data.

Second, the subroutine places a thick border around the updated cells. The previous step already selected the cells so in this step the subroutine can work with the current selection.

```
' Load the data in the XML document into a Word table
' in the currently active spreadsheet.
Sub LoadXmlTable(ByVal xml_file_name As String)
    Dim dom_document As DOMDocument
    Dim table_node As IXMLDOMNode
    Dim row_node As IXMLDOMNode
    Dim column_node As IXMLDOMNode
    Dim r As Integer
    Dim c As Integer
    Dim origin_row As Integer
    Dim origin_col As Integer

    ' Load the XML file into a DOM representation.
    Set dom_document = New DOMDocument
    dom_document.Load xml_file_name
```

```
' Get the Books node.
Set table_node = dom_document.documentElement

' Find the current cell's location in the workbook.
origin_row = ActiveCell.Row
origin_col = ActiveCell.Column

' Enter the data into the active workbook.
r = 0
For Each row_node In table_node.childNodes
    c = 0
    For Each column_node In row_node.childNodes
        ActiveSheet.Cells(origin_row + r, origin_col + c) = _
            column_node.Text
        c = c + 1
    Next column_node
    r = r + 1
Next row_node

' Autofit the new cells.
ActiveSheet.Range( _
    ActiveSheet.Cells(origin_row, origin_col).Address & ":" & _
    ActiveSheet.Cells(origin_row + r - 1, _
        origin_col + c - 1).Address).Select
Selection.Columns.AutoFit

' Give the new cells a border.
With Selection.Borders(xlEdgeLeft)
    .LineStyle = xlContinuous
    .Weight = xlThick
    .ColorIndex = xlAutomatic
End With
With Selection.Borders(xlEdgeTop)
    .LineStyle = xlContinuous
    .Weight = xlThick
    .ColorIndex = xlAutomatic
End With
With Selection.Borders(xlEdgeBottom)
    .LineStyle = xlContinuous
    .Weight = xlThick
    .ColorIndex = xlAutomatic
End With
With Selection.Borders(xlEdgeRight)
    .LineStyle = xlContinuous
    .Weight = xlThick
    .ColorIndex = xlAutomatic
End With
End Sub
```

Figure 9.5 shows the resulting Excel worksheet. In this example, focus was on the cell B2 when the subroutine began execution so the resulting data begins there.

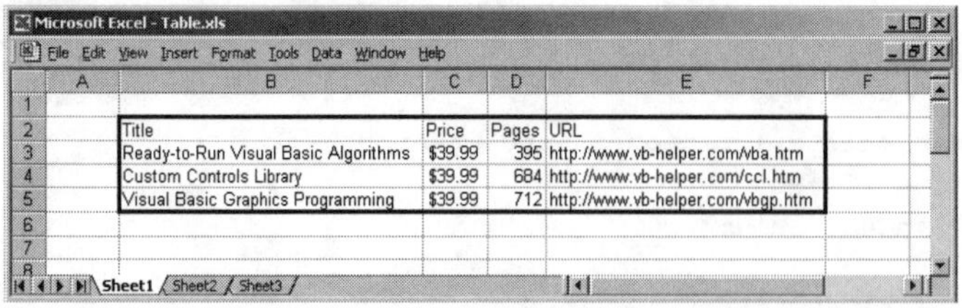

Figure 9.5 VBA subroutine LoadXmlTable copied this data from an XML document.

Excel: Pushing Table Data

VBA subroutine SaveXmlTable, shown in the following code, saves Excel data in an XML document. It begins by creating a new DOMDocument object and creating the document's Books element.

The subroutine then determines the first and last row and column currently selected in the active Excel worksheet. For each selected row, SaveXmlTable creates a Book element. For each cell in the row, the routine adds a BookInfo element to the row element.

After it has finished adding all of the cell data to the XML document, the subroutine saves the resulting document.

```
' Save the currently selected table in an XML file.
Sub SaveXmlTable(ByVal xml_file_name As String)
    Dim dom_document As DOMDocument
    Dim processing_instruction As IXMLDOMProcessingInstruction
    Dim table_element As IXMLDOMElement
    Dim row_element As IXMLDOMElement
    Dim cell_element As IXMLDOMElement
    Dim min_row As Integer
    Dim max_row As Integer
    Dim min_col As Integer
    Dim max_col As Integer
    Dim r As Integer
    Dim c As Integer

    ' Create the new DOM document.
    Set dom_document = New DOMDocument
    Set processing_instruction = _
        dom_document.createProcessingInstruction("xml", "version='1.0'")
    dom_document.appendChild processing_instruction

    ' Write the Books element.
    Set table_element = dom_document.createElement("Books")
    dom_document.appendChild table_element

    ' Find the rows and columns we need to process.
    min_row = Selection.Row
```

```
        max_row = min_row + Selection.Rows.Count - 1
        min_col = Selection.Column
        max_col = min_col + Selection.Columns.Count - 1

        ' Write the rows.
        For r = min_row To max_row
            ' Indent.
            table_element.appendChild _
                dom_document.createTextNode(vbCrLf & "    ")

            ' Create the Book element.
            Set row_element = dom_document.createElement("Book")
            table_element.appendChild row_element

            ' Write this row's columns.
            For c = min_col To max_col
                ' Indent.
                row_element.appendChild _
                    dom_document.createTextNode(vbCrLf & "        ")

                ' Create the BookInfo element.
                Set cell_element = dom_document.createElement("BookInfo")
                row_element.appendChild cell_element

                ' Add the cell's text.
                cell_element.appendChild _
                    dom_document.createTextNode(ActiveSheet.Cells(r,
c).Text)
            Next c

            ' Indent before the </Book> tag.
            row_element.appendChild _
                dom_document.createTextNode(vbCrLf & "    ")
        Next r

        ' New line before the </Books> tag.
        table_element.appendChild dom_document.createTextNode(vbCrLf)

        ' Save the DOM document.
        dom_document.Save xml_file_name
        Set dom_document = Nothing
    End Sub
```

Access

Microsoft Access is a database management tool. Visual Basic has many tools for working with Access databases so its relationship is a bit different from its relationship with
other Microsoft Office products such as Word and Excel.

For instance, there is little need to write Visual Basic subroutines that load XML data and write it into an Access database. DataSet objects, which represent the results of database queries in Visual Basic .NET, provide methods for loading and saving data in both Access databases and XML documents.

The following two sections explain how you can use Visual Basic's DataSet object to move data between XML files and Access databases. The two sections after that show how you can write VBA programs in Access that read an XML file, use its structure to create new database tables, and fill those tables with the XML file's data.

Access to XML with Visual Basic

Program XmlAccess, shown in Figure 9.6, moves data between an Access database and an XML document. Click the left button to copy data from the database's Books table into an XML file. Click the right button to copy the XML file's data into the database.

Program XmlAccess uses the TableXbToXml subroutine, shown in the following code, to copy data from the Access database to the XML file. The subroutine starts by composing a connect string to tell the system how to connect to the database. This example uses the Jet OLEDB engine to connect to an Access database. For other databases, such as those provided by SQL server, Oracle, or Informix, the program would follow similar steps but use a different connect string.

The program creates an OleDbConnection object and uses the connect string to open the database. Next it creates an OleDbCommand object that selects all of the records from the database's Books table, ordering them by the Title field. It connects this OleDbCommand to an OleDbDataAdapter object so the OleDbDataAdapter knows what data it will manipulate.

The subroutine then adds a new entry to the OleDbDataAdapter's TableMappings collection to tell the adapter that it should map the Access result named Table to a DataSet table named Books. Without this step, the OleDbCommand would create a DataSet containing data in a table named Table. When the program saved the DataSet into an XML file, it would create elements named Table instead of Books.

Next, the routine calls the OleDbDataAdapter's Fill method, passing it an empty DataSet object as a parameter. The adapter executes the command defined by its OleDbCommand object to fetch the data in the Books table. It names the result Books (instead of the default name Table) and loads the results into the DataSet.

The subroutine calls the DataSet's WriteXml method to write the data out into an XML file. It finishes by disposing of the data adapter and closing the database connection.

Figure 9.6 Program XmlAccess uses DataSet objects to move data between an Access database and an XML document.

```
' Copy Access data into an XML file.
Private Sub TableDbToXml( _
   ByVal db_file As String, ByVal xml_file As String)

    Dim connect_string As String
    Dim db_connection As OleDbConnection
    Dim data_adapter As New OleDbDataAdapter()
    Dim data_set As New DataSet()

    ' Compose the connect string.
    connect_string = _
        "Provider=Microsoft.Jet.OLEDB.4.0;" & _
        "Data Source=" & db_file

    ' Connect to the database.
    db_connection = New OleDbConnection(connect_string)
    db_connection.Open()

    Try
        ' Initialize the data adapter.
        data_adapter.SelectCommand = New OleDbCommand( _
            "SELECT * FROM Books ORDER BY Title", _
            db_connection)

        ' Tell the adapter to map the Access results Table
        ' to the DataSet table Books.
        data_adapter.TableMappings.Add("Table", "Books")

        ' Use the data adapter to fill the DataSet.
        data_adapter.Fill(data_set)

        ' Write the XML data.
        data_set.WriteXml(xml_file)

        data_adapter.Dispose()
    Finally
        ' Close the database connection.
        db_connection.Close()
    End Try
End Sub
```

The DataSet object's WriteXml method overwrites the XML file if it already exists so the result is an XML file containing exactly the same records as the database table. If you need to append the records to the XML file, you can load the XML file into a DataSet, as explained in the next section. Then you can load another DataSet with the table's data, merge the two DataSets, and write the merged results into the XML file.

These more advanced DataSet operations are a bit outside the scope of this book. For more information, consult a book on ADO.NET or consult the MSDN online help.

Subroutine TableDbToXml is relatively short. The objects it uses to move the data from the database to the XML file do a lot of work behind the scenes, but once you figure out which objects to use the subroutine itself is simple.

XML to Access with Visual Basic

Moving data from an XML file to an Access file using Visual Basic is just as easy as moving data the other way. Program XmlAccess uses the TableXmlToDb subroutine, shown in the following code, to load data from an XML file into a database.

The subroutine begins by creating a new OleDbCommandBuilder object and attaching it to its data adapter. This allows the data adapter to automatically create SQL commands to modify the database table. In this case, the data adapter uses the command builder to generate INSERT statements to add the XML data to the database table.

Then, like the subroutine described in the previous section, TableXmlToDb composes a database connect string and connects to the database. It also creates an OldDb-Command object that defines the selection of records from the database much as the previous subroutine does. This subroutine does not actually invoke the command; it just uses the command to tell the data adapter the format of the data it will manipulate.

As before, the subroutine adds an entry to the data adapter's TableMappings collection to map the default name Table to the database table's name Books.

Now the subroutine uses an empty DataSet's ReadXml method to load the XML file's data into the DataSet. It then calls the data adapter's Update method, passing it the DataSet. This makes the data adapter insert the values in the DataSet into the database table. The Update method returns the number of records it affects. The subroutine displays a message box telling the user the number of records added.

The subroutine finishes by disposing of the data adapter and closing the database connection.

```
' Copy table-like XML data into an Access database.
Private Sub TableXmlToDb( _
  ByVal xml_file As String, ByVal db_file As String)

    Dim connect_string As String
    Dim db_connection As OleDbConnection
    Dim data_adapter As New OleDbDataAdapter()
    Dim command_builder As OleDbCommandBuilder
    Dim data_set As New DataSet()

    ' Give the data adapter a command builder so it can
    ' automatically create INSERT commands.
    command_builder = New OleDbCommandBuilder(data_adapter)

    ' Compose the connect string.
    connect_string = _
        "Provider=Microsoft.Jet.OLEDB.4.0;" & _
        "Data Source=" & db_file

    ' Connect to the database.
    db_connection = New OleDbConnection(connect_string)
    db_connection.Open()

    Try
        ' Initialize the data adapter.
```

```
        data_adapter.SelectCommand = New OleDbCommand( _
            "SELECT * FROM Books ORDER BY Title", _
            db_connection)

        ' Tell the adapter to map the Access results Table
        ' to the DataSet table Books.
        data_adapter.TableMappings.Add("Table", "Books")

        ' Load the DataSet.
        data_set.ReadXml(xml_file)

        ' Update the data.
        MsgBox("Loaded " & _
            data_adapter.Update(data_set) & " records.", _
            MsgBoxStyle.Information Or MsgBoxStyle.OKOnly, _
            "Ok")

        data_adapter.Dispose()
    Finally
        ' Close the database connection.
        db_connection.Close()
    End Try
End Sub
```

This code adds the data in the XML file to the database table. If you call this routine again with the same XML file, you will create duplicate records in the database (assuming the table allows duplicates).

Building a Table from XML with Access

One of the more important uses for XML is making data available to many different kinds of applications on different hardware platforms. For example, if a company legacy system saves its customer data into an XML file, you can load that data into Access for analysis.

The following VBA code shows how you can load XML data into an Access database. In addition to the MSXML library used by the other Microsoft Office examples in this chapter, this example also uses the DAO object library. In Access, start the Visual Basic macro editor. Open the Tools menu and select References. Check the box next to the Microsoft DAO 3.6 Object Library (your version number may vary) and click OK. Now your VBA subroutines can use the objects this library provides to create and modify database tables.

This example loads an XML file with the following structure.

```
<?xml version="1.0" standalone="yes"?>
<BookData>
  <Books>
    <Title>Custom Controls Library</Title>
    <URL>http://www.vb-helper.com/ccl.htm</URL>
```

```
    <Image>http://www.vb-helper.com/ccl.gif</Image>
    <Price>$39.99</Price>
    <Pages>684</Pages>
  </Books>
  ... More Books records ...
</BookData>
```

The code loads the XML data and analyzes its structure to determine the name of the record elements (in this example Books). It creates a new database table with that name. It gives the new table database fields for each of the XML elements contained in the record element. Then it copies the XML data into the new table.

Subroutine TestBuildAccessTableFromXml uses the DOMDocument object provided by the MSXML library to load the XML data. It then calls subroutine Build-AccessTableFromXml, passing it the XML document's root node. In the previous XML file, that node is the BookData element.

Subroutine BuildAccessTableFromXml builds a new database table for the XML data starting at the node it receives as a parameter. Before it can build the table, the subroutine needs to know how big to make each of the table's fields. To find the field lengths, the subroutine loops through the XML data and determines the size of the biggest field of each type of element.

The routine begins by assigning the variable record_node to the first child of the table's root node. That makes record_node point to the table's first record element. It determines the number of children this record node has, in order to learn the number of fields it must create in the new database table. The program sets the dimensions of the field_length array so that it has room to hold field lengths for each field and initializes all of its values to a minimum field length.

Next, the subroutine loops through all of the record elements. For each record element, the subroutine loops through the record's field elements. For each field, the routine updates the corresponding field_length value. When it has finished, field_length holds the length of the largest piece of data for each field.

Now BuildAccessTableFromXml creates a new DAO TableDef object to represent the new database table it will create. It gives the table the same name as the table's root XML element (in this example Books).

Again the routine loops through the fields in a record element. For each field, the subroutine creates a new Field object to represent that field in the new table. It gives the field the text data type and assigns it the length it calculated earlier for this field. After it has defined the field, the subroutine appends the field information to the new TableDef.

When it has defined all of the table's fields, the subroutine appends the TableDef to the current database's TableDefs collection to create the new table. At this point the table is ready to receive data.

The subroutine opens the table using a Recordset object. It then loops through the table's record elements one last time. For each record, the routine calls the Recordset's AddNew method to start a new record. It loops through the record's field elements, adding their values to the Recordset's fields, and calls the Recordset's Update method to add the new record to the table.

```
' Make a table named after the XML document's root node
' with fields given by its children.
Sub TestBuildAccessTableFromXml()
    Dim dom_document As DOMDocument

        ' Open the XML document.
    Set dom_document = New DOMDocument
    dom_document.Load "C:\VB XML\Src\Ch10\Books.xml"

        ' Make the table using the root node.
    BuildAccessTableFromXml dom_document.documentElement, 40

        ' Close the XML document.
    Set dom_document = Nothing
End Sub


' Make a table named after the given XML node with fields
' given by its children. Fields are VARCHARs with lengths
' big enough to hold the data or a minimum of min_field_length.
' This routine requires a reference to the DAO object library.
Private Sub BuildAccessTableFromXml( _
  ByVal table_node As IXMLDOMNode, _
  Optional ByVal min_field_length As Integer = 100)

    Dim record_node As IXMLDOMNode
    Dim field_node As IXMLDOMNode
    Dim num_fields As Integer
    Dim field_num As Integer
    Dim field_length() As Integer
    Dim new_table As DAO.TableDef
    Dim new_field As DAO.Field
    Dim rs As DAO.Recordset

        ' See how many fields the table will have.
    Set record_node = table_node.childNodes(1)
    num_fields = record_node.childNodes.length
    ReDim field_length(0 To num_fields - 1)

        ' Initialize the minimum field lengths.
    For field_num = 0 To num_fields - 1
        field_length(field_num) = min_field_length
    Next field_num

        ' Find the maximum field lengths.
    For field_num = 0 To num_fields - 1
        Set field_node = record_node.childNodes(field_num)
        If field_length(field_num) < Len(field_node.Text) Then
            field_length(field_num) = Len(field_node.Text)
        End If
    Next field_num
```

```
        ' Prepare to create the table.
        Set new_table = CurrentDb.CreateTableDef(table_node.nodeName)

        ' Create the fields.
        For field_num = 0 To num_fields - 1
            Set field_node = record_node.childNodes(field_num)
            Set new_field = new_table.CreateField(field_node.nodeName, _
                dbText, field_length(field_num))
            new_table.Fields.Append new_field
        Next field_num

        ' Create the table.
        CurrentDb.TableDefs.Append new_table

        ' Connect to the new table.
        Set rs = CurrentDb.OpenRecordset(table_node.nodeName, dbOpenTable, _
            dbAppendOnly)

        ' Load the data into the table.
        For Each record_node In table_node.childNodes
            ' Load this record.
            rs.AddNew

            ' Load the fields.
            For field_num = 0 To num_fields - 1
                Set field_node = record_node.childNodes(field_num)
                rs.Fields(field_num).Value = field_node.Text
            Next field_num

            ' Save the new record.
            rs.Update
        Next record_node

        ' Close the Recordset.
        rs.Close
        Set rs = Nothing
    End Sub
```

This subroutine makes all of the new table's fields text fields with lengths large enough to hold the longest item in each field. You could add attributes to the XML fields indicating their data types and lengths, as shown in the following XML code.

```
...
<Books>
  <Title Type="Text" Length="80">Custom Controls Library</Title>
  <URL Type="Text" Length="80">http://www.vb-helper.com/ccl.htm</URL>
  <Image Type="Text" Length="80">http://www.vb-
helper.com/ccl.gif</Image>
  <Price Type="Single">$39.99</Price>
  <Pages Type="Integer">684</Pages>
</Books>
...
```

Alternatively you could load field type information from a schema. This example is already complicated enough, however.

Building Multiple Tables from XML with Access

Once you have written the BuildAccessTableFromXml subroutine described in the previous section, you can call that subroutine more than once to create multiple tables. This example reads an XML file with the following format.

```xml
<?xml version="1.0"?>
<Stuff>
    <Books>
        <Book>
            <Title>Ready-to-Run Visual Basic Algorithms</Title>
            <URL>http://www.vb-helper.com/vba.htm</URL>
            <Image>http://www.vb-helper.com/vba.gif</Image>
            <Price>$39.99</Price>
            <Pages>395</Pages>
        </Book>
        ... More Book records ...
    </Books>
    <Cars>
        <Car>
            <Make>Subaru</Make>
            <Model>Legacy</Model>
            <ModelYear>1998</ModelYear>
            <Miles>32012</Miles>
        </Car>
        ... More Car records ...
    </Cars>
    .... More tables ...
</Stuff>
```

The routine creates new database tables for each of the XML file's second-level nodes: Books, Cars, and so forth. It then loads the XML data in each of those nodes into the new tables.

The TestBuildManyAccessTablesFromXml subroutine, shown in the following code, opens an XML document and passes its root node to the BuildManyAccessTables-FromXml subroutine.

BuildManyAccessTablesFromXml loops through the root node's children, calling the BuildAccessTableFromXml subroutine for each. BuildAccessTableFromXml performs all of the interesting work.

```vb
' Make tables for each of the document node's children.
Sub TestBuildManyAccessTablesFromXml()
    Dim dom_document As DOMDocument
```

```
        ' Open the XML document.
        Set dom_document = New DOMDocument
        dom_document.Load "C:\VB XML\Src\Ch10\Stuff.xml"

        ' Make the tables.
        BuildManyAccessTablesFromXml dom_document.documentElement, 40

        ' Close the XML document.
        Set dom_document = Nothing
    End Sub

' Make tables for each of the document node's children.
Sub BuildManyAccessTablesFromXml( _
  ByVal document_node As IXMLDOMNode, _
  Optional ByVal min_field_length As Integer = 100)

    Dim table_node As IXMLDOMNode

    ' Make the tables.
    For Each table_node In document_node.childNodes
        BuildAccessTableFromXml table_node, min_field_length
    Next table_node
End Sub
```

Depending on your particular data, you could use similar techniques to build much more complex table structures. For example, suppose you have an XML file containing customer data that has fields giving the customers' names, addresses, and phone numbers. The previous examples show how you could pull this data into a new Customers table. Alternatively, you could write subroutines to generate two different tables, Customers and Addresses, that use a new AddressId field to link the two tables. The routines could use the index of the record elements in the XML file for the AddressId value.

Routines that build these sorts of relations are not hard to write. They make sense only in the context of a specific application, however, so this chapter doesn't include any detailed examples.

Outlook

Microsoft Outlook is more than a mail application. It also allows you to track contacts, track appointments, schedule meetings, organize to-do lists, keep notes, and a lot more. How XML might help you with all of these features depends on your particular application. One scenario that may be particularly common, however, is importing an address list into Outlook.

This example reads an XML file of the following format. Each record element in the file contains contact information for a person. It could contain a lot of other fields as well. For example, if the XML file contains a customer database, it might include company name, customer and company addresses, lists of purchases, and so forth. This example ignores any fields other than FirstName, LastName, HomePage, and EmailAddress.

```
<?xml version="1.0" standalone="yes"?>
<Addresses>
  <Entry>
    <FirstName>Rod</FirstName>
    <LastName>Stephens</LastName>
    <HomePage>http://www.vb-helper.com</HomePage>
    <EmailAddress>RodStephens@vb-helper.com</EmailAddress>
  </Entry>
  <Entry>
    <FirstName>Brian</FirstName>
    <LastName>Hochgurtel</LastName>
    <HomePage>http://www.advocatemedia.com</HomePage>
    <EmailAddress>brian@advocatemedia.com</EmailAddress>
  </Entry>
</Addresses>
```

This example uses the XML data to create entries in the Outlook contact database. You can use your contacts list to send emails, schedule meetings, keep track of addresses and phone numbers, track personal information such as birthdays and anniversaries, and even make Outlook dial phone numbers for you.

Subroutine ImportAddresses, shown in the following code, reads this XML file and creates Outlook contact entries for each Entry element. It begins by creating a DOM-Document object and using it to read the XML file. It loops through the record elements that are the children of the document's root node.

For each Entry element, the routine creates a new ContactItem object. It then loops through the field elements that are children of the record element. It checks the names of the field elements looking for the fields it wants. When the subroutine finds an XML node with a name it recognizes, it saves the node's text value in the appropriate ContactItem field. The subroutine ignores any field with a name it doesn't recognize.

After it has examined and stored all of the Entry element's field values, the routine calls the ContactItem's Save method to save the new values.

```
' Import the address information from this XML file.
Sub ImportAddresses(ByVal xml_file As String)
Dim dom_document As DOMDocument
Dim root_node As IXMLDOMNode
Dim entry_node As IXMLDOMNode
Dim field_node As IXMLDOMNode
Dim contact_item As Outlook.ContactItem

    ' Load the XML file.
    Set dom_document = New DOMDocument
    dom_document.Load xml_file

    ' Loop through the Entry elements.
    Set root_node = dom_document.documentElement
    For Each entry_node In root_node.childNodes
        ' Create a new address book entry.
        Set contact_item = Outlook.CreateItem(olContactItem)
```

```
' Loop through the field elements.
For Each field_node In entry_node.childNodes
    ' See which field this is.
    Select Case field_node.nodeName
        Case "LastName"
            contact_item.LastName = field_node.Text
        Case "FirstName"
            contact_item.FirstName = field_node.Text
        Case "HomePage"
            contact_item.WebPage = field_node.Text
        Case "EmailAddress"
            contact_item.Email1Address = field_node.Text
    End Select
Next field_node

    ' Save the contact information.
    contact_item.Save
Next entry_node
End Sub
```

Subroutine ImportAddresses looks for XML elements named FirstName, LastName, HomePage, and EmailAddress. It ignores any other fields it finds. Outlook's Contact-Item object has a huge number of fields including company information such as name, address, main phone number, and network name; assistant name, assistant telephone number, billing information, and callback phone number; home and business address, phone, fax, and homepage; personal information such as anniversary, birthday; spouse, children, car phone, and multiple email addresses; and much more. You could easily extend this example to look for other information in the XML file and store it in the appropriate ContactItem fields.

Conclusion

XML allows you to integrate widely differing applications. If one application exports data in XML format, other applications can load that data on widely scattered computers using different software, hardware, and operating systems.

Many Visual Basic programmers use Microsoft Office applications to build similarly integrated solutions. Using Visual Basic and VBA, you can tie Word, Excel, Access, and the other Office applications together to allow integrated data analysis and presentation. Adding XML to the equation makes these solutions even more powerful.

While Microsoft Office 2000's version of VBA does provide direct support for XML, you can easily add it using the MSXML library. Using XML, you can build Office applications that work not only with other Office applications, but also with any application that uses XML.

Internet Explorer

Microsoft had the foresight to build a lot of XML functionality into Internet Explorer (IE). While IE doesn't have all the functionality of Visual Basic .NET, it has enough capacity to be a useful tool during XML development. IE gets this capability from Microsoft's XML parser, msxml30.dll. This file is a *dynamic link library* (DLL) that can be called by any windows application including Internet Explorer.

The first part of this chapter describes the functionality that comes with IE 5.5 when you first install it. This functionality includes features that allow you to view XML, check well-formedness, and see if the syntax of a DTD (Document Type Definition) file is correct.

IE acts as a nonvalidating parser because it is not checking to see if the content of the XML document is correct according to the DTD. A plug-in available from Microsoft's Web site gives IE the ability to validate documents using DTD files and translate documents to another text-based format using XSL (eXtensible Stylesheet Language). These added features in IE let you avoid writing a program that calls the functionality that resides in msxml30.dll. You just use IE, a program that you probably already use frequently and that is easily available on your Windows desktop.

Built-in Capabilities

Internet Explorer has several handy features that help with the development of XML documents. The features that IE comes with are most often used to ensure that a document's syntax is correct and that the document is well formed. Chapter 1, "XML Overview," explains well-formed XML in detail. This functionality allows you to check your documents quickly and easily during development.

Viewing XML

To view an XML document, open IE and select the File menu's Open command. Click the Browse button and navigate to the directory that contains the XML file. This part is confusing because even though IE handles XML files, it does not list XML files as one of the file types it handles. To see XML files in the given directory, you have to select "All Files" as the file type. This will show all of the files in the directory including the XML file you want to open. Select the file and click Open in the file browsing dialog box. Then click the Open dialog box's OK button.

You don't need to restrict yourself to your local file system. IE will let you enter an XML document's path across the Internet or an intranet as well. For example, try opening the file www.vb-helper.com/XML/Ch10/Example01.xml. Figure 10.1 shows the Example01.xml document in Internet Explorer.

Notice that IE displays minus and plus signs next to the XML file's root and node elements. By clicking on these signs, you can expand or collapse the nodes to show or hide their child elements. This lets you easily view large XML documents.

If an XML file refers to a DTD file, IE will not display the DTD file; however, IE and the msxml routines do check the syntax of both.

You can view the file's raw source data by opening IE's View menu and invoking the Source command.

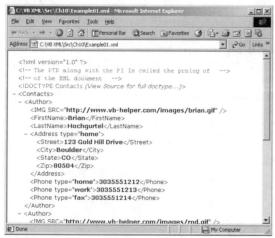

Figure 10.1 Internet Explorer can display XML documents.

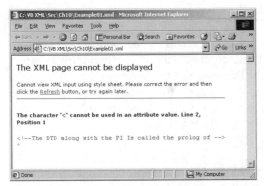

Figure 10.2   If Internet Explorer finds an error in an XML file, it tells you about it.

Checking Well-formedness and Syntax

If the syntax of your XML document isn't correct, IE will let you know about it. When IE loads an XML document, it calls classes and methods from msxml30.dll to check the syntax. If there is an error, IE displays an error message in the browser window. While these error messages can be cryptic and confusing, they do tell you where the error is occurring. For example, Figure 10.2 shows an error message for a malformed processing instruction. In this case, the closing quote in the document's XML declaration is missing.

The fact that the Processing Instruction is missing a closing quote is fairly obvious when you look at the code. Even if it wasn't obvious, IE displays the line number and position of the error, so you may not know what is causing the error, but at least you'll know where it is. Once you think you've corrected the mistake in your document, all you need to do is click IE's Refresh button to make it reload the document and check the syntax again.

Using DTD Files

Without installing a plug-in, IE cannot validate an XML document, although it will still check the DTD file's syntax. As you develop a DTD file, you can use the browser to see if the file's entity definitions are syntactically correct. If you wish to validate a document, you need to install the browser plug-in described in the following section.

Internet Explorer's XML Utility Plug-in

A plug-in is a small program that you can install to extend the functionality of a browser. Microsoft's XML Utility Plug-In allows IE to validate XML documents against a DTD file and use XSLT to translate XML into other text-based formats such as HTML. This plug-in is currently available from Microsoft's site at http://msdn.microsoft.com/downloads/default.asp?URL=/code/sample.asp?url=MSDNFILES/027/000/543msdncompositedoc.xml. Microsoft occasionally moves its links so the plug-in could move at some point. Check this book's Web page, www.vb-helper.com/xml.htm, for the latest location.

The installation of the plug-in is a little tricky because there isn't an installation program. Use Windows Explorer to navigate to the directory where the download wizard placed the files msxmlval.inf and msxmlvw.inf. Right-click on these files and select Install.

Validating with the XML Plug-in

If the XML document you are using has an associated DTD file, you can validate the document with Internet Explorer. Load the document in the browser window by either entering the document's URL or using the File menu's Open command.

For example, you can load the XML file shown in the following code by opening the URL www.vb-helper.com/XML/Ch10/Example01.xml. This document's prolog contains DTD code that defines the document's XML structure.

```
<?xml version="1.0"?>
<!-- The DTD along with the PI Is called the prolog -->
<!-- of the XML document. -->
<!DOCTYPE Contacts [
<!ELEMENT Contacts (Author+ )>
<!ELEMENT Author (IMG?,FirstName+, LastName+, Address+, Phone+)>
<!ELEMENT FirstName (#PCDATA ) >
<!ELEMENT LastName (#PCDATA )>
<!ELEMENT Address (Street+,City+, State+, Zip+ )>
<!ATTLIST Address type CDATA #REQUIRED>
<!ELEMENT City    (#PCDATA)>
<!ELEMENT Street (#PCDATA)>
<!ELEMENT State   (#PCDATA)>
<!ELEMENT Zip     (#PCDATA)>
<!ELEMENT Phone   (#PCDATA)>
<!ATTLIST Phone type CDATA #REQUIRED>
<!ELEMENT IMG EMPTY>
<!ATTLIST IMG SRC CDATA #REQUIRED>
]>
<Contacts>
  <Author>
    <IMG SRC="http://www.vb-helper.com/images/brian.gif"/>
    <FirstName>Brian</FirstName>
    <LastName>Hochgurtel</LastName>
    <Address type="home">
      <Street>123 Gold Hill Drive</Street>
      <City>Boulder</City>
      <State>CO</State>
      <Zip>80504</Zip>
    </Address>
    <Phone type="home">3035551212</Phone>
    <Phone type="work">3035551213</Phone>
    <Phone type="fax">3035551214</Phone>
  </Author>
  <Author>
    <IMG SRC="http://www.vb-helper.com/images/rod.gif"/>
    <FirstName>Rod</FirstName>
    <LastName>Stephens</LastName>
    <Address type="home">
      <Street>323 Nederland Place</Street>
      <City>Boulder</City>
```

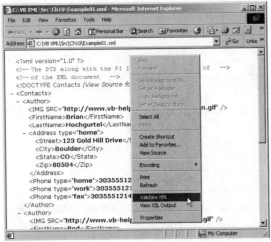

Figure 10.3 Right-click to make Internet Explorer validate an XML document.

```
        <State>CO</State>
        <Zip>80013</Zip>
      </Address>
      <Address type="work">
        <Street>869 Bug Blvd</Street>
        <City>Programmersville</City>
        <State>CO</State>
        <Zip>80808</Zip>
      </Address>
      <Phone type="home">3035551133</Phone>
      <Phone type="work">3035551144</Phone>
      <Phone type="fax">3035551155</Phone>
    </Author>
  </Contacts>
```

After you have the document in the browser, right-click on the document to display the menu shown in Figure 10.3. Be patient because it could take a second or two for the menu to load. Click on the Validate XML command near the bottom of the menu.

The dialog box shown in Figure 10.4 appears to tell you that the document follows the syntax required by its DTD file.

Figure 10.4 This message means the XML file is valid.

Figure 10.5 In this XML file, the Address tag is missing the required attribute "type."

If the XML document is not valid, the dialog box gives the line number that violated the DTD's rules. You can load the document at www.vb-helper.com/XML/Ch10/Example02.xml to see an example that is not valid. Figure 10.5 shows the browser displaying an error that is caused by having content that does not meet the requirements set in the DTD.

Fixing this error is easy because all that was left out was the attribute for address. Adding type="home" to the address element makes the error go away. See the previous example XML file for the address tag's requirements.

Transforming XML with the XML Plug-in

IE has the ability to transform XML documents using an XSLT file, but with IE versions 5.5 and below the parser, msxml.dll, does not handle standard transformations. This version of the parser was released before the XSL standard was complete so it does not handle all of the XSL described in Chapter 6, "XSL." The next version of IE Microsoft releases will probably have this problem fixed. If you currently have version 5.5 or lower of IE installed on your system, go to www.netcrucible.com/xslt/msxml-faq.htm to get information on making IE use the latest parser and XSLT specification.

After you install the latest version of the parser, IE can translate XML files. In your XML file, you must have the following *processing instructions* (PI) so that IE or any other parser or translation engine can find your XSL file.

```
<?xml version="1.0">
<?xml-stylesheet type="text/xsl" href="Example02.xsl" ?>
```

This code specifies the local fileExample02.xsl as the XSLT file that defines the translations. This could have just as easily been a file at a remote URI. With the plug-in installed, IE will instantly translate an XML file using the instructions in the associated XSLT file without forcing you to click on a menu command.

The following code transforms the XML document created in Chapter 1, "XML Overview," and displayed earlier in this chapter. Add the stylesheet command mentioned in the previous paragraph. Then use the following XSLT to display the information in HTML:

```
<?xml version="1.0"?>
<!--
Note that the first statement in an XSL file has to be the Processing
Instruction.

The stylesheet element is the root element of any XSL document, and it
sets up the namespace so we can use xsl directives.
-->
<xsl:stylesheet version="1.0"
    xmlns:xsl="http://www.w3.org/1999/XSL/Transform">


<!-- Execute the following code when the parser comes across the root
     element. -->
<xsl:template match="Contacts">
    <HTML>
        <HEAD>
            <TITLE>Translate Author Information</TITLE>
        </HEAD>
    <BODY>
        <B>Translated Author Information</B>
        <!-- Go to the XSL code that handles all the child elements of
             Author. -->
        <xsl:apply-templates select="Author"/>
    </BODY>
    </HTML>
</xsl:template>

    <!-- Process child elements of Author. -->
    <xsl:template match="Author">
      <P>
        <!-- Set up table to display data. -->
        <TABLE BORDER="1" CELLPADDING="1" CELLSPACING="1">
            <!-- Titles for each column in the table. -->
            <TR><TD><B>Element:</B></TD>
            <TD><B>Attribute:</B></TD>
            <TD><B>Value:</B></TD></TR>
            <!-- Loop through each child element of Author. -->
            <!-- Note only does one level of child elements.
                 Won't see child elements of the Address Element. -->
            <xsl:for-each select="*">
                <!-- Display the element's name. -->
                <TR><TD><xsl:value-of select="name()"/><BR/></TD>
                <!-- Display the element's attribute. -->
                <TD><xsl:value-of select="@type"/><BR/></TD>
                <!-- Display the element's value. -->
                <TD><xsl:value-of select="."/><BR/></TD></TR>
            </xsl:for-each>
        </TABLE>
      </P>
    </xsl:template>
</xsl:stylesheet>
```

If all goes well, your browser displays two HTML tables displaying all of the Author information. Figure 10.6 shows Internet Explorer displaying the translated XML as HTML.

When IE reads an XML file that has an associated XSLT file, IE picks apart the document. When it encounters elements identified in the XSLT file, it executes the XSLT code to process the data. The document is reassembled with a mix of HTML tags present in the XSLT file and XSLT directives to pull values and attributes from their elements. These values and attributes are then combined into HTML that is displayed by IE. Chapter 6, "XSL," has more to say about how specific XSL instructions work.

The file www.vb-helper.com/XML/Ch10/Example03.xml is an XML document that is translated if the plug-in is installed in your browser. If you open IE's View menu and select the Source command, you'll see the raw XML code. To view the HTML source code, right-click in the browser window and wait for the menu to appear. Select the View XSL Output command near the bottom of the menu to make IE display the HTML source code, as shown in Figure 10.7.

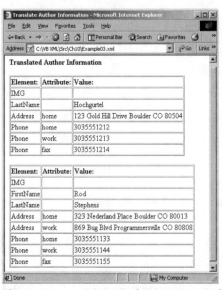

Figure 10.6 Internet Explorer automatically translates this XML file using its XSL stylesheet and displays the resulting HTML.

Figure 10.7 Internet Explorer can display HTML source code.

Conclusion

IE by itself cannot validate XML documents; however, it checks the syntax of the XML and any associated DTD and reports any errors. While the errors may be cryptic, they do report line numbers and positions to help identify where the problems lie. This makes IE a very useful tool during XML development.

If you install the Internet Explorer XML Utilities, IE will have the ability to validate XML documents that use DTDs. This may be helpful for checking the validity of older documents that still use a DTD. Schemas replace DTDs as a way of validating documents, and the .NET environment really focuses on them. There are plug-ins that support validating XML documents with schemas. The problem with these plug-ins is that they use an older schema standard that even Microsoft isn't supporting any more. Visit the book's Web site www.vb-helper.com/XML to see if new schema tools are available.

SQL Server 2000

Microsoft's enterprise database product, SQL Server 2000 (MSSQL), has the ability to return data in XML without using any scripting language. MSSQL integrates with Internet Information Services (IIS) as an Internet Server Application Program Interface (ISAPI) layer, and it allows direct access to data using HTTP. Each of these plays a role in displaying data to the end user with the XML functionality. MSSQL is a relational database that stores the data. Microsoft's Web server, IIS, handles browser requests and displays the end results. The ISAPI layer is the Dynamic Link Library (DLL) that IIS uses in order to communicate with MSSQL.

Microsoft's SQL Server 2000 and Internet Information Services products can work together to generate XML data without using any scripting language.

By itself, MSSQL is a powerful relational database that can store and manipulate large relational databases. It lets a program select records, sort them in various ways, insert, edit, and delete records, and perform all the other operations typically supported by a relational database.

IIS is a Web server engine that accepts browser requests and processes them. It can execute ActiveX Server Pages (ASP) and JavaScript code, and it can send the results back to the browser.

Separately, MSSQL and IIS are useful products. Using the Internet Server Application Program Interface (ISAPI), IIS can communicate with MSSQL so the two can work together. ISAPI is a dynamic link library (DLL) that provides a communication channel between MSSQL and IIS, as shown in Figure 11.1.

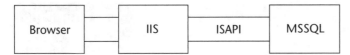

Figure 11.1   IIS and MSSQL can communicate using ISAPI.

This chapter guides you through the installation, setup, and security concerns of the ISAPI layer that glues MSSQL and IIS together. After the first sections show how to get the XML functionality working, the sections that follow demonstrate how to use SQL statements in a URL to return XML to the browser.

A slightly more secure way to execute queries is to use template files. If you specify the location of a template as part of the URL, SQL Server executes whatever query information it finds in that file. In addition, you can use a schema to retrieve data from the database. A template or schema constrains the information that MSSQL returns.

Once a template, schema, or URL query is complete, an HTML form can pull data from the database. This gives the visitor a complete interface to the data. Entering parameters into the form and clicking Submit sends the data to IIS. IIS sends the request to the database using the ISAPI layer and returns either XML or another format that an XSL (eXtensbile Stylesheet Language) file can transform.

It can be confusing to figure out which component of the XML functionality is doing what. IIS accepts and returns the HTTP requests. The ISAPI layer reads and writes the XML information. MSSQL stores and handles the SQL queries. These three layers work together to make all the functionality described in this chapter work. Instead of referring to all three of these tools, this chapter usually just refers to IIS because IIS is the Web server. You should keep in mind, however, that all three tools are working together behind the scenes.

Before you start reading the sections that follow, be warned that this chapter contains a lot of very long URLs. To make them fit on the page, these URLs are broken across lines. When you enter a URL in your Web browser, you must enter it all on one line even if it is broken in the text.

Configuring XML Support in IIS

To run the examples in this chapter, you need a system that has either Windows 2000 Professional or Windows 2000 Server installed on it and system administrator access to a local copy of MSSQL 2000. If you're using Windows 2000 Professional, MSSQL will allow you to install only a local copy for testing and development. MSSQL will not allow a user the full installation under Windows 2000 Professional.

During the MSSQL installation, try to install the XML examples. If the setup program cannot find the examples, search the installation disk looking for unzip_xml.exe. This is a compressed archive of all the XML examples that come with MSSQL. In addition to the examples, you will want to have the Northwind database available. This is the test database Microsoft installs with both Access and MSSQL, and many of the examples in this chapter use it.

The last piece you need to install on your system is IIS. The IIS Web server works with MSSQL to bring XML out through a URL. To see if IIS is installed on your system, click the Start menu's Settings command and open the Control Panel. Click on Add/Remove programs and insert the Windows operating system CD-ROM. Once the Add/Remove Programs dialog box is open, click on Add/Remove Windows Components in the lower left corner. This brings up a list of all the Windows components that are installed. If Internet Information Services is already checked, the Web server is already installed on your system. If IIS is not check, click the Internet Information Services checkbox to install it.

Setting Up IIS

To create a URL that can communicate directly with MSSQL, you must create a new virtual directory in IIS. This virtual directory not only defines a directory for templates, but it also associates a particular database within MSSQL with the URL.

To begin, click Start, go to Programs, and select Microsoft SQL Server. Click Configure SQL XML Support in IIS. Figure 11.2 shows the IIS Virtual Directory Management for SQL Server window that displays once the application is opened.

Making an IIS Virtual Directory

To make the examples in the rest of this chapter work, you need to add a new virtual directory that is associated with a database. Before you define the virtual directory, you need to create a physical directory on your hard disk. For this example, create a directory called C:\vbhelper.

When IIS first opens, the name of the server IIS is running should appear on the left-hand side. Click on the server name, and a list of available virtual directories should be displayed on the right-hand side below the menu bar. If there's nothing there, that means no virtual directories have been configured yet.

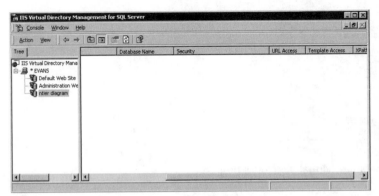

Figure 11.2 SQL Server lets you manage virtual directories for IIS.

To create a new virtual directory, right-click where the virtual directories should be listed. When you select the popup menu's New command, the dialog box shown in Figure 11.3 appears to help you step through the configuration process.

Initially, the dialog box displays the General tab. Give the virtual directory a name that is easy to remember. The name can be anything you want, but it should be something fairly simple because you will need to type it in your browser as part of a URL. For this example, give the virtual directory the name vbhelper. In general, this name does not need to match the name of the physical directory you created, but giving the physical and virtual directories the same name makes things less confusing.

At the bottom of the General tab, select the physical directory you created. In this example, you created a directory called C:\vbhelper.

Setting Virtual Directory Security

Next, click on the Security tab. As Figure 11.4 shows, there are three options for connecting to the database: Always log on as, Use Windows Integrated Authentication, and Use Basic Authentication (Clear Text) to SQL Server account. The choice you should use depends on how MSSQL was installed on the server.

Pick the Always log on as option when you need to use the same username and password for the MSSQL database for each query or template that executes. The user must be a valid SQL user and have the appropriate privileges to execute the desired SQL statements. By selecting the Windows user option, the specified Windows username and password are used for all requests.

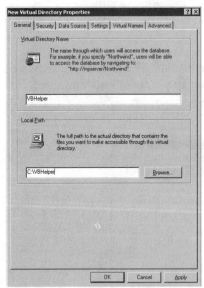

Figure 11.3 Define a new virtual directory's properties.

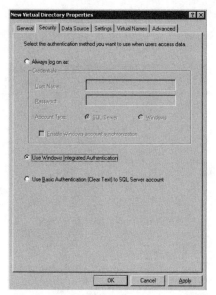

Figure 11.4   Select the authentication method for the new virtual directory.

Select the Use Windows Integrated Authentication option when the security of MSSQL has been integrated with the security of Windows on your computer.

Pick Use Basic Authentication (Clear Text) to SQL Server account when you wish to prompt a user for a username and password. Remember that the username and password the user needs to enter are a SQL server login rather than a login for IIS or Windows. This option brings up a dialog box in your browser when you access the URL that is set up as the virtual directory.

Talk with your system and database administrators to determine how to connect to the database. For this example, MSSQL was installed on a local machine with the security integrated with Windows.

Selecting the Virtual Directory's Server and Database

On the Data Source tab, shown in Figure 11.5, select the virtual directory's server and database. When you click the button next to the Data Source text box, the dialog box searches for all active MSSQL servers on the network. If you know the name of the server you want, enter the name in all capital letters.

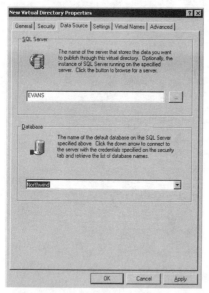

Figure 11.5 Specify the virtual directory's data source.

If security is set up correctly, a list of all the active databases for the server you selected is listed below the server name. Select the database you want to use for this virtual directory. To follow along with the examples in this chapter, select the Northwind database.

Selecting XML Functionality

The Settings tab, shown in Figure 11.6, allows you to choose what XML functionality is active in IIS. For the examples in this chapter, choose Allow URL queries, Allow template queries, Allow XPath, and Allow POST.

The Allow URL queries option lets IIS execute SQL queries as part of a URL.

The Allow template queries option lets IIS execute SQL statements contained in template files that reside on the server. Putting SQL commands in templates lets you hide the database structure from users.

The Allow XPath feature allows the execution of XPath queries when using a schema. Chapter 5, "Schemas," has more to say about XPath.

Finally, Allow POST allows the URL to accept the POST HTTP method from an HTML form. Note that a user can set the amount of information that the POST command will accept, and you may need to tweak the number of kilobytes that this method accepts.

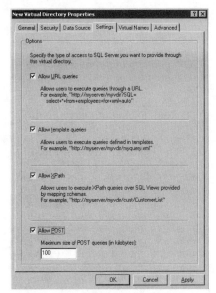

Figure 11.6   Pick settings for XML functionality.

Specifying Template and Schema Directories

Template and Schema directories give the XML functionality in SQL Server and IIS more security because they hide SQL statements from the user. To use templates, you must create a template directory and then map it for the virtual directory. For this example, create a subdirectory in the vbhelper directory called template. On the Virtual Names tab, select New to display the dialog box shown in Figure 11.7.

You can also create a similar directory for schemas here. To create a schema directory select schema as the type from the drop-down box rather than template. Be sure to specify a different directory than any template directory that may already exist.

Enter the virtual name you want to give the template directory. Select the template directory type using the drop box on the right-hand side of the screen. The drop-down box allows you to choose between a schema or template directory. Remember that template and schema physical directories must be different. In this example, map the template directory to C:\vbhelper\template and the schema directory to C:\vbhelper\schema.

Note that the virtual directory name doesn't need to match the physical directory's name, but using the same name makes things less confusing.

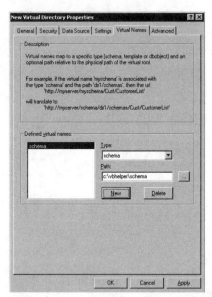

Figure 11.7 Using the Virtual Names tab to select a template directory.

After you finish setting up IIS as described in the previous sections, your physical and virtual directories should match those shown in Table 11.1.

Specifying an ISAPI DLL

If the ISAPI layer for the XML functionality of IIS and MSSQL changes, IIS needs to know where the new DLL resides. The Advanced tab shows the ISAPI DLL file used by SQL server and IIS. If the DLL location is incorrect, click the Browse button shown in Figure 11.8 and select the appropriate DLL. This should be necessary only if the there is an upgrade to the XML functionality.

Table 11.1 Example IIS Directory Structure

CONTENTS	PHYSICAL LOCATION	VIRTUAL NAME
Root directory	C:\vbhelper	vbhelper
Templates	C:\vbhelper\template	template
Schemas	C:\vbhelper\schema	schema

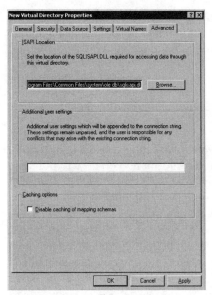

Figure 11.8   Use the Advanced tab to select the appropriate ISAPI dll.

Security Considerations

The XML functionality in IIS is very powerful and is a great way to get content from a database to the Web. You should consider what information you may be revealing to people when performing URL queries. As you'll see in upcoming examples, queries included as part of the URL might reveal the database's table names, column names, and even the names of stored procedures. This type of information should never be part of a production system because it reveals critical information to the users. Displaying this information could help someone figure out the structure of the database and gain unauthorized access to it.

If you want to use the XML functionality in SQL server, you are strongly encouraged to use templates. URL queries are useful during development to design the query that ends up in the template. Once you have the queries working correctly, move them into templates. Then, to prevent the use of URL queries, uncheck the Allow URL Queries box on the MSSQL Settings tab in the virtual directory setup dialog box.

Another consideration is the username and password used when creating a virtual directory. This user should not be the database system administrator (SA) or another user who has broad powers to create, insert, or remove tables. A visitor accessing the database does so with this user's privileges so granting that user too much power makes it more likely that a visitor can damage your database. It is safer to create a user within MSSQL that has permissions to use only select statements even when using templates. This prevents users from inserting and deleting data without your knowledge.

Executing Queries

MSSQL provides several ways to execute queries. You can type a query directly into the URL and pull XML data right into your browser. You can also use a template file containing information written in XML that provides information on how to pull data out of the database. A template file can also specify an XSL file that transforms the data into HTML for easy viewing. Parameters can tell the XSL file how to customize the display.

MSSQL has three query modes that allow you to retrieve XML from a database: AUTO, RAW, and EXPLICIT. You specify the mode by adding a simple statement such as FOR XML AUTO to the end of a query. AUTO tells MSSQL to name the elements in the returning XML file after the name of the table. Using RAW instead of AUTO makes MSSQL return each row of elements with the name "row." The EXPLICIT keyword lets the user specify the form of the XML document with the query. In this case, the user is responsible for ensuring that the returning XML is well formed and valid.

The following sections explain how to execute queries within a URL and from templates, and provide examples that use the RAW and AUTO keywords.

Using the URL to Execute Queries

Once you have configured the virtual directory, you can execute a query right in the browser's URL. Consider the following URL, which should be entered into the browser all on one line.

```
http://localhost/vbhelper?sql=select+*+from+products+
where+productID+=+6+FOR+XML+AUTO&root=ProductList
```

In this example, the URL uses localhost instead of a Web site because the database, Web server, and browser are all running on the same machine. You may need to specify a server name with a domain if you access the example over the Internet or an intranet.

The next part of the URL is the name of the virtual directory on the server. This example uses the virtual directory named vbhelper created earlier in this chapter.

The question mark indicates that the rest of the information in the URL is instructions to be passed on to the ISAPI layer. The plus signs within the SQL statement indicate spaces to the Web server. You could use the string %20 instead to indicate a space.

The FOR+XML+AUTO piece tells MSSQL to name the XML elements representing each row after the table. In this example, the resulting XML will use an element named "products" to represent each row of returned data.

The final statement, root=ProductList, names the root element of the XML document shown in the browser. Without the root declaration, Internet Explorer displays an error because the returning data is not valid XML.

The following code shows the output sent to the browser when it visits this URL. The results are unformatted so they normally appear on a single line of text sent to the browser. This database contains only one record with productID = 6 so the results contain only one row of data.

```
<ProductList>
<products ProductID="6" ProductName="Grandma's Boysenberry Spread"
SupplierID="3" CategoryID="2" QuantityPerUnit="12 - 8 oz jars"
UnitPrice="25" UnitsInStock="120" UnitsOnOrder="0" ReorderLevel="25"
Discontinued="0" />
</ProductList>
```

If the URL specified FOR XML RAW instead of FOR XML AUTO, the result would be the following code.

```
<ProductList>
<row ProductID="6" ProductName="Grandma's Boysenberry Spread"
SupplierID="3" CategoryID="2" QuantityPerUnit="12 - 8 oz jars"
UnitPrice="25" UnitsInStock="120" UnitsOnOrder="0" ReorderLevel="25"
Discontinued="0" />
</ProductList>
```

Notice that the only real difference is that the name of the element holding the data is now "row" rather than the table name.

You can change the row element name by specifying the new name after the table name in the select statement and using the FOR XML AUTO statement. Consider the following SQL in a URL:

```
http://localhost/vbhelper?sql=select+*+from+products+vbhelper+
where+productID+=+6+FOR+XML+AUTO&root=Productlist
```

The difference between this URL and the previous one is the addition of the name vbhelper after the table name. This URL produces the following results:

```
<ProductList>
<vbhelper ProductID="6" ProductName="Grandma's Boysenberry Spread"
SupplierID="3" CategoryID="2" QuantityPerUnit="12 - 8 oz jars"
UnitPrice="25" UnitsInStock="120" UnitsOnOrder="0" ReorderLevel="25"
Discontinued="0" />
</ProductList>
```

Renaming the XML row elements may let you use an existing XSL file to transform this XML data into another format. You can add a couple of parameters to the URL to make MSSQL send the resulting XML to an XSL file. Here's an example:

```
http://localhost/vbhelper?sql=select+*+from+products+vbhelper+
FOR+XML+AUTO&xsl=product.xsl&contenttype=text/html&root=ProductList
```

This URL is similar to the previous ones except the where clause has been replaced with two new directives. The xsl parameter specifies which XSL document in the virtual directory performs the transformation into HTML. The contenttype parameter ensures that the server and the browser know that the content being returned is in HTML and not some other format. If you omit the contenttype parameter, Internet Explorer may try to display the output as XML rather than HTML. Figure 11.9 shows the output created by this URL.

Passing Parameters

Sometimes composing a query directly in the URL can be awkward. Passing parameters in the URL gives you a little more flexibility. For example, consider the following URL.

```
http://localhost/vbhelper?sql=select+*+from+products+where+
UnitsInStock>=?+and+supplierid=?+FOR+XML+auto&param1=1&
param2=18&root=root
```

The select statement has two question marks that act as placeholders for the parameters that are added at the end of the URL. The values param1 and param2 are placeholders that represent the parameter values, and they must appear in the order of the question marks.

In this case, UnitsInStock uses the first question mark so param1 holds its value. The value of param1 is 1 so the query is looking for data where UnitsInStock is greater than or equal to 1.

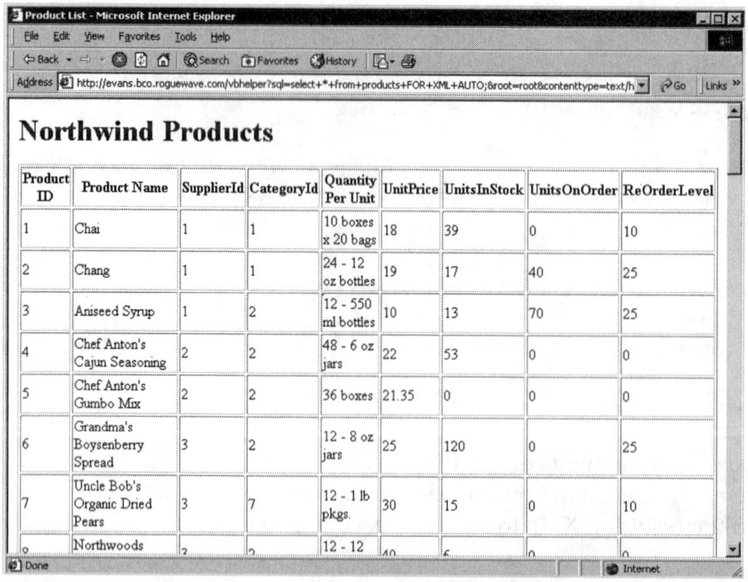

Product ID	Product Name	SupplierId	CategoryId	Quantity Per Unit	UnitPrice	UnitsInStock	UnitsOnOrder	ReOrderLevel
1	Chai	1	1	10 boxes x 20 bags	18	39	0	10
2	Chang	1	1	24 - 12 oz bottles	19	17	40	25
3	Aniseed Syrup	1	2	12 - 550 ml bottles	10	13	70	25
4	Chef Anton's Cajun Seasoning	2	2	48 - 6 oz jars	22	53	0	0
5	Chef Anton's Gumbo Mix	2	2	36 boxes	21.35	0	0	0
6	Grandma's Boysenberry Spread	3	2	12 - 8 oz jars	25	120	0	25
7	Uncle Bob's Organic Dried Pears	3	7	12 - 1 lb pkgs.	30	15	0	10
8	Northwoods	3	2	12 - 12	40	6	0	0

Figure 11.9 An XSL file transforms information into an HTML table.

The supplierid field uses the second question mark. The value of param2 is 18 so the query is looking for data where supplierid is 18. The results look like this:

```
<root>
  <products ProductID="38" ProductName="Côte de Blaye" SupplierID="18"
    CategoryID="1" QuantityPerUnit="12 - 75 cl bottles"
    UnitPrice="263.5" UnitsInStock="17" UnitsOnOrder="0"
    ReorderLevel="15" Discontinued="0"
  />
  <products ProductID="39" ProductName="Chartreuse verte"
    SupplierID="18" CategoryID="1" QuantityPerUnit="750 cc per bottle"
    UnitPrice="18" UnitsInStock="69" UnitsOnOrder="0"
    ReorderLevel="5" Discontinued="0"
  />
</root>
```

To specify an XSL file to transform the results into HTML, add the xsl statement after the parameter definitions like this:

```
http://localhost/vbhelper?sql=select+*+from+products+where+
UnitsInStock>=?+and+supplierid=?+FOR+XML+auto&param1=1&
param2=18&xsl=Templates\products.xsl&contenttype=text/html&root=root
```

Using Templates to Execute Queries

A template allows you to use the same functionality as the URL, but it also allows you to hide your queries, tables, and stored procedures from users. This adds a little security to the XML functionality in SQL Server 2000.

A template, unlike most files in Windows, does not have a file extension. That prevents users from displaying the contents of the template file in their browsers. If you add the xml extension to the end of the filename, the browser would display the contents of the file. For example, the template in the next example is just called products:

```
<root xmlns:sql="urn:schemas-microsoft-com:xml-sql" >
  <sql:query>
    select * from products FOR XML auto
  </sql:query>
</root>
```

The URL to execute this template looks like this:

```
http://localhost/vbhelper/template/products
```

Templates can handle parameters just like the previous examples using URLs that contain queries. Here's a template file containing a SQL statement that accepts two parameters:

```
<root xmlns:sql="urn:schemas-microsoft-com:xml-sql">
  <sql:header>
    <sql:param name="productid">%</sql:param>
    <sql:param name="unitsinstock">%</sql:param>
  </sql:header>

  <sql:query>
    select *
    from products
    where productid > @productid and unitsinstock >= @unitsinstock
    FOR XML AUTO
  </sql:query>
</root>
```

The URL now looks like this:

```
http://localhost/vbhelper/template/products?productid=1&unitsinstock=1
```

The parameters, productid and unitsinstock, need to have the same capitalization as the sql:param statements defined in the template file, or else no data returns to the browser.

Returning Data as Elements from a Template

So far, all the examples in this chapter return data in the form of attributes of tags that have either the name of the table in the database or a name you specify. By adding the ELEMENTS keyword to the template file, you can make the data appear in XML elements rather than attributes. In the following template, adding a comma and ELEMENTS after FOR XML AUTO is all it takes to show the data as elements.

```
<root xmlns:sql="urn:schemas-microsoft-com:xml-sql">
  <sql:header>
    <sql:param name="productid">%</sql:param>
    <sql:param name="unitsinstock">%</sql:param>
  </sql:header>

  <sql:query>
    select *
    from products
    where productid > @productid and unitsinstock >= @unitsinstock
    FOR XML AUTO, ELEMENTS
  </sql:query>
</root>
```

The data now looks like this in Internet Explorer:

```
<root xmlns:sql="urn:schemas-microsoft-com:xml-sql">
<products>
 <ProductID>76</ProductID>
 <ProductName>Lakkalikööri</ProductName>
 <SupplierID>23</SupplierID>
 <CategoryID>1</CategoryID>
 <QuantityPerUnit>500 ml</QuantityPerUnit>
 <UnitPrice>18</UnitPrice>
 <UnitsInStock>57</UnitsInStock>
 <UnitsOnOrder>0</UnitsOnOrder>
 <ReorderLevel>20</ReorderLevel>
 <Discontinued>0</Discontinued>
</products>
<products>
 <ProductID>77</ProductID>
 <ProductName>Original Frankfurter grüne Soße</ProductName>
 <SupplierID>12</SupplierID>
 <CategoryID>2</CategoryID>
 <QuantityPerUnit>12 boxes</QuantityPerUnit>
 <UnitPrice>13</UnitPrice>
 <UnitsInStock>32</UnitsInStock>
 <UnitsOnOrder>0</UnitsOnOrder>
 <ReorderLevel>15</ReorderLevel>
 <Discontinued>0</Discontinued>
</products>
</root>
```

You could also have converted data from attributes to elements using an XSL file. The section *Using XSL Files* later in this chapter shows how to use this approach.

Using XMLData to Create a Schema

IIS can automatically generate schemas for data if you add the XMLData keyword after FOR XML AUTO. When you specify XMLData, IIS returns the schema before the data in the resulting XML.

Unfortunately, this schema does not follow the standard adopted by the W3C so the syntax may not be what you expect. For more information about schemas, see Chapter 5, "Schemas."

The template file now looks like this:

```
<root xmlns:sql="urn:schemas-microsoft-com:xml-sql">
  <sql:header>
    <sql:param name="productid">%</sql:param>
    <sql:param name="unitsinstock">%</sql:param>
  </sql:header>

  <sql:query>
```

```
    select *
    from products
    where productid > @productid and unitsinstock >= @unitsinstock
    FOR XML AUTO, XMLData
  </sql:query>
</root>
```

With this template, IIS returns the following XML data.

```
<root xmlns:sql="urn:schemas-microsoft-com:xml-sql">
<Schema name="Schema1" xmlns="urn:schemas-microsoft-com:xml-data"
xmlns:dt="urn:schemas-microsoft-com:datatypes">
<ElementType name="products" content="empty" model="closed">
 <AttributeType name="ProductID" dt:type="i4" />
 <AttributeType name="ProductName" dt:type="string" />
 <AttributeType name="SupplierID" dt:type="i4" />
 <AttributeType name="CategoryID" dt:type="i4" />
 <AttributeType name="QuantityPerUnit" dt:type="string" />
 <AttributeType name="UnitPrice" dt:type="fixed.14.4" />
 <AttributeType name="UnitsInStock" dt:type="i2" />
 <AttributeType name="UnitsOnOrder" dt:type="i2" />
 <AttributeType name="ReorderLevel" dt:type="i2" />
 <AttributeType name="Discontinued" dt:type="boolean" />
 <attribute type="ProductID" />
 <attribute type="ProductName" />
 <attribute type="SupplierID" />
 <attribute type="CategoryID" />
 <attribute type="QuantityPerUnit" />
 <attribute type="UnitPrice" />
 <attribute type="UnitsInStock" />
 <attribute type="UnitsOnOrder" />
 <attribute type="ReorderLevel" />
 <attribute type="Discontinued" />
 </ElementType>
 </Schema>
 <products xmlns="x-schema:#Schema1" ProductID="76"
ProductName="Lakkalikööri" SupplierID="23" CategoryID="1"
QuantityPerUnit="500 ml" UnitPrice="18" UnitsInStock="57"
UnitsOnOrder="0" ReorderLevel="20" Discontinued="0" />
 <products xmlns="x-schema:#Schema1" ProductID="77"
ProductName="Original Frankfurter grüne Soße" SupplierID="12"
CategoryID="2" QuantityPerUnit="12 boxes" UnitPrice="13"
UnitsInStock="32" UnitsOnOrder="0"
ReorderLevel="15" Discontinued="0" />
 </root>
```

Using ELEMENTS and XMLData at the same time makes the schema quite a bit different. To do this, list ELEMENTS and XMLData after FOR XML AUTO. Here's the modified template:

```
<root xmlns:sql="urn:schemas-microsoft-com:xml-sql">
  <sql:header>
    <sql:param name="productid">%</sql:param>
```

```
      <sql:param name="unitsinstock">%</sql:param>
    </sql:header>

    <sql:query>
      select * from products
      where ProductId > @productid and unitsinstock >= @UnitsInStock
      FOR XML AUTO, ELEMENTS, XMLData
    </sql:query>
  </root>
```

Now the schema and the data look like this:

```
<root xmlns:sql="urn:schemas-microsoft-com:xml-sql">
<Schema name="Schema1" xmlns="urn:schemas-microsoft-com:xml-data"
xmlns:dt="urn:schemas-microsoft-com:datatypes">
<ElementType name="products" content="eltOnly" model="closed"
order="many">
 <element type="ProductID" />
 <element type="ProductName" />
 <element type="SupplierID" />
 <element type="CategoryID" />
 <element type="QuantityPerUnit" />
 <element type="UnitPrice" />
 <element type="UnitsInStock" />
 <element type="UnitsOnOrder" />
 <element type="ReorderLevel" />
 <element type="Discontinued" />
 </ElementType>
 <ElementType name="ProductID" content="textOnly" model="closed"
dt:type="i4" />
 <ElementType name="ProductName" content="textOnly" model="closed"
dt:type="string" />
 <ElementType name="SupplierID" content="textOnly" model="closed"
dt:type="i4" />
 <ElementType name="CategoryID" content="textOnly" model="closed"
dt:type="i4" />
 <ElementType name="QuantityPerUnit" content="textOnly" model="closed"
dt:type="string" />
 <ElementType name="UnitPrice" content="textOnly" model="closed"
dt:type="fixed.14.4" />
 <ElementType name="UnitsInStock" content="textOnly" model="closed"
dt:type="i2" />
 <ElementType name="UnitsOnOrder" content="textOnly" model="closed"
dt:type="i2" />
 <ElementType name="ReorderLevel" content="textOnly" model="closed"
dt:type="i2" />
 <ElementType name="Discontinued" content="textOnly" model="closed"
dt:type="boolean" />
 </Schema>
<products xmlns="x-schema:#Schema1">
 <ProductID>76</ProductID>
 <ProductName>Lakkalikööri</ProductName>
```

```
      <SupplierID>23</SupplierID>
      <CategoryID>1</CategoryID>
      <QuantityPerUnit>500 ml</QuantityPerUnit>
      <UnitPrice>18</UnitPrice>
      <UnitsInStock>57</UnitsInStock>
      <UnitsOnOrder>0</UnitsOnOrder>
      <ReorderLevel>20</ReorderLevel>
      <Discontinued>0</Discontinued>
    </products>
    <products xmlns="x-schema:#Schema1">
      <ProductID>77</ProductID>
      <ProductName>Original Frankfurter grüne Soße</ProductName>
      <SupplierID>12</SupplierID>
      <CategoryID>2</CategoryID>
      <QuantityPerUnit>12 boxes</QuantityPerUnit>
      <UnitPrice>13</UnitPrice>
      <UnitsInStock>32</UnitsInStock>
      <UnitsOnOrder>0</UnitsOnOrder>
      <ReorderLevel>15</ReorderLevel>
      <Discontinued>0</Discontinued>
    </products>
  </root>
```

In this version, the data values are included as elements rather than attributes so the schema defines them using ElementType statements rather than AttributeType statements.

Using XSL Files

Specifying an XSL file in a template is straightforward. Simply add the sql:xsl parameter to the root element of the template. The following example specifies an XSL file that transforms the data into HTML:

```
<root xmlns:sql="urn:schemas-microsoft-com:xml-sql"
      sql:xsl="products.xsl">
  <sql:header>
    <sql:param name="productid">%</sql:param>
    <sql:param name="unitsinstock">%</sql:param>
  </sql:header>

  <sql:query>
    select *
    from products
    where productid > @productid and unitsinstock >= @unitsinstock
    FOR XML auto
  </sql:query>
</root>
```

You can execute the template with this URL:

```
http://localhost/vbhelper/templates/products?productid=75&unitsinstock=2
```

The results look like this in the browser:

```html
<html>
  <head>
    <title>Customer List</title>
  </head>
  <body>
    <h1>Northwind Customers</h1>
    <table border="1">
      <tr>
        <th>ProductID</th>
        <th>ProductName</th>
        <th>SupplierId</th>
        <th>UnitPrice</th>
        <th>Quantity Per Unit</th>
      </tr>
      <tr>
        <td>76</td>
        <td>Lakkalikööri</td>
        <td>23</td>
        <td>18</td>
        <td>500 ml</td>
      </tr>
      <tr>
        <td>77</td>
        <td>Original Frankfurter grüne Soße</td>
        <td>12</td>
        <td>13</td>
        <td>12 boxes</td>
      </tr>
    </table>
  </body>
</html>
```

Nothing in this template tells the browser and server what kind of information the template returns. When making the call to the template file, the SQL is executed and the XSL file performs its transformation. The reason the results appear as XML rather than HTML is that the server and browser weren't told what the content was. If you add the contenttype=text/html parameter to the URL calling the template, the browser will receive HTML. Here's the proper URL:

```
http://localhost/vbhelper/templates/products?ProductId=75&UnitsInStock=2
&contenttype=text/html
```

Using an HTML Form to Call Data

In a real-world setting, making a user retrieve data using the URL just isn't practical. To make the XML functionality in SQL Server 2000 useful, the user must be able to use HTML forms to call the URL or template queries. The following sections, which show

how to use HTML forms with URLs and templates, will help get you started on integrating XML functionality into your Web site.

Forms with URL Queries

Although URL queries may pose security risks, you may still want to integrate a URL query into an HTML form for internal testing and reporting. They may also be useful on a secure intranet.

Calling a URL query from a form is quite simple, although the number of hidden fields needed for these examples can make it a little confusing at first.

The following HTML sends a query to a database. The paragraphs that follow describe the HTML code in detail.

```
<html>
<head>
    <title>Display Product Results</title>
</head>

<body>
<h2>Northwind Products</h2>
<!-- HTML comments are the same as XML comments. -->
<!-- Set up the form to do a post method to the URL -->
<!--    that executes the SQL statement. -->
<form method="post" action="http://localhost/vbhelper" >
    <!-- A hidden input field holds the sql statement to execute. -->
    <input type="hidden"
           name="sql"
           value=
"select * from products where UnitsInStock>? and supplierid=? FOR XML;">

    <p>
    <!-- Use a table for slightly better formatting. -->
    <table>
        <!-- Text Inputs for the two params we want to pass in. -->
        <tr><td>Units in stock >= </td>
            <td><input type="text" name="param1"></td></tr>
        <tr><td>Supplier ID >= </td>
            <td><input type="text" name="param2"></td></tr>
    </table>

    <!-- Hidden inputs specify the XSL file and the type of
         content that's returned. -->
    <input type="hidden" name="xsl" value="Templates\products.xsl">

    <!-- This hidden field specifies the content type that the returned
         data should be displayed in. -->
    <input type="hidden" name="contenttype" value="text/html">

    <!-- Specify the name of the root element. -->
    <input type="hidden" name="root" value="root">
```

```
      <input type="Submit" value="SendData"><br>
      <input type="Reset" value="Clear Form">
</form>
</body>
</html>
```

There are several hidden fields in this form that IIS needs in order to get the XML response from the ISAPI filter. They are hidden because the information contained in these fields does not require any user input. When the Web page posts this form, it passes the hidden information to IIS along with the parameters in the input strings.

The order of the fields is important only with the parameters. The parameters must appear in the same order as they appear in the SQL statement. Even though the order of the other fields is unimportant, their names must correspond to the names in the URL queries shown earlier in the chapter.

The first hidden field, sql, describes the SQL statement that the form executes. This field must be named sql for the form to work properly. The question marks in the SQL statement are placeholders for the query's parameters. Note that plus signs aren't needed in the hidden field because the post operation adds them when you click the submit button.

The SQL statement needs two parameters, unitsinstock and supplierid. The HTML form contains two text fields where the user can enter values for the parameters. These two text fields can have any names because only their order matters. The form's first text field is passed to the SQL query as its first parameter, and the form's second text field is passed as the second parameter. While you can give these fields any names you like, it makes sense to give them names like param1 and param2 that emphasize their relative positions on the form. In this example, param1 corresponds to unitsinstock, and param2 corresponds to supplierid in the query.

The hidden field named xsl specifies an XSL file that should transform the resulting XML. The last two hidden fields, contenttype and root, specify the type of content to be returned and the name of the root element in the document.

Figure 11.10 shows this HTML file as it appears in a browser window. Figure 11.11 shows the HTML that is returned when you enter 1 for both parameters and click the SendData button.

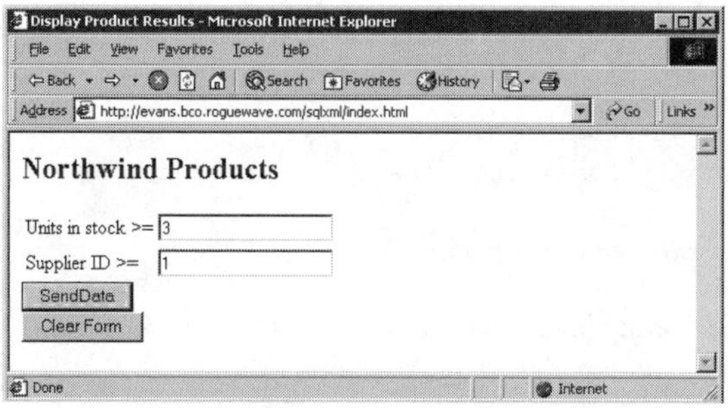

Figure 11.10   Enter parameters on this form.

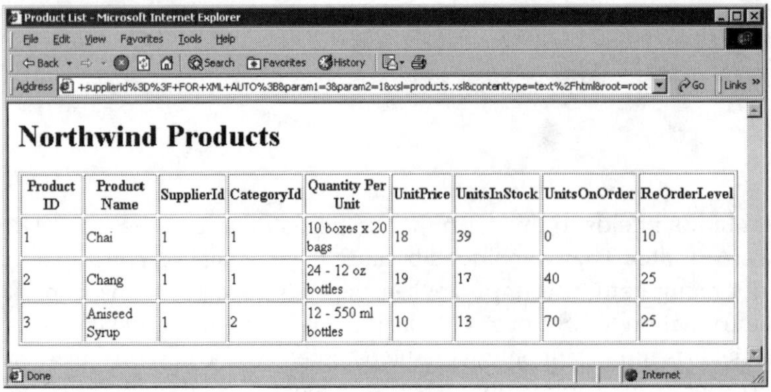

Figure 11.11 Data is returned in a HTML table.

Forms with Templates

Templates greatly simplify a form's HTML because the form doesn't need to specify either the SQL query or the XSL file. All this information resides in the template.

Unlike the case of using URL queries with forms, the parameters used with templates must have the same names as the parameters inside the template file, and the order of the parameters doesn't matter. Look at the following HTML:

```
<html>
<head>
    <title>Display Product Results</title>
</head>

<body>
<h2>Northwind Products</h2>
<!-- HTML comments are the same as XML comments. -->
<!-- Set up the form to do a post method to the URL -->
<!--    that executes the SQL statement. -->
<form method="post"
  action="http://localhost/vbhelper/templates/products" >
    <p>
    <table>
        <tr><td>Units in stock >= </td>
            <td><input type="text" name="unitsinstock"></td></tr>
        <tr><td>Supplier ID >= </td>
            <td><input type="text" name="productid"></td></tr>
    </table>
    <!-- Specify the type of content that's returned. -->
    <input type="hidden" name="contenttype" value="text/html">

    <input type="Submit" value="SendData"><br>
```

```
            <input type="Reset" value="Clear Form">
</form>
</body>
</html>
```

This form appears the same in the browser as the URL HTML example. This version contains fewer hidden input fields because the template holds much of the needed information.

The HTML action attribute of the form tag specifies the URL where the form's information should be posted. The products template file doesn't have an extension so visitors cannot view it with their browsers.

The products template file looks like this:

```
<root xmlns:sql="urn:schemas-microsoft-com:xml-sql"
        sql:xsl="products.xsl">
  <sql:header>
    <sql:param name="productid">%</sql:param>
    <sql:param name="unitsinstock">%</sql:param>
  </sql:header>

  <sql:query>
    select *
    from products
    where productid > @productid and unitsinstock >= @unitsinstock
    FOR XML auto
  </sql:query>
</root>
```

Notice that the input text fields have the same names, productid and unitsinstock, as the template file's SQL parameters. As in the previous example, the HTML file uses a hidden field to indicate that the returned data will have the content type text/html.

Using Schemas to Retrieve Data

Templates are small XML files that contain SQL statements and parameters describing how the data should be returned. Using Microsoft's schema standard within MSSQL, which is known as XML Data Reduced (XDR) schema, you can retrieve data without writing a SQL statement. As described in Chapter 5, "Schemas," a schema constrains XML data. In this case, schemas constrain the XML data returning from MSSQL.

Before you read the following sections, be warned that using schemas in this way is quite confusing. Microsoft's XDR Schemas are different from the accepted schema standard. There is no SQL executed here, at least at a level the user can see. Getting this method to work properly is much harder than using templates. Compared to the methods described previously, this method seems like a bizarre way to retrieve data from a database.

Although this chapter covers this technique, you might want to use the template files described in the previous section. Templates use SQL, which most Visual Basic

Programmers already understand, at least to some extent. Templates are also fairly flexible when it comes to passing parameters to an XSL file. The following sections are here more to make you aware that this functionality exists rather than as a recommendation.

The section *Configuring XML Support in IIS* earlier in this chapter shows how to configure a virtual directory for schemas. All the schemas described in the following sections must be in that schema virtual directory. For more information on schema syntax, see Chapter 5, "Schemas."

Calling Schemas Directly

The following schema is in the file products.xdr in the schema subdirectory of vbhelper:

```
<?xml version="1.0" ?>
<Schema xmlns="urn:schemas-microsoft-com:xml-data"
        xmlns:sql="urn:schemas-microsoft-com:xml-sql">
  <ElementType name="Products" sql:relation="Products" >

    <!-- Declare the columns to return. -->
    <AttributeType name="ProductID" />
    <AttributeType name="ProductName" />
    <AttributeType name="SupplierID" />
    <AttributeType name="CategoryID" />
    <AttributeType name="QuantityPerUnit" />

    <!-- Declare how the columns should be displayed. -->
    <attribute type="ProductID"  />
    <attribute type="ProductName"  />
    <attribute type="SupplierID" />
    <attribute type="CategoryID" />
    <attribute type="QuantityPerUnit" />
  </ElementType>
</Schema>
```

The ElementType declaration sets up the name of the returning element name, Products. The sql:relation statement tells MSSQL which table holds the data to grab.

At this point, the AttributeType and attribute elements aren't really doing a whole lot. They will become useful soon, but for now just realize they need to be there.

To retrieve data, use the following URL in your Web browser:

```
http://localhost/vbhelper/schema/products.xdr/Products?root=root
```

This returns the entire contents of the Products table for the columns we specified. Specifying root=root makes IIS place all of the returned XML row elements inside a root element named root. If you omit this statement, the resulting XML is not well formed.

To pass a parameter to a schema, add the parameter value in brackets after the name of the schema file. The following URL constrains the returned data so that it includes only rows where ProductID is 1.

```
http://localhost/vbhelper/schema/products.xdr/Products[@ProductID=1]
?root=root
```

The syntax that allows you to specify a parameter to the schema, Products[@-ProductID=1], is called XPath. XPath is a standard created by the W3C that allows a programmer to specify different nodes of an XML document during processing. This example processes a schema and passes in information using XPath to limit the returning data. For more information on XPath, see Chapter 6, "XSL," and the W3C's web site at www.w3c.org.

The following XML shows the results returned for this URL.

```
<?xml version="1.0" encoding="utf-8" ?>
<root>
 <Products ProductID="1" ProductName="Chai" SupplierID="1"
CategoryID="1" QuantityPerUnit="10 boxes x 20 bags" />
</root>
```

You can add other constraints on the schema's data. For example, the following URL selects records where ProductID < 10.

```
http://localhost/vbhelper/schema/products.xdr/Products[@ProductID<10]
?root=root
```

This URL returns the following results.

```
<?xml version="1.0" encoding="utf-8" ?>
<root>
 <Products ProductID="1" ProductName="Chai"
SupplierID="1" CategoryID="1" QuantityPerUnit="10 boxes x 20 bags" />
 <Products ProductID="2" ProductName="Chang"
SupplierID="1" CategoryID="1" QuantityPerUnit="24 - 12 oz bottles" />
 <Products ProductID="3" ProductName="Aniseed Syrup"
SupplierID="1" CategoryID="2" QuantityPerUnit="12 - 550 ml bottles" />
 <Products ProductID="4" ProductName="Chef Anton's Cajun Seasoning"
SupplierID="2" CategoryID="2" QuantityPerUnit="48 - 6 oz jars" />
 <Products ProductID="5" ProductName="Chef Anton's Gumbo Mix"
SupplierID="2" CategoryID="2" QuantityPerUnit="36 boxes" />
 <Products ProductID="6" ProductName="Grandma's Boysenberry Spread"
SupplierID="3" CategoryID="2" QuantityPerUnit="12 - 8 oz jars" />
 <Products ProductID="7" ProductName="Uncle Bob's Organic Dried Pears"
SupplierID="3" CategoryID="7" QuantityPerUnit="12 - 1 lb pkgs." />
 <Products ProductID="8" ProductName="Northwoods Cranberry Sauce"
SupplierID="3" CategoryID="2" QuantityPerUnit="12 - 12 oz jars" />
 <Products ProductID="9" ProductName="Mishi Kobe Niku" SupplierID="4"
CategoryID="6" QuantityPerUnit="18 - 500 g pkgs." />
</root>
```

You can change the names of the parameters of the elements that are returned when the schema activates. By adding a sql:field statement to the attribute declaration, you can map a return name to the corresponding field name in the database.

The following example declares the first two data fields to have output names ID and Name. Then when the schema declares the attribute types, it uses the sql:field statement to map these names to the Products table's ProductID and ProductName fields.

```
<?xml version="1.0" ?>
<Schema xmlns="urn:schemas-microsoft-com:xml-data"
        xmlns:sql="urn:schemas-microsoft-com:xml-sql">
  <ElementType name="Products" sql:relation="Products" >

     <!-- Attribute declarations for columns -->
     <AttributeType name="ID" />
     <AttributeType name="Name" />
     <AttributeType name="SupplierID" />
     <AttributeType name="CategoryID" />
     <AttributeType name="QuantityPerUnit" />

     <!-- Declare the instances -->
     <attribute type="ID" sql:field="ProductID"  />
     <attribute type="Name" sql:field="ProductName"  />
     <attribute type="SupplierID" />
     <attribute type="CategoryID" />
     <attribute type="QuantityPerUnit" />
  </ElementType>
</Schema>
```

The URL to invoke this schema is similar to the one used in the previous example. In the following code, the URL constrains the data's return name ID instead of the database field name ProductID.

```
http://localhost/vbhelper/schema/products.xdr/Products[@ID<5]?root=root
```

The results are similar to those of the previous example except the names ProductID and ProductName have been changed to ID and Name.

```
<root>
 <Products ID="1" Name="Chai"
SupplierID="1" CategoryID="1" QuantityPerUnit="10 boxes x 20 bags" />
 <Products ID="2" Name="Chang"
SupplierID="1" CategoryID="1" QuantityPerUnit="24 - 12 oz bottles" />
 <Products ID="3" Name="Aniseed Syrup"
SupplierID="1" CategoryID="2" QuantityPerUnit="12 - 550 ml bottles" />
 <Products ID="4" Name="Chef Anton's Cajun Seasoning"
SupplierID="2" CategoryID="2" QuantityPerUnit="48 - 6 oz jars" />
</root>
```

As with URL SQL queries, you can specify an XSL file to reformat the results and display them in the browser. The URL with the XSL file path and the contenttype added looks like this:

```
http://localhost/vbhelper/schema/products.xdr/Products[@ProductID<10]?
root=root&xsl=schema/products.xsl&contenttype=text/html
```

Figure 11.12 shows the result.

Using Schemas with Templates

As is the case with SQL queries, you can use templates with a schema to retrieve data. A template has the advantage of providing more security than calling the schema directly. Calling the template hides the name of the schema from the visitor and prevents the visitor from calling a schema file that has a file extension. Both of these measures prevent users from viewing the files in the browser, possibly revealing sensitive information about the database.

The templates that call schemas look similar to the templates used with SQL shown in the previous examples. Instead of the sql:query tag, however, these templates use the sql:xpath tag. The code shown between the start and end sql:xpath tags determines which data returns from the database. XPath syntax is described further in Chapter 6, "XSL."

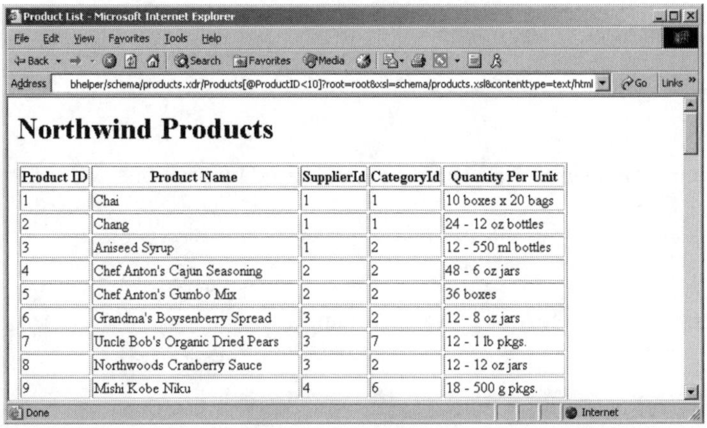

Figure 11.12   A URL can include a schema to format the returned data.

In the following template, /Products means data needs to come from the products table. The code within the brackets, [@ProductId = $ProductId], means the ProductId in the database table (@ProductId) must match the ProductId that was passed into the template from the URL ($ProductId).

```
<root xmlns:sql="urn:schemas-microsoft-com:xml-sql" >
  <sql:header>
    <sql:param name="ProductId">%</sql:param>
  </sql:header>

  <sql:xpath-query mapping-schema="products.xdr">
    /Products[@ProductId = $ProductId]
  </sql:xpath-query>
</root>
```

This template uses the first schema described in the previous section that does not use the sql:field parameter so the template calls the field ProductId. If the template were using the second schema that mapped the return name ID to the database field name ProductId, the template would refer to the schema's version of the field as ID as in [@ID = $ProductId].

You can add an XSL file to the template using the sql:xsl statement just as in previous examples.

```
<root xmlns:sql="urn:schemas-microsoft-com:xml-sql"
        sql:xsl="products.xsl">
  <sql:header>
    <sql:param name="ProductId">%</sql:param>
  </sql:header>

  <sql:xpath-query mapping-schema="products.xdr">
    /Products[@ID = $ProductId]
  </sql:xpath-query>
</root>
```

You can invoke the template using a URL similar to those used by previous examples.

```
http://localhost/vbhelper/template/productschema?ProductId=3
&contenttype=text/html
```

Figure 11.13 shows the HTML returned by this template.

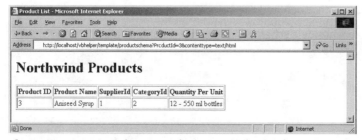

Figure 11.13   A template can select a particular ProductID.

Transforming to HTML

The XSL file used for the examples in this chapter is briefly explained here. Chapter 6, "XSL," gives a much more complete explanation of transforming XML into HTML.

To really understand what the XSL file does, you should examine some sample XML output that one of the previous examples might return.

```
<root>
 <products ProductID="38" ProductName="Côte de Blaye" SupplierID="18"
CategoryID="1" QuantityPerUnit="12 - 75 cl bottles" UnitPrice="263.5"
UnitsInStock="17" UnitsOnOrder="0" ReorderLevel="15" Discontinued="0" />
 </root>
```

The products element represents a row of data pulled from the database. The database field values are contained in the products element's attributes.

To display the data in HTML, the XSL file must loop through the products elements and display them. For each products element, the XML file must loop through its attributes and display the corresponding field data.

Products.xsl looks like this:

```
<xsl:stylesheet xmlns:xsl="http://www.w3.org/TR/WD-xsl">
  <!-- xsl:template means this is executed for the entire
         XML file we're mapping. -->
  <xsl:template match="/">
    <!-- Begin displaying HTML. -->
    <!-- When using HTML in an XSL file, all opening tags must have
           closing tags or the file isn't well formed. -->
    <html>
      <head>
        <title>Product List</title>
      </head>
      <body>
        <h1>Northwind Products</h1>

        <!-- Put the information in a table for easy viewing. -->
        <table border="1">
          <tr>
            <th>Product ID</th>
            <th>Product Name</th>
            <th>SupplierId</th>
            <th>CategoryId</th>
            <th>Quantity Per Unit</th>
            <th>UnitPrice</th>
            <th>UnitsInStock</th>
            <th>UnitsOnOrder</th>
            <th>ReOrderLevel</th>
          </tr>

          <!-- Begin processing the attributes of each products tag
                 returned, -->
          <xsl:for-each select="root/products">
```

```
        <tr>
          <!-- The following value-of statements display all the
               attributes returned by each products element. -->
          <td><xsl:value-of select="@ProductID"/></td>
          <td><xsl:value-of select="@ProductName"/></td>
          <td><xsl:value-of select="@SupplierID"/></td>
          <td><xsl:value-of select="@CategoryID"/></td>
          <td><xsl:value-of select="@QuantityPerUnit"/></td>
          <td><xsl:value-of select="@UnitPrice"/></td>
          <td><xsl:value-of select="@UnitsInStock"/></td>
          <td><xsl:value-of select="@UnitsOnOrder"/></td>
          <td><xsl:value-of select="@ReorderLevel"/></td>
        </tr>
      </xsl:for-each>
    </table>
  </body>
</html>
  </xsl:template>
</xsl:stylesheet>
```

Most of this XSL file contains HTML instructions. There are only a couple of places where any XSL code executes. The XSL file contains comments that explain what it does so only a few statements are worthy of further explanation.

The xsl:stylesheet element sets up the xsl file's namespace. For a more detailed explanation of namespaces see Chapter 1, "XML Overview."

The xsl:template directive makes the XSL file apply to the entire XML file. The match="/" clause makes IIS apply the XSL file to the XML document's root node.

The rest of the file contains simple HTML until the xsl:for-each statement. The statement select="root/products" makes XSLT apply the included code to all child elements of the XML root.

The xsl:value select="@AttributeName" statements display the values of each row's attributes one by one.

When the XSL file is finished, the browser receives HTML output that displays the selected data in a nicely formatted table that is easier to read than the raw XML.

Transforming to Other XML Formats

You don't always need to convert XML output into HTML because a Web browser isn't always the consumer of the data. For example, a business-to-business (B2B) application may require a certain format of XML. A voice recognition program may need data in VoiceXML format.

You can easily modify the XSL file shown in the previous examples to translate XML data into these other formats. Take a look at the following code:

```
<xsl:stylesheet xmlns:xsl="http://www.w3.org/TR/WD-xsl">
  <xsl:template match="/">
  <ProductListing>
    <xsl:for-each select="root/products">
```

```
        <Product>
          <ProductID><xsl:value-of select="@ProductID"/></ProductID>
          <ProductName><xsl:value-of select="@ProductName"/></ProductName>
          <SupplierID><xsl:value-of select="@SupplierID"/></SupplierID>
          <CategoryID><xsl:value-of select="@CategoryID"/></CategoryID>
          <QuantityPerUnit><xsl:value-of select="@QuantityPerUnit"/>
            </QuantityPerUnit>
          <UnitPrice><xsl:value-of select="@UnitPrice"/></UnitPrice>
          <UnitsInStock><xsl:value-of select="@UnitsInStock"/>
            </UnitsInStock>
          <UnitsOnOrder><xsl:value-of select="@UnitsOnOrder"/>
            </UnitsOnOrder>
          <ReorderLevel><xsl:value-of select="@ReorderLevel"/>
            </ReorderLevel>
        </Product>
      </xsl:for-each>
      </ProductListing>
    </xsl:template>
</xsl:stylesheet>
```

This XSL file is very similar to the previous one except that all the HTML directives are gone. The template and for-each commands are still present. Instead of surrounding the data with HTML, this XSL file converts the XML data into another form of XML. The document has the root element ProductListing. Each row of data has a Product tag.

You can invoke this template using the URL:

```
http://localhost/vbhelper/templates/products?productid=75&unitsinstock=2
```

The resulting XML looks like this:

```
<ProductListing>
  <Product>
    <ProductID>76</ProductID>
    <ProductName>Lakkalikööri</ProductName>
    <SupplierID>23</SupplierID>
    <CategoryID>1</CategoryID>
    <QuantityPerUnit>500 ml</QuantityPerUnit>
    <UnitPrice>18</UnitPrice>
    <UnitsInStock>57</UnitsInStock>
    <UnitsOnOrder>0</UnitsOnOrder>
    <ReorderLevel>20</ReorderLevel>
  </Product>
  <Product>
    <ProductID>77</ProductID>
    <ProductName>Original Frankfurter grüne Soße</ProductName>
    <SupplierID>12</SupplierID>
    <CategoryID>2</CategoryID>
    <QuantityPerUnit>12 boxes</QuantityPerUnit>
    <UnitPrice>13</UnitPrice>
    <UnitsInStock>32</UnitsInStock>
```

```
      <UnitsOnOrder>0</UnitsOnOrder>
      <ReorderLevel>15</ReorderLevel>
    </Product>
  </ProductListing>
```

Specifying the content-type in this case isn't necessary because the results are in XML, the default. It is important to note that adding the ELEMENTS keyword to the template could have provided this format as well without requiring an XSL translation.

Conclusion

The XML functionality available in IIS and SQL Server gives developers a quick and easy way to get information out of a database and onto a Web page. While there are some security issues, the use of a template file can hide a lot of critical information from the user. After building a template or a URL query, you can use an HTML form to give visitors easy access to the data. Developing XSL files to transform the data into HTML or another text-based format lets you format data in many different ways.

The combination of SQL Server 2000, IIS, and XSL makes an excellent tool for Web site content management. Storing content in a database and using XSL to format the data for display is a great real-world application of XML. In this scenario, the data is in one location and the formatting in another. When you change the data, you don't need to make any changes to the code that extracts and displays the data. Conversely, if you need to change the presentation format, you don't need to touch the content. If the content is fine but you want to change the Web site's look and feel, you need to modify only the display templates and XSL files.

Index